ceac

TULSA
1921

RANDY KREHBIEL

TULSA 1921

REPORTING A MASSACRE

FOREWORD BY KARLOS K. HILL

UNIVERSITY OF OKLAHOMA PRESS : NORMAN

This book is published with the generous assistance
of the Wallace C. Thompson Endowment Fund,
University of Oklahoma Foundation.

Library of Congress Cataloging-in-Publication Data

Names: Krehbiel, Randy, author.
Title: Tulsa, 1921 : reporting a massacre / Randy Krehbiel.
Description: Norman : University of Oklahoma Press, [2019] | Includes bibliographical
    references and index. | Summary: "Examines the events and players contributing to,
    participating in, and responding to Tulsa's 1921 race riot and massacre and the social,
    political and historical context in which it occurred"— Provided by publisher.
Identifiers: LCCN 2018054090 | ISBN 978-0-8061-6331-4 (hardcover : alk. paper)
Subjects: LCSH: Tulsa Race Riot, Tulsa, Okla., 1921. | Tulsa Race Riot, Tulsa, Okla., 1921—Press
    coverage—Oklahoma—Tulsa. | African Americans—Violence against—Oklahoma—
    Tulsa—History—20th century. | Greenwood (Tulsa, Okla.)—Race relations—History—20th
    century. | Tulsa (Okla.)—Race relations—History—20th century. | Racism—Oklahoma—
    Tulsa—History—20th century. | Tulsa world. | Tulsa tribune.
Classification: LCC F704.T92 K74 2019 | DDC 976.6/8600496073—dc23
LC record available at https://lccn.loc.gov/2018054090

The paper in this book meets the guidelines for permanence and durability of the Committee
on Production Guidelines for Book Longevity of the Council on Library Resources, Inc. ∞

1 2 3 4 5 6 7 8 9 10

To Lenzy and Jay,
and to the people of Tulsa.
May they always seek truth.

CONTENTS

ILLUSTRATIONS

Figures

Map

FOREWORD

KARLOS K. HILL

The Tulsa Massacre is the deadliest outbreak of white terrorist violence against a black community in American history. In 1921, Tulsa's Greenwood District, or "Black Wall Street," was the wealthiest black community in the United States. Yet, during the evening of May 31 and the early morning hours of June 1, 1921, Tulsa exploded. Enraged by rumors that a black man had attempted to rape a white woman, a white mob invaded the Greenwood District, indiscriminately killing any black person it encountered. It is estimated that more than three hundred people (mostly blacks) died due to the violence. Some black Tulsans fled for safety while others banded together to defend their lives and property. In the end, black resistance was futile. The white mob looted and then set ablaze practically every home and business in the Greenwood District. All told, in less than twenty-four hours, the thirty-five square blocks that constituted the Greenwood District—more than one dozen churches, five hotels, thirty-one restaurants, four drug stores, eight doctors' offices, two dozen grocery stores, a public library, and more than one thousand homes—lay in ruin.

The scale of destruction and loss of life unleashed upon Tulsa's black community was unprecedented in American history; however, it is important to note that the Tulsa Massacre was not an exceptional event. Over the course of American history, more than 250 episodes of collective white violence against black communities have occurred. Just two years prior to the Tulsa Massacre, similar large-scale outbreaks of white terrorist violence against black communities occurred in Dewey, Oklahoma, Elaine, Arkansas, Washington, D.C., and Chicago, Illinois. In fact, in Dewey, Oklahoma, a white mob burned down the "negro district" and drove twenty black families out of the town in response to a black man allegedly murdering a white police officer.

As with the white terrorist violence in Dewey, the Tulsa Massacre was not simply an example of white collective violence against a black community; it was also an attempted community expulsion. White Tulsans killed blacks indiscriminately and burned down every significant structure in the Greenwood District in order to terrorize blacks into leaving the city. When it was clear that black Tulsans were intent on rebuilding the Greenwood District, white city leaders attempted to block rebuilding through a proposed rezoning ordinance. Black Tulsans successfully resisted the rezoning ploy and subsequently were allowed to rebuild. Even though damages to homes and businesses and property loss amounted to approximately $4 million, local insurance companies denied every claim submitted by Greenwood business owners and residents. To make matters worse, Tulsa city leaders refused external financial assistance that could have filled the financial void created by unpaid insurance claims. Taken as a whole, the actions of the white mob and Tulsa city leaders can be seen in retrospect as a concerted attempt to banish Tulsa's black community. The efforts of black Tulsans to rebuild in the face of white intransigence is a testament to their courage and resilience.

Outbreaks of white terrorist violence against black communities as well as expulsions of black communities were common at the time and perhaps inevitable because of the culture of white supremacy that pervaded the United States. During the early twentieth century, there was near consensus within white society that "whiteness" or white skin was inherently and irrevocably superior to that of all nonwhite peoples. Conversely, whites viewed black people as inherently unequal to whites and all other racial groups. In order to perpetuate white racial superiority and black inferiority, white Americans excluded black people from every significant American institution, and when black people were included at all, it was always on an unequal basis. American newspapers and especially newspapers controlled by whites played a pivotal role in disseminating and justifying racist depictions of white terrorist violence against black communities. For example, during the late nineteenth and early twentieth centuries, it was common for American newspapers (regardless of region) to portray black lynching victims as criminals deserving of their fate and conversely depicted white lynchers as heroic defenders of their communities.

Despite the critical role that American newspapers often played in instigating or justifying mob violence against black people and black communities, there remains a dearth of case studies and particularly of book-length monographs that examine how specific newspapers reported outbreaks of white terrorist violence. *Tulsa 1921: Reporting a Massacre* fills this void by providing a narrative history of the Tulsa Massacre drawn largely from reportage from Tulsa's two largest newspapers—the *Tulsa World* and the *Tulsa Tribune*. The book will help readers understand two central questions: How did Tulsa's two largest newspapers report on the events of 1921, and, conversely, how did their coverage matter to the unfolding of events? By zeroing in on how the *Tulsa World* and the *Tulsa Tribune* reported on the Tulsa Massacre, the book illustrates perhaps better than any other book heretofore how the *Tulsa Tribune* played a pivotal role in instigating the massacre as well as how both newspapers helped consolidate the white opinion that the violence and destruction unleashed upon Tulsa's black community was a justified response to a "negro uprising." Additionally, the book sheds new light on other aspects of the Tulsa Massacre and should therefore be considered required reading for both general readers and serious students of Tulsa's history.

In short, *Tulsa 1921* makes a much-needed contribution to understanding the Tulsa Massacre, and I am thankful for the opportunity to contribute to its creation.

Norman, Oklahoma
October 2018

PREFACE

In the fall of 1999, the *Tulsa World* assigned me to take over its coverage of the Tulsa Race Riot Commission. As part of that, I was told to research the riot on my own and to compile an archive for our own use. It was an assignment that changed the course of my life and my career.

In 1999, the *World* clip files contained very little about the riot, and most of what was on file was relatively recent. The oldest clip was a single paragraph from 1949, and it was inaccurate. It should be said that this was not surprising; the *World* did not begin maintaining systematic clip files until the late 1940s. But it should also be said that it soon became apparent that some sort of taboo had been attached to the riot for decades. From late 1921 until the 1990s, it was rarely mentioned in the local papers.

I had some knowledge of the riot. I had read Scott Ellsworth's book *Death in a Promised Land* and have a vague recollection of a mention in my ninth-grade Oklahoma history textbook—though I may well be mistaken about that. And I had picked up bits and pieces of information since arriving at the *World* in 1979. A great deal has been made of the Tulsa riot not being taught in schools for many decades, but in my experience a great deal of the more unsavory aspects of the state's history were and sometimes still are glossed over. The purpose of teaching Oklahoma history was to make junior high school students feel good about their state, not to raise questions about it. The outright theft of American Indian and tribal freedman allotments, public corruption, segregation, civil rights, exploitation of poor whites, the Depression, and even the Dust Bowl were given scant attention or ignored altogether.

By the time I began covering the riot commission, a good deal of work had been done in interviewing survivors and preserving their stories. I was somewhat surprised, though, to find that very little effort had been put into reading the local newspapers of the day. The reason for this, I was told, was that it was assumed the newspapers were biased and part of covering up the truth. One common belief was that the morning *World* and the afternoon *Tribune* had not even reported on the riot and the aftermath. I was told entire issues of the *World* were missing from microfilm records. But, because so few people seemed to have actually looked at or for the old newspapers, and because part of my assignment was to recreate the archival record, I decided to give the microfilm a look.

What I found was a remarkably large volume of reporting on the riot and its aftermath.

In time, I read every issue—some multiple times—of the *World* from June 1, 1920, through the end of 1922, and every issue of the *Tribune* for the calendar year 1921. It was not great reporting by today's standards, but it was better than I had been led to believe. It was indisputably biased, but all reporting is in some way, intentionally or not. The trick is understanding those biases and allowing them to inform rather than distort. My reading yielded the names and dates that are the raw material of research and insights into the social and political context in which the riot occurred.

A few words about the *Tulsa World* and the *Tulsa Tribune*. Because they merged production operations in 1949, some have assumed a cozier relationship than actually existed. In fact, they were always competitors, until the *World* bought out the *Tribune* and closed it in 1992. In 1921, the two newspapers were bitter enemies. The *World*, in fact, was among the loudest of those trying to blame the *Tribune*'s loose reporting for the riot.

The *World* had been founded in 1905 as the organ of a local Republican faction. The *Tribune*, until 1920, was known as the *Democrat*, which accurately describes its allegiances. The *World* was the larger paper, the *Tribune* the feistier.

The newspapers were a starting point. From them I moved to other documents and publications. What follows is a product of those studies and my own experience covering the race riot commission and events stemming from it.

Everyone has his or her own perspective on history. This is mine. I would not presume it to be definitive. My hope is that it will be informative.

ACKNOWLEDGMENTS

This book began twenty years ago with an assignment from Joe Worley, then the *Tulsa World*'s executive editor, to find out everything I could about what was then commonly called the Tulsa Race Riot. Although none of us knew it then, the time and latitude Joe and Wayne Greene, then the *World*'s city editor, allowed me as I began my research and writing became the foundation for what you are about to read.

Those who helped me to better understand Tulsa's race massacre and the people and events surrounding it, and to assemble what I learned into this manuscript, are too numerous to count. But I shall try.

Tulsa World researchers, especially Hilary Pittman, have been indispensable. Hilary's diligence and ingenuity is remarkable. In a similar vein, I thank Marc Carlson, director of special collections at the University of Tulsa; Larry O'Dell and Bill Welge of the Oklahoma Historical Society; Ian Swart of the Tulsa Historical Society; the Tulsa Central Library staff; and Tulsa County clerks Michael Willis, Earlene Wilson, and Pat Key and their staffs. Early on, the late Robert Norris provided me with research related primarily to the Oklahoma National Guard, riots, and riot control.

Bob Blackburn, executive director of the Oklahoma Historical Society, has been very helpful in all aspects of my reporting and in the preparation of this book.

State representative Don Ross, who as a magazine publisher and then a lawmaker was so instrumental in the creation of the Tulsa Race Riot Commission, spent many hours explaining and discussing not only the riot but the culture, politics, and personalities of Tulsa and Oklahoma.

Julius Pegues, whose leadership created John Hope Franklin Reconciliation Park and the John Hope Franklin Center, has provided insight into black Tulsa and its history since the events of 1921. Many others have been similarly helpful, including former state senator Maxine Horner, Mike Reed, and Reuben Gant.

Scott Ellsworth, Alfred Brophy, and the late Danney Goble provided valuable information, through both their writing and in discussions with me.

I deeply appreciate the members of the Tulsa Race Riot Commission, especially Eddie Faye Gates, whose interviews with pioneer black Tulsans were invaluable, and Chairman Pete Churchwell, whose patience seemed to know no bounds.

Besides Bob Norris and Danney Goble, many others who have since passed on provided insight and guidance. These included John Hope Franklin, Robert Littlejohn, Beryl Ford, Dick Warner, Bill O'Brien, Otis Clark, and survivors still living when I began gathering information two decades ago.

The final product—this book—would not have been possible without the University of Oklahoma Press, and in particular acquisitions editor Kent Calder, managing editor Steven Baker, and copyeditor Kelly Parker. A special thanks to Oklahoma author John Wooley for a big assist, to Jay Krehbiel, and to Lenzy Krehbiel-Burton, who lent her copyreader's eye to the final proofs.

RK
Tulsa, 2019

TULSA
1921

1

MAY 30, 1921

The parade went on despite the rain.[1]

It formed up just before 9:00 A.M., even as dark, low clouds moved in from the west. The day's forecast was for heavy showers, and, sure enough, Tulsa would get them. But it was Memorial Day, and Tulsa would have a parade and a damn big one come hell or high water. This was a city that bought $33 million worth of war bonds, sent thousands of young men into military service, and prided itself on not just its patriotism but its *Americanism*.[2] It even observed an Americanism Day.[3] And when the 1920 U.S. census concluded that Oklahoma had the nation's highest percentage of native-born citizens, Tulsa celebrated that, too. "Oklahoma comes nearest to being a pure American state of any in the union," editorialized the *Tulsa World*. "We are tremendously proud of that classification."[4]

During the war, Tulsa had demonstrated its vigilance against foreigners, slackers, and reds, the more zealous going so far as to mete out beatings and hot tar to the local membership of the Industrial Workers of the World.[5] Others deemed insufficiently loyal to the cause were "made to see the light." A few were packed off to "insane asylums."[6] Now, two and a half years after the war's end, the fervor had scarcely waned. Despite the threat of rain, Tulsans lined downtown streets as motorcycle cops roared up Cincinnati Avenue from Fifth Street to Seventh, then west to Main and north through the heart of downtown. A seventy-piece band drawn from the local musicians' union followed.

And then came the veterans, scores of them, from the Grand Army of the Republic and the Confederacy through the recent war to end all wars—walking or conveyed by various means through the fat raindrops splattering down on the town that called itself the Magic City.[7] Written accounts are silent on whether Tulsa's black veterans, and there were many of them, were included in the procession, but it does not seem likely. Quite a few white Tulsans thought putting black Americans in uniform had been a mistake in the first place; soon, they would consider their opinions grimly vindicated.[8]

The parade had just reached its end at Second Street and Elgin Avenue when the skies finally opened full-throttle and chased everyone to cover, soaking hats and spring dresses and fresh linen suits; wilting the red silk poppies—handmade by the children of France—in every lapel. Every true Tulsan, every true American, wore the crimson flowers that morning as symbols of sacrifice and patriotism and also of American strength and generosity, for the poppy sales helped feed the starving children of Europe.[9]

As the parade wound down, participants and bystanders piled into their Nashes and Overlands, Buicks and Chevys, Maxwells and Mitchells and Hupmobiles. A few may have shoehorned into variations of the Tulsa Four, a little runabout made right there in town. Everyone drove five straight-as-an-arrow miles, along the Federal Drive to Rose Hill, the new cemetery on the east edge of town, where so many war dead were buried. The living stood in the downpour, heads bowed, listening to Tulsa's most decorated son of the Great War, Lt. Col. Patrick Hurley, a future secretary of war, eulogize his fallen comrades.[10] Little did they imagine that even as they memorialized the dead of distant battle, a deadly calamity of Tulsa's own had already been set in motion.[11]

A pervasive sense of invincibility, of destiny, blinded many Tulsans to the destructive passions simmering only a hair trigger below a white-hot rage. Tulsa was, after all, the Oil Capital of the World. The Magic City. And if the titles were pretentious, they were also apt. In twenty years, Tulsa had grown from a cow town of barely a thousand inhabitants to more than seventy thousand.[12] Flanked to the south, west, and north by major oilfields, whose value the military machines of the Great War multiplied many times over, Tulsa had become the financial and manufacturing center of the ascendant petroleum industry. Tulsa banks were the first in the world to cater to oilmen and, because of it, had profited hugely from the triumph of the internal combustion engine.[13]

Four rail lines served the city. The streets teemed with commerce of every kind. Convention Hall, built in 1914 at Brady and Main Streets, reverberated to the music of Caruso, Paderewski, and other great musicians of the day—and to the rumbling of passing trains. Tulsa High School, with some justification, claimed standing as one of the best in the country. Great mansions, opulent manifestations of the oil riches bought and sold in the lobby of downtown's Hotel Tulsa, rose on the bluff overlooking the Arkansas River.

But there was another side to Tulsa. Downtown, on First Street, where seedy hotels and boarding houses fronted for vice and misery, suicide and domestic violence were regular occurrences. In early May 1921, federal narcotics officer Charles C. Post declared Tulsa "overrun with narcotic peddlers,"[14] and said that eighteen had been arrested in the past month. A report by investigator T. L. Gosnell, entitled "Federal Report on Vice Conditions in Tulsa," identified fourteen houses of prostitution and claimed, "Gambling, bootlegging and prostitution are very much in evidence."[15]

West, across the river from the mansions, amid the stink and grime of the refineries, working men and their families lived in dirt-floor shanties along unpaved streets amid poverty and disease. Two social workers reported "an unusually large and greatly neglected 'slum' district in which large families are living in one-room tents or shacks." They noted, "We have heard it said several times that Tulsa has no slums. . . . As a matter of fact, Tulsa has an acute slum problem. In and around the city lie ragged spots of wretched housing where people live in any kind of miserable shelter, without sewers, water supply or garbage collection, many people crowded together in a shack or tent with no possibility of decent privacy and with no sanitary protection."[16]

Besides west Tulsa, continued the social workers, some of the worst areas were in the "negro district" that stretched more than a mile along either side of Greenwood Avenue north from Archer Street, on the northeast edge of town.[17] The "Black Wall Street of America," the name given Greenwood by Booker T. Washington during a 1913 visit,[18] was a bit of a misnomer. Greenwood had no formal financial institutions, no banks or brokerage houses.[19] In a sense, "Black Main Street of America" might have been more accurate, for Greenwood was alive with an enterprising spirit of commerce remarkable given black Americans' limited access to capital and markets in the early twentieth century. Something about Greenwood drew people from all over the United States. One of them, a young mother from New York named Mary E. Jones Parrish, operated a school where she taught typing and shorthand. Perceptively, Parrish described the place she so loved but which was held in such disdain by whites. "On leaving the Frisco Station," Parrish wrote, "going north to Archer Street, one could see nothing but negro business places. Going east on Archer for two or more blocks, there you would behold Greenwood Avenue, the Negro's Wall Street, and an eyesore to some evil-minded real estate men."[20]

There were not, as some have imagined, great mansions in the Greenwood District. But there were some very nice middle-class houses, especially along Detroit Avenue as it climbed Standpipe Hill on the eastern edge of black Tulsa's domain.[21] And, compared to the conditions under which most black Americans lived, particularly in the rural South, Greenwood was an improvement indeed. Here blacks achieved a measure of independence, able to come and go as they pleased, to work for whom they wished, to build lives of their own. This was not the case in much of the South, parts of rural Oklahoma included, where blacks lived in virtual peonage as sharecroppers and tenant farmers, tied to landlords by debt, intimidation, and courts with a very narrow interpretation of the Fourteenth Amendment.[22]

From the other side of the Frisco tracks, Greenwood looked like a sordid nest of sin and disease—and, razed and rebuilt as a warehouse district, a bonanza waiting to be realized. "Improvised shanties abounded with out-houses on stilts, and yards in conspicuous disorder," is how Amy Comstock, the assistant (and mistress) of *Tulsa Tribune* publisher Richard Lloyd Jones, described Greenwood. "It was in the sordid and neglected 'Niggertown' that crooks found their best hiding place," Comstock continued. "There were the low brothels where the low whites mixed with the low blacks. There were the dope vendors and the dope consumers. There crimes were plotted and loot hidden." The dreams of people like Mary Parrish were dismissed as the fantasies of "the childlike Negro mind."[23]

If whites scoffed at the notion of Greenwood as a "Black Wall Street," it was because they did not understand Greenwood was as much an idea as it was a place—or because they understood all too well. "I came not to Tulsa as many came, lured by the dream of making money and bettering myself in the financial world," wrote Parrish, "but because of the wonderful cooperation I observed among our people, and especially the harmony of spirit and action that existed between the business men and women."[24]

Some whites found this spirit disconcerting, particularly in the years after the Great War, when black military veterans returned home with a new sense of themselves.[25] From statehood, Oklahoma had tried to limit and ostracize blacks, imposing Jim Crow laws and attempting a series of maneuvers intended to keep African Americans from voting.[26] Some white Tulsa County voters expressed open alarm through letters to the editor when a black man, the Reverend E. N.

Bryant, won the 1920 Republican primary for county commissioner in the district that included Greenwood.[27] African American Tulsans asserted their rights and resolve in more muscular ways as well. A. J. Smitherman, editor of the weekly *Tulsa Star*, urged local blacks to arm themselves in response to the lynching of a black prisoner in the Oklahoma County jail. "While the boy was in jail," wrote Smitherman, "and while there was danger of mob violence any set of citizens had a legal right—it was their duty—to arm themselves and march in a body to the jail and apprize the sheriff or jail of the purpose of their visit and to take life if need be to uphold the law and protect the prisoner."[28]

In April 1921, the *Tulsa World* reported that one white law officer had been shot and another beaten when their car was hijacked by three black men in nearby Muskogee County. According to the report, the assailants freed two African American men the officers were transporting to the county jail to avoid a lynch mob in the small town of Oktaha.[29] The story, if true, suggests that Smitherman was not alone in advocating forceful intervention in such circumstances.

Usually, though, resistance was much less dramatic. In mid-May, an elderly black couple, Mr. and Mrs. Gilbert Irge, created a minor stir by refusing to move to the back of a Tulsa streetcar. Apparently more bemused than outraged, local officials fined Gilbert Irge ten dollars, chastised him for corrupting his wife, and sent the pair home.[30]

Much more disturbing, to at least some white Tulsans, was the perceived erosion of social and moral standards exemplified by the mixing of races in dance halls, speakeasies, and hotels along First Street and in the "negro quarter." Generally, the implication was that black pimps, drug dealers, and bootleggers were corrupting young whites, and particularly young white women. On May 20, 1921, the city's most outspoken segregationist and white supremacist, Southern Methodist clergyman Harold Cooke, told a court of inquiry that he and a companion had made the rounds of the city's questionable night spots and found them rife with illegal activity.[31] "At every single place we were informed that we could have girls and liquor according to our tastes," said Cooke. "Usually the deals were conducted through the negro porters. And let me say that they form the most damnable institution in the city today and should be put out of business at once." "Out in the negro section," said Cooke's companion, J. A. Hull, "we visited a place which perhaps was just outside the city limits. There we found whites and negroes singing and dancing together. Young white girls were dancing while negroes played the piano."[32]

This was shocking stuff in 1921—so shocking it became one of the more sensational aspects of a state attorney general's investigation of law enforcement in Tulsa. Attorney General S. Prince Freeling had been after Tulsa and Tulsa County for years.[33] His assistants, Kathryn Van Leuven and George Short, had spent months collecting evidence, and, with the backing of prominent citizens such as Hull and his wife, Lina (a friend of Van Leuven), and Jones's *Tribune*, Freeling must have envisioned a final vindication.[34]

Race was a factor but not the only concern in these proceedings. Black Tulsans also complained about lax law enforcement; Barney Cleaver, a black officer on the force since 1908, was fired in March 1921 after delving too deeply into Police Chief John Gustafson's relationship with a black drug dealer named Smithee.[35]

Claiming (not without some justification) a political witch hunt, local officials preempted Freeling with a court of inquiry, a sort of open and informal grand jury authorized by the city charter but not recognized by state law.[36] Witnesses who eagerly gave information to Freeling and his assistants behind closed doors fell silent in open court.[37] The investigation ground to a halt. To that extent, local officials were successful. But theirs was not much of a victory. In essence, the city and county's defense had been that, while the police and some county officers may have been incompetent, poorly equipped, dangerously undermanned, and corrupt, they were not criminally so.

Freeling's investigation had clattered to a standstill barely a week before Memorial Day. Now, on that solemn, rainy morning, while the rest of the city was occupied elsewhere, two of Tulsa's most insignificant residents—a white teenage divorcée recently arrived from Kansas City and a black youth variously described as a bootblack and a delivery boy—encountered each other on a downtown elevator.[38]

TULSA

In 1882, when the St. Louis–San Francisco Railroad reached the Arkansas River, a man named Josiah Perryman—part Creek Indian, part Caucasian, possibly part African—opened a store along the right-of-way, in the expectation that once the river was bridged and the tracklaying crews moved on, a town would remain. Perryman's was not the only store in the little draw drained by a stream called Cat Creek, nor had it been his idea to put a town there. But Josiah Perryman brought with him the little cubbyholed cabinet designated the post office of Tulsa, Indian Territory.[1]

That name—"Tulsa"—was about all that remained of a Creek settlement that sat on the heights overlooking the Arkansas River for nearly thirty years before disappearing into the cyclone of the American Civil War. Those heights had been the last stop on the Trail of Tears for the people of Lochapoka, a small village of Upper Creeks. Like all tribes of the southeastern United States, the Lochapoka Creeks had been expelled from their Alabama homeland at the demand of white settlers who wanted the Indians' land, and by a U.S. government without means or will to do other than comply. Transported by land and water to Fort Gibson, the army's westernmost outpost at that time, the Lochapokas traveled another fifty miles up the Arkansas, to the river's ninety-degree bend at the fringe of the new Creek Nation. Scattering the ashes of their old ceremonial fire at the base of a great oak tree, a place that became known as the Council Oak, the Lochapokas started life over.[2]

Already established in the vicinity were Plains Indians as well as early Creek and Cherokee settlers and frontiersmen of varied and often uncertain ethnicity. The writer Washington Irving, arriving at Fort Gibson in October 1832, described "stately" Osage warriors with "fine, Roman countenances, and deep broad chests," Creeks "quite oriental in . . . appearance," and "a sprinkling of trappers, hunters, half-breeds, creoles, negroes of every hue."[3] Traveling up the western bank of the Arkansas, Irving observed "Creek villages and farm houses, the inhabitants of which appeared to have adopted, with considerable facility, the rudiments of civilization and to have thriven to consequence. Their farms were well stocked and their houses had a look of comfort and abundance." Near present-day Tulsa, Irving and his party encountered Creeks "returning from one of those grand games of ball, for which their nation is celebrated." Their colorfulness again fascinated Irving. "They have a gypsy fondness for brilliant colors and gay decorations," he wrote, "and are bright and fanciful objects when seen at a distance on the prairies." A little farther, "on the verge of the wilderness," Irving's party encountered a white "settler or squatter,—a tall, rawboned fellow, with red hair, a lank lanthorn visage, an inveterate habit of winking in one eye."[4]

At some point, the when or how unrecorded, the Lochapoka settlement acquired the name "Tulasi"—"Old Town" in the Muscogee Creek language. Over time, "Tulasi" became "Tulsey" or "Tulsey Town," and finally "Tulsa." The bitter, highly personal violence of the Civil War in Indian Territory scattered Tulasi's inhabitants, but the name lingered, attached to an undefined area that included the sprawling fields and pastureland of the Perrymans. The family had been among the earliest Creek immigrants to the Indian Territory, arriving from Alabama in 1828 with a party that advocated voluntary resettlement beyond the Mississippi. The Perryman patriarch, Benjamin, was a man of prominence whose Muscogee name, Steek-cha-ko-me-co, translates as "Great King." He was among those who signed the Treaty of Fort Gibson of 1833 and represented the Creeks at a great intertribal conference the following year. In 1836, Benjamin and his oldest son, Samuel, sat for the portraitist George Catlin.[5]

Benjamin Perryman brought with him to Indian Territory six sons and two daughters. All became important figures in the Creek Nation and its history. One son, Lewis Perryman, established a trading post a few miles southeast of the Lochapoka settlement in about 1848. His large and diverse household included nineteen children and three or four wives, polygamy being common among the Creeks.[6] The naturalist S. W. Woodhouse, passing through the area in 1849, wrote that Lewis Perryman "showed evidently that he had considerable negro blood in him." A photograph of Lewis Perryman's son Legus, twice elected principal chief of the Creek Nation, also suggests possible African ancestry. Certainly, mixed parentage was not unusual among the Creeks. Blacks, free and enslaved, had been part of tribal society for decades.[7]

Benjamin Perryman's ancestry is uncertain, and the identity of his wife or wives is unknown.[8] So the notion that one of Tulsa's founding families might have been of African as well as Indian and European extraction is plausible. But that does not mean it has been widely embraced: the reference to Lewis Perryman's "negro blood" was excised from an edition of Woodhouse's journal published in 1992.[9]

Lewis Perryman and Talasi were both casualties of the Civil War. The small number of federal troops in Indian Territory was withdrawn at the war's outset, leaving the tribal governments little choice but to sign on with the Confederacy. In truth, their sympathies were mostly with the South, and many territory Indians readily volunteered for Confederate militia units. But many others either remained loyal to the Union or tried to stay out of what they viewed as a white man's war. Among these were the 7,000 men, women, and children, Indian and black, who set out for Kansas in November 1861, pursued by 1,400 Texan and Indian Confederates. The so-called loyalists, led by the ancient Seminole warrior Opothleyahola, and the Confederate forces commanded by Texan Douglas Cooper, fought three battles in the vicinity of Tulsa, the net result being the decimation of Opthleyahola's party. The survivors straggled half-naked and starving into southeast Kansas, only to be interned in miserable refugee camps for the remainder of the war. These battles so upset some Confederate Indians, they lost all enthusiasm for the Southern cause. Many switched sides.[10] Among them were several of Lewis Perryman's sons. When federal troops briefly occupied the Cherokee capital at Park Hill in the summer of 1862, the Perryman brothers abandoned the Confederacy for the Indian Home Guard of the Kansas militia. The Confederate recapture of Park Hill a few months later caused Lewis Perryman, well into his seventies, to flee to Kansas with his wives. He died there in December 1862.[11]

But the Perryman family, like the Tulsa name, endured. Lewis Perryman's son George settled after the war near his father's old place and eventually controlled sixty thousand acres of range and farmland. His older brother Josiah concentrated on commerce and in 1879 became postmaster of a stop on the overland mail route from Coffeyville, Kansas, to the Sac and Fox Agency near present-day Stroud. The post office, at George Perryman's combination ranch house and trading post, was called "Tulsa."[12]

A cousin, Alvin Hodge, another of Benjamin Perryman's innumerable grandchildren, grazed cattle on several thousand acres to the north of George Perryman's operation.[13] It was through the northwest corner of Alvin Hodge's holdings that the Atlantic and Pacific Railroad entered the Creek Nation and set up camp while its crews erected a bridge across the Arkansas River.[14]

Neither Hodge nor anyone else owned this land in the sense white Americans understood. No one in the Creek Nation or anywhere in all the Indian nations did. All land was held in common by the tribes, with citizens generally allowed to graze or farm as much they could care for. Non-citizens had no claim to tribal land, but they could lease it—sometimes from tribal citizens rather than the tribes themselves. In this way, by grazing the cattle of Texas and Kansas ranchers on land they controlled, George and Josiah Perryman increased their wealth in the last decades of the nineteenth century.[15]

Tribal law made no provisions for organizing towns or for the taxes necessary to pave streets and dig sewers and lay waterlines, or to educate the children of the ever-increasing number of noncitizen whites and blacks entering the territory. Tribal courts, schools, and institutions of all kinds were closed to the outsiders, who soon complained of these inequities, though all had come to the territory and remained of their own free will.[16]

Traders and other men of commerce required a license from the particular nation in which they conducted their business. The Cherokees, as the most Americanized of the tribes, were also the most savvy and therefore "difficult" to deal with. And that is why, as the new Frisco rails angled down from Vinita in the Cherokee Nation, paymaster H. C. Hall and his brother J. M. talked the chief engineer into moving a planned depot, roundhouse, and townsite two and a half miles southwest, to just across the line in the Creek Nation. The Creeks, the Hall brothers explained, were more "liberal" in their business dealings with whites.[17] H. C. Hall, known as "Harry," picked a spot along the surveyor's stakes not far from the big bend in the Arkansas. In August 1882, a little tent settlement—two stores, a doctor's office, a boarding "house," and a couple of residences—popped up in advance of the work crews. The only permanent structure in the vicinity was the cabin of Noah Partridge, a Creek living in the woods three-quarters of a mile south.[18]

Thus began modern Tulsa.

The settlement grew slowly at first, adding a general store here, a clapboard house there, a church, a livery stable, the Presbyterian mission school. There was no bank until 1895. Logging was a leading economic activity for a number of years. Veins of coal, barely concealed under the prairie sod east of town, were more important than oil, and cattle were more important than either. When communities were finally allowed to incorporate in 1898, Tulsa may have fudged the numbers a little to come up with the requisite one thousand residents.[19]

One of Tulsa's earliest, loudest, and most effective boosters was an erstwhile traveling shoe salesman named Wyatt Tate Brady. A native Missourian, Tate Brady arrived in Tulsa in 1890 as a twenty-year-old with not much more than ambition and drive. Declaring the village ripe with promise, Brady set down his sample cases and set up shop, establishing a mercantile business and later a hotel and marrying into a prominent mixed-blood Cherokee family. Short, stocky, energetic, Brady immersed himself in local and state politics and tribal affairs. He was one of the signers of the 1898 charter and an organizer of the booster trains that brought national attention to Tulsa. He invested extensively in real estate, particularly north of the Frisco tracks, in the soon-to-be-dissolved Cherokee Nation. His close friends included Oklahoma's first governor, Charles Haskell, and it was in Brady's hotel, in 1910, that the scheme was hatched to spirit the official seal from the existing state capital, Guthrie, to the new one, Oklahoma City, ahead of a voter-approved transfer.[20] Brady was also associated with and sometimes acted as a surrogate for Charles Page, a wealthy oilman and philanthropist who founded the town of Sand Springs a few miles west of Tulsa, and who exerted considerable influence over local affairs.[21]

Brady's vision began to take a more substantial shape in 1901, when oil was discovered five miles southwest of Tulsa at the village of Red Fork, the next stop on the Frisco line. The well produced too little, demand was too small, prices too low and transportation costs too high for this first strike to be profitable, but four years later, when the Ida Glenn No. 1 came a gusher one November night, the supply and demand trend lines had crossed. The petroleum age had arrived. The Glenn Pool, twelve miles southwest of Tulsa, became Oklahoma's first great oilfield, and one of the greatest in the world at that time. With the discovery of the Glenn Pool field, Tulsa went from town to city almost overnight.[22]

But there had been more to Tulsa's success than the Glenn Pool. Within a few years, even greater oilfields were discovered in the tangled, rock-strewn hills to the west and on the windswept Osage country to the northwest. Some other town, Jenks or Sapulpa or Red Fork or Kiefer, might have become the mid-continent hub of the burgeoning new oil and gas industry. Notwithstanding a natural gas flare that burned for a while from a pipe sticking out of the ground at the intersection of Boulder and Seventh,[23] Tulsa had no oil and gas production itself.

Drilling, in fact, was soon outlawed in the city limits.[24] What Tulsa did have was the ambition and foresight to turn itself into a railroad center, to build hotels, to start banks and opera houses, and to tolerate the saloons and gambling dens and bawdy houses where rough, hardworking men found entertainment.[25] Local businessmen put up "bonuses" to convince more railroads to come through town. Raucous, swaggering delegations of boosters chartered special trains to take them to Chicago, to St. Louis, to the East Coast, spreading their city's name and reputation.[26] Thus, when opportunity presented itself, Tulsa was ready. From a population of about 1,400 in 1900, Tulsa grew to 7,300 by statehood just seven years later. Three years after that, the 1910 census counted 18,000 Tulsans.[27]

Many of those eighteen thousand doubted that oil would be a lasting influence on the city's economy. The oil industry was young, but not so young that it had not already left a string of busted boomtowns in its wake. Agriculture and industry—not the carnival mayhem of oil—were the basis of a sound economic future. The Glenn Pool was still producing at full throttle when the Commercial Club, forerunner of the chamber of commerce, sponsored a contest to suggest a more substantial direction for the city once the Glenn Pool began its inevitable decline. The winning entry argued that Tulsa should aspire to asparagus capital of the world.

But the Glenn Pool was a start, not an ending. Discovery of the Cushing Field west of Tulsa in 1912 and the advent of competitive bidding for drilling rights in the former Osage Reservation to the northwest elbowed aside dreams of global asparagus domination. This new production, combined with increasing domestic demand and the onset of the Great War in Europe, made Tulsa one of the wealthiest, fastest-growing cities in the nation.[28] Tulsa's official population grew fourfold during the second decade of the twentieth century, to more than seventy-two thousand.[29] Many additions and subdivisions, including most of the black Greenwood District, lay outside the city limits, purposely excluded for various reasons, most of them financial in one way or another.[30]

The boosterism that drove Tulsans to pool their money to influence railroads and evangelize far and wide—and, in 1912, to build a modern hotel, the Hotel Tulsa, restoring the city's reputation for offering the best accommodations in the region[31]—reached unprecedented and at times dangerous proportions during and even before the war. Spurred by pride, shamed by the fiery harangues of patriotic speechmakers known as Four Minute Men, Tulsans subscribed to Liberty bonds and convinced or coerced their neighbors to do the same. Volunteers organized Oklahoma Ambulance Company No. 1, the first National Guard unit of its kind in the state and maybe in the country. A recruiting station, set up on Main Street, did a steady business.[32]

But this zeal, this enthusiasm to prove Tulsa the best, most loyal, most American of cities had its darker side. In November 1917, a week after an explosion at the home of a Carter Oil Company executive,[33] police raided rooms in the Fox Hotel at Main and Brady Streets, and arrested eleven members of the radical labor organization the Industrial Workers of the World, commonly called "Wobblies."[34] Six more were arrested a few days later when they appeared in court as witnesses for their comrades. Judge T. D. Evans fined each of the eleven originally arrested one hundred dollars for vagrancy and strongly recommended the lot of them leave town; the Wobblies were then loaded by police into three automobiles, ostensibly to be driven the few blocks to the Fox Hotel, where they would pack their bags and catch the first train out. The little motorcade had barely left the jail, however, when it was ambushed and the police supposedly overwhelmed by men in black robes and masks. These men, calling themselves the Knights of Liberty, drove the prisoners west of town; there, invoking "the outraged women and children of Belgium"—a reference to alleged German atrocities in the World War—they proceeded to administer an old-fashioned flogging, followed by an application of hot tar and feathers. Later, when one of the scourged union men dared return to Tulsa, the Knights quickly persuaded him to leave once and for all.[35]

The Knights of Liberty, said to have included Tate Brady as well as the chief of police and a local newspaper editor,[36] seemed to disappear as quickly and mysteriously as they materialized. They appeared only once more, near the end of the war, marching silently through the streets as a warning against those who did not buy their expected allotment of war bonds.[37] The same methods, however, would be repeated many times, with only slight variation, over the next half-dozen years. Undesirables—suspected drug dealers, wife beaters, adulterers, foreigners—were pulled in by the police and then either turned over directly to vigilantes or released in such a way as to make them easy targets. It would lead directly to at least one murder and countless beatings and ultimately contribute to dozens of other deaths and an unspeakable conflagration. Eventually, it would culminate in an extraordinary six weeks of martial law and military tribunals that laid bare a shadowy network of officially sanctioned violence and intimidation.[38]

This vigilantism began shortly after America's entry into the Great War, with the creation in Tulsa and throughout the state and nation of local councils of defense charged with monitoring everything from profiteers to draft resisters to Sunday sermons. In theory, Oklahoma's councils had limited legal authority, but that did not prevent them from imposing almost absolute rule. The Tulsa County Council, while accomplishing much in furthering the war effort, also exhibited little regard for the rights of individual citizens. Its investigation department tracked down "slackers" as far away as Florida and California and imposed its unofficial justice. A local clergyman, said to be unenthusiastic about the "voluntary" monthly sermon on patriotism, received a visit from council members who reported success in adjusting the preacher's attitude. Some Mennonites near Collinsville, twenty miles northeast of Tulsa, requested permission to continue their benedictions in German, and to have a monthly sermon in the language. Their request was declined, and a German-language school a few miles away near Skiatook closed. The council even opened a "detention center" whose exact nature is unclear except that its "patients" all seem to have been women who were interned as "a war measure whereby the morale and health of soldiers might be protected and advanced."[39]

At the council's disposal were the volunteer agents of the American Protective League, which today would be called a domestic spying agency, and the Home Guard, a one-thousand-member paramilitary force ostensibly created to replace National Guard units called to duty in Europe, but that acted more as an enforcement arm of the council. A "colored" company was even organized, trained, and led by black ex-servicemen, but never used. The American Protective League, an all-volunteer auxiliary of the Justice Department's Bureau of Investigation—later to become the Federal Bureau of Investigation—poked into the lives of hundreds of Tulsans, compiling files of photographs and reports passed to federal and local authorities. To be sure, many of these cases involved actual law violations, especially the Selective Service Act, but many others fell under nebulous categories such as "loyalty and character."[40]

The council's leadership, and the Home Guard's, included some of Tulsa's most prominent, respected, and generous citizens, but such was the level of hysteria feeding Tulsa's righteous and patriotic zealotry that few saw the potential dangers of such extralegal powers. Even the famous entertainer Eddie Foy was censured and reported by the council for unflattering remarks about the Home Guard made during an appearance at a local theater.[41] The end of the war in 1918 ultimately brought an end to the councils of defense, the Home Guard, and the American Protective League, but not the moralistic atmosphere of intimidation and intolerance they engendered and exemplified, and that would soon manifest itself in the likes of the Palmer Raids, the recurrence of the Ku Klux Klan, and the Red Summer of 1919.

Economic recession acerbated these social tensions. From 1919 to 1920, corporate profits declined nearly 90 percent, the Dow Jones Average fell 47 percent, and bankruptcies tripled.[42] To this bubbling cauldron of postwar America was added labor unrest, deteriorating race relations, woman suffrage, Prohibition, and immigration. The pot boiled over in summer 1919, with race riots breaking out in more than three dozen locations, from major cities such as New York, Chicago, and Washington, D.C., to remote rural communities such as Elaine, Arkansas, and northern factory towns like Coatesville, Pennsylvania. In Omaha, the army had to be sent in to restore order after a mob hung a black rape suspect and burned his body.[43] In Bisbee, Arizona, local police attacked the all-black U.S. Tenth Cavalry.[44]

Tulsa remained relatively quiet through all of this. There were strikes and threats of strikes, and loud complaints about the "high cost of living," but no outbursts of large-scale violence, not even when a black man was accused of shooting to death a white man.[45] But there is little doubt what Tulsans, white and black, thought about the racial conflict unfolding elsewhere. In July 1919, the *Tulsa World*'s evening edition asked four prominent locals, all white, for their opinions on the riot then raging in Chicago. Three of the four laid the blame squarely on blacks.[46] Three days later the *World* published a lengthy letter by Rev. H. T. F. Johnson, a black clergyman, taking issue with the assessment and warning of worse to come:

> After reading the comments referred to, I grew sad over the thought that possibly if all the white people of Tulsa had been interviewed, the same percent would have given black Tulsa the worst of it. And it did not help my spirits any to think that on the other hand, if all the [N]egroes had given opinions no less a majority would be against the white people. This plainly establishes the fact that whatever may be the cause or causes, there is a growing feeling of hate and prejudice between the races which must come to a crisis some day if the growth is not checked, and no peace-loving citizen of either race can think of the probable result without shuddering.[47]

3

GREENWOOD

How or why North Greenwood Avenue became the axis around which black Tulsa revolved is no longer clear. An oft-repeated story of recent years is that around 1905 a black man from Arkansas named O. W. Gurley bought forty acres that he reserved for African Americans.[1] This may be true but has not been verified by existing land records.[2]

Men and women of African ancestry had populated what became northeastern Oklahoma since at least the great Indian removal. Most came as slaves to mixed-blood Creeks and Cherokees; a few were adopted tribal members.[3] Some old Tulsa families will tell you that their people were never slaves, that they and the Indians shared common ancestors who crossed the Atlantic from Africa centuries before Europeans.[4] That this is contrary to most prevailing theory and scientific evidence matters not a whit to the believers. If anything, it is proof of the duplicity employed to deny them their heritage.

In any event, the black residents of the Creek Nation were concentrated on the rich farmland of the Choska Bottoms at the confluence of the Grand, Verdigris, and Arkansas Rivers, well south of Tulsa. Emancipated after the Civil War, the former slaves among them became full citizens and received allotments with the rest of the tribe's members when the tribal governments were dissolved and the tribal land parceled out in the early 1900s.[5]

By various means, outsiders filtered into the Indian nations after the Civil War, sometimes with the tribes' permission but often without.[6] They were looking

Downtown Tulsa and the Greenwood District, 1921. *Map by Steve Reckinger.*

for a foothold, a head start on the boom that would come with statehood. And statehood would come. Everyone knew it except the Indians, and even they, deep down, knew it, too. By 1900, whites outnumbered Indians in Indian Territory six to one. Blacks were a still-smaller minority, about thirty-seven thousand in all, of whom probably a quarter to a half were "state Negroes"—blacks not born in the territory and not brought there on the great migration of seventy years earlier.[7]

Where and how many African Americans lived in and around Tulsa from the arrival of the railroad until the special statehood census of 1907 is unknown. J. M. Hall, in his account of those years, mentions only two black residents, a man named Shanks, who dug the town's first water well, and a "mulatto negro" named Sorrel who was the first barber.[8] The 1907 census counted 6,611 whites, 638 Negroes, and, remarkably, only 49 Indians in Tulsa.[9] By then, blacks were moving into Tulsa's northeast corner.[10]

Brothers Gus and Dan Patton had been hired in 1900 to prepare a townsite plat so that lots could finally be transferred to private ownership.[11] The Pattons' survey extended and formalized the grid that had evolved with the Frisco tracks as its baseline. Because the tracks ran a few degrees from true east and west, the streets laid out parallel and perpendicular to it were equally off-kilter, and the entire townsite sat at an angle to the world. Thus, its northern edge, which was also the northern boundary of the Creek Nation, cut diagonally through city blocks. Near the northeast corner, Greenwood Avenue extended only a block and a half above Archer, the first street north of the Frisco tracks.[12]

The Pattons had suggested numbering east-west thoroughfares "streets" and naming north-south thoroughfares "avenues." Main Street divided east and west; the Frisco tracks, north and south. Avenues east of Main Street generally would be named for cities east of Tulsa. Avenues west of Main were mostly named for cities west of Tulsa. The first street south of the divide was First Street South, the next, Second Street South, and so on. The same pattern applied north of the tracks, but almost immediately it was decided to name those streets for cities, too—and then, just as quickly, the first few were named instead for pioneer Tulsans. Thus, First Street North became Archer Street, named for a merchant killed when a drunken customer fired a gun into a barrel of black powder. Second Street North was named for the indefatigable Tate Brady. Those were followed by Cameron (possibly Missouri), Davenport (Iowa), and Easton (Pennsylvania). The avenues east of Main were Boston, Cincinnati, Detroit, Elgin, and Frankfort.[13] Greenwood Avenue was likely named for Greenwood, Arkansas, the Pattons' hometown.[14]

The land records' earliest entry for North Greenwood is March 1903, when the Creek Nation transferred one lot and part of another in Block 46 of the original townsite to a James Salts. Block 46 is the first block north of Archer on the west side of Greenwood. Block 47 is the first block on the east side. The earliest records for Block 47 show the Creek Nation had deeded it entirely to E. M. Rambo, a white real estate developer, by June 1906. Whether any of this property was previously occupied under license from the Creek Nation is not known.[15]

Whether Gurley, an enterprising and politically active black businessman, truly founded Greenwood is probably a matter of interpretation. Certainly he was important in establishing it as a black community. The Gurley name first appears in the land records in May 1906 when Emma Gurley, O. W.'s wife, acquired property in Block 46 from Giuseppe "Joe" Piro, a white man. Gurley's hotel and store may have been the first businesses on Greenwood north of Archer. In 1911, the Gurley Hill Addition was platted just north of the town's original boundary. But Gurley was not early Greenwood's largest property owner. Land records suggest he and his wife Emma never owned more than a few lots; whether his involvement in Gurley Hill Addition extended much beyond the use of his name is unclear. Records show the land was owned by a William Campbell and platted by J. Roff Burnham.[16]

Salts kept his property only a year before selling it to W. F. Jones, who became one of the leading property owners in the neighborhood. Other early owners included Piro, Rambo, G. F. Blevins, C. F. Parker, and William and James Miller. Besides the Gurleys, John and Loula Williams were among the first African Americans established on Greenwood Avenue.[17] They came to Tulsa in the early 1900s after John took a job operating the steam engine at a creamery. He soon left that job and opened an automobile repair shop, and over the next decade and a half Williams added a three-story building at Archer and Greenwood that included Loula's confectionary, and another building that housed a theater and a rooming house.[18]

If North Greenwood's identity as a black neighborhood was not established at the outset, it evolved very quickly. In 1906, the first few blocks north of the original town boundary were platted as the Turley Addition,[19] and it was then that names more familiar to the history of Greenwood began to appear: Cleaver, Cherry, Bridgewater, Stradford, Lockard.[20]

Barney Cleaver was a lawman in the tradition of the legendary Bass Reeves, tough and smart and adept at the delicate art of being a black man of authority, however limited, in a white world. By and large, Cleaver seems to have been respected on both sides of the Frisco tracks and was perhaps even a little feared. Born in Virginia soon after the Civil War, Cleaver is described in the 1870 and 1880 census records as a mulatto, the son of a black father and mulatto mother. In 1900, he was working as a coal miner in the Choctaw Nation. He moved to Tulsa a few years later, maybe to work in the coal mines east of town. By 1908, he was on the Tulsa police force.[21]

Cleaver settled in the new Turley Addition, at the "n end Greenwood," according to the 1910 city directory. That same year he married for the second time, to Vernon "Vernie" Harrison of Joplin, Missouri, who brought with her a one-year-old daughter named Chloe. The Cleaver home, soon assigned the address

508 North Greenwood Avenue, apparently became a rather large one, for by 1920 it housed not only Barney, Vernie, and Chloe, but five boarders as well. Cleaver remained on the force until he was dismissed for continuing to poke around in vice operations outside the city limits after he had been ordered to stop. He briefly worked for the Burns Detective Agency before becoming a Tulsa County deputy sheriff. All the while, he invested in real estate and acted as a broker.[22]

Jim Cherry was a plumber from Texas who became one of Greenwood's most successful black property owners. Like many financially secure black Tulsans of the era, Cherry seems to have been constantly on the scout for financial opportunity. Between 1909 and 1921 he operated a pool hall, ran a grocery store, took in boarders, traded real estate, and served as a deputy sheriff. His brother William and son Jasper were also in the building trades, making it reasonable to assume the three of them also remained active in construction during those years.[23]

Dr. Robert Tyler Bridgewater was born in Taylor County, Kentucky, in 1879, but in 1906, when he married Mattie Halmer in Sedalia, Missouri, Bridgewater gave Tulsa, Indian Territory, as his address. The 1909 city directory listed him as one of Tulsa's two black physicians. Bridgewater originally lived and saw patients on North Hartford, one block east of Greenwood, but in 1918 he moved his office to 103½ North Greenwood and joined the prominent African Americans living on North Detroit. He could be testy—to hear whites tell it, anyway—but was sufficiently respected to be appointed assistant county physician.[24]

Joe Lockard was born in Indian Territory to native Texans. His wife Rina was also born in the territory, to parents who appear to have been tribal freedman. Joe and Rina operated a rooming house at 20 North Boston Avenue, then opened a diner a few blocks away at 316 East Archer.[25]

Andrew Smitherman and his younger brother John were born in Alabama, but by 1900 the family had moved to Lehigh, near Cleaver's family in the Choctaw Nation, and where their father worked as a coal miner.[26] Eight years older than John, Andrew soon moved to Muskogee, where he became a protégé of Dr. W. H. Twine, a prominent member of the community and publisher of the *Muskogee Cimeter*. Andrew Smitherman also dealt in real estate while in Muskogee and married his wife, Ollie. The Smithermans moved to Tulsa around 1913, where they established the *Tulsa Star*, a feisty weekly that did not hesitate to throw darts at both white and black leadership.[27]

John Smitherman followed his older brother to Tulsa in probably 1916 or 1917, when he would have been in his midtwenties. He first appears in the 1917 city directory, when he is listed as living with his mother, Bessie, in a rooming house at 14 North Cincinnati Avenue.[28] His draft registration from that same year indicates that John was also responsible for the care of a twelve-year-old brother.[29] John Smitherman was already working as a deputy sheriff and may have been a private detective on the side.[30] By 1920, he was married with a small daughter and living in a house at 322 North Elgin, which his family shared with ten boarders, including Deputy Sheriff Staley Webb.[31]

John B. Stradford was a glowering Kentuckian whose full name, according to some sources, was John The Baptist Stradford.[32] Certainly he possessed the prophet's righteous zeal. In 1912, when a conductor ordered Stradford out of a first-class car for which he had a ticket, Stradford sued. He lost, as he probably knew he would, but his point was made.[33] Stradford (sometimes spelled "Stratford") was born in Kentucky during the Civil War.[34] He may have lived a while in St. Louis, where his brother Ben was a barber.[35] He attended Oberlin College and went to law school in Indiana.[36] After his wife, Bertie, died around 1903,[37] Stradford moved briefly to Coffeyville, Kansas,[38] where his brother then lived, but in 1906 he bought three lots in the Turley Addition, apparently with money he borrowed from Dick Bardon, a white pawnshop owner.[39] The 1911 Tulsa city directory lists Stradford as operator of a pool hall at 26 North Boston Avenue. Within a short time, the pool hall moved to 407 East Easton, and Stradford opened a real estate office at 103½ North Greenwood. He had also remarried; his second wife, Augusta, was nineteen years' Stradford's junior, and is listed in the 1919 city directory as a city librarian.[40]

J. B. Stradford's crowning achievement, the Stradford Hotel, was completed around 1920,[41] and was emblematic of Greenwood's accelerating growth. In 1911, the only "colored" hotel in Tulsa was Gurley's. There were five black churches, three black attorneys, two black physicians, and no black theaters.[42] Ten years later, the city directory listed a dozen black churches, fifteen black physicians, a black hospital, and two black theaters.[43] The Hunton YMCA on North Greenwood reported five hundred members.[44] Booker T. Washington High School, perhaps the first secondary school in the state for African American students, had opened in 1913 at the corner of Haskell Street and North Exeter Place. Younger students attended Dunbar, on Hartford between Cameron and Easton Streets.[45] The neighborhood, by this time practically a city unto itself, reached from Detroit Avenue, three blocks west of Greenwood, to Madison, three blocks east of Greenwood, and north from Archer Street to Pine and even a little beyond.[46] Arguably, the best houses, or at least the most prized, lined the east side of Detroit Avenue as it rose along the brow of Standpipe Hill—so named because early Tulsa's water supply depended on a standpipe atop it. With front porches that faced white neighbors across Detroit Avenue lived the likes of Andrew Smitherman, surgeon A. C. Jackson, Booker T. Washington principal E. W. Woods, Dr. Bridgewater, and others.[47]

But the heights of Sunset Hill, which projected eastward along Fairview Street almost as far as Greenwood Avenue, and at whose foot set a brick plant, were occupied by working-class whites.[48] Thus, the heart of Greenwood sat in a poorly drained valley with mostly unpaved streets, no sanitary sewers, and little or no running water. Rev. H. T. F. Johnson, in his 1919 letter to the *World*, said, "The unsanitary condition of the negro section is the city's outstanding disgrace."[49] When, in March 1921, 350 blacks petitioned the city commission to annex their subdivisions into the city limits, and to provide sewers, running water, paved streets, and a fire station, they were practically laughed out of the room.[50]

And yet Tulsa must have had its attractions. From 1910 to 1920, the city's African American population swelled fourfold, from just less than two thousand to almost nine thousand, a rate somewhat greater than for whites.[51] Mary Jones Parrish, the young black woman who came to Tulsa from Rochester, New York, said this migration was prompted by economic opportunity but also a sense of purpose and community. "Every face seemed to wear a happy smile," she wrote.[52]

A half century after the Emancipation Proclamation, African Americans lived a sort of shadow existence, somewhere between the forced servitude of their forbearers (or even their own youth) and real freedom. Where they lived, what they did, even what they aspired to be, were grimly circumscribed. This was particularly true in the South, where many black Americans labored in conditions not much removed from slavery, bound to landowners through intimidation, chicanery, and perpetual debt, in a condition known as "virtual peonage."[53] During the opening months of 1921, two sensational cases came to light. In March, a Georgia plantation owner and his black foreman were accused and subsequently convicted of murdering eleven black farmhands to keep them from "squealing" about the conditions under which they lived, worked, and ultimately died.[54] Two months later, former Florida governor Sidney Catts was charged with keeping blacks in a state of servitude on his plantation.[55]

Educational and occupational options for African Americas were limited; even the few who managed to achieve professional status could not expect to earn as much as their white counterparts.[56] Blacks were effectively excluded from the political process through much of the country, and only marginally included most everywhere else.[57] Thus the ballot box, the schoolhouse, and even the barest chance at a decent life were denied millions of African Americans.

In Tulsa, they at least saw a glimmer of light. The schools were not nearly as well-equipped nor the teachers nearly as well-paid as those for whites, but still they were better than most available to black children elsewhere.[58] There were plenty of jobs, and while they may not have been the best jobs, or the highest paying, they beat picking cotton or living under the thumb of a despotic landlord. And there was opportunity, maybe not the same opportunity that made white men into millionaires, but enough to fashion a comfortable life through hard work and diligence.

Most black Tulsans made their living across the Frisco tracks or across the crest of Standpipe Hill, as domestic workers, cooks, waiters, porters, shoeshines, laborers, truck drivers. Some were in the building trades, skilled and semiskilled: plumbers, carpenters, mechanics, bricklayers.[59] They worked for whites, by and large, but were not bound to them. They could leave a job they did not like, could spend money with whomever they wanted. Mostly, they spent it in Greenwood. It was not that downtown businesses necessarily barred African Americans; some did, especially restaurants and hotels, and stores that did not outright refuse service to blacks often humiliated them. But, in the end, most were more than willing to take black people's money. But black Tulsans consciously kept their money in their community—so much so that William Redfearn, a white man who owned a store and a theater in Greenwood, complained that potential customers were being intimidated.[60] "No man, be he pauper or millionaire, had more pride in Tulsa than her upstanding, forward looking colored citizens," wrote G. A. Gregg, executive secretary of the YMCA's Greenwood branch.[61]

Greenwood became a town within a town. Even many of the street names were different, particularly in the subdivisions soon spreading to the north. This was common practice in white additions, too, but in Greenwood it contributed to the sense of insulation and isolation. In Greenwood, Frankfort Place became Exeter Place. Independence Street became Gurley Boulevard. Marshall Street became Dunbar. Oklahoma Street became Center Street. Iroquois became Pocahontas. King became Bryant.[62]

The postal service maintained a substation in Economy Drug at 108 North Greenwood.[63] A public library, perhaps affiliated with the downtown public library and perhaps not, was operated by an "efficient colored librarian" named Mrs. Bankhead. The *Tulsa World*, in a story soliciting donations for the undertaking, reported that Mrs. Bankhead had with her own money bought and moved to Tulsa a one-room house for this purpose, but that it had no furniture and very few books and received no money from the city.[64]

Politics were lively. Early attempts to suppress the black vote statewide through a so-called grandfather clause amended to the state constitution proved largely ineffective in Tulsa. The *Tulsa Democrat* warned in 1912 that Tulsa would be overrun by blacks—"Muskogeeized," as editor William Stryker called it—if the town let African Americans become overly familiar with the ballot box.[65] For some reason, this does not seem to have concerned white Tulsans much. The grandfather clause, which subjected most African Americans to literacy tests but excluded most whites, seems to have been enforced only once in Tulsa, in a 1912 municipal runoff primary. It was a disaster. Whites as well as blacks were inconvenienced, and a Republican poll watcher and former police commissioner named John Oliphant was arrested when he tried to intervene.[66] Thereafter, Tulsa election officials allowed the grandfather clause and its literacy test to languish in judicial limbo until the U.S. Supreme Court, in 1915, ruled it unconstitutional. That case, *Guinn v. United States*, was the first civil rights lawsuit to involve the National Association for the Advancement of Colored People (NAACP).[67]

Oklahoma's grandfather clause belonged to the ruling Democratic Party's fevered efforts to not only disenfranchise but subjugate African Americans,[68] and was spurred in part by the 1908 election of a black man, A. C. Hamlin, to the Oklahoma House of Representatives. Amended to the state constitution with the aid of a dubious provision by which unmarked ballots counted as votes for the amendment, the grandfather clause helped prevent Hamlin's reelection in 1910.[69] Undiscouraged by the Supreme Court's decision in *Guinn*, Oklahoma erected new barriers to the ballot box targeting poor rural whites as well as blacks. Alarmed by the election of six Socialists to the legislature in 1914, lawmakers limited voter registration to a single two-week period and declared those missing the deadline banned for life from voting in Oklahoma. This latter provision does not seem to have been rigorously enforced, at least not in Tulsa County, but it remained on the books until overturned by the courts in 1939.[70] Oklahoma, meanwhile, would not elect another black legislator until court-ordered reapportionment in the 1960s.[71]

In truth, despite the fearmongering claims of "Negro domination," Oklahoma's black population was never large enough to win more than a few local elections. The same was true for Tulsa.[72] But there were enough black votes to influence city and county elections, and white politicians were as likely to try to win those votes as to suppress them.[73] White office seekers, especially Democrats, advertised in A. J. Smitherman's *Tulsa Star*.[74] They appeared at neighborhood functions and met with black leaders.[75] Although civil rights were the leading issue for black Tulsa voters, there were other, more prosaic considerations: schools, jobs, public safety. The political aspirations and ambitions of men and women like E. N. Bryant and A. C. Hamlin owed something to rutted, unpaved streets and poor sanitation as surely as they did to high-blown ideals.[76]

Yet even these issues were shaped by race. The idea that blacks should expect the same streets, sanitation, schools, and police and fire protection seemed ludicrous and even arrogant to many whites. Whites often claimed at least cursory acceptance of "legal equality," the principle that all races deserved equal treatment under the law, but "social equality"—the integration of society—was something else entirely. Some whites might argue for a black person's right to vote or get some semblance of a fair trial, but that did not mean they wanted to sit next to black people in a theater or send their children to school with African American kids. In April 1921, when the Harding administration proposed appointing a black man registrar of the Treasury, Oklahoma congressman Charles Carter—an American Indian—protested on the grounds that "five hundred white women" would be working for him.[77]

That same month, the *World*'s editorial page complained loudly about U.S. senator Boise Penrose of Pennsylvania using his influence to get that state to pass a law guaranteeing black people equal access to public accommodations such as hotels and restaurants. Of Tulsa's two daily newspapers, the *World* was the more progressive—or at least the more reserved—on race, but that did not preclude it from being staunchly segregationist. "Never," editorialist Tom Latta wrote of Penrose, "did he transgress the laws of decency and practical reason more outrageously than in his impossible declaration for social equality for the black men of the nation."[78]

A week later, a letter writer to the *World* lashed another reader, named C. W. Joshua, who had defended Penrose. "I do not know C. W. Joshua, but . . . I am compelled to list him as being either a saddle-colored coon or a degenerate white man, emanating from that small class that believes in the social equality of whites and negroes," wrote Gid Graham of Nowata, a town northeast of Tulsa. "No man could write such a [letter] as this in whose veins flowed pure Caucasian blood."[79] J. T. Bailey of Tulsa wrote, "Had God intended the negro to be the equal of the white man He would have straightened his kinky hair and flat nose, thinned his thick lips and then bleached his skin. Social equality is absolutely and positively impossible—no decent white person will even think of it, let alone advocate it."[80]

This deceit, that "equality under the law" could exist independently and without regard to social and economic discrimination, had been validated by the U.S. Supreme Court's 1896 *Plessy v. Ferguson* decision. Against it, African

Americans grew increasingly frustrated, and began to push back. Nationally, the first two decades of the twentieth century witnessed the rise of what would become known as the "New Negro": assertive, independent, ambitious.[81] Not coincidentally, the first two decades of the twentieth century also witnessed a rise in racial violence.[82]

In Tulsa, the loudest African American voice was A. J. Smitherman's *Star*. Unlike most politically active blacks of that era, Smitherman was a partisan Democrat;[83] the *World*, in fact, implied that the *Star* was subsidized by the Democratic Party.[84] Smitherman feuded with the "poor, pedantic little editor" of Oklahoma City's *Black Dispatch*, Roscoe Dunjee,[85] who was arguably the most respected and influential black man in the state. Willing but skeptical, Smitherman joined in Governor J. B. A. Robertson's interracial conferences, which were largely ignored by the white press, and mocked the *World* for claiming that influential blacks favored segregation.[86] "If, as the *Tulsa World* says," Smitherman wrote, "there are leading Colored men who favor the 'Jim Crow' railroad transportation laws of Oklahoma, it is the opinion of the Star these so-called black leaders are ripe for a full coat of tar and feathers and a swift ride on fence rails out of any community in which they live."[87]

The black intellectual W. E. B. DuBois, then leader of the NAACP, visited Tulsa while on a tour of Oklahoma in March 1921, but while DuBois was one of the two or three most famous African Americans alive, the white press ignored him except for a brief advance notice in the *World* that misspelled his name.[88] (The *Star* undoubtedly covered the great man's visit, but no copies of those issues survive.) In all likelihood, DuBois would have at least touched on the subject of lynching. At about the same time DuBois came through Tulsa, the NAACP began distributing a brochure composed entirely of headlines related to the abduction and murder of Henry Lowery,[89] who was burned to death in the Arkansas delta for allegedly killing his white employer and his employer's daughter. Lowery had escaped to El Paso, but for some reason did not cross into Mexico before sending a postcard to relatives back home. Authorities intercepted the card, Lowery was arrested, and he was being transported back to Arkansas by train when vigilantes seized him in Mississippi. Newspapers and wire services filed frequent updates as Lowery was driven to Memphis—where the ringleaders paused for dinner and to hold court at the Peabody Hotel—and then across the Mississippi River back into Arkansas. Originally, the plan to was to hang Lowery at the place where he was supposed to have killed the two whites (he does not seem to have denied the charges), but when that did not work out he was tethered to a tree and a fire was started. Instead of being put in the fire and thus swiftly consumed, Lowery was slowly roasted until someone finally put a bullet in him. Throughout the ordeal, law enforcement officials insisted there was simply nothing they could do.[90]

The story was on the front page of newspapers, including Tulsa's, for days, sharing space with developments in the case of twelve black men convicted of murder during the Phillips County, Arkansas, race war of 1919. That incident, which some believe was the deadliest of the many racial conflicts of this era, involved black sharecroppers trying to organize a union against the wishes of the white landowners. When law officers arrived at the rural black church where this nascent association was meeting, gunfire erupted, resulting in the death of a white railroad detective and the wounding of a deputy sheriff. Five hundred armed whites, later joined by a similar number of regular army troops, swept through the county in a deadly retaliation justified by calling what had happened a "Negro insurrection." At least five whites and an unknown number of blacks were killed. Hundreds of African Americans were arrested. The twelve convicted of murder and sentenced to die ultimately went free, the result of landmark legal proceedings that stretched on for more than five years.[91] But such a reprieve seemed unlikely in the spring of 1921, when hardly a day went by without a black man somewhere in the country being strung up, shot, burned, or otherwise dispatched in the name of quick justice.[92]

It is not surprising, then, that some in Greenwood feared and expected the worst when they heard about the trouble in the Drexel Building, on Main between Third and Fourth Streets. The Rowland boy, the one sometimes known as "Dick," had in some way interfered with a white girl—innocently maybe, but that hardly mattered once the white girl screamed.

"THE STORY THAT
SET TULSA ABLAZE"

Later it would be said that Sarah Page and the young man called Dick Rowland were acquaintances and maybe quite a bit more. A half century after whatever happened on that downtown Tulsa elevator, a woman who claimed she was Dick Rowland's adoptive mother would say he and Page had been lovers.[1] Perhaps they were. But the story Damie Rowland told and Ruth Avery recorded, now another half century ago, contains just enough inconsistencies to make one wonder how much Damie Rowland knew firsthand and how much she acquired secondhand and thirdhand over the intervening years.[2]

The fact is, remarkably little is known about these two central characters in the drama that was about to unfold. This is particularly true of Page. Unnamed in initial reports that referred to her as an "orphan" working her way through business college,[3] she was later identified as a fifteen-year-old divorcée from Kansas City who had come to Tulsa while the dust settled on the ruins of a brief and unhappy marriage.[4] Rowland is described by various sources as the biological son of David and Alice "Ollie" Rowland; the adopted son of Dave and Ollie; their biological grandson; and their adopted grandson. The only Richard or Dick Rowland in the city directories of the period was white,[5] but Dave and Ollie did have a sixteen-year-old John Roland living with them at the time of the 1920 census. "John Roland" is listed as a grandson born in Texas.[6] Damie Rowland, Dave and Ollie's daughter, said in her 1972 interview that Dick Rowland's real name was Jimmy Jones, that she had taken him off the streets in Vinita when he was a small boy, and that he was born in Arkansas.[7] Alice Andrews, who had just turned nineteen that fateful morning, told interviewer Eddie Faye Gates in the 1990s that Dick Rowland—and she referred to him by that name—was the son of David "Dad" Rowland and was a "well-off boy" who "didn't have to work" but did.[8] Robert Fairchild told Gates that he "knew Dick when he was a star football player at Booker Washington High School. He had a reputation of being a 'good-looking ladies' man.'"[9] Dick Rowland is generally identified as a bootblack, but sometimes as a delivery boy. There is a suggestion, but no more than that, that he may have also been engaged in less honorable pursuits.[10] So elusive is the truth about Dick Rowland and Sarah Page that even the one thing history has been most sure of, that they were together in an elevator in downtown Tulsa on the morning of May 30, 1921, is sometimes disputed.[11]

The story told by police and reported the next afternoon in the *Tulsa Tribune* is that Rowland got into the elevator operated by Page on the third floor of the Drexel Building at 319 South Main Street, and that somewhere on the way to the ground floor the two came into contact. Page screamed, attracting the attention of an employee of Renberg's Department Store, which occupied the first two floors of the four-story building. The unnamed employee summoned police while Rowland fled. He was arrested the next morning.[12]

Exactly when the elevator incident is supposed to have occurred is unclear. The *Tribune* says it was "early" in the day,[13] suggesting the morning; it seems unlikely, though, that it happened during the Memorial Day parade, which passed right by the Drexel Building.[14] In that case, there almost certainly would have been more witnesses. Also, Renberg's was closed because of the holiday,[15] which has caused skeptics to question the entire story. Why, they ask, would the unnamed store clerk have been present? For that matter, why was Dick Rowland in the Drexel Building, since most if not all of the offices on the upper floors were likely closed?

These questions play into a parallel narrative, one in which all that followed was not about race but about real estate; a scheme in which whites and blacks conspired to create a pretext for turning Greenwood into a warehouse district adjacent to the rail yards. Certainly, an effort was made to exploit the riot for that purpose.[16] Whether the riot was planned and instigated toward that end is a more sinister mystery that may never be definitively solved.

The presence of Rowland and the store clerk is probably easily explained. Something must have been going on in the building if the elevator operator was on duty—unless that was made up, too. The *Tribune* identified "Diamond Dick" Rowland as a delivery boy.[17] The *World*, on June 1, said he was a "bootblack."[18] Either occupation would have given him a legitimate reason for being on the third floor of the Drexel Building, even on a holiday. The third and fourth floors of the building were occupied almost entirely by offices of small oil-related enterprises.[19] So, Rowland, in fact, could have been delivering—or attempting to deliver, if the office was closed—a pair of shoes or boots or some other package. Another story, told by Robert Fairchild, is that Rowland had gone into the building to use the restroom. At least two of Gates's informants, Fairchild and a white woman named Clara Forrest, said the Drexel Building elevator was notoriously difficult to operate, shaking and shuddering and often leaving an uneven step at the threshold that caused passengers to trip as they exited.[20]

There is no record that anyone thought Page's or the unnamed store clerk's presence odd. Perhaps the clerk was stocking shelves or waiting for a delivery. Perhaps he was going over accounts. That neither newspaper reported the witness's name may—or may not—suggest something else: that the witness was someone more prominent than a store clerk, perhaps even storeowner Sam Renberg, a major advertiser the newspapers may have been loath to identify.

Tulsans did not have a general knowledge of the incident until more than a day later, on May 31, when a short front-page story in the afternoon *Tribune* reported Rowland's arrest that morning by two Tulsa police officers—one white and one black.[21] Why it took a day to bring in Rowland is unclear, and he actually may have been arrested the night before. Chief John Gustafson, during his trial in July, said Rowland was arrested the day of the incident and spent a night in the city jail before being transferred.[22] In any event, Rowland's identity seems to have been known quickly, and perhaps immediately. On June 1, the *World* reported that Rowland had been hiding.[23] Whatever the case, the alleged assault of a white girl by a black man should have been sensational news, yet it was not reported in the May 30 *Tribune* or the May 31 *World*. Whether the police kept the situation under wraps or the press did we do not know.

And then there it was, on the front page of the *Tribune*. It was not the lead story. The banner headline went to a wire service account of disarmament talks, and the largest element on the front page was a grouping of ten photographs and a story on a beauty contest promoted by the *Tribune*. The story of Dick Rowland's alleged attempted assault and arrest was just five paragraphs at the bottom of the right-hand column. But the headline—"Nab Negro for Attacking Girl in Elevator"—was certain to grab attention.

A negro delivery boy who gave his name to the public as "Diamond Dick" but who has been identified as Dick Rowland, was arrested on South Greenwood avenue this morning by Officers Carmichael and Pack, charged with attempting to assault the 17-year-old white elevator girl in the Drexel building early yesterday.

He will be tried in municipal court this afternoon on a state charge.

The girl said she noticed the negro a few minutes before the attempted assault looking up and down the hallway on the third floor of the Drexel building as if to see if there was anyone in sight but thought nothing of it at the time.

A few minutes later he entered the elevator she claimed, and attacked her, scratching her hands and face and tearing her clothes. Her screams brought a clerk from Renberg's store to her assistance and the negro fled. He was captured and identified this morning both by the girl and the clerk, police say.

Tenants of the Drexel building said the girl is an orphan who works as an elevator operator to pay her way through business college.[24]

The story was freighted with racially charged language, from the headline to the final sentence. In the circumspect code words of the day, it accused a young black man of attempting to rape an innocent white girl.[25] Men had been murdered for less, from Atlanta to Duluth.[26] To round out the picture, the brief story portrays Rowland as the sort of "shifty Negro" who would refer to himself as "Diamond Dick" and hung about deserted hallways looking for something to steal; the sort who was impertinent to white women and attacked teenage orphans working their way through school, tore their clothes, ravished them in public elevators, and ran cravenly away.

Whether the story was intended to precipitate some sort of confrontation or merely grab readers' attention cannot be said with certainty. Perhaps it simply reflects the sensibilities—and insensitivities—of the time. The *Tribune's* publisher, Richard Lloyd Jones, belonged to the clique that brought Attorney General S. Prince Freeling and his assistants to town. Among their complaints were race mixing, vice, and crime they associated with Greenwood and the city's black population.[27] Jones's circle also included the industrialist and oilman Charles Page, from whom Jones had bought his newspaper two years before, and the ubiquitous Tate Brady. Page—no relation to Sarah Page—and Brady sometimes worked toward the same ends, and had common financial interests in both the black and white sections of north Tulsa.[28] The extent to which these moral, social, and economic factors may have influenced the *Tribune*'s judgment is a matter of conjecture. What is certain is that no reader, black or white, could have missed the story's implications.

Sex-related lynchings in Oklahoma were rare, but newspapers regularly reported the gruesome vigilante justice visited on black men elsewhere accused of forcing or trying to force themselves onto white women.[29] Just being in the wrong neighborhood could be dangerous. On January 2, a black man spotted "shuffling along" at Fifteenth and Baltimore, in the white section of town, raised an alarm that resulted in police firing more than twenty shots, all of which miraculously missed the suspect and everyone else in the vicinity. The man, when finally detained, was determined to have been minding his own business and was released.[30]

Over the years, many people have maintained that the May 31 *Tribune* also contained another, even more inflammatory piece, an editorial that called directly for Dick Rowland's lynching. In most accounts, this editorial was headlined "To Lynch Negro Tonight." No example of this editorial is known to exist.[31] In 1921, The *Tribune*'s editorials normally appeared on the back page of the newspaper. When its file copies were microfilmed in the 1940s, the front-page arrest story and about half the editorial page had been torn out.[32] When this happened, under what circumstances, and by whom are unknown. The arrest story had been reprinted in other publications, and so copies of it still exist,[33] but not the supposed editorial. In 2002, an intact copy of a *Tribune* that appears to be identical to the May 31 microfilmed edition, except that it is dated June 1, was discovered.[34] This edition, apparently intended for mail subscribers, was probably printed on May 31 but dated a day later because that is when it would have been delivered in mailboxes. This no doubt explains why an early researcher, Loren Gill, cited the June 1 instead of the May 31 *Tribune* when he wrote about the riot in the 1940s.[35]

This June 1 edition, however, does not clear up the matter of the editorial. In the space missing from the microfilmed May 31 edition is an editorial about European disarmament. There is nothing about Rowland.[36] The most common explanations for the fact that no copy of the offending editorial can be found is that it appeared in only one, limited-run edition that *Tribune* management suppressed, or that the presses were stopped and the "To Lynch Negro Tonight" piece was pulled before many copies were printed, with only a few of those making it onto the street. These explanations are certainly possible, but they also pose problems.

First, the assumption that only a few copies of the editorial made it into general circulation is contrary to the assertion that it incited widespread anger and violence among white Tulsans. Rumors or secondhand accounts of such an editorial may have circulated, but that is not the same as actually reading the piece as it is described.

That leads to a second, more difficult point to overcome: None of the *Tribune's* most vocal critics—not the *World*, not Roscoe Dunjee's *Black Dispatch*, not the NAACP's Walter White, who arrived in Tulsa a few days after the riot to investigate—ever mentioned a "To Lynch Negro Tonight" editorial. None of the three had reason to hold back knowledge of such a piece. Instead, they cited exclusively the front-page arrest story. The *Black Dispatch* reprinted the story under the headline "The Story That Set Tulsa Ablaze."[37] White, writing in the *Nation*, attributed the riot to the Tribune's careless use of the word "assault."[38] The *World*, on June 2, quoted a police official blaming the *Tribune's* "yellow journalism" for what occurred.[39] It followed that story a few days later with a similar statement from state adjutant general Charles Barrett, and generally did all it could to cast as much blame as possible on its rival publication.[40]

The missing editorial may not, in fact, have existed in the form often described, but that does not mean that it was invented from thin air. Clearly, the arrest story was inflammatory on its own. And readers, it must be said, often do not distinguish between news articles and editorials. That the arrest story could have been interpreted as an open call to violence, especially in the telling and retelling, would be understandable. The *World's* June 1 report of Rowland's arrest—also on page one—and how it contributed to the previous night's violence could be read as supporting evidence for either conclusion regarding the editorial. "There was a movement afoot, it was reported, among white people *to go to the county courthouse Tuesday night and lynch the bootblack*," the story reads. It is not clear what is meant by "reported." This could refer to the missing *Tribune* editorial, it could refer to general rumor, or it could refer to Police Commissioner James Adkison's statement that he was warned of such an attempt by an anonymous caller.[41]

If the *World* story does not refer to the supposed *Tribune* editorial, it might, in fact, be a source of the editorial legend. In the confusion of that day and the days that followed, the *World's* after-the-fact reporting could have become conflated with the *Tribune's* earlier story into a single, cold-blooded call for Dick Rowland's murder.

The *Tribune* and *World* both reported that Rowland was arrested on South Greenwood, which seems odd but is likely accurate precisely because it is odd. It is the sort of fact that would be checked, certainly by one copy editor and probably by two. After his arrest, Rowland was taken to police headquarters at 109 East Second Street and jailed. At some point, he seems to have made a statement to the police, in which he said he accidentally stepped on Sarah Page's foot.[42]

Six weeks after the riot, Adkison testified that he received a telephone call at three o'clock in the afternoon—some accounts say four—threatening Rowland's life. "We are going to lynch that negro tonight," Adkison said the caller told him, "that black devil who assaulted that girl."[43] Thus, in news reports of Adkison's remarks, the phrase "to lynch that negro tonight" did appear in print, but in a different context than ascribed to the missing *Tribune* editorial, and a month and a half after the fact. By then, stories about the supposed editorial seem to have already been in circulation. Druggist P. S. Thompson mentioned it in the account he gave Mary Jones Parrish, who had been hired soon after the riot to take down the stories of African American witnesses.[44]

After the call, Adkison hurried to the police headquarters, where he consulted with Chief John Gustafson and then ordered Dick Rowland moved to the Tulsa County jail. This was a reasonable decision. The city jail was easily accessible and none too secure.[45] The county jail was on the fifth floor of the limestone Tulsa County Courthouse, and while embarrassingly easy to get out of—twelve men had escaped a few days earlier by sliding down a forty-foot rope made from bed sheets[46]—it was undeniably difficult to break into if willingly defended. The jail could be reached only by a single elevator and a closed stairwell that could be locked from the inside. Nevertheless, after turning the prisoner over to Tulsa County sheriff W. M. "Bill" McCullough, Adkison and Gustafson urged the sheriff to get Rowland out of town. This was a standard tactic for defusing such situations, but McCullough refused to go along with it. Rowland was much safer in the jail, he said, than on the open road. McCullough called in all of his deputies and vowed that no one would take his prisoner.[47]

This was not a decision or a pledge McCullough took lightly. Ten months earlier, on the same weekend as the Oklahoma City lynching that had so outraged A. J. Smitherman, a white prisoner named Roy Belton was taken from the Tulsa County jail and hanged from a billboard southwest of town, near the present intersection of Southwest Boulevard and Union Avenue. Belton was charged with shooting and beating cab driver Homer Nida as Belton and two companions, posing as passengers, relieved Nida of his cab near the Texaco tank farm on the road to Red Fork. Belton—who first gave the name Tom Owens—was captured after one of his accomplices, Marie Harmon, confessed and identified the man she knew as Owens as the actual killer. Dramatically, in a face-to-face confrontation in Nida's hospital room, the taxi driver identified Belton as his assailant before dying of his injuries.[48]

James Woolley, the Tulsa County sheriff at the time, would later say he did not take rumors of a lynching seriously. When twenty-five men entered the courthouse and took Woolley prisoner, he told the jailer to do all he could to protect the prisoner but to not get anyone hurt. Belton, in fact, was quickly handed over and taken in Nida's taxi to the scene of the crime at the head of a long procession of automobiles, including an ambulance. Belton was hung from a Federal Tire sign on the Jenks road, just south of where it forked off the main thoroughfare from Tulsa to Red Fork and on to Sapulpa, a road that in a few years would become known as U.S. Route 66. Tulsa police, it was reported, helped direct traffic at the scene; Gustafson, on the job only four months at the time, denied the charge but admitted that officers stood by and watched the lynching because they did not want to endanger "innocent bystanders" with gunplay. "I do not condone mob law—in fact, I am absolutely opposed to it," Gustafson said, "but it is my honest opinion the lynching of Belton will prove of real benefit to Tulsa and vicinity. It was an object lesson to the hi-jackers and auto thieves, and will be taken as such."

Gustafson blamed the sheriff's office for not asking for help sooner. "The county officers waited too long to notify us, and we got there a little too late," said Gustafson. Outraged, Governor J. B. A. Robertson ordered an investigation and offered a reward for information on those responsible for Belton's death, but no one was ever charged.[49]

McCullough defeated Woolley in the general election later that year.[50] The two were old friends who had traded the sheriff's office back and forth for a decade, McCullough the Republican and Woolley the Democrat. A former cowboy with an impressive handlebar moustache and a pearl-handled revolver he seldom wore and even more seldom used, McCullough, in 1911, carried out the county's only execution, the hanging of a black man called Frank Henson, who had been convicted of killing a deputy in the outlying community of Dawson. In a scene straight out of the Old West, McCullough built the scaffolding, tied the hangman's noose, and dropped Henson to his death. Late in life, the man known as "Uncle Bill" would say that this was the most difficult thing he ever did.[51]

McCullough was no fan of Gustafson, a private detective who had been fired from the Tulsa Police Department (TPD) five years earlier. McCullough claimed to have advised against Gustafson's appointment, and considered him to be of questionable character.[52] Evidence gathered by Freeling, Van Leuven, and Short in their admittedly one-sided investigation supported McCullough's conclusion.[53] This distrust between the two lawmen may have figured into McCullough rejecting the recommendation to sneak Rowland out of town. It also may have factored into the drama about to unfold.

The news that Rowland might be in danger reached Greenwood, or at least the Gurley Hotel, by way of Reverend Bryant, the same Reverend Bryant who had run for county commissioner the previous year, and who in the African American community was called "Doctor Bryant." He delivered the lynching rumor to Gurley, and together they sought out Deputy Sheriff Barney Cleaver. Cleaver contacted McCullough, who insisted he had things under control.[54]

By six or six-thirty, a crowd was gathering in the street outside Gurley's hotel. Cleaver would later testify that he tried to disperse this "advance guard" gathering in Greenwood but was laughed at and threatened.[55] Gurley, who had briefly been a deputy during one of McCullough's previous terms,[56] agreed to go to the courthouse with a man named Webb—presumably Staley Webb—to talk to the sheriff and assess the danger to Rowland. Cleaver also went to the courthouse at about this time, but it is unclear whether he and the other two men went together.[57]

Men gathering at the *Star*'s new printing plant on North Greenwood seethed with angry suspicion approaching certainty. Their confidence in the local authorities was nil. They were convinced that Dick Rowland would be taken, regardless of what anyone said. A man identified as Henry Jacobs, who said he was present, told investigators that J. B. Stradford told the men, "Boys, we will send and get the Muskogee crowd, and you go on up [to the courthouse] and lay there till they come."[58]

When Gurley returned with reassuring news, he said later, one of the men gathered at the *Star*'s new printing plant on North Greenwood loudly proclaimed him a liar and might have killed Gurley had lawyer Isaac H. "Ike" Spears not intervened. A larger group, this one numbering perhaps twenty-five or thirty, loaded into cars and trucks and headed for the courthouse. When they arrived, McCullough told Cleaver to "go out and see what they wanted." "The boy is upstairs in the cage," Cleaver told them. "He's locked up and no one is going to get him."[59]

The white crowd around the courthouse grew steadily. Initially, it does not seem to have been particularly unruly or even hostile, and may have been more curious than violent. It had no identifiable leadership or organization and, as events would soon suggest, was not armed or equipped to the extent one might expect for a planned assault on a fortified position such as the courthouse jail. And, no serious attempt to take Rowland seems to have occurred. But a lot of people, white and black, believed there would be, or that there was a good chance of it, and they acted accordingly.[60] "Since the lynching of a white boy [Belton] in Tulsa, the confidence in the ability of the city officials to protect its prisoner had decreased," wrote Mary Jones Parrish. "Therefore, some of our group banded together to add to the protection of the life that was threatened to be taken without a chance to prove his innocence."[61]

Parrish operated a secretarial school in a building on Greenwood. After her last class ended at about nine o'clock, her young daughter called Parrish's attention to "cars full of people" and "men with guns" in the street outside. "I am told this little bunch of brave and loyal black men who were willing to give up their lives, if necessary, for the sake of a fellow man, marched up to the jail were there were already 500 white men gathered, and that this number was soon swelled to a thousand," Parrish wrote.[62]

As courageous as these men and as honorable as their intentions no doubt were, their appearance alarmed and then angered the white population.[63] McCullough and Cleaver convinced the first party of African Americans to go home, and then a second. McCullough, though, had no such success with the increasingly abusive whites. He ordered, pleaded, harangued, and cajoled to no effect. So, apparently, did other prominent white citizens.[64] They were greeted with boos and jeers from a determined knot "at the south entrance of the courthouse heckling speakers who attempted to disperse them."[65]

Between eight and eight-thirty, three white men entering the courthouse were met by McCullough and Ira Short, who had been elected county commissioner but had not yet taken office. When McCullough ordered them out, the men rather meekly complied and returned to their automobile. McCullough watched as a "crowd of 20 or 30" gathered around the car. McCullough told his deputies to run the elevator to the top floor, disable it, and barricade themselves in the jail. Then he crossed the street to the car containing the three potential troublemakers.[66] "I was jeered by the men in the car and by persons standing around on the street and sidewalk," McCullough told the *St. Louis Post-Dispatch*. "They called me a 'nigger-lover,' but the men in the car drove off."[67]

This rather half-hearted attempt to reach Rowland may have quickly fizzled, but it fed the spiraling racial fear, anger, and hatred the way heat and air feed fire. It, and the whites' refusal to go home, would bring yet another wave of concerned African Americans, this one even larger and better armed than the ones before.[68] Word soon reached Greenwood's two movie theaters, the Dixie and the Dreamland, and guns were passed around in at least one of them.[69] Cars and trucks were commandeered.[70] Some may have thought Sheriff McCullough asked for them.[71] All were determined to make a statement, to stand up not just for Dick Rowland but for their race.

So the inability of McCullough, Gustafson, police captain George Blaine, and a few others to disperse the whites at the courthouse was crucial. Sheriff McCullough probably did not have the manpower to do it, and certainly not after ordering his available deputies to barricade themselves inside the jail. The city police did have the manpower—barely—had it been properly organized and deployed, but it was not. The local National Guard units, especially in conjunction with the police, would have made a difference had they been brought to bear during the early stages of the crisis, but no one asked for them until it was too late.[72]

By ten o'clock, there were perhaps two thousand whites at the courthouse. Perhaps three hundred blacks—estimates of both groups vary widely—had joined them, with many more conspicuous on the downtown streets.[73] "[A] negro," noted someone looking out a window of the *Tulsa World* Building at 317 S. Boulder Avenue, two blocks south of the courthouse, "walked into the middle of the street in front of the office, carrying a long shotgun loosely under his arm . . . in a few minutes a big car drew up beside. 'Disarm?' one of them was heard to say. 'You bet I won't disarm.'"[74]

Gustafson and Adkison had essentially washed their hands of the situation after McCullough spurned their suggestion to take Rowland out of the city. Now they grew uneasy. Early on, when trouble first began bubbling to the surface, City Commissioner C. S. Younkman had found the police chief at the station and asked him what was going on. Gustafson said he did not know but he had heard that there was a crowd at the courthouse. Oddly, he seemed more worried that mob violence would be turned against police headquarters than he was about the county jail holding the supposed focal point of the seething ill will.[75] But, as dusk approached and tension mounted, the chief and his boss, Police Commissioner Adkison, began to grasp the seriousness of the situation. In so doing, however, they did virtually nothing to break up or subdue the hostile whites.[76] Even Younkman's order to turn fire hoses on the whites surrounding the police station was ignored.[77] Instead, Gustafson and Adkison addressed only the black side of the equation. Adkison dispatched one of his black officers, Henry Pack, to Greenwood on a reconnaissance mission, and sent "all available police" to "keep the negroes from coming to town." Gustafson ordered Detective Ike Wilkerson, Sergeant Claude Brice, and Officer Sid Jackson to intercept a band of blacks forming at Second and Cincinnati, about six blocks northeast of the courthouse and a block and a half north of the Frisco tracks; Gustafson himself went out with Captain George Blaine, probably the TPD's boldest and most fearless officer. At the courthouse, Gustafson and Blaine observed the large crowd and concluded it would be "suicide" to try to disarm anyone. Driving on, they encountered "three carloads" of blacks about six blocks away at Fourth and Elgin. Gustafson and Blaine followed them back to the courthouse, then returned to the police station, badly shaken.[78] Shortly after ten o'clock, Gustafson asked Major James A. Bell of the local National Guard for men to "clear the streets of negroes."[79]

Bell had learned of the courthouse disturbance sometime earlier, not from law enforcement or city authorities, but from two of his men, a Private Canton and a Sergeant Payne. At about nine, the pair "came to my door and reported that a crowd of white men were gathering near the Court House and that threats of lynching a negro were being made, and that it was reported the negroes in 'Little Africa' were arming to prevent it," Bell wrote about a month later. "As I had heard rumors of this kind on other occasions that did not amount to anything serious I did not feel greatly worried," Bell continued.[80]

Nevertheless, Bell sent Canton and Payne back to the courthouse to get more information, then called McCullough and Gustafson. McCullough told Bell everything was under control, but Gustafson was less confident. "The chief reported that things were a little threatening, that it was reported that negroes were driving around town in a threatening mood," Bell wrote.[81]

Bell suggested that city officials contact Governor Robertson and ask him to authorize use of the National Guard. Next, Bell notified the commanding officers of the three National Guard units based in Tulsa to "quietly" assemble as many of their men as possible. As Bell was changing into his uniform, a messenger arrived with the news that whites had shown up at the National Guard Armory, across the alley from Bell's house, demanding rifles and ammunition. The armory was about a half mile east of the courthouse on Sixth Street, across from what was then Central Park. Summer training camp at Fort Sill, in the southwestern part of the state, was only a few days away, and some of the men were at the armory preparing for the trip.[82]

Bell recounted, "Grabbing my pistol in one hand and my belt in the other I jumped out of the back door and running down the west side of the Armory building I saw several men apparently pulling at the window grating." After chasing those men away, Bell went to the front of the building and found "a mob of white men three or four hundred strong" clamoring for admission. "I asked them what they wanted," Bell recalled. "One of them replied, 'Rifles and ammunition.' I explained to them that they could not get anything there. Someone shouted, 'We don't know about that, we guess we can.'"[83]

Backed by National Guard captain Frank Van Voorhis, TPD motorcycle officer Leo Irish, and "a citizen named Williams," Bell told the crowd the armory was full of armed soldiers who would "shoot promptly" anyone trying to get inside. This finally did the trick. The mob dispersed, and Bell ordered a guard around the armory with "one man on the roof."[84] It was at this point that Bell called Gustafson the second time and Gustafson asked for men "to clear the streets." Bell said he had to have an order from the governor and "urged haste" in doing so "before it was too late."[85]

That point had already been reached. Wilkerson, Brice, and Jackson had intercepted the group of black men at Second and Cincinnati and had almost talked them into withdrawing when Deputy Sheriff John Smitherman arrived. "'What the hell are you trying to do here?'" Wilkerson later testified Smitherman asked. When Wilkerson said he was assuring the blacks that Rowland was safe, Smitherman replied, "Yes, damn you, you're one of them. Come on, boys!"[86]

This remarkable exchange, assuming Wilkerson recounted it accurately, hangs in the air a century later. What did Smitherman mean by "You're one of them?" One of what? One of whom? Those planning harm to Dick Rowland? Who could not be trusted? Wilkerson said he did not know, and if Smitherman ever explained himself, it is not recorded.

Led by Smitherman, the men pushed past the three white officers and headed for the courthouse.[87] There, some white citizens had taken it upon themselves to disarm the black men arriving in ever-greater numbers. Somewhere in the roiling tumult, E. S. MacQueen decided to be a hero. A former investigator in the county attorney's office, MacQueen had finished a distant second in the 1920 Democratic sheriff's primary. A man of less-than-sterling reputation, by the spring of 1921 MacQueen was reduced to the dubious position of deputy constable for a justice of the peace. Perhaps intent on demonstrating that he, not Bill McCullough, should be in charge, MacQueen confronted an African American man, identified in some sources as Johnny Cole, and demanded Cole's pistol. Cole refused in no uncertain terms. MacQueen grabbed for the gun; Cole resisted.[88]

The pistol discharged.[89]

All hell broke loose.

5

CHAOS

It was nearly midnight when Major Charles Daley, approaching the city from the southwest on the Sapulpa road, encountered sentries on the Arkansas River bridge leading into Tulsa. What, he demanded, was going on? "All hell is breaking loose," replied one of the men, "and the Negroes are trying to take over the city."[1] Daley did not wait to hear more. Engaging his automobile's transmission, he roared off toward the center of the action.

At thirty-seven, Charles Daley had already lived a remarkable life. Born in Brooklyn to Irish immigrant parents, Daley ran away from home at eleven, went west, and by 1904 was a trick rider in Zach Mulhall's show at the Louisiana Purchase Exhibition in St. Louis. He was a prize fighter and a vagabond who settled in Tulsa in 1911 and opened a cigar store. In 1916, Daley became the first man to enlist in Tulsa's National Guard Company C. Discharged on medical grounds, he underwent a "dangerous and expensive" operation—perhaps for a hernia—in order to qualify for service. He was eventually commissioned a first lieutenant and raised companies in Tulsa, Sapulpa, and Claremore, but never saw active duty.[2] Politically connected, Daley accompanied the Oklahoma delegation to the 1920 inauguration of Mexican president Alvaro Bergeron. The group included Lieutenant Governor Martin Trapp, Adjutant General Charles Barrett, and Colonel Baird Markham,[3] who in 1923 would become the first commanding officer of the Forty-Fifth Infantry Division, comprising the Oklahoma, New Mexico, Arizona, and Colorado National Guard.[4] On the night he stopped on the bridge into Tulsa, Daley was both a major in the Oklahoma National Guard, assigned to the inspector general's office, and inspector and assistant chief of the Tulsa Police Department, where he seems to have been installed to keep an eye on Gustafson and a force with a less-than-stellar reputation.[5]

Arriving in downtown Tulsa, Daley found confusion bordering on chaos. "Thousands of persons . . . including several hundred women, and men armed with every available weapon in the city taken from every hardware and sporting goods store, swarmed on Second street from Boulder to Boston avenues watching the gathering volunteer army or offering their services to the peace officers," reported the *Tulsa World*.[6]

The sentry's casual assertion that black rioters were trying to take over the town was not true, but seems to have been white Tulsa's prevailing opinion. What black Tulsans thought of as protecting a fellow African American through a display of unity, whites interpreted as an armed uprising.[7] Indeed, any sort of defiance was liable to be construed as an act of rebellion. Police and then National Guardsmen were deployed not to the point of conflict, but to the power plant and waterworks, to major entrances into the city, and later to the Midland Valley Railroad Depot, in anticipation of a broader attack.[8] Auto patrols were sent into the white residential neighborhoods in the expectation that African Americans living in servants' quarters would rise up against their employers.[9]

These concerns may not have been entirely groundless. Attorney B. C. Franklin, in the autobiography edited by his son John Hope Franklin and published many years later, recounted a remarkable story in which he said he witnessed two men—one white, one black—urging Greenwood residents to go start fires in the white part of town. Franklin had moved to Tulsa a few months earlier, leaving his young family behind in the all-black town of Rentiesville, fifty miles to the south. The separation was to be temporary, until Franklin could establish himself, and he had taken up residence in a rooming house at 420 East Easton Street. As night fell, a "huge, menacing crowd" gathered on a nearby corner. "There is talk of taking Rowland from jail and lynching him, and that some young Negroes say it won't be," Franklin's agitated landlady told him. Franklin rushed outside to investigate.

> I soon spotted the leaders, one white and a Negro. . . . There was no doubt that these men had seen active service in World War I; they fired up the crowd by telling about their exploits in the different battles; how they spent nights together in the same foxholes; that winning a battle did not always

depend on numerical strength, but on strategy and surprise attack. That's when the white solider suggested that someone should proceed across town immediately and set fire to houses in different parts of the city; that would take the pressure off the Negro part of the city and cause the governor to immediately dispatch soldiers to the scene. He said, "If you don't do this, they are going to burn you out before this thing is finished."[10]

Tulsa Chamber of Commerce secretary Clarence Douglas, perhaps not an entirely objective observer on this point, wrote a few months after the event that blacks "had been worked upon by a lawless element of white agitators, reds and bolshevists."[11] "Reds and bolshevists" made convenient villains, and if they were too convenient by half, few whites cared to notice. The panic, fear, and anger loosed by those first shots at the courthouse chased all reason from the streets of Tulsa.

"People were gathered in front of the [police] station running with guns of all kinds," Daley wrote in his National Guard after-action report. "It was at this point that I requested all men to stand still and I picked out a half dozen ex-service men to act as my assistants. Separating the crowd[,] placing men with pistols on one side and men with rifles on the other, and gave final instructions that all men under 21 years of age be disarmed as the City would not be responsible for any accidents that might occur in the discharge of firearms in the hands of boys."[12]

The shots at the courthouse had been fired between ten and ten-thirty.[13] Confused newspaper reports and eyewitness accounts conflict on some details but generally convey the sense of the mayhem that ensued. Central High School students, intending to drag Main after returning from a school outing near Sand Springs, found themselves surrounded by gun-wielding rioters. "Looking west down toward the courthouse," one of the teens, James Leighton Avery, recalled nearly sixty years later, "there was a mob of black and white men in confrontation, lots of yelling, screams of women, and the firing of many guns. Cars were driving haphazardly, and no policing of the streets could be seen. . . . Not wanting to get any of my passengers hurt, I analyzed the situation and rushed them all home."[14]

The panicked crowd scattered as wild shots pierced the summer night. At least two men—one white, one black—fell wounded. A white oil company employee named Walter Daggs, who lived near the courthouse, caught a fatal bullet to the head. His friends said he was running away from the scene when he was hit.[15] Daggs may have been the riot's first fatality, although newspaper reports and a death certificate suggest that a white oilfield worker named Cleo Shumate was fatally wounded by a "negro auto party" as early as 8:30 P.M., nearly two hours before the shooting at the courthouse.[16] Sapulpa city clerk A. B. Stick was gunned down on the steps of the Hotel Tulsa, possibly by whites who mistook him for a black man in the deepening gloom;[17] alternately, the hotel's assistant manager reported "carloads" of armed black men firing into the lobby at about the same time.[18]

Automobiles careened through the streets; one tipped over on Boulder, spilling its passengers onto the pavement. Police captain Blaine, manic in his determination, leaped onto a truck loaded with black men and dragged one off. Four whites chased a black man into an alley behind the *Tulsa World* and either killed him or did not, depending on who told the story; a more dubious version, first recorded some time later, had the black man chased into a theater and shot down on stage. At the police station, Adkison began passing out "special commissions" to select volunteers. Across the street, men too impatient for someone to show up with the keys broke into the Bardon and Magee sporting goods stores and helped themselves to guns and ammunition; other, similar establishments were looted once the first two had been picked clean.[19]

While certainly ill-advised and ultimately disastrous, neither of these last two actions was as extraordinary as one might think. Tulsa in 1921 was not so far removed from the days of posses and Old West justice. A generation earlier, the citizens of Coffeyville, Kansas, seventy-five miles north of Tulsa, shot to pieces the notorious Dalton gang with firearms readily distributed by the town's hardware dealers.[20] And court testimony and news reports indicate that the Tulsa police and other law enforcement agencies often relied on informally deputized citizens. The previous December, Adkison advised Tulsa businessmen to hire armed guards with instructions to shoot to kill.[21] In January, the commissioner told persons "holding special commissions" to be ready for duty on liquor raids outside the city limits.[22] These special commissions apparently were not limited to whites, either; Barney Cleaver claimed that Gustafson had given one to a black drug dealer named Smithee, who may or may not have been acting as an informant.[23]

As for Magee's and Bardon's, city records indicate that they were a regular source of ammunition for the police department[24]—which, in any event, does not seem to have been heavily armed, especially by today's standards. On the night of the riot, the TPD appealed to the National Guard for rifles; turned down, it obtained twenty-five such weapons from the Cosden refinery across the river.[25]

Adkison, and many others beside, apparently were so obsessed with putting down the "negro uprising" that it did not occur to them how extraordinarily reckless it was to pass out guns and the authority to use them in the middle of a riot. Adkison would later say he trusted people he should not have. "We were unable to limit the commissions to our choice," he would testify. "I usually talked to the men and those I thought would remain cool headed I commissioned."[26] This astounding statement, uttered in self-defense, impressed many people then and in the decades since as preposterously lame if not completely unbelievable. At best, Adkison demonstrated shockingly poor judgment. He "usually" talked to the men commissioned, which implies that sometimes he did not. "We were unable to limit the commissions to our choice," he said, but that was not true at all. Adkison could have simply refused to commission anyone who was not his first choice. He could have commissioned no one. Either decision would have been better than the one he made.

The alternative is that Adkison knew exactly what he was doing, or thought he did, and the special deputies were part of a carefully laid plan to destroy Greenwood.[27] If so, someone badly miscalculated, for the special deputies began by shooting up downtown Tulsa "with much promiscuous firing," as the *Tulsa World* described it.[28] Bardon's and Magee's were ransacked, stripped of not only guns and ammunition but just about everything else of value. All told, downtown Tulsa suffered more than $40,000 in damage and theft during the early stages of the riot, and whites seem to have been responsible for all it.[29] To be sure, this was negligible compared to the subsequent destruction of Greenwood, but it weighs against the idea that the entire riot was a carefully planned scheme. Surely, if the objective was to wipe out the black section of town, a pretext could have been found that did not include running gun battles the length and breadth of the white business district, resulting in white deaths and the looting of white-owned stores.

Whatever Adkison expected of these special deputies, the commissions do not seem to have been entirely indiscriminant. Laurel Buck, a twenty-six-year-old bricklayer and son of a local building contractor and Greenwood District property owner, said he was turned down when he tried to volunteer at the police station. Asked what he could do, the sergeant on duty told him to "get a gun and get a nigger." Buck said he did indeed sign for a pistol at the Tulsa Hardware Co., but did not "get" anybody with it.[30]

The available local National Guard troops were deployed shortly after the shooting began. This had been done at the order of Adjutant General Charles Barrett, who had been apprised of the situation by one of his staff officers, Major Byron Kirkpatrick.[31] A Spanish-American War veteran and son of a Kansas congressman,[32] Kirkpatrick lived about six blocks east of the courthouse near Fifth Street and Elgin Avenue. He said a boarder told him at about ten that evening that "a large number of armed negroes, approximately 150[,] had congregated" nearby. Soon after, Kirkpatrick heard shots being fired. "These shots, as far as I can learn, were fired into the air and no casualties resulted therefrom," Kirkpatrick wrote in his after-action report.[33]

The Oklahoma National Guard at this time consisted of about 2,750 officers and men divided into the Second and Third Infantry Regiments and the First and Second Artillery Batteries. Each infantry regiment was divided into three battalions; each battalion had a headquarters company, three rifle companies, a machine gun company, a service company, a howitzer company, and a sanitary company. The Third Infantry was essentially made up of men from eastern Oklahoma.[34] Its commanding officer, Lieutenant Colonel L. J. F. Rooney, had served with the Sixty-Ninth New York Infantry during the Spanish-American War and moved to Tulsa in 1909. An engineer by training, Rooney was one of the city's leading businessmen and most respected citizens, and commanded Tulsa's Home Guard during World War I.[35] Bell, the senior officer called to the armory as the situation deteriorated, commanded the First Battalion, three elements of which were based in Tulsa.[36] Only one of those—Rifle Company B—was a combat weapons unit. The other two were a service company concerned with transportation and supply, and a sanitary detachment of medical personnel. A fourth unit, an artillery company, had been organized but not federally recognized or equipped.[37]

Rooney arrived at the armory about 10:40 P.M., while Bell was talking to Barrett by telephone. About fifty guardsmen had reported by this time, and Rooney loaded fifteen to eighteen men onto the supply company's truck and headed for the police station, accompanied by Kirkpatrick. Bell, at Rooney's direction, organized and dispatched squads to the Public Service Oklahoma power plant on First Street, the waterworks just west of town on the Sand Springs road and the PSO substation on Archer between Boston and Cincinnati. This last location had come under fire, apparently from African Americans, "causing the cutting off of the current from several buildings, among them the Brady Hotel" at Main and Archer. In securing this substation, the National Guard suffered its only reported casualty, a bullet wound to Sergeant W. R. Hastings.[38]

The guardsmen carried standard-issue .30 caliber Springfield M1903 rifles, but at the armory were at least six Browning Automatic Rifles,[39] capable of firing five hundred rounds a minute and with an effective range of up to 1,500 yards. The BAR had been used as a light machine gun during the First World War and was the most powerful weapon in the local National Guard's arsenal.[40]

How many of these high-powered weapons were on hand is unclear; Bell, in any event, adamantly insisted that none ever left the armory "because of the danger to non-combatants long distances away if we attempted to use them."[41]

Rooney and his men arrived at the police station to find "125 to 150 men with guns drawn up in military formation." Unsure of this crowd's temperament or intent, he approached from the rear prepared for a fight but discovered it to be an impromptu assembly of "Legion men," members of the new organization for returned war veterans, the American Legion. As far as they were concerned, they were answering the call of their community just as they had answered the call of their country. But at this particular moment they were one more problem, one more mass of armed men that had to be dealt with.[42] Gustafson asked Rooney to clear them from the street in front of the police station, a task Rooney assigned Kirkpatrick. Kirkpatrick divided the Legion men into two groups, appointed officers, and ordered them to patrol the business district and the area around the courthouse, reporting back to the police station every fifteen minutes.[43] Whether Kirkpatrick thought they would actually do some good or he just wanted to keep them busy and out of the way is impossible to say. Rooney later testified that he thought seeing organized patrols in the streets would calm the white general public.[44] In any event, their assignment was a safe one; the tidal wave had already passed, flowing northeast, from the courthouse to Greenwood, from white Tulsa to black.

Booker T. Washington High School's senior class play was in progress earlier that evening when a small boy rushed in to announce: "They are trying to lynch a colored man downtown, and the colored people are going down to prevent it."[45] Similar messages were being conveyed at the Dixie and Dreamland theaters. At the Dixie, owner William Redfearn, the white Greenwood merchant, observed "a colored girl . . . going from one person to another, telling them something." Upon inquiry, Redfearn was told that a lynching was going to be attempted; he emptied the theater, locked it, and headed for the courthouse.[46]

Across the street at the Dreamland, the house manager, a Mr. Cotton, told projectionist Henry Sowders to stop the second feature and turn up the house lights.

"Why do you have a gun?" Sowders asked.

"Looking out for No. 1," Cotton replied.[47]

Sowders then became aware of "a bunch of guns" at a side door, and that they were being distributed by "four or five men." The six or seven hundred people in the theater cleared out in minutes, Sowders among them. Sowders was white, and when he reached his car he found the top down and nine black men in it.

Sowders asked for his car; instead, a "husky negro" picked up Sowders, set him in the back of a Ford truck, and told him to stay there. The big man then gave some money to one of his comrades and told him to take Sowders to the police station. As he was being driven through the crowd, Sowders saw Officer Henry Pack, one of the two officers to arrest Dick Rowland earlier in the day, vainly trying to hold back the army mobilized for Rowland's presumed defense. The truck nearly "ran over" a black man "standing in the street and shooting" on First near Cincinnati, and dropped Sowders, as promised, somewhere near the police station. Still bewildered, Sowders heard the sound of breaking glass, saw guns being carried out of Dick Bardon's store, and asked what was going on. Go home, he was told. Stay out of it.[48]

The battle was now only a few blocks away. At First and Cincinnati, the blacks retreating from the debacle at the courthouse turned and made a stand, reinforced by men in cars and trucks, some of them carrying the guns handed out at the Dreamland Theater.[49] In an instant, at the crack of a pistol shot, their mission had been transformed, from saving a solitary black man from lynching to saving themselves, their families, their homes, every last thing each of them owned. For that was the pattern. In America, in 1921, any act of African American rebellion was answered with gunpowder and fire. In taking up arms against white authority, they had committed a sin far more serious than any real or imagined offense charged to Dick Rowland. In these frantic minutes or hours—afterward no one was sure which—a fierce exchange of gunfire left men dead and injured. A white policeman, arriving in town from the north and oblivious to the turmoil, was surrounded by angry black men clamoring for blood, but a black preacher put his arms around the officer and bargained for his freedom.[50] A white man named Slinkard was reportedly run over on Main Street at the Frisco tracks; a story, apparently erroneous, went around that three Frisco switchmen and a brakemen were killed by whites for refusing to take them into the African American quarter on a switch engine. Sometime after midnight, a little house on Boston Avenue just north of the tracks went up in flames; when firefighters arrived to put out the fire, white rioters shooed them away at gunpoint.[51]

And, as daylight approached, an automobile dragged the body of an African American man through downtown. "At 5:30 [A.M.] . . . reports to police headquarters from members of the white bands that had been at 'the front' between the line of armed whites and 'Little Africa' said they had counted the bodies of more than a dozen negroes stretched in the street," the *World* reported in an extra.[52]

For Mary Jones Parrish, the exhilarating pride of only a short time earlier faded into fearful realization. "It was hours before the horror of it all dawned upon me," she wrote a few weeks later. "I had read of the Chicago riot and the Washington trouble, but it did not seem possible that prosperous Tulsa, the city which was so peaceful and quiet that morning, could be in the thrall of a great disaster. When it dawned upon me what was really happening, I took my little girl in my arms, read one or two chapters of Psalms of David and prayed that God would give me courage to stand through it all."[53]

6

"MOB SPIRIT AND FEVER HEAT"

Charles Daley never really explained where he got the machine gun. "We dug it up," is all he told Lieutenant Colonel Rooney.[1]

This was sometime after midnight,[2] after Rooney and Kirkpatrick had run the looters and the vigilantes out of Magee's Hardware and locked it up,[3] and Daley had ordered in the self-appointed auto patrols "running wild over the city without any head or anyone to give instructions."[4] Rooney would later testify that he had never seen or read of a situation quite like this one, with thousands of armed men in groups of two hundred or more wandering aimlessly through the city, looking for a fight. "The mob spirit and the fever heat was there," the *World* quoted him as saying. "Any interference without plenty of help would have been a battle."[5]

Rooney wanted to "segregate" the African American district—that is, surround it with a cordon of men to keep the combatants separated—but he and Daley agreed that they did not have nearly enough men to do it.[6] Fewer than thirty National Guardsmen were at their disposal,[7] and while the Tulsa Police Department numbered sixty-four men—thirty-two patrolmen, fourteen plainclothesmen, and eighteen traffic officers—many were of questionable value or absent altogether.[8] Chief of Detectives J. W. Patton and another officer, for instance, spent the night "guarding" an ice plant and watching the mayhem from the building's rooftop.[9] Gustafson later testified that assembling his men was complicated by an end-of-the month shift change, which involved officers on day duty switching to night and vice versa.[10] Most of those who did report seem to have been kept as far from the center of action as possible.[11]

But even with every policeman, National Guardsman, ex-serviceman, former Home Guardsman, and all the various hangers-on stomping about, Rooney did not think he could secure Greenwood. "When I first reported at the station," Rooney said, "it would have taken at least one thousand men to restore any degree of order, and to have put an effective guard line around the negro district would have required that many more."[12]

Kirkpatrick, who would later serve as Tulsa County attorney, had managed to get both Barrett and Governor J. B. A. Robertson on the phone, and at Rooney's instructions asked that two rifle companies and a machine gun company be sent immediately. Barrett ordered Kirkpatrick to prepare a telegram to that effect and have it signed by Gustafson, McCullough, and a district judge. In the meantime, Barrett advised, he would begin gathering the additional troops in Oklahoma City; even so, it would be morning before the men could reach Tulsa. Kirkpatrick did as directed and set about obtaining the requisite signatures.[13]

Mayor T. D. Evans—the former municipal court judge—all but abdicated during the crisis, and for this he would be severely criticized. Despite warnings from whites and blacks that trouble was brewing, he remained mostly silent and entirely invisible.[14] Thus Rooney, Daley, Gustafson, and Adkison were making most of the decisions at this point, and despite their alarm at the number of armed white men roaming the city, they continued to see the situation primarily as a "Negro uprising" possibly extending beyond Tulsa. "Information" reached police headquarters "that large bodies of negroes were coming from Sand Springs, Muskogee and Mohawk (an outlying settlement), both by train and automobile," causing Daley to send out "auto patrols with instructions to cover the roads which the negroes might come in on."[15]

Daley also organized foot and motorized patrols to canvas white neighborhoods "to preserve order and to assist in gathering up all negroes," who were to be brought to the police station. "No one was to fire a shot unless it was to protect life after all other methods had failed." Daley ordered even African Americans living in servants' quarters in white neighborhoods brought in, saying later, "I thought some of the bad negroes may set fire to homes of white people causing a lot of destruction to property and a possible loss of life." Each car was assigned an "ex-service man" and as many police officers as available. According to the *Tulsa World*, these squads also included "home guards"—presumably members of the wartime Home Guard.[16]

At about one in the morning, Daley told Rooney about the machine gun.[17] "It was old and worn out," Rooney later testified. "The shells were dirty and there was water in the gun."[18] Captain John McCuen, commander of the rifle company, said he "understood some ex-service officer had brought it from Germany as a souvenir."[19]

Whether the gun was of German, American, or some other manufacture is unclear. The German Maschinengewehr 08, a version of the American-designed Maxim gun, was probably the most common heavy machine gun of World War I. The British Vickers gun, another variation of the Maxim design, is another possibility. Both were water-cooled—that is, the barrel was encased in a water-filled jacket that slowed but did not prevent overheating—which may explain Rooney's reference to "water in the gun."[20]

According to testimony, the gun could be fired only with great difficulty and then only a round at a time. As a weapon it was practically useless, but it looked scary, so Rooney had it mounted on the back of his supply truck and driven around town.[21] "We decided to use it more for a demonstration against the crowd than anything else," he explained. [22]

None of Rooney's men knew how to operate the gun, so a war veteran named E. L. "Ed" Wheeler—a bystander who had just moved to the city—and two other ex-servicemen were recruited for the job. The truck was driven by the service company commander, Captain Frank Van Voorhis, and—besides the machine gun crew—carried six enlisted men under the command of Lieutenant Ernest Woods and, at least part of the time, Rooney himself.[23] Rooney's written report suggests that he went with the truck immediately to the "danger spot" on North Detroit, between Archer and the foot of Standpipe Hill, and began marching the rifle company up and down the street with the machine gun prominently displayed.[24] Van Voorhis gave a slightly different account, saying the truck was "ordered to various parts of the city where there was firing" until sent to Standpipe Hill about 3:00 A.M.[25]

As Rooney worked his men into position along Detroit Avenue, word arrived that five hundred blacks from Muskogee—presumably the African Americans allegedly summoned by J. B. Stradford—were approaching aboard a hijacked Midland Valley Railroad train.[26] In one account, from the *New York Times*, authorities were said to have been tipped off by a telephone operator who put through a call from Tulsa to Muskogee, which fits Henry Jacobs's statement that Stradford promised to make such a call.[27]

This story was among the most sensational of the rumors swirling through Tulsa that night and in the days ahead. In this particular case, there is some question about whether there was even a train. Rooney said there was not.[28] Daley, reporting in more detail, contradicts this. He said that one hundred "Legion men" under the direction of a "Mr. Kinney" were marched to the Midland Valley depot a few blocks south of Archer and Greenwood.[29] "Instructions were given that the men form a line on both sides of the track with instructions to allow no negroes to unload but to hold them in the train by keeping them covered," reported Daley. But when a train arrived, its only passengers proved to be a bewildered freight crew.[30]

Why Rooney said no train arrived when one almost certainly did was never explained, at least not in the public record. Perhaps Rooney returned to Standpipe Hill before the train came in, and in the confusion assumed that it never did.

A better question might be why the one hundred "Legion men" summoned to the Midland Valley depot in the expectation of an armed confrontation were not redeployed more advantageously once it became clear that there was in fact no threat rolling in by rail. Daley might have sent them to reinforce the National Guardsmen under Rooney or to stop the skirmishing along the Frisco tracks, where several buildings were ablaze and mobs had driven off firefighters responding to the alarm. Instead, he simply told Kinney "to take his men and use them to the best of advantage in maintaining order throughout the city."[31]

The black residential district extended two blocks west of Detroit, to Boston, along Archer and Brady Streets.[32] Some of these "negro shacks," as the *World* described them, were set on fire around 2:00 A.M.; at least two fire trucks sent to fight the blaze were warned away by armed men.[33] One driver said that he went to the same location twice more over the next three hours, once seeing three black men inside a burning house, and that on both occasions he was again chased off.[34] A driver from another station, though, reported that Chief R. C. Alder ordered alarms from the riot zone be ignored.[35] "It would mean a fireman's life to turn a stream of water on one of those negro buildings," Alder said. "There is not a chance in the world to get through that mob."[36]

Again, there are discrepancies. Daley said the blaze was eventually extinguished after Rooney assigned a six-man detachment to guard the firemen.[37] The *World*, too, initially reported that the fire had been put out;[38] later, in a subsequent edition, the paper said the fire went out on its own. The next paragraph in the same story in the same edition says that the fire destroyed all but one house on the block, and that five of six blacks snipers within one of the buildings were gunned down as they fled from the flames.[39]

Who these vigilantes were, and why the National Guard or police did not directly confront them, are not just unanswered questions. They were, at the time, largely unasked questions. And blacks were not the only ones targeted. Captain McCuen's rifle company took fire from both sides as it tried to separate the warring sides throughout the early morning;[40] Wheeler, the volunteer machine gunner, was seriously wounded trying to disarm a white rioter.[41] Sometime during the night, two riflemen directed their weapons on snipers in the belfry of Mt. Zion Baptist Church, who, according to Van Voorhis, immediately fell silent.[42]

It would be said later that most of the white combatants were oilfield workers, many of whom lived in the cheap boarding houses and hotels just south of the railroad tracks. There is some evidence this is at least partly true. Arthur Janes (spelled "James" in some references), the only person whose death is specifically listed as having occurred "during the gun battle at Archer and Cincinnati," is described as a thirty-six-year-old divorced driller from West Virginia. All but one or two of the twelve whites known to have died as a result of riot injuries—all from gunshots—fit the profile: young, unattached, working-class male.[43] At least one, a hotel clerk named Ira James Withrow, was one of Gustafson and Adkison's "special deputies."[44]

From the testimony of Fire Marshal Wesley Bush, these deputies seem to have been in and out of the police station throughout the night. He did not identify them as such, only as "bunches of men," who "would leave the police station and go out and come back—they were out and in, all of them."[45] In the confusion, two men arrested the previous week on vagrancy and weapons charges managed to saw through the bars of their cell in the city jail and were about to go through an outside window when they were caught.[46]

Inside Greenwood, only a few blocks removed from the flames and gunfire on Archer between Boston and Cincinnati, with bullets whizzing overhead, most people tried to sleep. Or said they did. Given what followed, it is understandable that most survivors described their own activities on this fearsome night in the blandest terms possible. "We sat up at our houses until about midnight, and then we decided to go to bed," James T. A. West, a teacher at Booker T. Washington High School, told Mary Parrish. "There was little sleeping, for the noise of guns kept us awake all night."[47]

It is no wonder West did not get much rest. He seems to have been living with principal E. W. Woods and family at 531 North Detroit Avenue, a little more than a block from Mt. Zion Baptist Church at 421 N. Elgin Avenue.[48] The new $85,000 church featured a structure on one end variously described as a tower or belfry—a photo in the April 10 *Tulsa World* suggests the former—from which one or more snipers exchanged gunfire throughout the night with both the rioters on Archer and residents of the white neighborhoods overlooking Greenwood from the heights to the north.[49] And if that were not enough noise, there were "people of all description going up and down [Detroit Avenue] and most of them were armed," according to J. C. Latimer.[50]

City health inspector C. F. Gabe's odyssey from Greenwood to the courthouse and back again reveals the confusion, violence, and brutality of the moment. Gabe was a Greenwood pioneer, having arrived around 1906, and, as one of the few African Americans employed by the city in a professional capacity, he was also a man of some standing in the community. This is also suggested by Gabe's statement that he was asked on the evening of May 31 to "see about" Dick Rowland's safety.[51]

For reasons not explained, Gabe apparently was armed, because he made a point of testifying that he "went home and pulled off his gun" before going to the courthouse. There, he saw Barney Cleaver and O. W. Gurley, and estimated the crowd at seven to eight hundred. Someone—he did not say whom—yelled at Gabe to "get these niggers away from here"; African Americans, meanwhile, urged Gabe to go home and get his gun because he was going to need it. A carload of whites pulled alongside. "Let's go to the armory," Gabe heard one of the passengers say.[52]

Someone pointed a gun at him, so Gabe headed back to Greenwood. At Archer and Boston, he encountered a churning crowd of African Americans the like of which he had never seen, maybe five thousand in all, though he readily agreed that he was not sure. He went back to the courthouse, left, and was four blocks away when he heard a gunshot. Gabe tried to get back to the courthouse and was intercepted by Adkison, the police commissioner, who told him to get away before he got hurt. And then he ran into John Smitherman, the deputy sheriff who Tulsa police officers said had quarreled with them only a short time before, but who now asked Gabe to "help stop the thing." So Gabe went to see J. B. Stradford, presumably at Stradford's hotel. He asked Stradford to come with him, to use his influence to intervene, but Stradford refused. So Gabe went to Cincinnati and Archer on his own, where he saw two men shot while they tried to set a house on fire, and a third finally succeed. And at that point he finally gave up and went home, to 422 East Easton Street, and went to sleep.[53]

Mary Parrish, huddled in an apartment with her child, was wide awake. "About 1:30 o'clock the firing had somewhat subsided, and it was hoped that the crisis had passed over," she wrote. "Someone on the street cried out, 'Look, they are burning Cincinnati!' On looking, we beheld columns of smoke and fire, and by this we knew the enemy was surging quickly upon Greenwood." But the line of defenders held. Parrish compared them, somewhat surprisingly, to the doomed Confederate general Thomas "Stonewall" Jackson. "Our boys stood 'like a stone wall,'" Parrish wrote, "offsetting each and every attempt to burn Greenwood and the immediate vicinity."[54]

Andrew Smitherman, staunch in his belief that Dick Rowland would have been lynched if not for the intervention of the men Smitherman helped organize, later wrote a long poem projecting the events of this night as a reverse image of the "Negro uprising" imagined south of the Frisco tracks. In this version, the whites were the shameless aggressors, the blacks heroic and righteous.

> Thus responding to their duty,
> Like true soldiers that they were,
> Black men face the lawless white men
> Under duty's urgent spur.

Thwarted in their attempt to get at Rowland, in Smitherman's telling the whites turned on his defenders.

> Rallied now with reinforcements
> Brave (?) white men five thousand strong
> Marched upon the Black defenders
> With their usual battle song:
> "Get the niggers" was their slogan
> "Kill them, burn them, set the pace.
> Let them know that we are white men
> Teach them how to keep their place."

And so they squared off, reportedly perforating at least one passenger train unfortunate enough to happen along the Frisco tracks, whites succeeding in setting a few fires along the southwestern edge of the African American quarter but unable to advance much farther.

> Rapid firing guns were shooting.
> Men were falling by the score.
> 'Till the white men quite defeated
> Sent the word "We want no more."[55]

By three or four o'clock in the morning, it seemed that perhaps the worst had passed. Henry Pack, the black police officer, started toward the police station thinking he might soon clock out but encountered gunfire near Archer and Elgin.[56] Barney Cleaver decided the jail was sufficiently secure for him to go home;[57] Dick Rowland, it developed, had become the safest man in Tulsa the moment the first shots were fired at the courthouse. In the furor, he seems to have been forgotten by everyone except Sheriff McCullough and the deputies guarding him. They had so resolutely barricaded themselves inside the jail that Kirkpatrick could not talk his way in to get McCullough's signature on the telegram to the governor and adjutant general. McCullough finally admitted a *Tulsa World* reporter he trusted, and the reporter convinced the sheriff to sign.[58] Incredibly, McCullough does not seem to have realized the mayhem raging outside his fifth-floor fortress.[59] "We believe we have the situation well in hand without further help from the [N]ational [G]uard or the state militia," McCullough told the reporter. "While I do not feel the situation warrants help from the outside yet it is always best to play safety first."[60]

Cleaver may have thought Rowland safe enough, but he had his doubts about the rest of the city and especially Greenwood. When he left the courthouse, it was to check on his family members, apparently with the intention of removing them to a farmhouse he owned somewhere well clear of the city. Nothing on Cleaver's journey to his home on North Greenwood dissuaded him. He and two companions encountered armed and hostile patrols on both sides of the tracks. First, they were accosted by a series of automobiles filled with whites wanting to know who they were and where they had been, and threatening to shoot the three men if they did not keep moving. Whether these were some of Daley's "auto patrols," Cleaver did not say. Once in Greenwood, they were met by "fifteen or twenty boys with guns" who wanted to know if Rowland had been lynched. Cleaver told them no and urged them to go home.[61] "White man lover," one of the men said.[62]

Throughout the neighborhood, African Americans stood in their yards, guns ready for the attack they hoped would not come but that they knew in their hearts almost certainly would. They asked if they could go into the second floor of the building at Easton and Greenwood that Cleaver owned with Jim Cherry, or maybe they went without asking, Cleaver following. A man named Anderson had a grocery on the first floor; the second floor was the meeting hall for the black chapters of the Knights of Pythias and the Masons. It was almost light by now, approaching five o'clock, and they all knew that whatever was going to happen would happen soon.[63]

And then the whistle blew.

Believed to be Tulsa's first African American police officer, Barney Cleaver was a Tulsa County sheriff's deputy at the time of the Tulsa riot. Cleaver was also a substantial Greenwood property owner and suffered one of the largest financial losses from fire and looting. *Photo courtesy of Greenwood Cultural Center.*

Oklahoma attorney general S. Prentiss "Prince" Freeling. *Photo courtesy of the Oklahoma Historical Society.*

The Drexel Building (*second from right*). *Photo courtesy of the Tulsa Historical Society.*

Mary Jones Parrish provided the best reporting from an African American perspective of what she called "the Tulsa Disaster." *Photo courtesy of the Tulsa Historical Society.*

Dr. A. C. Jackson, murdered in front of his house on June 1, 1921, was the most prominent Tulsan to die during the violence. *Photo courtesy of the Tulsa World.*

Opposite top. Attorneys Isaac Spears and B. C. Franklin continued their practice in a tent after their offices were destroyed in the fire. The identity of the woman in the photo is not known. *Photo courtesy of the Tulsa Historical Society.*

Opposite bottom. Early Tulsa African American lawman John Smitherman near the end of his career. As a sheriff's deputy, Smitherman clashed with Tulsa Police Department officers on the night of May 31 and was jailed more than a month as a result, yet went on to spend another three decades with the sheriff's office and police department. *Photo courtesy of the Tulsa Historical Society.*

Tulsa County Courthouse, where the violence started on the night of May 31, 1921. *Photo courtesy of the Tulsa Historical Society.*

Tulsa police chief John Gustafson.
Photo courtesy of the Tulsa World.

Nab Negro for Attacking Girl In an Elevator

A negro delivery boy who gave his name to the police as "Diamond Dick" but who has been identified as Dick Rowland, was arrested on South Greenwood avenue this morning by Officers Carmichael and Pack, charged with attempting to assault the 17-year-old white elevator girl in the Drexel building early yesterday.

He will be tried in municipal court this afternoon on a state charge.

The girl said she noticed the negro a few minutes before the attempted assault looking up and down the hallway on the third floor of the Drexel building as if to see if there was anyone in sight but thought nothing of it at the time.

A few minutes later he entered the elevator she claimed, and attacked her, scratching her hands and face and tearing her clothes. Her screams brought a clerk from Renberg's store to her assistance and the negro fled. He was captured and identified this

A photograph of the front page of the June 1, 1921, state edition of the *Tulsa Tribune*. The June 1 state edition, which was mailed to subscribers in outlying areas, is identical to the May 31, 1921, final edition later microfilmed for archive purposes, except the "Nab Negro" story was torn from the lower right corner of the front page of the May 31 final edition before microfilming. The June 1 copy also has a complete editorial page, while the May 31 copy does not. *Photo courtesy of the Tulsa World.*

Opposite bottom right. This *Tulsa Tribune* report headlined "Nab Negro for Attacking Girl in an Elevator" was described by the *Oklahoma City Black Dispatch* as "the false story that set Tulsa on fire." The story appeared in at least some editions of the May 31, 1921, *Tribune*, as well as the "state," or mail edition, dated June 1, 1921. This photo was taken from a copy of the latter edition in the collection of the late Beryl Ford. *Photo courtesy of the Tulsa World.*

RETRIBUTION

Many people heard the whistle, but no one seemed to know what it was or where it originated. C. F. Gabe, exhausted from his night's wanderings, was awakened by it.[1] Green Smith, a carpenter installing an air cooling system in the Dreamland Theater, heard the siren and went to a window to investigate.[2] A few blocks farther up Greenwood, on the second floor of his building and surrounded by armed neighbors, Barney Cleaver heard the whistle, too.[3] So did James T. A. West, the teacher boarding with principal E. W. Woods a quarter mile to the west on Detroit Avenue. "About five o'clock a very peculiar whistle blew," West told Mary Parrish. "This seemed to be a signal for a concerted attack by the whites, for immediately a terrible gunfire began. Aeroplanes also began to fly over very low; what they were doing I cannot say, for I was in my room."[4]

Just down the street, Dr. R. T. Bridgewater heard the whistle as he, his wife, and his niece fled their home. A phone call a few minutes earlier had summoned Bridgewater to attend two wounded men, but it must have been a ruse, for as he opened the front door a bullet grazed his leg. Bridgewater jumped back inside; his wife Mattie stuck her head around the corner and was greeted by bullets thudding into the door frame. Time to get out, she told Bridgewater. "Shortly after we left a whistle blew," Bridgewater said.[5]

Some have theorized that the noise came from the steel plant adjacent to the east edge of the black district; more likely, but by no means certainly, it was the "fire steam whistle" installed the previous November at the Public Service Oklahoma generation plant. News accounts said the PSO whistle could be heard for twenty miles around and would be used for "announcing changes of shift, 'election returns' and other 'news' of public interest."[6]

Not everyone who recounted the early stages of this invasion, for that is what it was, heard the whistle; or, if they did, they failed to mention it. But those who did interpreted it as West did—as a bugle call for a final, vengeful assault on Greenwood. "The shots rang from a machine gun located on the Standpipe Hill near my residence and aeroplanes began to fly over us, in some instances very low to the ground," Bridgewater said. "A cry was heard from the women saying, 'Look out for the aeroplanes, they are shooting upon us.'"[7]

The details of the next few hours are as murky as the origin and purpose of West's "peculiar whistle." Written and oral histories differ from and even contradict each other, and arguments over these details sometimes obscure an irrefutable and essential truth: a terrible retribution was exacted upon Tulsa's African American community, and the best that can be said of local authorities is that they did not do much to stop it.

In his report to Colonel Rooney written five weeks after the riot, Charles Daley said the fire at Boston and the Frisco tracks was extinguished around 3:15 A.M., and that soon thereafter some of the white attackers took up positions on the platform of the Frisco depot on the south side of the tracks.

> I immediately went to the depot and found a large crowd gathered on the platform of the Frisco station[,] also on the Frisco tracks where several of the men were firing over into the black belt. At this point I called for volunteer guards to handle this crowd and to prevent further shooting. About twenty men with rifles stepped forward. They were placed in a triangular formation from Boston Avenue to the end of the Frisco platform on Cincinnati Avenue, and back across the Frisco tracks with instructions to keep the crowd back and to prevent any further firing into the negro district.[8]

A more colorful account, appearing in the *Tulsa Tribune* four days after the riot, says that for almost two hours Daley "single-handed[ly]" held back "a crowd of nearly 400" that was "being incited to shoot up and burn the colored district." Citing "Frisco employees and other policemen," the *Tribune* story recounts that Daley, dressed in civilian clothes, "threatened the storming mob with his revolver and fists while guns were pointed at him and he was cursed by the leaders of the gang for opposing their plan." Witnesses, continued the *Tribune* report, "expected Daley would be shot at any moment."[9]

Daley told the *Tribune* that he returned to the Frisco depot about dawn to find his "pyramid line" of volunteers "submerged in the crowd."

> The leaders of the mob were egging them to start burning and shooting and they were just about to cut loose. . . . I drew my gun and told them I would shoot the first man that crossed a line I drew on the platform.
>
> Then I sent call after call to the police station for help. But everyone was out on the hills or in other parts of town protecting people or conveying negroes into camp. For about an hour and a half I stood there and argued and threatened with that mob, while some of the leaders kept pushing 'em on.
>
> They finally drew their guns on me from one side and I had to crack one fellow hard to keep him back. The crowd kept getting larger and larger, until finally the mob burst past me and ran for the business blocks across the tracks."

Daley went on to say that he knew who the riot ringleaders were, and that "I've got one in jail now and he's not the only one who ought to be there."[10]

Daley's story includes several interesting points, beginning with his statement that his direct confrontation with the mob began at dawn—about the same time West and the others say the invasion of Greenwood began—and *continued for an hour and a half*. This implies that the rioters were not the first whites into the African American district. This is somewhat supported by his reference to the police being occupied "conveying negroes into camp." This loosely fits recollections of both blacks and whites, and the explanation offered by authorities, that the initial move into Greenwood was by National Guardsmen, police, and volunteers told to take into custody more or less the entire black population of Tulsa, ostensibly for its own safety, and officials' assertion that the destruction that followed was an unforeseen consequence of that.[11]

The reality was probably messier, and the motives more suspect.

The *Tulsa World*'s second and third extras, published in the early- and mid-morning of June 1, described a "circle of steel" surrounding "Little Africa" at dawn, and a "continuous rattle of rifle and revolver fire." "Sixty or seventy automobiles filled with armed men were in the line drawn about the black belt and there were many reports to the effect that they planned to range through the negro settlement and 'clean it out,'" the *World* reported.[12] In practice, few of the cars seem to have ventured into Greenwood. Mainly, they seem to have transported armed whites to the edge of Greenwood and taken away black detainees.[13]

Mary Jones Parrish, who lived in the Woods Building on the northeast corner of Archer and Greenwood, "saw carloads of men with rifles unloading up near the granary, which is located on the railroad tracks near First Street. Then the truth dawned upon us that our men were fighting in vain to hold their dear Greenwood."[14]

McCuen's rifle company, with its service company detachment, had continued patrolling the first few blocks of North Detroit Avenue, taking black residents into custody, who were then "turned . . . over to the police department automobiles that kept close to us at all times." The cars, said McCuen, "were manned by ex-service men, and in many cases plain-clothes men of the police department."[15]

Van Voorhis said he left McCuen and Lieutenant Wood about 6:30 A.M. "with orders not to fire until fired upon." Van Voorhis returned to the armory for breakfast and reinforcements, and returned an hour later with six men in a touring car driven by a "civilian." He went as far as the brick plant at the foot of Sunset Hill in the northwestern corner of the Greenwood District. Unable to find McCuen and his command, Van Voorhis, his men, and their driver turned east on Cameron Street to Greenwood, then "proceeded north three (3) blocks when I discovered negroes fleeing to the northeast. We immediately proceeded to overtake them and when overtaken they were commanded to halt and put up their hands, which orders were promptly complied with."[16]

Van Voorhis left two of his men in charge of the prisoners and continued north on Greenwood. "I discovered more armed negroes, and having overtaken and disarmed them, sent my men in various directions with orders to search all houses for negroes and fire arms." By this time, the little squad had accumulated "twenty (20) to thirty (30) negro prisoners" when suddenly "white civilians on Sun Set Hill opened fire on us and caused us to suspend operations." Van Voorhis moved his prisoners behind a building for protection until the shooting subsided, then took them south on Greenwood until "police patrol cars arrived."[17]

The men then "proceeded up Sun Set Hill," apparently from the east, but came under fire from black snipers to the north of them. Sergeants Len Stone and Ed Sanders were slightly wounded, according to Van Voorhis, although this seems to contradict Major Bell's report, which stated that Sergeant Hastings, shot earlier at the electric substation, was the National Guard's only casualty. At any rate, Van Voorhis's command continued without returning fire and at last found McCuen and his men "deployed in a prone position with the old machine gun in position."[18]

Van Voorhis asked for volunteers to go back into Greenwood, but before he left he ordered McCuen to "see that the [white] civilians immediately ceased firing" from Sunset Hill into the "negro settlement" below. Neither Van Voorhis nor McCuen says how this was done, only that "the firing ceased." At about 8:00 A.M., Van Voorhis said he deployed men along Davenport Street for two blocks between Detroit and Greenwood, where he established a "receiving station" for blacks taken into custody.[19] This description is probably incorrect. The distance between Detroit and Greenwood was four blocks, not two, and Davenport did not go through between the other two streets. Perhaps they were one block farther north on Easton, which did go through, or even two blocks north on Haskell.[20] Van Voorhis said one of the "first prisoners captured" was Dr. Charles B. Wickham, who lived on the southwestern corner of Haskell's intersection with Elgin. Wickham, said Van Voorhis, "proved to be a very valuable aid in having the negroes surrender to me." This, he said, "they willingly did upon finding out we were there to protect them and to preserve order."[21]

Thirty to forty people were taken into custody between Detroit and Greenwood and sent on foot to Convention Hall, accompanied by a National Guard detail. At Greenwood, Van Voorhis turned north again. He took another 150 prisoners, and a 5-man detail under the command of Sergeant James Concannon collected another 171 in a nearby park. These, too, were marched to Convention Hall.[22]

The first black people swept up by authorities were taken to the city jail, city hall, and possibly the county jail as well,[23] and some wound up at the big downtown churches.[24] These locations, however, were wholly inadequate for the "protective custody" plan devised by Rooney. By early morning of June 1, black citizens were being held at Convention Hall,[25] a red brick building at Brady Street and Boulder Avenue constructed in 1914. Claiming to be the largest concert hall between Kansas City and Houston, the municipally owned theater had hosted some of the world's most famous performers.[26]

But even Convention Hall was too small. By late morning, it, too, was full, and those taken into custody were forced to travel, by foot and in the back of trucks, a mile-long gauntlet to the minor league baseball stadium, McNulty Park, at Tenth Street and Elgin Avenue.[27] There they were kept under guard—both to confine and protect them—until either a white person vouched for them[28] or they were transferred to the fairgrounds, located several miles to the northeast in the Whittier neighborhood near present-day Admiral and Lewis.[29]

Sometime after daylight—the exact time is unclear—a white woman named Ida Gilmore was shot six times as she stood on her porch at 225 East King Street, on Sunset Hill overlooking Greenwood. With Gilmore believed dead or mortally wounded—she actually survived, and filed an unsuccessful $25,000 claim against the city—police directed McCuen to move his men and truck-mounted machine gun up Standpipe Hill.[30] "Some time after day light," McCuen wrote in his report to Rooney, "it may have been 8 or 9 o'clock in the morning, by urgent request of the police department[,] the service company and 'B' company moved north to Sunset Hill to stop negroes from firing into white peoples' homes."[31]

This action probably happened earlier than McCuen remembered, judging from Van Voorhis's report and other accounts, but at any rate McCuen marched his men to the crest of the hill, where they were forced to lie down "because of the intense fire of the blacks who had formed a good skirmish line at the foot of the hill to the northeast among the outbuildings of the negro settlement which stops at the foot of the hill."[32] This seems to match Van Voorhis's account of finding McCuen's men "deployed . . . in a prone position" shortly before eight o'clock.[33] But McCuen's after-action report to Rooney does not mention reuniting with Van Voorhis, or the gunfire from the white neighborhood overlooking Greenwood. Less detailed than Van Voorhis's, McCuen's report nevertheless suggests a bloodier, more deadly operation. He ordered his men to train their rifles on the valley below, and "after about 20 minutes [of] 'fire at will' at the armed group of blacks the latter began falling back to the northeast."[34]

The Tribune, apparently relying on secondhand information, gave a more spectacular account of this exchange. "The bodies of half a hundred negroes . . . are lying in the valley at the base of Standpipe Hill, according to reports. . . . These blacks were killed in a three-hour engagement early this morning which finally ended when national guardsmen turned a deadly fire from two machine guns into the valley."[35]

This story is no doubt one reason, and perhaps the primary one, that local National Guard officers went to such great pains to document the absence of operational machine guns under their command, and that their Browning Automatic Rifles, which amounted to light machine guns, were kept under lock and key throughout the battle. The Tribune insisted that two reporters interviewed "two young men in semi-civilian clothes" who had turned a single machine gun—not two, as it said a day earlier—on the African Americans below Standpipe Hill. "When asked if they were members of the National Guard[,] they replied, 'Yes,'" the Tribune said.[36]

The "semi-civilian clothes" suggest that the two men either had no connection to the National Guard or were the two war veterans recruited to operate the truck-mounted machine gun. But this weapon seems to have been virtually useless, based on the testimony of several witnesses. Perhaps what some took as machine gun fire was actually McCuen's "20 minutes 'fire at will,'" which would match West's "terrible gunfire" at about the same location. But West said that the skirmish occurred between five and six in the morning;[37] McCuen put it between eight and nine.[38] At any rate, this seems to have been the beginning of an intense exchange that resulted in an unknown number of deaths in the ranks of the African Americans who chose to stand and fight.

The holdouts retreated into the neighborhood, and while McCuen and his men initially followed with little opposition, they eventually encountered "some negroes who had barricaded themselves in houses." These, McCuen wrote, "refused to stop firing and had to be killed." And that is all he says about it. The number killed—or that McCuen thought were killed—could have been one or two, a dozen, or many dozens. And that was not the end of it.[39]

"At the north-east corner of the negro settlement," McCuen wrote, "10 or more negroes barricaded themselves in a concrete store and a dwelling and stiff fight [sic] ensued between these negroes on one side and guardsmen and civilians on the other. Several whites and blacks were wounded and killed at this point. We captured, arrested and disarmed a great many negro men in this settlement and sent them under guard to the convention hall and other points where they were being concentrated."[40]

Exactly where this battle occurred is unclear. A possibility is the Mann Brothers Grocery at 1294 North Lansing Avenue and the adjoining residence.[41] One of the brothers, O. B. Mann, was identified by O. W. Gurley as a leader of the armed black men at the courthouse, a "tall, brown-skinned" man who had "come back from France with exaggerated ideas about equality and thinking he can whip the world."[42] Mann would be indicted by a grand jury[43] and, according to family tradition, he fled town and stayed away for years.[44]

T. J. Essley, a National Guard sergeant interviewed in the late 1980s, seemed to put the battle a little farther out, saying McCuen was "pinned down . . . just north of Pine Street and east of Peoria." Leading a twenty-two-man "platoon," Essley circled to the east and persuaded the black men fighting McCuen to surrender by convincing them that he had a machine gun. To complete the ruse, Essley ordered his men to concentrate a single volley on an outhouse in the middle of a field. The outhouse disintegrated under the fusillade, and the combatants "throwed [sic] down their guns and some of them stood up and held their hands up and others went down praying and I shouted at McCuen to cease fire."[45]

The reliability of Essley's recollections after more than sixty-five years is uncertain, but his story generally fits with McCuen's and Van Voorhis's reports. McCuen, though, said his last big skirmish of the morning was at a grocery store and a house, while Essley's description sounds more like an open field or a tract under development. He reported that McCuen and his men had taken cover behind trees that had been "pulled over" to make room for "a new addition."

Essley also gave details—sometimes reluctantly—that McCuen either did not know or chose not to include in his report. Most dramatic was a three-way confrontation somewhere north of Latimer Street on Lansing Avenue involving Essley, one of his men, a black man barricaded in his basement, and three white vigilantes trying to get to him. Essley said a brick had been "knocked out of the foundation" and the black man, firing through the hole, "was knocking off white people. He . . . knocked off three that I, uh, saw." Posting a private outside the house, Essley said he went inside and was about to descend into the basement when three white men approached intent on killing the black sniper. When the private tried to stop them, they said, "'Get out of the way, or we'll shoot you, too, you nigger-loving son of a bitch.'" The private, said Essley, got out of the way.

Apparently the men opened fire on the house, because Essley said "wooden partitions and splinters was flying out of there . . . some of them six to eight inches long. And I had to get outta there. I took my pistol and knocked the window glass out of the window just over where that [black] man was and put my gun on him and told him, 'Throw that gun away, or, or, you can't live any longer. I'll blast you.' And he threw that gun away." After disabling the black man's weapon, Essley ran outside to confront the whites, but one of them fired at him with a rifle, grazing his neck. "It knocked me to the ground," he said. "As hard as you'd hit me with a . . . ball bat and it was just as hot as any poker you ever felt."

At this point in the interview, Essley demanded that the recorder be turned off, for reasons that became evident once he relented and resumed his narrative. "I rolled right up on my knees and the guy says, 'Well, I missed him.' And he started at me again and I hit him with a .45 . . . automatic with dum dum bullets and stopped him." At that point, the private returned with the rest of the platoon and forced the other two whites to surrender. Essley explained that the men's long guns were wrapped around a tree and the cylinders removed from their revolvers. "They just hollered their heads off," said Essley. "'Oh, we'll get killed, oh, we'll get killed with nothing to protect us.' I said, 'They're all up and down the railroad track with loud speakers telling you not to come over here. Now, you just get back the way you got over here.'"

McCuen, in his report, refers several times to "both negro settlements," by which he apparently meant the older African American neighborhood and newer additions to the north and east. "Fires were started in all parts of both negro settlements and a continuous discharge of fire arms was in progress. Very often it was difficult to tell where bullets came from owing to the fires and also to the fact that so much ammunition exploded in the buildings as they were being consumed."[46]

This matter of "exploding ammunition" and the extent to which black Tulsans were prepared for a fight was an important point and a contentious one in the months and even years ahead. In 1937, Van Voorhis claimed that many African Americans were wearing World War I uniforms and were armed with "long range Winchesters."[47] Cleaver disputed this, telling the *Tulsa World* and the *St. Louis Post-Dispatch* that no arsenal existed.

> When questioned about reports that the negroes had long been preparing for a race war, Cleaver said there was no truth in the rumor. He denied there had been any organization of negroes for a conflict with white people, or that negroes had been furnished arms by any central organization. He branded as untrue a report that a quantity of guns and ammunition were [sic] taken Sunday into a church, which was the center of much of the rioting and in which a number of negroes hid themselves and fired at whites.[48]

"Many of the negroes shot were innocent of any wrong-doing," Cleaver said.[49]

In this, Van Voorhis agreed. "There is no doubt," he said, "but what some factions had been preparing for a revolt of some kind, but the mass of the negroes were innocent victims."[50]

Not to mention frightened, bewildered, outraged, and humiliated.

"About 5:30 someone called up our home and said for the men not to fight, that the Home Guard were visiting the homes and searching them but that they would harm no one," teacher James West told Mary Parrish. "A few minutes after that, some men appeared with guns drawn and ordered all men out of the house." West said he was told to raise his hands, was searched, and then was put in a line with other men in the street. His request to get his hat and his "best shoes" was "abusively" rejected; West recalled that another man was not allowed to put on shoes at all. Finally, when thirty or forty black men were rounded up, they were forced to run through the streets to Convention Hall. "While we were running," said West, "some of the ruffians would shoot at our heels and swore at those who had difficulty keeping up."[51]

When a bullet smashed into C. F. Gabe's piano shortly after the whistle sounded, he went to the door of his house to find two white men outside. They first ordered him out, then recognized him and said he could stay—but advised him to take cover. Gabe said both men were shot as they walked on up the street. Two more white men came, and this time they insisted Gabe leave his home. One wanted to kill him, but his companion prevented it and sent Gabe along to one of the groups of detainees.[52]

Incredibly, some Greenwood residents went to work, or tried to, as if nothing was amiss. One of them, John Wheeler, reported to work as a porter at the First National Bank but told his supervisor that he did not feel well. Upon examination, it was discovered the elderly Wheeler had a bullet wound. He died later that day and was buried in his work uniform.[53] Gabe would testify that one of the men who came to his door—presumably the one that wanted to kill him—said that he had shot a man whose description seemed to match Wheeler's.[54]

Adding to the confusion and fear on the ground were a half-dozen airplanes buzzing overhead. Officials insisted the planes were used for observation purposes only, communicating with the ground by notes dropped in metal canisters, but many African Americans and some whites said otherwise. Bombs, both explosive and incendiary, fell from the planes, they reported. Bullets rained down on women and children as they fled north. There was even a report that black riflemen managed to bring down one of the planes. Subsequent reports in the *Chicago Defender* and other publications bolstered the belief that Greenwood was the target of an aerial assault.[55]

A particularly vivid account came to light in 2016, when a ten-page manuscript attributed to B. C. Franklin and dated 1931, ten years after the riot, was found among some discarded family belongings. In it, Franklin never specifically says he saw anything dropped from airplanes, but that he heard a sound "like hail" on the roof of his building; going outside, he saw buildings "burning from the top," and he "knew all too well why."[56] There are questions about the nature of the manuscript. In it, Franklin implies that he lived in Tulsa in 1917, which seems to contradict his subsequent autobiography. Franklin also appears to introduce fictional characters into the 1931 account. And, one must wonder why Franklin made no mention of bombing in the lawsuits he filed on behalf of clients following the riot—as rival attorney Elisha Scott did—or incorporate the language from the 1931 manuscript into his autobiography.

One plausible answer is that the 1931 account is a dramatized version of events intended as short fiction. Franklin's son, John Hope Franklin, said his father was something of a frustrated writer who turned out a number of unpublished manuscripts during his lifetime.[57] The 1931 manuscript happened to be produced at about the same time Frances Prentice, a white woman who had lived in Tulsa at the time of the riot, published a short story titled "Oklahoma Race Riot," which was a thinly disguised fictionalized account of the Tulsa calamity.[58]

Even if it is fiction, B. C. Franklin's manuscript is no doubt based on what he saw the morning of June 1 and what others told him they saw. All of that said, there is also reason to think the airplanes were more effective psychologically than tactically.

Most if not all of the aircraft were probably Curtiss JN-4s, commonly known as "Jennies," wood-and-canvas biplanes that were easy to fly and relatively inexpensive because so many went on the market as surplus after the war. The planes were sold and serviced at a Tulsa airfield and readily available.[59]

According to at least one account, "turpentine balls"—a type of torch hurled with a stick—were thrown from the planes.[60] Other flammables, and nitroglycerin and dynamite, were also allegedly tossed from the cockpits.[61] But explosives seem unlikely, if only because no explosions were reported—except, perhaps, for what Van Voorhis said was ammunition. Greenwood burned; it was not blown up. Some of the fires might have been set from the air, but this seems unnecessarily dangerous and inefficient. And every account of the airplanes says that they did whatever they were doing simultaneously with the invasion of Greenwood. If so, bombs thrown or dropped from the air were as likely to hit allies as enemies. Lighting an incendiary and dropping it with any accuracy would have been roughly the equivalent of lighting one in a convertible or the back of a pickup truck moving forty-five to fifty miles an hour and then throwing it at a target in the opposite ditch—only more difficult and more dangerous.

Built of flammable materials with the pilot sitting on top of the gas tank, Jennies were more or less flying Molotov cocktails just waiting for a spark.[62] Turning one into an impromptu bomber would have required igniting the turpentine balls or kerosene soaked rags in an open cockpit, against the wash of the propeller and the flow of air around the moving aircraft, without setting the airplane on fire, and then hurling the incendiary clear of the biplane's lower wingspan. This seems foolhardy, especially when the whites on the ground were setting all the fires they wanted, and with much greater precision. However, that does not mean that it did not happen, for foolhardiness ruled the day.

Shooting from a Jenny would, likewise, have been difficult. Possibly some of those running for their lives believed gunfire from Sunset Hill, which overlooked their escape route, or possibly the granary mentioned by Mary Parrish, came from the sky. More accounts taken at the time mention the gunmen on the hill than gunfire from airplanes, and certainly gunfire on the ground was more effective. Still, the fact is that more than one riot survivor went to the grave absolutely certain that the planes were sent to kill them. "There was a great shadow in the sky," wrote Mary Parrish, "and upon a second look, we discerned that this cloud was caused by fast-approaching aeroplanes. It then dawned upon us that the enemy had organized in the night and was invading our district, the same as the Germans invaded France and Belgium."[63]

"Fires were started in all parts of both negro settlements," McCuen said.[64] Whether he meant his men started them or someone else did is not clear. All things considered, he probably meant the latter, but the widespread suspicion at the time and ever since is that the fires that consumed so much of the African American quarter on the morning of June 1, 1921, were set at the direction of, and in some cases with the active participation of, white authorities.

The official story was that the fires were set by white rioters and looters after the National Guard, with the assistance of police and white civilians, had removed all but a handful of the residents from Greenwood. Some evidence indicates that this sequence is generally true, but there is also evidence that fires were set simultaneously with the evacuation, and that men under the color of uniform and badge applied the fuel and flame that destroyed the Black Wall Street.

Some of the most startling testimony came from Deputy Sheriff V. B. Bostick, who said that he and his family were ordered from their home by men whose leader wore the uniform of a Tulsa traffic officer. This officer, recalled Bostic, poured "oil" on the porch and set the house on fire as the Bostic family was driven away in an automobile.[65]

Barney Cleaver told a similar story. He said a "police officer and other men with guns" appeared in front of his house. The policeman called out, "Barney, what are you going to do?"[66]

Cleaver said he did not know. "I hate for my place to get burned up."

"I will help you take your stuff out and put it out on the street," the officer replied.

It was after that that Cleaver returned to the courthouse and with McCullough drove Dick Rowland to Cleaver's farm.

Green Smith, the workman at the Dreamland Theater, testified that a "gang" came up Greenwood "knocking on the doors and setting the buildings afire." Asked who the men were, Smith replied, "Policemen, I guess." Smith said he was accosted by a group of "ten or twelve" wearing "what they call special police and deputy sheriff's badges. . . . Some had ribbons and some of them had regular stars."

Smith may have been mistaken about the deputy sheriffs; no one else mentioned their presence, and McCullough was severely criticized for keeping himself and his men barricaded in the jail until after the riot was over. In any event, this "bunch," as Smith called them, relieved him of fifty dollars. He wound up at the First Baptist Church and later the ballpark before being released about four o'clock in the afternoon.

O. W. Gurley's hotel was emptied by men "wearing khaki suits" who warned Gurley, "You better get out of that hotel because we're going to burn all of this Goddamn stuff." Gunfire raked Greenwood Avenue, causing Gurley to take cover under Dunbar School at 326 North Hartford Avenue. He abandoned this hiding place and surrendered when the school was set on fire.

Whites, too, said police officers were among the "arson squads" systematically torching the African American neighborhood. Laurel Buck, whose father owned property in Greenwood, said a policeman stopped him at Cincinnati and the Frisco tracks on the morning of June 1, and kept him back while two other officers entered buildings a short distance away and that "a few moments after they made their exit smoke began to pour out."[67]

Laurel Buck's father, I. J. Buck, said a uniformed officer stopped him from getting to "a large brick building" he owned. "He told me that I didn't have any business to build buildings for negroes to live in," the elder Buck testified six weeks after the riot. "I went on and he stopped me again, and told me to keep out or I would get my head shot off. My building was not set fire that I could see. It caught from adjoining buildings."[68]

These accounts of police, or men who appeared to be police, being chiefly responsible for the fires that burned Greenwood come with two caveats: first, none of the witnesses could or would identify the police involved, although several said they recognized the men;[69] second, each account was given after it became known that most insurance policies would not be honored unless the owners could prove that the fire that swept through Greenwood did not result from the riot, but from a deliberate act such as police acting at the direction of city officials.[70] Whether this influenced any of the testimony is impossible to know, but the Bucks, Gurley, Cleaver, and Bostick all had vested interests in convincing a court that the police, acting in an official capacity, burned their property. That, in fact, was the purpose of the court case in which Gurley, Cleaver, Green, Gabe, and others testified. It was a lawsuit brought by white businessman William Redfearn against his insurance company, seeking payment for his store and movie theater.[71]

Scores of lawsuits were filed in the wake of the riot. Most never went to trial. And the Oklahoma Supreme Court's adverse ruling in *Redfearn v. American Central Insurance Co.*, issued on January 12, 1926, effectively ended all hope of restitution for Greenwood property owners.[72]

Of all the wanton mayhem during these hours, none was more craven than the murder of Dr. A. C. Jackson. A noted physician and surgeon, unarmed and absolutely no threat to anyone, Jackson was shot dead in front of his house, hands raised in surrender. "I heard him holler and looked up and saw him coming about twenty-feet away from me or thirty, with this hands up, and he said . . . 'Here am I, I want to go with you, or words to that effect," said Jackson's white neighbor, John Oliphant[73]—the same John Oliphant who had tried to intervene in the 1912 municipal elections.

"I said to the fellows, 'That's Dr. Jackson, don't hurt him,'" Oliphant testified. The "fellows" were seven or eight men who appeared in front of Jackson's home at 523 North Detroit Avenue shortly before 8:00 A.M. Oliphant lived around the corner at 119 East Easton Street, and had been trying for some time to get law officers to the vicinity.[74]

"I wanted to get some policemen to help me," the seventy-three-year-old former police commissioner said. "I thought I could stop that whole business but I guess I was mistaken." By this time, said Oliphant, "The fight was all over and had been for an hour and a half. There was no shooting at that particular time because there were no negroes to shoot at" except Jackson and "one old man that was sick."

Oliphant's testimony, preserved in the state archives, is important not only because it is detailed—garbled as it sometimes is—but because it is free of any real or perceived taint of self-interest. Though he tried to save Dr. Jackson, Oliphant was forthcoming in saying he tried to stop the arsonists who followed not out of concern for his neighbors but because he feared that the fire would spread to his own property. And his house, in fact, was spared, so he had no claim against a doubtful insurer, and a professed friendship with the city administration did not cloud his judgment of their handling of the crisis. Oliphant said he called and sent for help from the police, the sheriff, and the National Guard; no one arrived until long after Jackson was murdered and the fine homes along Detroit had been looted and burned.

Oliphant said two men in "civilian" dress shot Jackson but that several others in "khaki uniforms" were nearby. They put the doctor into an automobile and said they were going to a hospital with him. Oliphant insisted he could not identify any of those in uniform and seemed uncertain of their connection, if any, with the shooters. "I probably knew some of them because I am well acquainted here, but I don't remember," he said. "The excitement was pretty heavy, and I had as many things to think about that . . . I couldn't remember just who was in the party."

The looters arrived soon after, "a hundred or two" strong, said Oliphant, women and children as well as men, stealing everything in sight and having a good time as they did. "Some were singing," he said, "some were playing pianos that were taken out of the buildings, some were running victrolas, some dancing a jig and just having a rolic[k]ing easy good time in a business which they thought . . . was upright." The looters hauled off "oceans" of property from African American homes. "They absolutely sacked all the houses and took everything out. . . . Pianos, victrolas, clothing, chairs, musical instruments, clothing of all kinds[;] men, women and children would go in the house and fill up pillow cases, sheets and clothing and carry them out and carry them away."

Oliphant said he talked "three or four crowds of fellows" out of setting fire to the Negro homes near his own property by telling them he would make sure no blacks moved back in. "I didn't know if I could make good or not but I was going to try it," he said.

But he could not hold off four men who showed up a little after ten o'clock, dressed in civilian clothes but wearing badges and claiming "they had been ordered to destroy—that ain't the word they used. I don't remember the word he used but it was to the effect that they were to make the destruction complete."

Oliphant said one of the four was a "red-complected" man called Brown; a policeman, Oliphant thought, but whether Brown was on the force at that time or had been, or Oliphant was mistaken, the old gentleman could not or would not say with certainty.

He was definite about one of the others, a bootlegger, roadhouse operator, and all-around bad actor named E. L. "Cowboy" Long. When Daley said he knew who the riot ringleaders were, he may well have had Long in mind; it was Long, said Oliphant, who was giving the orders on Detroit Avenue that morning. "When they called his name I feared him because I had heard about him," Oliphant said. "They threatened that when he came he would fix them houses quick, and he did."

By noon, it was over. All but a handful of Greenwood residents had fled or been taken into custody; most of those who remained were old or infirm or both. The National Guard, reinforced from Oklahoma City and elsewhere, controlled the district's perimeter and established an eerie order over the smoldering city.[75] The shooting stopped and the fires died out, but the smoke and the smell of death lingered.

The destruction was not quite complete, but near enough. The Black Wall Street of America lay in ashes, barely one brick on top of another, from Archer to at least the Gurley Hill Addition a half mile north. "Greenwood avenue, principal business district in the negro district, is a mass of broken bricks and debris," reported the next day's *World*. "Only gas and water pipes, bath fixtures, bedsteads or other metal fixtures remain to mark the places where homes once stood. The negro residences remaining intact can almost be counted on one's hand. There is not an undamaged business building owned by negroes in the entire district." [76]

More than 1,200 buildings were destroyed. Those left standing, with very few exceptions, were looted and vandalized.[77] For white and black alike, the scene called to mind the barbarity of World War I. "The colored section of the town was wiped out, and a long line of hopeless, destitute, pitiful refugees fled northward from the burning town," the *World* wrote in a June 2 editorial. "The German invasion of Belgium with its awful consequences was no more unjustified or characterized with any greater cruelty."[78]

"I watched this awful destruction from where I sat on the hillside," recalled one of Parrish's informants, unidentified but probably Mrs. C. L. Netherland. "As I sat and watched my modern 10-room-and-basement home burn to ashes, an old white man came by. Addressing me as 'Auntie,' he said, 'It's awful, ain't it?' and offered me a dollar to buy my dinner with."[79]

8

AFTERMATH

Two infantry companies and a machine gun company, maybe a hundred men in all, arrived by train from Oklahoma City at 9:30 A.M.[1] Adjutant General Barrett, who arrived with the troops, said their first task would be to "disarm most of the disorganized band of whites who are riding about the city armed to the teeth," as the *World* put it;[2] right away, though, some wondered just how quickly these reinforcements deployed. The shooting seems mostly to have been over by 9:30, but the looting, vandalism, and arson were in full swing. John Oliphant, clearly, was disappointed that guardsmen did not come to his aid sooner.[3] Former Tulsan Frances Prentice's fictionalized account of the riot, published in *Scribner's* magazine a decade later, reinforced the notion of a less-than-speedy entry into the fray by having the guardsmen eat a leisurely breakfast before venturing out against the vigilantes.[4]

In a four-volume history of Oklahoma published in 1939, Barrett said his men were on the ground and ready for formation "by the time the [rail] cars were fully halted." The problem, Barrett said, was that he could not find anyone to report to. Protocol called for him and his men to present themselves to the sheriff, and he and his men marched to the county courthouse for that purpose, but McCullough—apparently at Cleaver's farmhouse with Rowland—could not be found.[5] "It was evident from the start that neither [McCullough] or any other civil authority could at that time restore order," Barrett wrote.

Trucks, loaded with scared and partially clothed negro men and women[,] were parading the streets under heavily armed white guards and the troops began there by taking over the trucks and disarming those who had them in charge. . . . While there is no doubt that what was left of civil authority was trying to protect [African Americans] by placing them in impromptu places of refuge, it was beyond question that many of the most active in dragging these inoffensive people from their homes, were real leaders in the frenzied mob that earlier in the night had taken over the complete control of affairs.[6]

Setting up his headquarters at city hall, Barrett advised Governor Robertson that the situation called for martial law. Robertson wired back almost immediately, at about 11:15 A.M., authorizing the adjutant general "to do all things necessary" to restore and maintain order and protect lives and property.[7]

Barrett had already drafted a declaration and ordered it printed and distributed as soon as he received Robertson's reply. The declaration ordered civilians off the streets and nonessential businesses to close between 6:00 P.M. and 8:00 A.M. Private automobiles were banned from 7:00 P.M. to 6:00 P.M. "After the publication of this order," it concluded, "the man or woman, white or black, found with arms in their hands without written permission from military authority or by virtue of proper commission under the civil law, will be considered as public enemies and treated accordingly."[8]

The arriving National Guardsmen probably just took a while to become oriented and organized, and when they did, they may have spelled local troops who had been on duty all night. Barrett explained that "all available troops" were "concentrated to aid the fire department in suppressing the widespread conflagration" and "disarming all unauthorized persons bearing arms."[9]

The general was quite appalled by what he found in Tulsa, and adamant in his condemnation of it. He immediately ordered further reinforcements[10] and laid a blistering lecture on city leaders, telling them that they would take care of the displaced blacks "not just today and tomorrow" but indefinitely.[11] According to the New York Times, Barrett demanded to know how it was that "twenty-five thousand whites, armed to the teeth, were ranging the city in utter and ruthless defiance of every concept of law and righteousness."[12]

Barrett's estimate of twenty-five thousand is probably high, or maybe a misquote; there might not have been that many able-bodied white males in the entire city.[13] But whether the mob was twenty-five thousand or twenty-five hundred, it had wreaked havoc. Dozens of people, at the very least, were dead, and an estimated twenty-five fires had been set.[14] Barrett said those who "could give no satisfactory account of themselves and their actions" during the riot were locked in an "improvised guardhouse."[15] The location of this guardhouse is not recorded, and no other accounts mention such a place. The *Tulsa Tribune*, though, reported seventy-five whites arrested and thirty jailed over the next two days, mostly for looting and possessing stolen property.[16] A dozen whites, including Cowboy Long, were indicted three weeks later on riot charges.[17] But prosecutions, much less convictions, would be exceedingly few—microscopically so, given the thousands, according to Barrett, still rampaging when he and his troops arrived, and the hundreds gleefully robbing the homes of John Oliphant's African American neighbors.

Although he had belonged to the territorial and state militia since 1896, and would be adjutant general for nearly two decades,[18] Barrett was more of a political operative than a military man, and for that, Tulsa was probably fortunate. He summoned the local authorities, the chamber of commerce, and other leading citizens to an auditorium in city hall and told them exactly what they were going to have to do to get their town back. Barrett's exact words were not recorded, except for a fragment of a quote in the *World*, but they must have humiliated his audience down to its toes. Governor Robertson, Barrett told them, could not fathom their incompetence. How, he wanted to know, could the situation have gotten so completely out of control? Any reply except dead silence is difficult to imagine.[19]

At Barrett's direction, Mayor T. D. Evans appointed a short-lived, ten-member "military commission" to run the city during martial law. Their No. 1 task, Barrett told the commissioners, was to take care of the dispossessed black people scattered through town and across the countryside.[20]

Mary Parrish and her daughter Florence Mary had joined the great exodus northward, up Greenwood Avenue to Pine, and away from the city on the back of a truck. "I did not take time to get a hat for myself or Baby, but started out north on Greenwood, running amidst showers of bullets," Parrish wrote. A machine gun, she said, fired down on them from the top of the granary. "Someone called to me, 'Get out of the street with that child or you both will be killed,'" Parrish said. "I felt that it was suicide to remain in the building, for it would surely be destroyed[,] and death in the street was preferred, for we expected to be shot down at any moment."[21]

But they were not. And as they continued on, they encountered neighbors riding on a truck. Mary Parrish and her daughter climbed aboard and were soon in the country, passing farmhouses whose white occupants watched silently, "as if we were animals escaping a forest fire," thought Parrish. "We passed many of our group," she wrote. "The most pathetic sight was an old couple struggling along on foot. How I longed to get off and give them my seat, but I dared not leave my little girl alone to perish."[22]

Parrish said they passed an "aviation field," where men with "high-powered rifles" climbed into waiting airplanes. But Parrish's party was not molested, and traveled on, stopping at the farm of a black woman and her family, but then pushing on at word that trucks loaded with food were coming to feed them and take them home. Parrish and the others with her believed it was a trap. "After spending such a dreadful night and day witnessing so much destruction, how could we trust a race that would bring it about?" Parrish wrote. "At that hour we mistrusted every person having a white face and blue eyes." Physically and emotionally spent, Parrish and the others found refuge a few miles farther on, where they were fed and allowed to spend the night.[23]

It was the same along virtually every road leading north and east from Greenwood. Forty miles north, several dozen blacks spent the night in Bartlesville's city park, guarded by members of the American Legion. A few miles away in the African American section of Dewey, a woman fleeing the riot gave birth. African Americans from Collinsville and Owasso, small towns near Tulsa, were also reported to be in the caravan.[24] Thirty-five blacks were held for authorities at Catoosa.[25] Two hundred were detained at the Arbon airfield—perhaps the one Parrish's party passed—northeast of town.[26] A few African Americans fled into the wild Osage Hills northwest of Tulsa;[27] many went to Oklahoma City.[28] Some just kept going and never looked back.[29]

Those who did not flee, who surrendered or were taken prisoner, did not have that option, at least not initially. By shortly after noon almost all were confined to Convention Hall and the minor league ballpark at Tenth Street and Elgin Avenue.[30] A significant number had taken shelter in the downtown churches, and most of those apparently were allowed to remain for the time being.[31] Frizzell, the city's black hospital, had burned,[32] so the wounded and injured were taken first to the city jail and later the National Guard Armory for treatment; the most serious cases were soon transferred to Morningside Hospital on North Boulder Avenue, where Major Paul Brown, a doctor and the commanding officer of the National Guard's sanitation company, commandeered space.[33]

In all, the unhappy band numbered upwards of five thousand men, women, and children. They were fed, provided basic necessities, and both protected and held prisoner by the National Guard. Some of those interviewed later by Mary Parrish said they were treated well enough inside the Convention Hall and the ballpark,[34] but that hardly compensated for the humiliation of being marched and otherwise transported through the streets to the shouts and jeers of angry white onlookers, or the trauma of the morning's death and destruction.

At the ballpark, *World* reporter Faith Hieronymus encountered a phalanx of guardsmen with weapons at the ready, ordering sightseers back as African Americans entered the impromptu stockade. Written by a "girl reporter" so new that an editor misspelled her byline, Hieronymus's tale is generally sympathetic but reveals as much about white stereotypes and prejudices of the time as it does the plight of the detainees.

> The white sun beat blankly down on the unloading refugees lugging their meager possessions with them into the park; upon trucks filled with ice, huge boxes of food, tubsful of coffee; upon rickety wagons filled with huge bundles bursting open with their contents of clothing, and with household goods, from trunks to phonographs that the refugees had picked up in their flight.
>
> Inside the park was color and heat—stifling, odorous heat—the crying of babies, the sound of many voices and the moaning of women; and negroes—thousands of negroes huddled together as far as the eye could see from one end of the grandstand to the other.[35]

Hieronymus says that the majority of those thus confined "accepted the inevitable" with "good cheer," which suggests that she either badly misread the mood or that blacks were so resigned to this sort of treatment that it had become an expected if not necessarily accepted fact of life.

> Seated on the floor, an old woman with a gray handkerchief tightly knotted about a wrinkled face that might have been carved from dark oak rocked gently back and forth, moaning softly. In her hand she held the quart measure of hot vegetable soup that was being doled out by the hundreds of Red Cross workers. Someone bent over and touched her on the shoulder.
>
> "Sister," she asked, "why don't you eat your soup?"
>
> Tears stole out from under the half-closed eyelids.
>
> "Oh, Lawdy," she moaned. "Me an ole woman what has worked so hard all huh life, and now eve'thing gone! Mah house burned, mah chaihs [chairs] burned, mah chickens burned. Nuthin' have I got but the clothes

on mah back. Oh, Lawdy, that I should live to see such trouble come to me!" and she rocked back and forth in her misery.

Nearby, a "comely young negro woman" wept over the loss of her and her husband's home, rental property they owned, and their every other earthly possession. A middle-aged woman, "cool and immaculate" in a maid's uniform, read from the Bible to a little group of "pickaninnies," as Hieronymus called them, while a "mulatto woman" nursed a "light-skinned baby" with blue eyes, and conversed with the reporter in "excellent English." Hieronymus tells her readers of a girl wandering about in what seems to be a silent, stunned daze; a woman in charred shoes who had lost everything, including her husband, in the confused mayhem of the early morning.

Hieronymus portrays those at the ballpark as victims—but victims of Dick Rowland's allegedly provocative behavior. Her interview subjects not completely bewildered by what has happened uniformly blame Rowland for the calamity and want him punished. Implicitly, Hieronymus reassures white readers that they have nothing to fear from these people, that they are good Negroes who had nothing to do with the previous night's "uprising."

Hieronymus seems to have been the only white reporter to interview the suddenly destitute refugees and to tell their stories, and the overall tone of her piece is sympathetic. But a bold-faced line, inserted by an editor to break up the block of type, reveals the psychological limitations of even well-intentioned whites, stating simply: "Black—but human."

No one knows exactly how many people died as a result of the Tulsa race riot. It is unlikely anyone ever will. The uncertainty began that very first day, on the afternoon of June 1, when the National Guard and local officials began sifting the ashes of north Tulsa and rumors of corpses hauled to secret graves first circulated. A *Tulsa Tribune* headline from the archived June 1 edition puts the death toll at sixty-eight blacks and nine whites, but a bulletin just below it quotes Major Charles Daley as saying he expected at least 175 fire fatalities.[36] The next morning's *World* reported an even one hundred deaths—ninety blacks, ten whites[37]—but by afternoon that had been revised all the way down to twenty-seven, after Daley and Major Forrest Dutton reported finding no more bodies in the burned district.[38] The official count reached thirty-six on June 10, when a black man identified only as "H. Johnson" died in Morningside Hospital.[39]

Although there was an effort later to downplay the possibility that the real death toll was much higher than the confirmed total, officials initially admitted that they did not know how many people, especially blacks, were killed. The *Tulsa World*, citing Major Byron Kirkpatrick, said the "difficulty in determining the number of dead negroes is caused by the fact that the bodies were apparently not handled in a systematic manner." None, explained Kirkpatrick, was picked up by the National Guard, and "a number" were reportedly "removed in motor trucks operated by citizens." Whether these bodies were "placed at some point for later attention, if they were dumped into a large hole, or thrown into the Arkansas River," Kirkpatrick did not know. By the evening of June 1, the *World* went on, the remains of fifteen African Americans had been delivered to a local funeral home; how they arrived, and who brought them, is not disclosed. "Reports heard over the city indicate that five to eight times that number of negroes were killed during the riots," the *World* concluded.[40]

Thus began the stories that have echoed through the past century. The Tulsa newspapers soon were dismissing and even condemning the unconfirmed rumors, but to no avail. Nearly sixty years later, in 1980, James Leighton Avery remembered watching from the roof of Tulsa Central High School as "city trucks [drove] up and down Tulsa streets filled with dead bodies, black and white, all headed in different directions."[41] The Red Cross's Maurice Willows, in a report dated December 31, 1921, said estimates of the dead ranged from 55 to 300.[42] Commonly told stories had bodies disposed of in the city incinerator,[43] thrown in the Arkansas River,[44] and taken away in freight cars to be dumped in the coal mines east of town.[45] The NAACP's Walter White, citing a Salvation Army official named O. T. Johnson, said 120 blacks were buried in unmarked graves at a remote and unknown location.[46] A former Tulsa police officer thought they might have been dumped in a trench cut into an embankment just west of downtown.[47] Some blacks asserted that their own casualties were actually exaggerated by authorities, and that far more whites were killed than was admitted. In the early 2000s, a local black historian named Robert Littlejohn said that as a boy he was told hundreds of dead whites were taken away by blacks who ground up the bodies and spread them for fertilizer.[48] While implausible, the story speaks to the heroic status assigned the defenders of Greenwood.

Just as Littlejohn's story seems unlikely, so, under closer examination, do others. The city's incinerator, for instance, had not worked for some time,[49] thus creating a well-documented health hazard and complaints from the public about the smell of decomposing and improperly burned animals emanating from the city dump only a mile or so west of downtown.[50] The disappearance of a large number of bodies into the Arkansas River seems almost equally unlikely, although this was among the first rumors to be heard.[51] But the river was generally not deep, even in those pre–flood control days, and the corpses surely would have been much in evidence downstream. As far as can be determined, none were every reported. And, surreptitiously removing hundreds of bodies in broad daylight, transporting, and disposing of them, either in hand-dug graves or into coal mines, would have required scores of men, none of whom ever revealed the secret.

Yet the fact remains and cannot be ignored: from Day One, whites and blacks alike believed more people died during the riot than were accounted for. The search continues still, with the city planning a new investigation into possible mass burial locations, but the truth remains as elusive now as it was then.

The men J. B. Stradford and Andrew Smitherman sent to the courthouse to defend Dick Rowland and the law officers and public officials who chose not to disarm them were blamed for the disaster. The *World*, some of the police, and even General Barrett tried to shift at least some of the responsibility to the *Tribune*, and at least some blacks agreed. The influential Roscoe Dunjee and his *Black Dispatch* thought so; Walter White said the newspaper's careless use of the word "assault" set the stage for what followed. The *World*, quoting Chief of Detectives J. W. Patton, said that Rowland was never even charged and had been kept in jail for his own protection. Patton maintained that Page and Rowland told essentially the same story—that he had grabbed her arm, she screamed, and he ran away.[52] On the evening of June 1, Patton told the *World*:

> The police were quietly conducting an investigation of the alleged assault before taking any decided action.
>
> But when an afternoon paper [the *Tribune*] came out with a colored and untrue account, so far as we had been able to ascertain, of the entire affair, we concluded that it would be best for the safety of the negro to place him behind the bars of the county jail. The story incited such a racial spirit upon the part of the whites and under the impression there would be a lynching the armed blacks invaded the business district. If the facts as told the police had only been printed I do not think there would have been an[y] riot whatever.[53]

Patton's statement was self-serving, and he no doubt had a grudge against the *Tribune*; the attorney general's investigation the newspaper instigated had turned up embarrassing information on Patton.[54] But General Barrett also said "yellow journalism" was responsible for touching off the riot.[55] Like Patton, Barrett quickly backed off, but nearly two decades later, in his history of Oklahoma, Barrett wrote, "The bloody clash between the races had its beginning in a little spat and scuffle between a young negro janitor and a white girl elevator operator and the fantastic write-up of the incident in a sensation-seeking newspaper."[56]

The *Tribune* fought back. It published a statement from Patton denying most of the *World* story.[57] Civic leaders, including former Mayor L. J. Martin, were quoted prominently decrying "a complete fall down of the city government, police authorities, and county sheriff's office."[58] Whispers of a shadowy, perhaps imported, insurgency were heard, too. The *New York Times*, with a horror of radical influences, reported, "The negroes were either expecting or preparing for trouble," and claimed that explosions in some of the burning buildings were ammunition caches. "The police say that the I.W.W. and other malcontents had been stirring up animosity . . . for months," said the *Times*' correspondent,[59] who may have been photographer Alvin Krupnick.

Rev. Harold Cooke, the incendiary Southern Methodist preacher, told a chamber of commerce gathering: "This thing is not over. . . . Every white man knows we are not to blame for this thing." Allowing black men into the military during the Great War "and their recognition by the United States government as soldiers on the same plane as the white soldier" was the leading cause of the riot, Cooke said.[60] Stradford and Andrew Smitherman were regarded as the chief instigators; both managed to slip quietly from the city, although Smitherman may have been held for several hours at Convention Hall.[61] Barney Cleaver identified Will Robinson, "a dope peddler and all-around bad negro," as a ringleader.[62]

Not everyone blamed African Americans. District Judge Redmond Cole, in whose courtroom John Gustafson would soon be tried, told a friend that "the same group of rough necks and hoodlums who mobbed Belton" were chiefly responsible. He listed MacQueen and several others, including someone "known among the underworld as Yellow Hammer," as leading suspects.[63]

As ready as most whites and even some blacks were to blame Dick Rowland and his would-be defenders, considerable anger and scorn were also heaped on the city government, especially on Evans and Gustafson, and on Sheriff Bill McCullough, whose single-minded protection of Rowland while the city descended into chaos earned him nothing but ridicule from white Tulsans. A firmer hand at the outset, disarming and perhaps shooting a few of the black men coming through downtown Tulsa, would have put an instant stop to the situation, according to this line of thinking. Governor Robertson, furious at this second collapse of law and order in Tulsa in less than a year, told the *World* that a few men "who possessed guts" could have averted the riot "even though they had been forced to kill the negroes who first appeared on the streets."[64]

At best, Evans, Gustafson, and McCullough misread the situation badly, individually and collectively. At worst, they consciously facilitated one of the deadliest riots in U.S. history.

Certainly, all three were in over their heads.

Evans, a Republican, was elected as a reformer—as most Tulsa mayors claimed to be in those days—who promised to settle the long-standing dispute over the best way to solve Tulsa's chronic shortage of potable water.[65] He defeated incumbent Democrat Charles H. Hubbard by 207 votes in a year in which all but one elected city official was replaced.[66] Reserved and dignified, Evans was primarily a title attorney and banker, but in 1917 had been the municipal judge who presided over the IWW trial. As mayor, his powers were somewhat limited. Tulsa's modified commission form of city government consisted of four commissioners and a mayor, all elected at-large to two-year terms, and an elected city auditor. The mayor assigned responsibilities for various areas of city government to the four commissioners, but the appointments had to be approved by the commission voting as a group.[67]

Evans was warned several times on the evening of May 31 that trouble was brewing, both at the courthouse and in Greenwood,[68] but exercised little or no leadership. His order for white Tulsans to disarm on the morning of June 1 came too late to make much difference and was ignored in any event;[69] later he would dismiss complaints about his handling of the situation by saying simply that once the riot began there had been no way to stop it.[70]

McCullough, also a Republican, was a well-meaning relic of Tulsa's not-so-distant days as a little cow town on the Frisco line. Born in Clay County, Indiana, McCullough became a ranch foreman southeast of Tulsa in 1891; later, he farmed, operated a country store, and served as a rural postmaster. In 1910, with no real law enforcement experience, McCullough was elected Tulsa County sheriff; as such, it fell to him the following year to execute a black man using the name Frank Henson—there was some question about his true identity—who had been convicted of killing a Tulsa County deputy.[71]

The chief complaint against McCullough was that he did not pursue bootleggers, moonshiners, and other flouters of the state's (and later nation's) prohibition on alcohol with sufficient zeal. Attorney General Freeling filed suit to have McCullough removed from office in 1917 on those grounds,[72] and prepared but never filed similar charges in early 1921.[73] McCullough protested that he did not have enough men to close down every still, roadhouse, and honky-tonk in Tulsa County, and he was not going to unduly risk the lives of the men he did have with night raids into uncertain circumstances. McCullough rarely carried a firearm, and claimed with some pride to have never shot anyone, saying he preferred talking to gunplay. His may have been a noble approach, especially in light of more recent events, but it was one Tulsans judged far too passive once the enormity of the disaster of their own making was realized.

Whatever their failings, Evans and McCullough were essentially honorable men. Chief John Gustafson, if even a fraction of the information gathered by the industrious Kathryn Van Leuven was true, was considerably less so. The dossier compiled by Van Leuven and her associates portrays him as a shady character involved in blackmail and possibly embezzlement, armed robbery, and even murder. Gustafson had been fired from jobs as a railroad detective and private investigator in Kansas City and, in 1916, from the Tulsa Police Department. He became police chief in 1920 over several seemingly more-qualified candidates, apparently with the support of an "open town" faction. While chief, Gustafson maintained a private detective agency to which, it was alleged, he referred individuals with cases that might have been more properly handled by the police.[74]

Whether the department was actually more corrupt under Gustafson is debatable. Some of his predecessors were not exactly paragons, and complaints about lax vice enforcement predated Gustafson's arrival.[75] Once on the job, he and Commissioner Adkison advocated a larger, more professional force,[76] and, according to the *Tulsa Star*, some officers were fired for mistreating blacks.[77] But the scandals did not end. Allegedly, a teenage girl was arrested and held until her stepfather came up with the twenty dollars he owed a police officer.[78] A traffic cop was peddling moonshine on the side.[79] Several officers complained that assistant chief of detectives Harry Sanders "had been repeatedly taken away from homes in negro town, upon the complaint of negro men that he was interfering with their negro women, and on one occasion they actually took him from a negro house in a nude condition."[80] Patton, the chief of detectives, was caught engaging in sex with a female prisoner in an office at the police station.[81]

One of Gustafson's officers, Roy Meacham, punched the Reverend Rolfe Pomeroy Crum, rector of Trinity Episcopal Church, in the face—at the police station, no less—while the two argued about a citation for "jay-driving."[82] Meacham also supposedly "went out" with a woman being held for immigration authorities[83] and, most seriously, was suspected of involvement in an automobile theft ring operated by—who else?—the department's auto theft detail.[84] Owners complained that the police were arranging for automobiles to be stolen and then either sold or turned in for rewards.[85] Lending some credence to this accusation was the fact that the son of the detail's chief investigator was a well-known car thief.[86]

Gustafson reported directly to Police Commissioner J. M. Adkison, a real estate and insurance salesman by trade who saw no conflict of interest in writing most of the city's surety bonds while in office.[87] Some were surprised that Evans slotted Adkison, a fellow Republican, as police commissioner, given that one of the other city commissioners, Democrat Herman Newblock, had twice been police chief. Evans did initially indicate that Newblock would be in charge of the police and fire departments, but changed his mind and retained Newblock as finance commissioner, the position he had held in the previous administration.[88] But Adkison seems to have taken the job seriously. He promised to modernize the department by instituting civil service and professional practices, visited police departments in the East, and attended a "modern practices" convention in New York.[89] Among Adkison's more novel initiatives was an attempt to ban taxis from parking downtown, apparently in the belief some were fronts for vice. "Some taxi men seem determined to work against the police department instead of with it," Adkison said. "It is this latter class we hope to see quit, fold their tents and leave."[90]

Adkison insisted that he and Gustafson were not to blame for any real or perceived shortcomings in the department. The two of them complained about easy bail,[91] the lack of witnesses willing to testify in vice cases,[92] and county attorney W. F. Seaver's reluctance to try all but the most airtight cases.[93] (In response, Seaver—his name often spelled "Seavers"—pleaded lack of money, manpower, and even the correct forms.[94]) Adkison warned that labor agitators and the growing number of unemployed nationwide would likely cause an increase in crime locally,[95] and asked for thirty-five additional officers to meet the challenge.[96] He and Gustafson also advised businesses to hire their own guards and to order them to shoot to kill. "By this I don't mean the promiscuous taking of human lives," Adkison explained, "but I insist that if a few robbers are killed in the act of pulling off robberies—if they are caught redhanded and dealt with summarily—there will be an immediate and noticeable decrease in the number of holdups."[97]

But for all of their tough talk, Adkison and Gustafson were indecisive when a show of strength might have squelched the crisis; then, they threw gasoline on the fire by unleashing a deputized mob.

When it came out on the afternoon of June 1, the *Tulsa Tribune* more or less blamed everybody in a front-page editorial headlined "Restore Order.": "Lynch law leads not to law but to lawlessness and lawlessness is a repudiation of government.

Lynch law is a fire brand in the hands of those who thoughtlessly elect to establish mob rule for law and order. Lynch law is an impassioned appeal to the hatreds of prejudice. It brings ignominy and disaster to any community that fails it victims."[98]

African Americans were released from Convention Hall and McNulty Park that day as soon as they could get a white person to vouch for them.[99] For some, this happened fairly quickly. Domestics, many of whom had been taken from servants' quarters in white neighborhoods only hours earlier, were picked up by their employers.[100]

A laborer named A. J. Newman telephoned his employer, who came for New-man in a truck and took him to search for his wife and daughter; the daughter, it developed, had been hospitalized with an epileptic seizure. "White friends" called for attorney Richard Hill and his wife at about 2:00 P.M., and took them to the Hill's house, where they found "everything considerably tumbled around, but no serious damage done." A white man and his son "and a few neighboring white friends" had "prevented any further molestation of our home." The men said they "were ready to stay with us all night if we thought it necessary to insure that we would not be molested."[101]

The school district's black teachers and their families were retrieved from various locations by the superintendent, E. E. Oberholtzer, and taken to the old high school, vacant and scheduled for demolition, in downtown Tulsa. The men remained there overnight, while the women were taken to the homes of white principals. The next day the families were reunited and those without shelter installed in rooms at Booker T. Washington High School.[102]

Black Tulsans who either could find no one to get them out of detention or had no place to go once they were released stayed at the detention centers. Late in the afternoon, trucks and cars began transporting those left at McNulty Park and Convention Hall to the fairgrounds on the eastern edge of the city, near present-day Lewis Avenue and Admiral Place. A large exhibit hall built in 1913 for the International Dryland Farming Congress was turned into a makeshift dormitory; cooking and sanitary facilities were set up. Thousands of displaced African Americans spent the night of June 1 there, while in the large downtown churches, elderly blacks slept on cots or on the floor.[103]

In the countryside, hundreds or perhaps thousands of men, women, and children, Mary Parrish and her daughter Florence among them, bedded down for the night in fields and barns.[104] In the twilight, they could see their homes, their lives, in some cases their loved ones, dissolving into a distant orange glow, and began to wonder where they would go and what they would do next.

9

"WOUNDS OF PASSION"

The *Tulsa World* appealed to false honor more than true justice the next morning. In a commentary headlined "The Disgrace of Tulsa," editorialist Tom Latta wrote: "There is but one way Tulsa can rehabilitate itself either in its own eyes or the eyes of the outside world. That is by rebuilding that which has been destroyed. . . . Restitution, not because of affectionate regard for the colored man, but because of an honorable and intense regard for the white race whose boast of superiority must now be justified by concrete act."[1]

Latta's blithe disregard for those actually most affected by the riot may have been, to some extent, a rhetorical attempt to convince the broadest possible audience. On race, the forty-eight-year-old journalist's views seem illogically bifurcated and even immoral today, but in his time they passed for moderately progressive. He was a segregationist and believer in the superiority of not merely the white race in general but white Anglo-Saxons specifically. But he also believed in legal equality, a tortured, tentative step toward real equality. Latta did not want blacks living in his neighborhood or attending his children's schools, he might not have thought most blacks capable of anything except menial labor, but neither did he want them cheated, robbed, and murdered. These were not inconsistent positions in an era when "separate but equal" was the closest America could come to addressing civil rights.[2]

"Pride of race" and the "impudence of the negroes" in coming armed through downtown Tulsa, Latta wrote, "permits something to be said for those who responded to the riot impulse" on Tuesday evening. But, he quickly added, "nothing that the mind is capable of conceiving permits a word of defense or excuse for the murderous vandalism which set in at daybreak. . . . Hundreds of thousands of dollars' worth of property—the homes of women and children, black in color to be sure but guilty of no other offense—went up in smoke. Semi-organized bands of white men systematically applied the torch while others shot on sight men of color."[3]

Murder, arson, and robbery were bad enough, but in Latta's view, and others', the worst sin was embarrassing the Magic City.

> Members of a superior race, boastful of the fact, permitted themselves to . . . deal their home community the foulest blow it has ever received in its history.
>
> _____
>
> The entire "race war" was as unjustified as it was unnecessary. Because of it Tulsa is blazoned as a community where tolerance does not exist, where the constitution of the United States can be enforced or suspended at will, where prejudice and race bigotry rules and law and order haltingly flexes the knee to outlawry. Ten thousand citizens have been rendered homeless and made exiles on the face of the earth!
>
> Will Tulsa accept such a reputation willingly? Will this city tolerate such injustice—accept meekly the sudden ending to its dream of primacy and glory? . . . There is but one way in which Tulsa can rehabilitate itself either in its own eyes or the eyes of the outside world. That is by rebuilding that which has been destroyed.
>
> _____
>
> Not else can the wounds of passion be healed or the scars of intolerant hatred be soothed. In this moment the men of Tulsa stand at the crossroads in the city's destiny. One way leads to a greater and more glorious future, the other certainly leads to retrogression and decay. There must not be, there cannot be, any hesitating.[4]

One of the trucks sent out to bring back the Greenwood refugees found Mary Parrish's party at nine o'clock Thursday morning. The weary refugees did not resist. "We did not enter [Tulsa] through our section of town, but they brought us in through the white section, all sitting flat down on the truck looking like immigrants, only that we had no bundles," Parrish wrote.[5]

She felt the eyes of spectators seen and unseen upon her, and her humiliation deepened when the truck reached the fairgrounds.[6] Barrett had ordered all blacks released from detention, albeit with identifying tags,[7] but many had no place to go. So they remained at the fairgrounds, standing in long lines for food and clothing, "people who formerly had owned beautiful homes and buildings, and people who had always worked and made a comfortable, honest living." Parrish was at least spared this embarrassment; the home of the friend with whom she had been traveling remained miraculously intact, and the woman invited Parrish and her daughter to stay with her.[8]

> Soon we reached the district which was so beautiful and prosperous looking when we left. This we found to be piles of bricks, ashes and twisted iron, representing years of toil and savings. We were horror stricken, but strangely we could not shed a tear. For blocks we bowed our heads in silent grief and tried to blot out the frightful scenes that were ahead of us. . . . At last we reached my friend's home to find it still standing, but with everything torn up and part of her things gone.[9]

Every African American whom Parrish's party encountered wore paper cards bearing the words "Police Protection" prominently displayed.[10] Two versions of these seem to have been issued, one under the auspices of martial law the day after the riot[11] and another by civil authorities a few days later.[12] Ostensibly, these were to warn off attackers. And they may have done so; there were no major incidents and very few minor ones in the days following the riot. Mostly, though, these tags were supposed to calm nervous whites by identifying "good Negroes"—those judged neither guilty of fomenting trouble leading up to the riot nor likely to cause more of it later. Conversely, those without a green card were quickly marked as malingerers, interlopers, and agitators.[13]

"Between 5,000 and 6,000 negroes were cared for at the fair grounds last night," the June 2 *Tribune* reported. "The women slept on cots and the men slept on the floors in the buildings. The Red Cross workers expect by tonight to have beds for all of them."[14] A heavy "white rain" fell that afternoon, extinguishing the last glowing embers in Greenwood. Inside the exhibit hall, "babies wept . . . women lamented as they remembered the ashes that were once their homes, and the men sat about, listless." From time to time, the *World* reported, "a negro officer went down the aisle between the cots bawling the name of someone who was wanted by a white employer at headquarters. When such persons were identified, they were given badges and driven into town by their employers."[15]

Men, women, and children continued arriving from outlying areas and from the downtown churches, but by evening the tumult had somewhat subsided, calmed by exhaustion and the relief workers' relentless efficiency. Everything from bedding to clothes to food to armed guards appeared practically on command—much to the congratulatory approval of the newspapers eager to salvage what they could of the city's image.

> Orderly rows of cots filled with sleeping women and children, long pine tables bare and clean after the evening meal, a little group of negroes in one corner putting away the last of the food and cleaning up things generally, armed sentries pacing back and forth in the cleared space nearest the door, the occasional fretful cry of a child soon stilled by the soothing voice of the mother, the lights shining through the windows of the men's quarters in the next building—all this was part of the Red Cross central camp at the old free fair grounds Thursday night.

In just one day, the camp's population fell to about a thousand, although it was thought that number might rise slightly as more blacks came in from the surrounding countryside or were transferred from churches. Presumably, the military sentries would have repelled any assault from without and quelled any disturbance within, but their primary duties seem to have been frisking blacks for weapons and keeping them busy while in the camp.

> Aside from the fact that lack of proper military protection made it possible for the negro men to come and go without proper search . . . the negroes' inherent respect for the uniform and bayonet and his entire willingness to obey the orders of such uniforms presented another difficulty: with the exception of a few men who did all they could, the negroes were reluctant to do the bidding of civilians, and there was much to be done. . . . Negroes were working for the one guard on duty Wednesday night making temporary sanitation provisions, and when he was recalled to town, work stopped.
>
> But with the sending of soldiers Thursday afternoon, under the direction of Red Cross workers the floors were swept, cots arranged, tables arranged and order brought out of chaos.

Despite everything they had been through, the trauma and humiliation, the loss of homes and possessions and in many cases family and friends, African Americans were expected to go immediately back to work, either for their regular employers or by building camp furniture and digging latrines.[16] By Friday afternoon, they would be put to work clearing away the smoldering remains of their homes and businesses and paid some minimal amount, most likely twenty-five cents an hour.[17]

Several hundred blacks remained at downtown churches on Thursday, which caused Barrett to briefly ban church funerals for "those killed during the riot." Bringing blacks and whites together under such "conditions of emotional stress" could be disastrous, Barrett wrote in Field Order No. 3.[18] "Every downtown church has been turned into a relief station for the negroes," the *Tribune* said. "They will continue to be cared for there as long as necessary, but the Red Cross is making an effort today to get them removed to the fair grounds as soon as possible. Some of them are still being cared for at the ball park."[19]

"The basement of the First Methodist church was established as a center for the wounded, who were taken there from other churches" the *World* reported. "On the orderly rows of cots lay men and women, either slightly wounded, burned or otherwise injured in the riots. Volunteer doctors and nurses gave medical attention while women of the church assisted in nursing and preparing food, assisted by uninjured negro women." Among those finding refuge was Seth Holts, a pipeline company employee who had arrived from Beaumont, Texas, and woke up in his boarding house room Wednesday morning "to find white men making off with his clothes, his savings of $180 and everything else except the bible given him by his mother." Though badly burned, Holts stoically maintained that he was "doing as well as could be expected."[20]

Nearby, Boston Avenue Methodist—affiliated with the denomination's southern branch—started Thursday with about three hundred blacks in the church basement and a tent. By evening, only forty remained. "The same scenes," the *World* explained, "were repeated and the same help given at the First Baptist, the First Presbyterian and the First Christian churches, and in the basement of the Holy Family [Catholic] School. Refugees dwindled during the day, but those who went out to find work or homes returned for meals and to spend the night."[21]

Mary Parrish found herself at the Red Cross offices on the morning of June 3, ragged and dispirited, as much by the circumstances of her fellow African American refugees as her own.

> I found long rows of women, men and children waiting their turn to receive clothing, such as was obtainable. And the thing that I could not understand was why these innocent people, who were as helpless as babes, were placed under guard. Nevertheless, heavily armed guards were all around the building. Some were kind and manly, others were beasts dressed in

uniforms. These poor people stood for hours waiting their turn; some were seen to sicken and faint. The nurses would immediately take them out of line and give them treatment.

I finally succeeded in getting inside of the door, where I was met by a guard who asked what I wanted. On being told he directed me to a room where I was registered. From here I went upstairs into the clothing room in quest of a change of clothing for my little girl. Here I found stacks of clothing and shoes. Having worked hard always for an independent living, thereby being able to have what I wanted within reason, this was wormwood and gall to me, just to be standing around waiting to a get a change of secondhand clothing, but what could I do?[22]

Meanwhile, the search continued for those who had fled. Louis Lefko, secretary of the Better Business Bureau and a reserve army officer, took a group of men into the Osage Hills northeast of town on the morning of June 2 and found Drs. R. R. Robinson and B. H. White and their wives, one of whom was "quite seriously ill."[23] The next day, a black man hiding near Sperry, ten miles north of Tulsa, told Red Cross volunteers that a black girl had drowned trying to get away from marauding whites; two other girls, ages twelve and fourteen, had run away into the hills.[24]

The *World* and *Tribune* emphasized the charity and good intentions of the "better class" of white Tulsans. Consciously or unconsciously, the newspapers and those they interviewed tried to counter the unflattering images of their city appearing on front pages of newspapers across the country. A Mrs. Elmer Vick, it was said, had worked at Boston Avenue straight through from noon on Wednesday until Thursday evening. Mrs. M. V. Cadman, with an address on Sunset Drive in one of the newer and more exclusive south Tulsa neighborhoods, took in her servant's entire family. A neighbor named Brown did the same for another black family.[25] And one unnamed woman housed "in addition to her own maid, a man and his wife, their four children, and the woman's sister." The woman also crammed into her automobile the black family's sole remaining possession, a baby carriage.[26]

Governor Robertson, who had arrived in Tulsa on Wednesday evening, departed the next morning, pausing just long enough to formally direct district court judge Valjean Biddison to empanel a grand jury. Robertson said he had "scant hopes of any good result," given the unsatisfactory outcome of the Belton inquiry, "yet it is our duty to do the best we can under the circumstances."[27]

In a letter dated June 3, Robertson dispatched Freeling to Tulsa to oversee the proceedings, writing, "I am determined that the causes of this riot shall be ascertained and the responsibility for the same fixed and the guilty parties brought to justice."[28]

Sated on blood and fire, the passions that flared so violently subsided as quickly as they had emerged. "No cross-roads village, where citizens go to bed at 8 o'clock, could be more quiet," the *World* said in describing downtown Tulsa on Wednesday night, just hours after the last shots had been fired.[29] Barrett, satisfied that peace had been restored, on Thursday issued field orders that, as a whole, loosened the constraints of martial law and relieved out-of-town National Guard units to return home. Civil control was restored to the city and county government.[30]

But the city was not quite as tranquil as it perhaps seemed. A meeting of white business and civic leaders on Thursday morning resulted in something very close to an overthrow of the elected city government. Mayor Evans and the police and sheriff's departments were loudly denounced, and an ad hoc committee formed that, in the weeks ahead, would clash sometimes bitterly with Evans and the city commission. This committee does not seem to have had a formal name, and was identified at various times by various sources as the "reconstruction committee," "citizens committee," "board of control," and "public welfare board." In an early proclamation, it called itself the "Welfare Expenditure Committee."[31] Within a few days, "Public Welfare Board" became the generally accepted name.[32]

By acclamation, recently retired judge L. J. Martin, a former mayor, was named chairman of an executive committee that also included H. L. Standeven, Grant McCullough (no relation to Sheriff McCullough), H. C. Tyrrell, C. F. Hopkins, and Cyrus Avery.[33] All were prominent men in the community. Standeven and McCullough were bank executives,[34] and McCullough had been responsible for bringing a Carnegie library to Tulsa.[35] Standeven, a former county judge,[36] had been one of the first two donors to the *Tulsa World* relief fund.[37] Tyrrell, an oilman, was a major supporter of the University of Tulsa, which had only that year changed its name from Henry Kendall College.[38] Hopkins had been an unsuccessful mayoral candidate in 1920, was vice president of the chamber of commerce, and had interests in oil, refining, and auto parts.[39] The peripatetic Avery was, among other things, deeply involved in creating the national highway system and would be chiefly responsible for the routing of America's Main Street, U.S. 66, from Chicago to Santa Monica, California. Of more immediate interest, he had platted at least one of the additions north of Archer Street along Greenwood Avenue and seems to have had the trust of many African Americans.[40]

"We have neglected our duties and our city government has fallen down," Martin told the forty men gathered in the city hall auditorium. "We have had a falling police protection here and now we have got to pay the costs of it. The city and county is legally liable for every dollar of the damage which has been done. Other cities have had to pay the bill of race riots, and we shall have to do so probably because we have neglected our duty as citizens." The *Tribune* said "smashing applause" greeted Martin's pep talk, although this may have been an exaggeration, given the newspaper's animosity for the Evans administration.[41]

Judge though he might have been, Martin did not let the finer points of law cloud his view of where authorities went wrong or how to proceed. Most of the damage, he said, was done by "criminals" who should have been "shot on the spot." Some of the worst criminal activity had been perpetrated by informally organized "special deputies," yet Martin advocated more of essentially the same thing—authorizing a "detachment" of one hundred American Legion men to be kept "in readiness for every outbreak during the coming period."[42]

Martin and the others, the *Tribune* reported, were "to assume full charge of the relief situation as it exists in the aggregate and have permanent responsibility for immediate relief work and financial measures of rehabilitating the colored district." The very next sentence, though, notes that "responsibility for immediate relief work" was to remain with the Red Cross, "which assumed active work in those lines early [Wednesday]."[43]

The situation was not quite as confused as it sounds—although at times it came close. The Public Welfare Board was to raise money and to a certain extent set policy. The Red Cross was to do the actual work and provide operational expertise.[44] In a time long before the most rudimentary federal or state disaster services, improvised partnerships were not only the norm but a necessity. Tulsa's Red Cross, led by general director Clark Fields and board chairman A. L. Farmer, a forty-year-old businessman with interests in several enterprises including an insurance agency and a medical laboratory, mobilized quickly.[45] With the help of local merchants and churches, the Red Cross got food and water to those being held in the detention camps,[46] helped reunite families,[47] and, as early as the afternoon of June 1, began assessing the situation in what remained of Greenwood.

> A pair of Red Cross relief workers, on horse back, were making an inspection tour of the devastated negro section Wednesday afternoon. There is a little fringe of houses that were pillaged but not burned and from one

of them, a tumbledown hut covered with vines[,] hobbled a white-haired and grizzled "uncle" of pre–[Civil] war days. His name is Ofie Page, and before the [Civil] war he was a slave. He went to meet the two men and his old eyes lighted at the sight of the red crosses on their sleeves.

"Praise d'Lawd," he ejaculated. "Ah knew the white folks would help us. . . . They's misery 'cause of what's happened this day: crazy niggers and crazy white folks, they is."[48]

The little reconnaissance party found an elderly woman wandering along a burned-out street clutching a guitar; another rushed from her tiny house waving a bit of white cloth. "Some of the negroes," said one of the men, "believing that their homes were still standing, told workers at relief centers that they had safe places of shelter where they could go, came back to ashes instead of home."[49]

Farmer and Fields needed help and knew it. They appealed to national Red Cross leadership for assistance, not so much for financial aid as for experience. The Red Cross sent them Maurice Willows. The forty-four-year-old Willows had actually left his position with the American Red Cross in St. Louis on May 31, the day the riot began, and was to begin a new job the following day. The national Red Cross headquarters intervened, however, and persuaded Willows, with his new employers' acquiescence, to go to Tulsa instead. Taking an overnight train from St. Louis, Willows arrived early Thursday morning to find the entire city, by his own description, in a state of shock.[50]

"Crowds of both whites and negroes were milling about," Willows wrote many years later. "In front of the Y.M.C.A. building was a crowd of negroes being fed, handout fashion. Their homes had been burned out, families had been scattered and no one seemed to have authority in control." Three hours after arriving in Tulsa, Willows met the Public Welfare Board at city hall, where "the Red Cross man"—whether this was Willows or one of the locals is unclear—was asked to take charge of the relief effort. Willows hesitated. It was not, he explained, the policy of the Red Cross to get involved in "man-made disasters." By this, he apparently meant he did not want to commit the organization to what was already a politically charged situation. So he called the national headquarters.[51]

Founded in 1881, the American Red Cross was a relatively small organization until World War I, when it became an important civilian component of the U.S. war effort. It grew from 17,000 members to more than 30 million adult and junior members in 1918. After the war, it took on responsibilities related to the care of veterans and resumed its peacetime programs in emergency services safety training, home health care, and first aid.[52] Willows told his superiors that he was not sure whether the Tulsa riot fit any of those categories.[53]

"I called Washington with the report that: there was an unknown number of homeless refugees, all negroes; there was no adequate relief organization in town; on account of the divisions between the whites and negroes, a political situation complicated everything. . . . What should I do?" "We will take your advice," Washington told him. "Go ahead and report further. We will back you."[54]

So Willows went back to the Public Welfare Board—or, as he called it, the citizens committee—and said the Red Cross would take on the assignment under three conditions: relief administration would be financed by the national Red Cross, so as to avoid local pressure; the city and county government would pay for all the operating expenses, including the costs of caring for refugees; the city government, including the mayor and police chief, would "abdicate" for sixty days in favor of the Public Welfare Board. The board readily agreed to the proposal; the mayor and city commission, it appears, had no say in the matter.[55]

The newspapers were not as straightforward in their explanation of the arrangement. Although it soon became clear that Evans and the commission were being largely ignored—much to their annoyance—it was not specifically stated. Nor was it explained whether Martin's abrupt refusal of outside assistance was related to the Red Cross's condition that the city and county pay relief expenses.[56] If so, Willows himself came to regret the decision, eventually telling city leaders it had stunted fundraising efforts.[57]

Willows asked for and received $25,000 from the Red Cross, and with it began organizing relief efforts. The local Red Cross office was moved from downtown to the Booker T. Washington High School, which had somehow survived the conflagration. O. V. Borden, a local and national officer in the Purchasing Agents Association, was drafted to acquire the necessary supplies; nurses and other paid and volunteer helpers were brought in from around Oklahoma and nearby states. Rosalind McKay, state director of public health nursing, arrived on June 3 with eight nurses. Major Paul Brown, the National Guard physician, remained in charge of medical care; a rooming house near Morningside Hospital was refitted as a clinic for African Americans, and two white hospitals set up maternity wards for black women. A missing person bureau was established at the YMCA, then was moved to Washington High School. Clothing was collected at First Baptist Church and the YWCA.[58]

"With the coming of Director Willow[s] from St. Louis to take charge of the organization work here we have the situation well organized now," Fields told the *Tribune* on the morning of June 4.[59] But there remained one glaring problem: money.

For all the brave talk about restoring Greenwood and setting things right, cash donations to the cause were shockingly light, especially for a city that had so recently raised millions for war bonds. Almost immediately, Martin and the Public Welfare Board announced that no outside contributions would be accepted[60] and challenged one thousand businessmen to underwrite the relief work.[61] No one seems to have taken the pledge. The *World*, which had started a relief fund on June 1 with a thousand dollars of its own, turned over $4,447 to the Public Welfare Board late the next day.[62] The *Chicago Tribune* sent a thousand dollars, but it was returned per Martin's instructions.[63] Otherwise, the money came in drips and drabs. Somebody brought in fourteen dollars in change he had collected on East Second Street.[64] The local pool halls kicked in their Saturday receipts. A shoe store donated one hundred pairs of shoes.[65]

"Contributions to date have been distressingly small," Grant McCullough, finance chairman for the Public Welfare Board, said on June 4. "I earnestly appeal to [the public] for immediate and generous contributions." Besides the *World* fund, only $775 had been collected.[66] Insurance and real estate appraisers, meanwhile, put the losses in Greenwood at $1.5 million to $2 million.[67] The committee itself said a minimum of $500,000 would have to be raised.[68] "These funds are not needed for any sentimental purpose or for pampering or favoring anybody," committee treasurer Cyrus Avery said in an impassioned and exasperated plea. "They are absolutely necessary for buying food and shelter and plain necessities of life for about five thousand negroes now charges of this city. . . . We shall not have to have hundreds of dollars, but hundreds of thousands of dollars before this restoration work is complete, even in the most rudimentary state," Avery said.[69]

Avery's remarks reveal the difficulty he and others committed to the cause had convincing the community at large that the entire relief effort was not some sort of scam, or more likely a well-intentioned blunder, that rewarded blacks of the city for their own foolish rebellion. Allowing them to live at the fairgrounds, providing them with food and clothing, and showing sympathy for their plight would only give them ideas and "spoil" them.

Four days after the riot, the *Tribune* published a letter from a J. M. Jones warning that it was "a great mistake" to pay high wages to unemployed blacks. "Pay a fair price for help and then if you feel that the servant is worthy and needs help give it to them as a gift . . . but to pay high wages through sympathy will ruin them after things are settled again." As proof, Jones offered the case of a "negro domestic woman" who had had the temerity to refuse his wife's offer of two dollars a day and meals, insisting instead on at least forty-five cents an hour.[70]

So there it was. White Tulsa was willing to give their African American neighbors their old clothes and a meal or two. They were willing to let their servants and their servants' families live in their detached garages and servants quarters and give them jobs at depressed wages. They might even go so far as to give financial help to a few "worthy servants." But they were not willing to do something that disrupted the status quo—that is, loosened their economic hold on the African American community. Direct assistance to those deemed deserving might be okay; a general aid program run by a bunch of do-gooders was not.

The ban on downtown church funerals did not prevent families from saying goodbye to their dead. Services for John Wheeler, the black First National Bank employee fatally wounded as he walked to work the morning of June 1, were held that very afternoon; his porter's uniform served as his burial suit.[71] The first funeral for a white fatality, sixteen-year-old Homer Cline, was held the next day in the home of his parents. The youngest known fatality, Cline was reportedly shot to death near the Frisco Depot on the morning of June 1.[72]

Many remains were shipped out of town at the families' request. This included Dr. A. C. Jackson, who was buried at Guthrie.[73] Others were buried hastily—some would say suspiciously so—and this contributed to the endless speculation about the number actually killed during the riot. On June 2, the *Tribune* reported that the bodies of eighteen black men killed in the riot were being held at two local funeral parlors while the city and county argued over who would dig graves for them in the potter's field section of Oaklawn Cemetery.[74] The next morning the *World* reported that thirteen blacks, five of them unidentified, "were buried separately and in plain caskets" in Oaklawn, just southeast of downtown. Although the story says eight of the bodies were identified, it names only seven: Curly Walker, Henry Walker, Ed Adams, George Muller, George Lewis, Sam Ree, and Ed Howard.[75] Dr. Clyde Snow, who analyzed the riot-related death certificates for the Tulsa Race Riot Commission, said six bodies were unidentified, which may account for the discrepancy.[76] "Some trouble was experienced in getting graves dug," the *World* said, "but finally several blacks volunteered for the work."[77]

White embalmers typically did not handle black bodies, and vice versa, so the city's only black embalmer, S. M. Jackson, was put to work preparing the African American dead for burial.[78] Interviewed in 1971 by Cyrus Avery's daughter-in-law, Jackson said he was paid $12.50 each to prepare bodies for burial. Jackson's own mortuary burned during the fighting, and one of the riot's countless small mysteries is what happened to the four corpses inside at the time.[79]

As these accounts suggest, considerable confusion surrounded the dead and injured. The morning *World* of June 2 said officials estimated one hundred deaths;[80] that afternoon's *Tribune* put the known dead at twenty-seven.[81] The figure rose to thirty-six over the next few days as injured men succumbed or their bodies were discovered in the ashes of Greenwood and in outlying areas.[82] Three were brought by truck from north of the city.[83] On June 7, a badly decomposed body was found near the Curtiss flying field north of Dawson.[84]

Hospitals remained crowded with injured blacks and whites. Major Paul Brown, the National Guard doctor, and Tulsa physician in civilian life, had used his authority and influence to move his African American patients into Morningside Hospital's basement.[85] Only a few blocks from Greenwood at 512 North Boulder Avenue, Morningside said it treated six whites and sixty-one blacks on June 1, and performed "22 major operations."[86] According to Brown, a few African Americans were taken to the Oklahoma and Tulsa Hospitals.[87] Most whites were treated at the Tulsa, Oklahoma, and Physicians and Surgeons Hospitals on the other side of town. According to the *Tribune*, a total of forty-five whites were at those hospitals on the morning of June 2, but many others had been treated and released or simply walked away. The same report said fifty-five injured African Americans were at Morningside.[88] Black patients would soon be shifted to accommodations next door, and to a building owned by a "negro preacher" named Hill.[89] Later, those remaining would again be moved, this time to the Red Cross hospital that became the forerunner of today's Morton Health Center.

"The negroes were too sick to talk even among themselves, though cots touched shoulders in the crowded space," the *World* reported from Morningside on June 3, describing conditions of the previous afternoon and evening. "Their quiet was also due in part to the opiates administered to dull suffering. . . . C. E. Arnley, a builders' assistant and an older man of seeming stability and character, who was shot through the leg, said, 'They did not shoot the negroes who had the guns. They shot the innocent parties.'" Intriguingly, the story goes on to say that a "negro woman doctor" appeared in the late afternoon, accompanied by several other black women, to care for the patients. The story does not name the doctor, who would have been unusual on account of both sex and race.[90]

Some people simply disappeared with no accounting of their fate or whereabouts. "R. E. Love, negro, has searched for his family since Wednesday morning," noted a brief story in the June 4 *Tribune*. "He has not seen or heard from his wife or four children, one of them a baby one month old. Mrs. M. R. Travis [wife of a prominent oilman] of 1702 S. Boulder, who is in charge of this case, is anxious to hear from anyone who knows the whereabouts of Mrs. Love and the children."[91] It is not clear whether the Love family was ever reunited.

On June 3, a man named C. D. Dodson pleaded guilty to "petit" larceny on a charge of stealing clothing from the home of Dr. R. T. Bridgewater. Like many whites caught with the goods, Dodson claimed he was taking the clothes to protect them. He was fined twenty-five dollars and costs, thus becoming the first white person—and, as it turned out, one of the few—actually hauled into court for looting the black district during the riot.[92]

Authorities do seem to have made an effort to recover stolen property. In a locked room at the county courthouse, the *World* reported, were "four phonographs, two pianos, several dining room tables . . . and numerous other articles." At the police station were "three phonographs, two finely upholstered parlor chairs, two leather-bottom mahogany dining room chairs, two new trunks, a quantity of bedding, clothing and miscellaneous household articles." Even a couple of crates of chickens turned up.[93]

The recovered items, of course, would have amounted to a tiny fraction of the possessions stolen and destroyed. But authorities dutifully pursued charges, at least initially, against those implicated in what police called an "organized plundering expedition." Perhaps they were motivated as much by the opportunity to run some public nuisances out of town as they were a sense of justice. In any event, about one hundred whites were arrested;[94] most were released and promptly left town,[95] which the authorities must have known would happen, and which probably suited them fine. It saved the trouble and expense of prosecution and achieved more or less the same end—ridding the community of an undesirable element. And if they forfeited their appearance bonds in the process, so much the better.

The opportunistic thieving class did not limit themselves entirely to Greenwood. A couple was charged with looting the home of Ida Gilmore, the white woman shot several times on the morning of June 1.[96] One of the eight automobiles reported stolen was taken from in front of the First Baptist Church while its owner was inside; a truck disappeared from outside Convention Hall.[97] A woman living on the west side of Detroit Avenue complained that a "special police officer" came into her house and made off with $18.47.[98]

Sometimes the search for stolen goods yielded unexpected results. On June 4, police raided the Bee Hive Cleaners on Haskell Street between Main and Boston and found not only a stash of purloined furniture but "the largest still ever captured in Tulsa county." Besides the copper and zinc still, the police found fifty gallons of corn whiskey, five hundred gallons of mash, and some cognac "used as coloring."[99]

The *Tribune*, especially, seemed to make light of black Tulsans' plight, even as it commanded white Tulsans to contribute to the relief fund. On June 2, it featured a black man identified only as "Mose," who the newspaper said owned a "shack" just north of the Frisco tracks on Boston Avenue. The *Tribune* said the building was used as an "ambuscade" [*sic*] during the previous night's fighting, from which blacks fired on whites at the Frisco station. Five black men had died there, according to the newspaper, and the building burned to the ground. Mose, the account continued, hurried to the ruins as soon as possible, where he "scraped around in the ashes" until he found his sole remaining financial asset, six hundred dollars in gold coins melted into a single large lump. "I sho' is glad gold won't burn," Mose was quoted as saying before returning to Convention Hall, "content to go to the fair grounds with the other homeless negroes."[100] The story's lighthearted tone implies that something is not quite right with Mose and his six hundred dollars, but then what else could be expected from conniving, hapless Negroes.

If *Tribune* readers found Mose's story amusing, they must have been rolling in the aisles over the June 4 account of blacks collecting their possessions at police headquarters.

> A bit of humor was injected into the proceedings this morning when Harrison Rector, negro . . . identified as his own a brown handbag.
>
> "It ought to be full of clothes," he told the police.
>
> When opened the bag was empty.
>
> "Gimme it and let me get out of this town," he said as he reached for the handbag.[101]

Martial law ended on the afternoon of June 3.[102] The chamber of commerce, perhaps influenced by the Reverend Harold Cooke's fiery warning that "this thing is not over,"[103] urged Barrett to extend military rule at least a week. He dismissed their concerns, and ordered the Tulsa-based National Guard units to leave as planned on June 4 for summer camp at Fort Sill. "I believe that all danger of further disorders is entirely removed throughout the county," said Barrett. "I recommend that the people of Tulsa discount ninety-nine percent of every rumor they hear for the National Guard has not yet found any truth in a single one of the many rumors we have run down."[104]

To calm the jittery public, Martin's executive committee asked Patrick Hurley, the local hero and future secretary of war, to recruit fifty battle-tested veterans as a sort of quasi-military unit ostensibly attached to the sheriff's department. Hurley assured reporters that his men could "quietly and quickly" put down any riot that erupted after the last National Guardsmen left town on the morning of June 4.[105]

Hurley was one of Tulsa's most respected citizens; as his chief lieutenant he chose another, Horace Greeley Barnard, an oilman and cattle rancher who "at one time . . . had to deal with a criminal and lawless pioneer element." "I believe this force is capable of dealing with virtually any body of lawbreakers that might be disposed to start something," Hurley said. "There isn't a man in the bunch who hasn't faced death in probably a dozen different ways, and a mob would hold little or no terrors for them."[106]

In fact, the greatest danger to the general population seems to have been from all the armed men going about in military uniforms. On the evening of June 5, three whites returning to Tulsa from a picnic near Sand Springs were run off the road and fired upon by a carload of men they took for hijackers. The men—two dressed as soldiers, two in civilian clothes—claimed to be American Legionnaires on patrol for roving bands of Negroes. A man named R. L. Osborne was fatally wounded in the fracas and his sister seriously injured. Although Osborne's family pressed Governor Robertson and other officials on the matter, no action against the supposed guards seems to have been taken.[107]

To the handful of black residents who managed to remain in their homes through the mayhem and destruction were soon added an increasing number of hardy souls pitching tents on the desolate ruins of their former lives. The first tents up, perhaps as many as thirty of them, were reported on June 3. "This afternoon negroes, paid by the reconstruction committee, are at work clearing away debris and erecting tents," The *Tribune* reported. The county was providing men and equipment for the task, which was being supervised by the American Legion. By evening, hundreds of black men, women, and children were expected to take up residence in the tents, which had been furnished by the Red Cross.[108]

"Little stores and shanties are being opened up for business by the negroes," the *World* reported a few days later, "selling everything from fresh meat to ice cream cones, and the blacks are rapidly getting on their feet again."[109]

As was already becoming apparent, not everyone was pleased by that.

"IT MUST NOT BE AGAIN"

A little after noon on June 2, emissaries from the local Real Estate Exchange, forerunner of today's Realtors' Association, approached the Public Welfare Board with a proposition: move out Greenwood's black residents, and turn the burned district south of Easton between Cincinnati and the Midland Valley Railroad tracks into a "wholesale and industrial site."[1]

The Exchange proposed to do this by creating a corporation that would buy up the old Greenwood District and resettle the residents and business owners farther north and east. This, it was argued, would serve both economic and social interests, since this would be a better use of the land and would put more distance between blacks and whites. The real estate men also touted the public health benefits of the move, saying the new homes would be built on a higher elevation with better drainage, thus facilitating sanitation. As part of the proposal, the Real Estate Exchange offered to appraise the burned property, and recommended that the county clerk suspend all title transfers in the affected area.[2]

Those with losses to report were directed to a tent at the corner of Greenwood and Brady, in the midst of the ruined business district, to submit their claims. This applied to white as well as black property owners and to renters who had lost household goods in the conflagration. Claimants, interestingly, were advised not to consult attorneys because "competent legal advice will be furnished free of charge" by the Real Estate Exchange. The organization further promised to try to "collect the insurance on the properties destroyed," even though it had already been established that such claims were unlikely to be paid.[3]

The Public Welfare Board accepted the Real Estate Exchange's offer to appraise the affected area, and also prevailed upon General Barrett to issue a field order temporarily stopping title transfers, but it took no action on the larger, pivotal issue of vacating the black district south of Sunset Hill between the Midland Valley and Santa Fe tracks and Cincinnati Avenue. Indeed, the Real Estate Exchange and the Public Welfare Board agreed that it was not their decision to make, that "the plan could only succeed if the property owners in the area saw the financial advantage to themselves and were generally willing to sell their property for industrial purposes."[4]

The June 3 *World* devoted less than a paragraph to the buyout proposition, but included a very salient bit of information. "The value of the vacant property," the *World* said, "for negro residence[s] . . . is only $500 per lot while for industrial purposes the valuation would average about $1,700, it was stated."[5] That afternoon's *Tribune* went into much more detail, publishing the Real Estate Exchange's written proposal in full under the headline "Plan to Move Negroes into New District."

> We believe that the vacant lots with proper railroad facilities will bring enough money to enable the negroes to rebuild in a more removed section.
>
> We further believe that the two races being divided by an industrial section will draw more distinctive lines and thereby eliminate the intermingling of the lower elements of the two races, which in our opinion is the root of the evil which should not exist.[6]

So there it was. The solution to the problem was not to bring blacks and whites together, but to keep them farther apart. The Exchange claimed that its proposal would "add much to our city both from a business and a civic standpoint."[7]

Thus began a concerted campaign to relocate Tulsa's black district. Quite early, suspicion arose that this scheme was in fact the invisible hand behind the riot, perhaps orchestrating even Sarah Page's scream in an all-but-deserted Drexel Building. And this may have been the case; someone certainly seemed to be intent on provoking a fight that could only end in disaster for Greenwood. More likely, on balance, is the possibility that the arson squads that invaded the black neighborhoods on the morning of June 1 were organized by someone with a stake in the Real Estate Exchange proposal. But even that is uncertain; if this was a grand conspiracy, the supposed conspirators were woefully ill-prepared and undercapitalized, especially since the idea of converting the area to a warehouse district seems to have been around for a while.

Initial reception to the plan was mixed. Whites generally approved but, by and large, in a disinterested way that deprived the real estate syndicate of decisive public support. The *Tribune* was fully behind the proposal, but the *World* remained circumspect. Ultimately, it called for the scheme to be dropped and property owners allowed to rebuild free of the obstacles being thrown up by the would-be developers and their allies on the city commission.

Several black property owners told the *World* and the *Tribune* that they were open to the idea, depending on financial terms;[8] even Maurice Willows, who later would bitterly denounce the deal and those behind it, at first offered a muted endorsement.[9] The Real Estate Exchange promised paved streets, sanitary sewers, and running water—all of which Greenwood residents had been pleading for—and new homes removed from the noise and grit of the rail lines running through their old neighborhood.[10] So the deal may have been appealing, at least at first. Or, given the show of force so recently visited upon Tulsa's African Americans, an outright "no" may have seemed less than prudent.

The rapidly shifting focus of white Tulsans, and especially those with an interest in the proposed real estate transaction, can be tracked by the newspapers' editorials, and especially the *Tribune*'s. On June 1, on page 1, it severely chastised those responsible for the riot. "Lynch law is a fire brand in the hands of those who thoughtlessly attempt to establish mob rule," the editorialist, probably Richard Lloyd Jones, wrote. "Lynch law is an impassioned appeal to the hatreds of prejudice."[11] On June 2, still on the front page, the *Tribune* insisted that "Every citizen, every civic organization, every newspaper, every church should unite in one great effort to redeem our lost name."[12] Columnist H. M. Stivers said the previous day's looters had "about as keen moral concept as a grave robber."[13] But already the tone of the reporting, and white Tulsa's view of the riot, was changing. At the back of that day's *Tribune*, in the standing space reserved for editorials, a long piece clobbering local officials and exhorting Tulsans to "restore" the homes and possessions of "thousands of colored people, most of whom are innocent," began with the words "Acres of ashes lie smoldering in what was once 'Niggertown.'"[14]

The next day, June 3, the paper printed on its front page a coupon to be sent with checks or pledges to the Public Welfare Board;[15] inside appeared a Real Estate Exchange form asking for information on lost and destroyed property.[16] The lead editorial pleaded for contributions to the relief fund, saying, "Most of these people have lost their homes through no fault of their own, and they will not have another home soon unless this city that should protect does protect by giving them at least that which they lost." But this was after the editorialist poisoned the well with a first sentence that informed readers, "A thoroughly bad element in the negro district has for some time past been collecting firearms and ammunition."[17] The front page carried details of the Real Estate Exchange proposal, as well as a story on the following day's funeral services for Ira James Withrow, one of Gustafson's "special deputies" killed in the fray, and whose family ran one of the hotels the *Tribune* found so objectionable.[18] Page 1 also carried a story, headlined "Police Say They Knew of 'War' Plans," in which Police Commissioner Adkison said he and Gustafson had "headed off what promised to develop into a serious situation a short time ago. We went over there and told a group of negroes of the better class that we placed the entire responsibility on them for whatever should happen."[19]

Adkison immediately complained that his words had been misrepresented, that while he had had general concerns about unrest in Greenwood, he had no inkling of "war plans." The *World*, publishing the morning of June 4, buried Adkison's comments, and similar ones by Mayor Evans, behind Reverend Cooke's rant about whites not being to blame for the riot, and former mayor L. J. Martin's attempt to cool inflammatory rhetoric.[20] But its lead editorial was headlined "'Bad Niggers!'"

> There are those of the colored race who boast of being "bad niggers." These it was seizing the merest semblance of an excuse they armed themselves and, invading the business district of the city, defiantly sought to take the law into their own hands. If possible harmony between the races is to be restored these "bad niggers" must be controlled by their own kind.
>
> The innocent, hard-working colored element of Tulsa faces both a dangerous and unescapable duty if the work of those who seek to restore and tranquilize is to accomplish anything. They must co-operate fully and with vast enthusiasm with the officers of the city and county in ridding the community of the worthless, boasting, criminal "bad niggers."
>
> While the very work of mercy and restoration is going on, while the community is exerting itself to heal the wounds and assuage the suffering, these loose-mouthed impudent men are indulging in talk that can but start anew the holocaust.[21]

Who these "loose-mouthed impudent men" were, and what they were saying, was left unsaid. References to them as "non-working worthless negroes," though, would seem to exclude suspected ringleaders John and A. J. Smitherman and

J. B. Stradford. All three were gainfully employed, or were before the riot, and none was in position to be making speeches. John Smitherman sat in the county jail, held for the moment without bond, and Stradford and A. J. Smitherman were on the run.[22] Perhaps the editorialist—probably Tom Latta—was referring to the usual suspects that Barney Cleaver and others were beginning to name as troublemakers at the courthouse, and would soon be named in grand jury indictments. Or perhaps these nefarious characters were more necessary creation than flesh and blood. In any event, the *World* followed its first editorial with a second exhorting "the black men of Tulsa" to "school yourselves to a becoming attitude in your associations." Whites are the "dominant race," black Tulsans were reminded. "Avoid the boastful intriguers who speak to you of race equality. There has never been such a thing in the history of the world. Nor will there ever be. There is no equality recognized or practiced in the white race nor in your own."[23]

The *Tribune* took up the theme that afternoon. "A ride through the burned district yesterday afternoon," noted H. M. Stivers, "revealed many groups of able-bodied negroes standing about in more or less careless mood."[24] A news story about Red Cross work noted, "Darkeytown was an unsightly place before the devastation hit it. . . . The whole district is so different than the city Tulsans think of as their city that it might be in a foreign city as far as any resemblance to the real Tulsa is concerned."[25]

The lead editorial was headlined "It Must Not Be Again," but the subject matter was not what one might expect three days after a race war. It was a call to finish the job the arsonists and looters had begun.

> Such a district as the old "Niggertown" must not be allowed again in Tulsa. It was a cesspool of iniquity and corruption. It was the cesspool which had been pointed out specifically to the Tulsa police and to Police Commissioner Adkison, and they could see nothing in it. Yet anybody could go down there and buy all the booze they wanted. Anybody could go into the most unspeakable dance halls and base joints of prostitution.
>
> In this old "Niggertown" were a lot of bad niggers and a bad nigger is about the lowest thing that walks on two feet. Give a bad nigger his booze and his dope and a gun and he thinks he can shoot up the world.[26]

Summoning the paper's earlier assertion, that Adkison and Gustafson had failed to decisively quash the "war plans" of the real or imagined agitators, the *Tribune* editorialist declared, "The bad niggers started it. . . . Why were these bad niggers not made to feel the force of law and respect the force of law?"[27]

The point of the editorial was to heap coals on the city administration for not keeping the black population in line. The effect, undoubtedly, was to neutralize sympathy for the destitute African Americans—a fact driven home by another plea for contributions to the relief fund, not for the sake of blacks (who, given the editorial's phrasing, apparently did not qualify as real Tulsans), but for the "honor of Tulsa" and its "commercial stability."[28]

From the very first, whites blamed the riot on the black men who went to the courthouse on the night of May 31. That was somewhat balanced, though, by an equal disdain—publicly, at least—for the whites who burned and pillaged Greenwood. Within days, if not hours, that balance began to tilt in ways reflected and perhaps driven by local newspaper reporting. Appeals to white Tulsans were blunted by editorialists and public figures suggesting that black Tulsans brought their destruction on themselves by failing to control their unruly elements. And, with the Real Estate Exchange's proposal came an assurance that the means for a new and better African American district was in place if only the black property owners themselves would take the offered deal.

W. F. Seaver, the parsimonious county attorney who never seemed to have enough money in his budget to prosecute any but the simplest cases, hoped to resolve the criminal indictments arising from the riot without a grand jury. He thought the less formal—and presumably cheaper—court of inquiry route would be sufficient.[29]

He must have been the only person in America who did.

Just about everyone from President Harding[30] on down demanded a thorough investigation. The Justice Department announced its own probe—a perfunctory one, it turned out—in part because the postal substation on North Greenwood had burned.[31] Nationally, newspapers and public figures clamored for justice.[32]

Governor Robertson was ahead of them. On June 2, he formally asked Judge Valjean Biddison to call a grand jury, and followed up by detailing the ambitious and sometimes bombastic state attorney general Prince Freeling to oversee it.[33] "There will be a grand jury empaneled in a very short time," Robertson wrote in his instructions to Freeling, "but I think it very necessary that you be on the ground to preserve evidence for when the grand jury convenes. . . . I am determined that the causes of this riot will be ascertained with responsibility for the same affixed and brought to justice."[34]

Many whites and probably some blacks expected such an investigation to find most or all of the guilty parties to be African American. Barrett, while still in charge, ordered Stradford's arrest, citing statements by "numerous refugees" that the hotel owner was the "principal agitator of open rebellion against the whites and was mostly responsible for fanning into flames the spark that was ignited Tuesday night" by the African Americans' repeated forays to the courthouse.[35] Stradford, though, was long gone. Jailed briefly in Independence, Kansas, where his brother lived,[36] he made bail and left the state before extradition could be arranged.[37] Eventually settling in Chicago, Stradford tried unsuccessfully to sue his insurance company in the Illinois courts, saying he could not do so in Oklahoma because he feared "a Ku Klux Klan jury."[38]

A. J. Smitherman also fled. He called Sheriff McCullough on June 3 from an undisclosed location and promised to surrender himself "in a few days,"[39] but never did. Instead, he made his way to Boston, where he wrote and published his long poem about the riot. Later he moved to Buffalo, New York, where he started a newspaper and spent the rest of his life.[40] Smitherman's younger brother John, the deputy sheriff who got into a shouting match with police detective Ike Wilkerson and a TPD sergeant during the heat of the riot, was jailed June 3.[41] Two black men, Henry Jacobs and John Henry Potts, told investigators that John Smitherman had taken an active role in organizing the courthouse sorties;[42] that, and his intemperate harangue, kept John Smitherman behind bars for more than a month, until two women posted bond.[43]

Some African Americans tried diverting attention from Stradford and the Smithermans. A few said they blamed Dick Rowland.[44] O. W. Gurley, under scrutiny himself, conceded that guns and ammunition were distributed at the *Tulsa Star*, but that A. J. Smitherman told his followers "not to precipitate trouble."[45] Barney Cleaver said an "all around bad negro" named Will Robinson led the black men at the courthouse, and that most of the others were "ex-servicemen with an exaggerated idea of their own importance and wanted to show the white folks that nothing could intimidate them." They had cost him everything he owned, Cleaver said, and he intended to see them locked up.[46] But two years later, just before the statute of limitations tolled, Cleaver told a different story. He joined dozens of property owners, white and black, in filing lawsuits that alleged a conspiracy involving local officials and business interests.[47]

Whites, too, went to jail, but mainly for possession of stolen property. Cowboy Long, the acknowledged leader of the arsonists and a likely candidate in the Jackson murder, was not arrested until June 20.[48] During the interim, he was able to get a district court injunction stopping the police from raiding his drug store on East Second Street,[49] even though Long had been known as a bootlegger and all around bad actor since at least 1917.[50]

Summonses went out on June 4 for a grand jury to convene on Wednesday, June 8, just one week after the riot.[51] Freeling arrived in Tulsa on Sunday, June 5;[52] he ultimately consented to an extraordinary "court of inquiry" at the chamber of commerce offices on the fourth floor of city hall, where he was to hear secret, unofficial testimony behind closed doors on Tuesday afternoon.[53]

The burden for carrying out Governor Robertson's directive fell heaviest on Freeling, his assistants Kathryn Van Leuven and George Short, and Seaver's assistant John Goldsberry.

A Tennessee native and Harvard graduate, the grandly named Sargent Prentiss "Prince" Freeling was, in the words of early Oklahoma journalist Walter Harrison, "as handsome a human being as ever faced an audience. His voice was mellifluous. His knowledge vast. His presence charming. He was a man's man."[54] Freeling hung out his shingle in Shawnee, thirty miles east of Oklahoma City, in 1900, and soon was appointed assistant county attorney. He became county attorney in 1908 and attorney general in 1914.[55] As the state's top lawyer, Freeling was prone to pontificating and to personally prosecuting high-profile cases.

In February 1921, Freeling had taken charge of the sensational Clara Smith Hamon murder trial at Ardmore. The beautiful young Clara was accused of fatally wounding Jake Hamon, a wealthy oilman who was expected to have a prominent role in the new Harding administration. Clara was the married Hamon's mistress and secretary, and the wife of his nephew. Lingering six days before dying, Jake Hamon initially claimed to have accidentally shot himself, but there was never much doubt that Clara had fired the gun. She disappeared the night of the shooting and became the subject of a national search before eventually surrendering in Mexico. At trial, Clara said she shot Hamon in self-defense to escape his physical and mental abuse. The jury deliberated thirty-nine minutes before acquitting her.[56]

Robertson then ordered Freeling to take over a Tulsa County bank robbery case that Seaver was not prosecuting to the satisfaction of the Oklahoma Bankers Association.[57] The three men charged with holding up a bank at Sperry, a small town north of Tulsa, admitted guilt but claimed that they had been talked into the heist by the state's star witness, a man named Saunders, who had been recruited by Oklahoma City's chief of detectives to infiltrate the gang.[58] Three separate trials, more entertaining than suspenseful, were jazzed up by such dramatic touches as the courtroom arrest of two suspected conspirators in the robbery,[59] spectators rowdily cheering the outlaws,[60] and a witness sending a defense lawyer through a glass pane.[61] Against this backdrop, Freeling touted

Van Leuven's ongoing investigation of crime in Tulsa and Tulsa County, and promised a thorough cleanup.[62] During his closing argument for the first Sperry bank robbery trial, Freeling told the jury:

> No longer will places clutter up Tulsa county, places where booze runs like water, where robber gangs gather and plan right at the doors of your homes, for their nefarious business. I am going to see that there is something done to stop it.
>
> I want to serve notice on the lawless element in this county that no longer will they have places to gather at and plan. Tulsa County is going to be cleaned up. No longer, not if I can help it, will Tulsa County be the gathering place for crooks from not only from all over the state but the union.[63]

Meanwhile, on April 3, Seaver's investigator F. J. Bays arrested a taxi driver and small-time scammer named Calvin O. Brady. Brady—no relation of Tate Brady—was charged with being part of an auto theft ring preying on the area. Chief Gustafson, though, tried to get Brady released, claiming that he had been doing undercover work for the police. Bays was outraged. The ring Brady worked for, Bays said, was led by none other than the head of the TPD auto detail, Bay Ward, and included several officers[64] as well as Ward's son Buck, who had a reputation for boosting automobiles.[65] Bays claimed that the scheme involved not only stealing and selling cars but "recovering" them for reward money.[66] Ward denied the allegations, but by the end of the second Sperry bank robbery trial in early April, Freeling was ready to pursue those charges and others against the Tulsa Police Department, as well as the city commission and possibly Sheriff McCullough.[67]

Though he himself claimed disinterest, Freeling was being touted as a candidate for governor in 1922.[68] In early May, he was introduced at a meeting of the state Hereford Association as "the next governor of Oklahoma."[69] The *World*, on April 15, said Freeling's investigation of local officials was being conducted in bad faith and "for mere partisan purposes and factional advantage."[70] The paper was more pointed a month later, when it charged that Freeling, Van Leuven, Richard Lloyd Jones, and others were part of a "cabal in which intrigue, personal pique and selfish ambition seek to realize their aims through ways that are dark and tricks that are vain."[71]

Freeling, it was true, did belong to the Democratic machine that had ruled since statehood, while Tulsa remained one of the few places of Republican refuge.

Politics almost certainly influenced him. But the *World* was hardly a disinterested bystander in this matter. It was, by and large, a Republican paper and a supporter of the Evans administration—largely on T. D. Evans's promise to put through the Spavinaw water bonds.

Certainly there was some justification for Freeling's apparent fixation on Tulsa. Gambling, alcohol, and prostitution had operated with little to no impunity since the city's early days. But whether Tulsa was worse than Oklahoma City or many another place in the state is debatable. Some of the oil boom towns were squalid, violent places straight out of the Wild West, and the state capital had its own problems with vice, corruption, and scandal. In any event, Freeling committed a good deal of his office's limited resources to investigating Tulsa, and kept Van Leuven in town off and on for months interviewing informants and compiling a dossier said to run more than one hundred pages.

Fascinating and now largely forgotten, Kathryn Van Leuven was a steely, petite single mother said to be the country's first female assistant attorney general at a time when few women entered law or professions of any kind. Born Kathryn Nedry in Fort Smith, Arkansas, probably in 1888 (various sources also list 1882, 1883, and 1892), Van Leuven was described by *Daily Oklahoman* reporter Edith Johnson as a "just-too-cute-for-words type . . . not much bigger than a minute." She married attorney Bert Van Leuven in 1905 and gave birth to her son and only child, Kermit, two years later. She studied law under her father and husband and passed the bar exam in 1913, at about the same time she and Bert Van Leuven divorced. In 1925, she told Johnson she became a lawyer because she "couldn't teach music." Van Leuven was briefly an assistant county attorney for Nowata County, northeast of Tulsa, then lived in Oklahoma City for a while and was general counsel of an Okmulgee oil company when Freeling hired her in 1920.[72]

Despite her status as a divorced single mother and professional woman, or perhaps because of it, Van Leuven was well-connected socially, especially with the circle of well-to-do women intent on straightening up and sobering up the state. Proud, direct, and perhaps slightly jaded, Van Leuven had no patience for the ineffectual Seaver and thought Gustafson devious and unreliable even before the riot. On May 13, she wrote of Seaver that, "being an old man, he was not much help as he appeared to be feeble of body and seemed so in mind." She appraised Gustafson as a "pretty smooth article," who one of her informants believed had had two men "waylaid" and "bumped off" before he became chief.[73] Without naming sources, the *World* on May 21 said Van Leuven had told insiders that she would drop her investigation if the city fired John Gustafson.[74] At the same time, she was also building dossiers on Akdison and fellow city commissioner O. A. Steiner. Steiner, Mayor Evans's closest ally on the city commission, sold tires and other auto parts to the city though a store he owned. Besides being Gustafson's boss, Adkison earned commissions on the bonds he wrote for city employees. Some people, Van Leuven apparently among them, saw this as, at best, a conflict of interest, but the two city commissioners did not.[75]

George Short, the other assistant attorney general involved in the race riot cases, intended to move up to the top job when Freeling left after the 1922 election. He had been the subject of some scandal shortly before the riot when a state House of Representatives committee accused Short of impropriety for representing shareholders of a private corporation while working for the state, but Freeling had ignored the complaint.[76] John Goldsberry, who worked with Freeling on the Sperry bank robbery trials, represented the county. At fifty-five, he was an experienced trial lawyer with a successful private practice before agreeing to become Seaver's chief deputy. Later he would become U.S. attorney in Tulsa.[77]

This was the prosecution team. Within days, it began building its case.

We do not know what was said in the surviving African American churches on the Sunday morning following the riot, or whether the congregations that lost their buildings gathered somewhere else to observe the Sabbath. No written records remain, if any ever existed. We know plenty about the messages delivered from the pulpits of the large white churches of the city, the same churches that had sheltered black refugees only a few days before. The *World* carried side-by-side front page stories on the subject that Monday morning. The afternoon *Tribune* relegated its coverage to a single but lengthy story inside as the news cycle and breaking developments near and far grabbed page 1.

Everything from lax observance of the Sabbath to nefarious "agitators" were blamed for the riot, but the overarching theme, hammered home by even the most moderate and sympathetic of clergymen, was summarized by Rev. C. W. Kerr of the First Presbyterian Church. "The colored people must understand they started it," said Kerr. "The fact of their arming and coming up through the city was an outrage to the citizenship of Tulsa."[78]

Kerr had been a leading figure in the community for twenty years, and would be for another thirty until his death in 1951. He was widely admired as a kind, courageous, and fair-minded soul. Whites, he said, had not done enough to foster relations with "good negroes," and most of his sermon dealt with what he called "the growing spirit of lawlessness." But not even the beloved Dr. Kerr was immune from the prejudices of his generation and untold generations before.

Kerr's remark about the black forays to the courthouse being "an outrage to the citizenship of Tulsa" suggests that the black residents of the city were not themselves real citizens of it.[79]

Bishop E. D. Mouzon, speaking Sunday evening at Boston Avenue Methodist Church, speculated that the April visit of W. E. B. DuBois—"the most vicious negro man in America," he said—had something to do with the riot.[80] Vaguely, he linked DuBois to the guns and ammunition so widely rumored to have been stockpiled in Greenwood.

> If it is true that our wives, our children and the people of Tulsa were threatened with being at the mercy of armed negroes, then the white man who got his gun and went out in defense with it did the only thing a decent white man could have done.
>
> It is true that somebody blundered. Civilization broke down in Tulsa. ... The mob spirit broke and hell was let loose. Then things happened that were on a footing with what the Germans did in Belgium, what the Turks did in Armenia, what the Bolshevists did in Russia.

Blame fell on white Tulsa, Mouzon said, for paying insufficient attention to city government, and by permitting "petty pilfering" by black household staff and "immorality in your servants' quarters." Greenwood was "one of the blackest spots in Oklahoma.... There were all sorts of 'joints' operating there. Certainly everything bad was going on there—but that was Little Africa." Whites had erred, and erred badly, by not keeping a tighter rein on their black neighbors, and in letting them suppose they might aspire to something they could never achieve.

> There is one thing upon which I would like to make myself perfectly clear. That is racial equality. There never has been and never will be such a thing. It is divine ordained. This is something that the negroes should be told very plainly. Steps toward racial equality are the worst possible thing for the black man.
>
> There has been too much of this social equality, and the low-down white trash are responsible.

When Mouzon said, "Race hatred and contempt must die out; there is no place for it, and we must have cooperation for the good of both races," he mostly meant that African Americans should accept the status quo, enforced by the firm, paternal hand of white America.

There may be some of you here tonight who are members of the Ku Klux Klan. The other day members of that organization marched down the streets of Dallas, masked and robed. Such an organization may have been justified once, in the days following the [Civil] war, when civilization went wrong. But it is not justified here and now. Although civilization broke down in Tulsa the other day, we are not willing to turn over to men who disguise themselves this problem of modern life. It is more than unsafe; it is dangerous.

Rev. L. S. Barton, pastor of Boston Avenue Church, had delivered a more temperate message that morning. "The riot was not born in a day," he explained.

You must go back of the day when it burst upon us last week. It was not an occasion but a cause. It needs to be brought back to the people who take insufficient interest in public welfare. . . . Right up until the present time we have had choc joints in Tulsa and the lower down the people the more these joints have flourished. I think you will find the negroes were dominated by people who frequent these places. . . . With such breeding places of iniquity . . . is it any wonder we have a reign of hijacking, burglary and at last this riot?[81]

Two blocks away, at First Methodist, Rev. J. W. Abel said the black population itself knew it was to blame for the riot.

We must not make a martyr of the negro, even though many hundreds of them have suffered innocently. There are all too many of the so-called leaders of the negro race who habitually discredit the white race as to our willingness to give the negro a chance under all of the rights to American citizenship. What other nation in all human history has done as much . . . as the white race has done for the race which but a brief half-century ago emerged from slavery? A race which even in slavery was a thousand times better off than the black princes who ruled their race in Africa.

We tax ourselves to educate him; we help him to build churches, we are careful to keep him supplied with work at a good wage, and trust him with a ballot, and all we ask of him is to behave himself and prove himself worthy of our trust.[82]

African Americans, Abel said, protected members of their own race that they knew to be lawbreakers. Instead of marching on the courthouse, he said, "how much more respect we would have had for the leaders of the race had they presented themselves to the authorities and asked for the privilege of meting out their wrath on the criminal who had disgraced their race."[83]

That Dick Rowland might have been innocent, or that black "leaders of the race" might have had reason to fear for his safety, does not seem to have occurred to Abel. He proceeded to heap coals upon the heads of the city's leadership for tolerating "a spirit and condition of lawlessness" that corrupted whites and blacks alike.[84] Calling for a "loan" fund to help blacks "by putting a premium on industry and morality," scarcely tempered Abel's message.[85]

The harshest assessment, not surprisingly, was delivered from the pulpit of Centenary Methodist Church by the crusading Harold Cooke. "There has been a great deal of loose-mouthed and loose-minded talk about the white people of Tulsa being equally to blame with the blacks," he thundered. "This is not true. Any person that makes that assertion makes an assertion that is false to the core." The crowd of whites at the courthouse, said Cooke, was no mob, but "curious, unarmed and innocent" bystanders, stirred to action only by the appearance of "armed and liquor-frenzied niggers."[86]

In hindsight, it could be said the armed African Americans did exacerbate the situation; the courthouse hangers-on may have, in the beginning, been more titillated than bloodthirsty. But the fact they showed up in such numbers on the chance of witnessing a lynching disqualifies them as innocents. Would any of them have interfered if a concerted effort to storm the jail had been made? Less than a handful, maybe, but otherwise there is nothing to suggest that Cooke's curious, innocent spectators would have lifted a finger in Dick Rowland's defense.

The problem, posed Cooke, was that whites and blacks had gotten too chummy. "It should be a lesson learned, once and for all," Cooke said, "that the colored man is a colored man and a white man is a white man, and there can never be anything like social equality between the two races. Many negroes realize this and are the better element of the colored race."

Two classes of whites were particularly to blame for the blurring of the color line. The first, while perhaps well-intentioned, "would allow the negro to come up and mingle with them on the plane of the white." These do-gooders, said Cooke, "are the cause of a great deal of agitation taking place over this country today. They, through their shallow-brained ignorance, are plunging this country into wreck and ruin."

The second class of whites, Cooke said, "will leave the plane of the white man and permit themselves to mingle with the black on his plane." These, he continued, "are not worthy to be classed as members of the white race, and are too polluted and degraded to be tolerated by the negro." Such an outcast, Cooke concluded "forfeited his claims to membership in the human family."

Finally, he demanded that a new black quarter not rise from the ruins of the old. "'Little Africa' should never be rebuilt in the heart of the city," Cooke said. "It has been a festering sore in the heart of this city for many years. . . . The property rights of the colored people should be preserved, and they should receive all their property is worth. But the most absurd thing in the world would be to rebuild it where it has stood."

How much this was Cooke's own conviction, and how much driven by the desires of his friends and parishioners with a financial interest in seeing the burned district repurposed is a matter of conjecture. His church on North Denver Avenue was practically across the street from Tate Brady's home, a recreation of Robert E. Lee's Arlington House. Brady was a member. He also was among the most insistent advocates of relocating the black district.

Ironically, this first Sunday after the riot had some time earlier been designated "National Peace Sunday." Rev. Rolfe Crum at Trinity Episcopal and Rev. S. S. Kaufman of First Lutheran took note of this, and preached on the dangers of ready access to guns and ammunition—particularly in the hands of unruly blacks. "If the negroes had had no arms or ammunition or if they had been disarmed at the outset, there would have been no bloodshed," said Crum, "but because they went through the city armed they were the cause of their own undoing."[87] Kaufman said that Tulsa "must redeem her folly as warring nations must. To restore the property losses of the unfortunate is the least that Tulsa can do."[88]

But how anyone could have expected hearts or wallets to open after such denigration of Tulsa's African Americans, and from the city's pulpits no less, is beyond imagining. Tulsans returned their attention to existing philanthropic pursuits. By the end of that Sunday, the relief fund stood at about $10,000.[89] On that same day, First Methodist—a Northern Methodist congregation—raised that same amount for what is now Oklahoma City University, and promised to reach its $50,000 quota within a few days.[90] Meanwhile, Bishop Mouzon announced that Boston Avenue and other local affiliates of the Methodist Episcopal Church, South—the Southern Methodists—had met their $50,000 apportionment for a proposed (and ultimately aborted) Southern Methodist college to compete with the Presbyterian-affiliated University of Tulsa.[91]

Church services for African Americans were held that Sunday afternoon at the fairgrounds and in a tent next to Booker T. Washington High School. The

World allotted one long paragraph to them, the *Tribune* nothing at all. The *World* assured its readers that the "negroes seemed responsive and attentive" and "fairly shouted the negro songs." But the services were led by white clergymen, the same white clergymen who had belittled and condemned these same congregants only a few hours earlier. In this service, only "simple gospel sermons, with no allusion to the events of the last week, were preached," with no pontification on the inherent waywardness of the black race and the blame they bore for their own destruction.[92]

Looking north on Greenwood Avenue from Archer Street around 1938. Despite its destruction in 1921, the Greenwood District rebuilt and reached its peak just after World War II. *Photo courtesy of Greenwood Cultural Center.*

Left: Oklahoma assistant attorney general Kathryn Van Leuven led investigations of the Tulsa Police Department and prosecuted TPD chief John Gustafson. *Photo courtesy of Oklahoma Hall of Fame.*

Right: Adjutant General Charles Barrett of the Oklahoma National Guard. *Photo courtesy of the Oklahoma Historical Society.*

Oklahoma National Guard troops march African Americans under "protective custody" through the streets of Tulsa. *Photo courtesy of the Oklahoma Historical Society.*

Oklahoma National Guardsmen assemble outside the Tulsa Police Department headquarters, probably on June 1. The machine gun on the truck at left may be the derelict weapon "dug up" by Major Charles Daley on the night of May 31 or a functional one brought by an Oklahoma City–based machine gun company the next morning. *Photo courtesy of the Oklahoma Historical Society.*

Mt. Zion Baptist Church pastor R. A. Whitaker (*at left in tie and jacket*) administers to riot survivors. Although this house seems to have survived the fire, the ruins of another building—perhaps Mt. Zion—can be seen in the background. Whitaker was among the plaintiffs in the lawsuit that ultimately stopped the attempt to relocate Greenwood residents during the summer of 1921. *Photo courtesy of the Oklahoma Historical Society.*

This 1921 photo includes Tulsa's city commission and other prominent citizens, among them: Mayor T. D. Evans (*seated, second from right*); City Auditor Mary Seaman (*seated, at right*); Police Commissioner J. M. Adkison (*standing, far right*); Cyrus Avery (*standing, fourth from right*); Water and Sewer Commissioner C. S. Younkman (*standing, fifth from right*); Finance Commissioner Herman Newblock (*standing, sixth from right, against wall*); Street Commissioner O. A. Steiner (*standing, center, in front of door*); and City Attorney Frank Duncan (*standing, middle row, fifth from left*). *Photo courtesy of the Tulsa Historical Society.*

In an effort to recover their losses, Tulsa's African American property owners formed the East End Relief Committee. Members included hotel owner O. W. Gurley (*second from left*) and Rev. E. N. Bryant (*center, head turned to left, wearing dark hat, suit, and tie*). *Photo courtesy of the Tulsa Historical Society.*

Attorney P. A. Chappelle was among those who fought black Tulsans' legal battles during the summer of 1921 and beyond. Grandson Carlos Chappelle became Tulsa County's first African American presiding judge, and great-grandson Danny Williams served as U.S. attorney for the Northern District of Oklahoma, based in Tulsa. *Photo courtesy of the Tulsa Historical Society*

The Greenwood District after the fires and devastation of June 1, 1921. *Photo courtesy of the Tulsa Historical Society.*

Red Cross worker Marguerite Watkins (*left*) and director Maurice Willows (*second from left*) outside some of the temporary facilities constructed in June 1921. The Red Cross provided vital services and support during the summer and fall of 1921. Others pictured are Red Cross worker Clarence Dawson, Sam Jule, and Charles "Andy" Anderson, a former Tulsa police captain. *Photo courtesy of the Tulsa Historical Society.*

The heart of the Greenwood District was reduced to smoldering ruins by midmorning of June 1, 1921. *Photos courtesy of the Tulsa Historical Society.*

11

DIRECTED VERDICT

As if Tulsa had not had enough of amateur cops with guns and badges, the Public Welfare Board announced after its Sunday morning meeting of June 5 that it had authorized a "business men's protective organization" of "250 men who have shown ability in law enforcement and dealing with the criminal element." These "minute men," the committee said, would "meet any emergency that might arise."[1] This announcement may have been an attempt to calm jittery whites who continued to hear and no doubt repeat rumors of up to fifty thousand armed men gathering in rural black communities such as Red Bird, Boley, and Wybark. Officials did their best to dispel these reports, even sending Captain Blaine on an aerial reconnaissance mission, from which he reported no sign of invaders. Blacks in these outlying areas were equally keen to distance themselves from the Tulsa troubles, so much so that residents of Red Bird, a tiny black community twenty-five miles to the southeast, published a letter in the *World* earnestly denying any plans to attack Tulsa.[2]

Armed guards were placed on the major roads into town, which was supposed to further reassure residents. But, as mentioned previously, one patrol mortally wounded a hapless white picnicker on Sunday evening,[3] and another shot a grocer headed to a meat-packing plant before daylight the next morning.[4]

Some of this fear and suspicion was stoked from the outside. The *Sunday Oklahoman* said Mt. Zion Baptist Church had been "an arsenal of Black Bolshevists."[5] The *St. Louis Post-Dispatch*, in a lengthy report on the situation, blamed the riot on the "arrogance" of returning black military veterans and "agitation" for racial equality by whites as well as blacks.[6] And the *New York Times*, which seemed almost obsessed with militant African Americans, reported that prominent equal rights advocate Hubert H. Harrison had called black New Yorkers to arms. "I should not be surprised," Harrison said, "if we saw three splendid race riots by next September."[7]

Perhaps most alarming to white Tulsans was the *Times'* assertion that a shadow army of black Communists called the African Blood Brotherhood (ABB) was probably behind the riot. On June 4, citing unnamed "authorities," the newspaper's equally anonymous correspondent—perhaps photographer Alvin Krupnick—reported that ABB organizers were thought to have "passed through Oklahoma about sixty days ago and organized a chapter of the secret society in Tulsa."[8] The time frame matches W. E. B. DuBois's tour of the state, but DuBois was in no way affiliated with the African Blood Brotherhood. Its founder, Cyril Briggs, rejected DuBois and the National Association for the Advancement of Colored People as out of touch with the majority of American blacks and too accommodating to whites.[9] Briggs is not known to have ever visited Oklahoma, but he did claim—after the fact—to have a "post" in Tulsa.[10]

The thirty-three-year-old Briggs was born on the island of Nevis to a black mother and white father, and followed his mother to New York in 1905. Sometimes called the "Angry Blond Negro," the tall, handsome, and light-skinned Briggs joined an influx of West Indian radicals immigrating to New York in the early years of the twentieth century. Briggs became a reporter for the *New Amsterdam*, a leading black newspaper, where he attracted the attention of postal inspectors and intelligence officers with his blunt black nationalism and increasingly radical politics. At various times, Briggs was linked with Marcus Garvey's Universal Negro Improvement Association and African Communities League and George Wells Parker's Hamitic League, both of which advocated African repatriation. By the time of the Tulsa riot, though, Briggs was aligned with the Communist Party and was involved in its campaign to discredit Garvey; some authorities say Briggs was largely responsible for Garvey eventually going to prison for mail fraud.[11]

If Bishop Mouzon and other leading whites quailed at the mention of W. E. B. DuBois, they no doubt were even more agitated to learn that the likes of Cyril Briggs may have had a foothold in their city. In the first issue of his magazine the *Crusader*, published in 1918, Briggs verified his credentials as one of the most extreme and outspoken radicals of the era. "The Fight is on," Briggs wrote. "The War begun for Negro freedom throughout the world." Espousing a bare-knuckled fusion of revolutionary Marxism and black nationalism, Briggs organized the African Blood Brotherhood for African Liberation and Redemption, commonly known as just the African Blood Brotherhood, along the lines of the Irish Republican Brotherhood, the secret Irish independence organization of the late nineteenth and earlier twentieth century. Through the *Crusader*, Briggs advocated meeting force with force and taking whatever steps necessary to defend blacks from white aggression and injustice. The ABB was to be the instrument of this resistance, a secret militia to answer America's reconstituted Invisible Empire.[12]

As with the Ku Klux Klan, far more people shared the ABB's philosophy, all or in part, than actually belonged to it. At the time of the riot, Briggs claimed 150 chapters with fifty thousand members,[13] but later admitted his group never numbered more than three thousand, mostly concentrated on the East Coast. W. A. Domingo, the ABB's publicist, said years later that in his opinion it was "nothing more than a paper organization." Experts on the ABB doubt it had much if any real presence in Tulsa; Briggs himself seemed to eventually admit as much. True, his fiery rhetoric on the subject of lynching and self-defense was very similar to A. J. Smitherman's and J. B. Stradford's, but they differed on other matters. Briggs was a Communist Party insider.[14] Stradford and Smitherman, for all their fire, were essentially middle-class businessmen with fairly conventional politics. Membership in the Democratic Party seems to have been the extent of Smitherman's radicalism. Stradford had been a delegate to the Republican National Convention.[15]

Smitherman argued vigorously for change, but within the existing system. White Democratic candidates advertised in his newspaper, as did white merchants—including City Commissioner C. S. Younkman's pharmacy in the Brady Hotel.[16] And Smitherman's call for armed resistance to lynch law was issued long before the rumored ABB organizer was supposed to have "passed through" in April 1921.[17] None of this precludes an ABB presence; certainly some formal or informal organization seems to have been in place ahead of the riot. The best evidence and expert opinion, though, suggests that any local sympathizers were more likely fellow travelers than dues-paying members.

Briggs answered the *New York Times* claim of African Blood Brotherhood involvement in the Tulsa riot in the newspaper's June 5 issue. He said the ABB taught members to "hit back" against "wanton attack."

> Certainly the available facts in this case show that the casus belli was supplied by the whites, and that the whites were the aggressors, the act of

a white man in attempting to unarm a negro precipitating in the general
fight which followed. Haven't negroes the right to defend their lives and
property when they are menaced, or is this the exclusive prerogative of
the white man?

And were not the negroes who gathered to defend the Tulsa Jail against
attack by a white mob, and to defend a prisoner confined in that jail against
the murderous intentions of white hoodlums out for a lynching bee—were
not these negroes acting in behalf of law and order, and in defense of the
prisoner's Constitutional right to a legal trial by his peers and with due
process of law?[18]

Vague allusions to outside agitators notwithstanding, the local papers made
no mention of the African Blood Brotherhood. Presumably, they had the same
or better access to information as the *Times'* correspondent, but they may have
been afraid injecting the name of an organization like the ABB into the situation
would be more than the skittish public could handle. Perhaps the *Times* gave
Briggs too much credit. A few weeks later, in the July *Crusader*, Briggs would
publish a report from a "Tulsa post commander,"[19] but confided to Marcus Garvey
that the account was not "literally true."[20]

Another story that might not have been "literally true" involved a party of
African Americans from Okmulgee County, just south of Tulsa, who arrived in
New York shortly after the riot. On June 3, the NAACP announced that the eight
black travelers, led by Stella (or Estelle) Harris, fled Oklahoma in fear of their
lives. The group claimed that notices posted on their doors ordered them out
and that a similar notice addressed to all African Americans had been published
in an Okmulgee newspaper. They said that their house had been burned and
that they had narrowly escaped with their lives. Later it was reported that they
attributed the riot to a dispute over oil rights.[21]

There had been grumblings about trouble in Okmulgee County in March,
when two blacks were accused of killing a white man, but nothing came of it.[22]
On June 2, the day before the stories about the Harris party first appeared, the
general contractor on a seven-story hotel in the town of Okmulgee received an
anonymous demand to fire all of his African American employees. He ignored it.[23]
Quoting a "negro deputy sheriff," a June 4 Associated Press story said the Harris
group had left on its own accord at the urging of a phony "African potentate"
who claimed to have founded a new colony "in the land of their ancestors." Stella
Harris's house, said the deputy, was still standing.[24]

The lack of a name for the "negro deputy" raises a red flag, but then the Harris party's tale is suspect, too. In all likelihood, its departure from Okmulgee County had no direct connection to the Tulsa riot. But perhaps it was a reflection of broader conditions. On June 12, a deputy sheriff had to rescue a black father and son accused of beating up a white oilfield worker near Beggs, thirty-five miles southeast of Tulsa.[25] By June 21, tensions were such that the Okmulgee County sheriff banned the sale of guns and ammunition in Beggs and confiscated them from homes west of town.[26]

On Monday morning, June 6, the Tulsa county attorney's office filed criminal complaints against J. B. Stradford and three other African Americans, whom the newspapers did not identify except to say that they had "not been apprehended." The four men were charged with inciting a riot, which under state law meant that they could be held accountable for anything that had happened during the melee, including murder. Prosecutors also requested extradition of Stradford from Kansas, where they believed—incorrectly, as it turned out—he was being held.[27] Even before Stradford skipped bail in Independence, Oklahoma officials admitted that they were far from certain that Kansas governor Henry J. Allen would return Stradford; a year earlier, Allen resisted extradition of an African American wanted in connection with the Phillips County, Arkansas, race war. Allen, though, was saved a decision in Stradford's case. An extradition hearing in his Topeka office was set for June 18, but Stradford failed to appear.[28] Prosecutors insisted that the four men would by no means be the last charged.[29]

Some whites accused of theft, looting, and possession of stolen property continued to appear in court. On June 6, a white man named B. W. Wallace was bound over by Judge S. C. Maxey on a complaint of stealing a Hudson automobile from African American Charles Scott, although it is unclear whether the alleged crime was connected to the riot.[30] The following morning, county attorney Seaver charged thirty-two whites with grand larceny, including for the theft of a shotgun from a downtown pawnshop and the looting of the home of Ida Gilmore, the white woman initially reported shot to death just outside the black district. Seventeen of the accused, according to the *Tribune*, were already in jail.[31]

That same morning, June 7, Attorney General Freeling and the Public Welfare Board met to discuss the ongoing investigation and impending grand jury. In the *Tribune*'s telling, the *World*'s snippy editorials casting shade on Freeling's frequent poking about in Tulsa made the attorney general reluctant to lead the proceedings. It is inconceivable that Freeling seriously considered for an instant relinquishing control of the riot prosecutions or the spotlight that went with it. This was not just a matter of vanity; the state had good reason to believe that Seaver, left in charge, would make a hash of the case. Nevertheless, the committee soothed Freeling with promises of complete cooperation, assuring him, "No one entertained any thought of the state administration playing politics in the investigation."[32]

This, of course, was hokum, and both sides were guilty of spreading it. The *Tribune*, Freeling, local critics of the Evans administration, and those intent on avoiding blame were quite keen to pin responsibility on the mayor, Adkison, Gustafson, and McCullough. This was soon proved out when the grand jury and Gustafson's trial turned out to be at least as much about stolen cars as about the recent death and destruction on Tulsa's streets. Conversely, the *World* had every reason to defend the "splendid citizens and well-meaning and devoted officials" besmirched by the "miserable machinations of politics being hurled against the local government."[33] It supported Evans, distrusted Freeling, and particularly loathed *Tribune* publisher Richard Lloyd Jones and the sanctimonious tone of his newspaper.

Freeling convened the closed-door court of inquiry that afternoon on the fourth floor of city hall. This meeting apparently was intended as a sort of dry run for the grand jury scheduled to begin taking testimony only a few days hence. Summoning an unknown number of witnesses, beginning with Deputy Barney Cleaver, the attorney general and his associates reviewed their testimony and no doubt gleaned a few new details. He did not, however, get what he wanted out of the TPD's five black officers. Calling them individually into the conference room, Freeling pressed them for the identities of the African Americans at the courthouse on the night of May 31. Each insisted that he did not know—possibly because they had been sent to Greenwood and were not at the courthouse. Enraged, Freeling demanded that Adkison take the officers' badges; when Adkison refused, Freeling ripped them from the men's shirts. Despite Adkison's indignant protests, Freeling kept the badges and the men's guns for two weeks before returning them.[34]

With its usual lack of self-awareness, the June 7 *Tribune* reported, "A long list of eye-witnesses . . . will be called, also several leading negroes."[35] Apparently no African Americans, not even "leading" ones, qualified as eyewitnesses. The *Tribune* said reporters, local officials, and law officers would be called before the court of inquiry, but there is no indication, in the newspapers themselves or the surviving records, that statements were actually taken from members of the press—including those responsible for the reckless *Tribune* story some believed set the fuse to burning.

"This inquiry particularly seeks to find the facts as to the inception of the riot and if it could reasonably have been prevented by the peace officers," Freeling told the *Tribune* before testimony began on the afternoon of June 7. "In the securing of this evidence, if individual acts of murder, arson or burglary are found, the facts will be presented by me to the grand jury to be impaneled by Judge Biddison tomorrow."[36] Thus, Freeling confirmed that his first priority was the events at the courthouse on the night of May 31; all that followed was of secondary interest, if that. If someone went to jail for murdering Dr. Jackson or burning down Greenwood, it would be coincidental to proving Tulsa's local government and law enforcement weak, corrupt, and much too tolerant of troublemaking blacks.

Freeling told the *Tribune* that the court of inquiry would operate parallel to the grand jury, but he suspended it after a brief Tuesday evening session and never resumed proceedings. On Wednesday morning, June 8, Freeling and Van Leuven began examining potential grand jurors. Remarkably, only twenty-four were initially summoned; of those, twelve were immediately eliminated, either because they did not appear or because they were disqualified for cause. Among the questions Freeling put to the prospective jurors were the following: Would they recommend removal of officials if it could be "shown the officers could have saved life and property by disarming the mob?" Would they recommend removing officials "if it should be shown that drinking, gambling, bootlegging and prostitution were running wide open in the negro district and the whites and blacks were permitted to mingle indiscriminately and the officers did not do all in their power to stop these conditions?" And "If it is shown that a band of armed men came uptown in automobiles and started a riot in which men were killed [would you] hold them for murder even if they did not do the killing?" The prospective jurors, all white men, were asked if they held any prejudices that might prevent them from treating African Americans fairly. They do not seem to have been asked if they had any qualms about prosecuting a white man for killing blacks.[37]

Here Freeling again signaled the direction he would take the grand jury. The *Tribune* applauded with a lengthy editorial extolling the attorney general's virtues; those who thought otherwise, the *Tribune* said, were "associated with a background that is not the best." It veered off into a self-righteous condemnation of motion picture theaters that had pulled advertising from the newspaper because of its crusade against "crime-suggestive pictures," lauded Reverend Cooke as a potential mayor, and finished up with a blast at Seaver and Tulsa's "national reputation as a crime-infested city."[38]

The *World* was more circumspect. Coverage of the grand jury selection appeared on the back page,[39] and a convoluted editorial tiptoed around the newspaper's continued skepticism about Freeling's motives. The attorney general's investigation, the *World* said, must avoid "even the semblance of partisanship." But the editorialist did not sound optimistic in this regard. Voters would take care of public officials who failed in their duty, he wrote, "but mere criticism based on insufficient knowledge of the circumstances . . . will but divide the citizenship at a time when division above all things is not desirable." Worse, the *World* continued, it would divert the grand jury from what should be its true purpose, which was to root out and punish the "leaders . . . of that colored ring which both white and black now agree precipitated the conflict."[40]

So either way, African Americans were going to be blamed for the riot. The only question was whether those who had gone to the courthouse on the evening of May 31 would be primary or secondary targets.

In addition to its tortured editorial, the *World* of Thursday, June 9, carried two letters of some interest. J. H. Welch of Tulsa chided the newspaper for its "Bad Niggers" editorial, saying it should have been paired with one headlined "White Scum." Blaming the riot on a "lawless element of the black race," Welch said, ignored "the white riff-raff that tried to start the lynching" as well as "the white police force that collapsed so utterly."[41] The second letter, by B. F. Ingraham of Tulsa, defended law officers, and said if Barney Cleaver, "the best negro officer whom I ever knew," thought it would have been unwise to attempt disarming the black men at the courthouse, that was good enough for him. "There seems to have been between 50 and 150 mad negroes armed with high powered guns," Ingraham wrote. "The streets were lined on either side with white people. An attempt there to quell the negroes by force might have caused many white people to lose their lives."[42]

Freeling finished choosing his grand jury before noon the next day, and Judge Biddison swore them in. The jurors' names, addresses, and occupations were published in the newspapers. Foreman C. A. Cloud was the local manager for meat-packing giant Swift and Company. According to the *Tribune*, the two most prominent jurors were a shoe store owner named Lyon and oil broker H. H. McFann. The others were Sand Springs Church of God pastor A. A. Kinion, Tulsa barber D. F. Wynn, Tulsa oil broker B. F. Schaff, Jenks banker Quay V. Johnson, Sand Springs retired farmer L. M. Dixon, Tulsa loan and real estate broker Frank Thompson, Sand Springs farmer W. C. Harvey, Red Fork refinery worker J. W. Arrington, and Tulsa building contractor D. W. Quinn.[43]

Even as Biddison gave the grand jury detailed instructions, sheriff's deputies were dispatched from the courthouse to locate witnesses.[44] By early afternoon, some fifty police officers jammed the corridor outside the grand jury's third-floor room, waiting—anxiously, no doubt—to be called to testify.[45] They, and the entire Tulsa Police Department, were about to go on trial.[46]

At the same time the Public Welfare Board met with Prince Freeling on the morning of Tuesday, June 7, the Tulsa City Commission took steps to guarantee that Greenwood would not be rebuilt. At the behest of the Real Estate Exchange, it voted 4–0, with Commissioner Younkman absent, to extend the city's fire code to all the burned district south of the Sunset Hill brick plant and Haskell Street. New construction would have to be of fire-resistant materials and meet modern standards. At first blush, this might seem prudent and even noble, but the commission's motives were made clear by the *Tribune*'s triumphant headline: "Negro Section Abolished by City's Order."[47]

The fire code, the *Tribune* explained, would make rebuilding impossibly expensive for blacks, leaving them with little alternative but to accept the Real Estate Exchange scheme.

> Thirty-five blocks of the negro district . . . now in ruins following the fire of last Wednesday morning will never again be a negro quarter but will become a wholesale and industrial center. This was accomplished this morning when the city commission passed an ordinance extending the fire limits to include this section, including the negro business section on Greenwood avenue. Because of the building requirements laid on the district it is believed impossible that the negroes will again build there.[48]

Real Estate Exchange president Merritt J. Glass told the commission that his group would "at once secure industrial purchasers" and "options on land farther to the north so that the negroes may build their homes and locate a new negro business district." Glass admitted that the plan had one serious weakness—coming up with the money to buy out the black property owners—but "made it plain that the real estate men are not seeking financial returns in the transaction but are working for the good of Tulsa and not for private interests."[49]

It is doubtful that anyone took this claim seriously. These men may not have been out to unduly chisel black property owners, but they certainly intended to profit in the long run. In the meantime, they were asking everyone to trust them. But Tulsans, black and white, were not in a trusting mood. Black property owners understandably wanted to see cash, and a lot of it, before committing to the deal, but whites seem not to have been very enthusiastic either. Glass's group must have had trouble raising capital, because the day after his presentation to the city commission, Judge L. J. Martin and the Public Welfare Board discussed the possibility of creating a "housing corporation," capitalized at between $500,000 and $1 million, to finance reconstruction as well as helping "wage-earning white men" buy homes.[50] In effect, they were talking about what today would be a government-backed housing authority.

"The housing corporation plan has become most successful in many cities where it has been worked out," Martin told the board. "I have a letter from a big concern in Chicago backed by the biggest business men in Chicago, which promises to give us co-operation and service at the present time in building homes on a large scale. Some means of united effort is necessary, and I believe this offers the best solution for quick work."[51] The relocation scheme was kicked around for months without anything coming of it. The reasons for this failure are a little fuzzy but essentially boiled down to disinterest. If Tulsans were not inclined to donate money to the rehabilitation of Greenwood, they were even less inclined to invest in an iffy real estate deal involving it.

The nation's focus shifted only a few days after the riot, when a freak storm on the upper Arkansas River valley flooded Pueblo, Colorado, killing as many as 1,500 people. Even in the Tulsa papers, the flood became the lead story for several days.[52] Thus, with little private money coming in and national interest already waning, on June 6 the Public Welfare Board worked out a deal to borrow $25,000 backed by twenty-five "leading business men."[53] This proved unnecessary, however, after the county excise board came up with the money for the city to pay more than $37,000 in expenses already accumulated. Most of this went to cleaning up the burned area and to pay the "special officers" recruited in the aftermath of the riot.[54]

The actual care of the dispossessed African Americans was left to Maurice Willows and the Red Cross. Contributions to the relief fund remained distressingly small, prompting the *World* on June 7 to suggest that the decision to turn down outside assistance had been ill-advised.

> The *World* would have tremendously enjoyed Tulsa being permitted to bear the financial load necessary to replace that which has been destroyed—as far as humanly possible to right the great wrong. . . . Yet what can one say to the magnificent overtures of assistance made by other American communities? . . . Since the tenders have been made, what in sound reason can

we do but accept in the spirit it is offered and hold ourselves in readiness
to reciprocate when some other fellow-community feels the red-hot iron
in its soul?[55]

A few days later, the frustrated Public Welfare Board turned over fundraising
to the Red Cross, which had the effect of lifting the ban.[56]

Maurice Willows's administrative ability, meticulous honesty, and innate
fairness quickly won him the respect, albeit sometimes grudgingly, of whites
and blacks alike. He quickly reorganized relief services, infusing a professional
efficiency that cleared the long lines of African Americans waiting forlornly for
assistance.[57] The Red Cross headquarters were moved from Fourth and Cincinnati
downtown to Booker T. Washington High School,[58] where clothes and other
items were already being distributed.[59] A grocery and clinic were added, and
an employment office set up.[60] Whether through personal conviction or his
understanding of the charitable public, Willows encouraged self-sufficiency
among the refugees; employers were urged to pay their black workers daily in
cash so they would not be dependent on handouts or credit.[61] African American
men without jobs were given make-work at twenty-five cents an hour,[62] which
seems to have been the going rate for unskilled casual labor at the time—and
was the first national minimum wage instituted more than a decade later.

Even at this early date, there were complaints about blacks being "spoiled."
The *World*, especially, assured readers that refugees were expected to pay for
as much as possible, whether food, clothes, or even medical care. Women still
living at the fairgrounds were expected to do the camp's cooking and cleaning.
Meals were provided to men working for the Red Cross at a cost of twenty cents,
which was deducted from their daily wages. Black doctors, re-equipped with the
help of the Tulsa County Medical Association, set up practice on a cash basis.
"While these physicians are working under the direction of the Red Cross," the
World said, "they are not paid by that organization and services rendered by
them to patients will be paid for by such patients."[63]

Local officials still concerned about idle blacks renewed efforts to keep tabs
on them. Adkison ordered police to round up unemployed black people living
with relatives and friends in servants' quarters in the white neighborhoods,
and to take them to the fairgrounds. Furthermore, blacks "seen on the streets"
without a green identification card pinned to their clothes were to be arrested
and taken to the fairgrounds for "permanent identification." The cards—apparently different from those issued immediately after the riot—were to carry the

wearer's identity and the signature of an employer;[64] within days, eight thousand were in circulation.[65] Adkison's order was expected to more than treble the four hundred people remaining at the fairgrounds camp, but in the end added very few.[66] Anecdotally, it appears that many African Americans simply got tired of the hassle and left town[67]—which may well have been the purpose all along.

On June 7, a committee of the county bar association, with Freeling in agreement, determined that neither Tulsa County nor the City of Tulsa could be held liable for riot damages. The lawyers expressed regret at their finding, and said citizens ought to voluntarily assume responsibility.[68] This suggestion was ignored, and the legal opinion did not deter property owners, white or black, from seeking redress. The first to do so, apparently, was Dr. Charles Wickham, the physician who had convinced his neighbors to go peacefully with the National Guard on the morning of June 1. Wickham's assistance did him no good, for his house at 544 North Elgin Avenue was torched. On June 7, Wickham filed a tort claim with the city for $7,300.[69] More than three hundred such petitions followed. A few claims from the stores supplying guns and ammunition were paid, as were at least one white riot victim's funeral expense, but those for property damage—with one exception—were not.[70] Mrs. Bankhead, the black librarian, was paid $250 for "library building burned in riot."[71] Bankhead also appealed for and was granted her June salary after the city commission dropped her from the payroll.[72]

While white Tulsa as a whole may not have been keen on blanket assistance to riot victims, it was by no means indifferent to individual circumstances. A white attorney originally from Alabama, Mather Eakes, challenged the new fire code limits on behalf of black property owners.[73] Medical care seems to have been quite good—so much so that Reverend Cooke complained that it was better than whites were receiving—and included natal care and vaccinations for smallpox and typhoid.[74] Willows, so critical of much he found in Tulsa, had nothing but praise in this regard, saying, "To the everlasting credit of Tulsa and the Red Cross, it should be said that the very best surgical and medical care obtainable has been given the negro patients."[75] Anecdotally, it appears that a fair amount of selective, personal assistance was given, despite an official directive "not to give to any negroes money or assistance in any other way, but that they refer them to the Red Cross headquarter."[76] To the dismay of authorities, "excess" blacks were allowed to move into servants' quarters and even occasionally main houses in white neighborhoods,[77] and white employers or acquaintances seem to have helped African Americans they knew and considered deserving get back on their feet. Gypsy Oil, for instance, completed a house for an employee named Aaron

Ellis just eight days after the riot and said it would build at least two more.[78] In midsummer, a group of blacks threatened a lawsuit, claiming that C. F. Gabe and others were receiving preferential treatment from white authorities.[79] George Buckner, who visited Tulsa on behalf of the Urban League several times in the year following the riot, claimed that a few blacks were allowed to rebuild on "open credit," some were extended loans at exorbitant interest rates, and "the great majority" could not get credit at all.[80] No doubt this, to a large extent, determined which African Americans remained in Tulsa after the riot and which did not.

One week after the riot, on June 8, a small newspaper called the *Oklahoma Sun* was published by Theo Baughman, a former employee of A. J. Smitherman at the *Star*.[81] Backed by the Tulsa Chamber of Commerce,[82] it had been in the works for more than a year[83] and may have actually begun publication before the riot; the record in this regard is hazy. In any event, the *Sun*'s first editorial after the riot was significant not only because it encouraged its readers to stay put but because the *World* reprinted it. Taken together, the chamber's sponsorship and the *World*'s broadcast of the *Sun*'s message surely hint of simmering opposition to the buyout scheme.

> A great many would ask themselves this question? "Does it pay to stay? Should we not sell out what little we have and move to some other city? Should we not ask for transportation to some faraway place? Will Tulsa be fair to us? Will she recompense us for our loss?" . . . The earnings of a lifetime should not be sacrificed without reason or excuse. . . . Act with firmness. Move with caution. Talk little, cooperate with the efforts of the best people to restore a status quo and all will be well.
>
> In the midst of our dilemma, loan sharks and conniving persons will suggest you sell out and leave. They will tell you that fate is against you if you remain in Tulsa. Such persons should be spurned for they are not your friends. They will profit through your temporary misfortune and embarrassment.[84]

On the same day the grand jury began its work, the *World* carried a brief story reporting that six African American men scheduled to die in Arkansas's electric chair had been granted stays of execution.[85] The six were among the dozen convicted of murder and sentenced to die in connection with the Phillips County race war of autumn 1919. This conflict, fought out over three days in a remote sliver of the Arkansas Delta seventy miles below Memphis, matched or exceeded the Tulsa riot for violence. Estimates of the dead range from 25 to 850;

500 regular army troops from Camp Pike, near Little Rock, sent in to restore order may have actually joined in the killing.[86]

The fighting broke out on September 30, 1919, when two whites—a deputy sheriff and a railroad detective—with a black jail trusty interrupted a meeting of African American sharecroppers at a rural church. The sharecroppers were organizing a union to demand fairer treatment by the white landowners whose fields they worked. A gunfight broke out between the two whites and at least some of the black farmers; one of the whites was killed and the other wounded. In the aftermath, hundreds of African Americans were held in hastily constructed stockades, and at one point 285 were confined to a county jail built for 48. Governor Charles Brough told local authorities to handle the situation any way they wanted, as long as there were no outright lynchings.[87]

The first twelve men put on trial, in October 1920, were found guilty of murder and sentenced to death; thus intimidated, sixty-five others promptly pleaded to lesser offenses, and received prison sentences of up to twenty-one years. By June 1921, six of the twelve death sentences had been temporarily overturned on a technicality; all six of those men would eventually go free. The remaining six, those mentioned in the *Tulsa World* story, were less than twenty-four hours from death when a chancery-court judge issued a stay. The judge, in fact, lacked legal authority to intervene, but he created enough confusion that the condemned men's attorneys were able to secure a stay through federal court. Their case would eventually reach the U.S. Supreme Court as *Moore v. Dempsey* and become one of the foundational decisions by which the federal government began imposing some semblance of equal protection on state courts.[88]

Freeling's rhetoric—and the pages of the *World* and especially of the *Tribune*—indicates that Oklahoma contemplated the same legal response to the Tulsa riot as Arkansas had to Phillips County: blame African Americans espousing unreasonable notions of equality for stirring up racial tension, prosecute the ringleaders for murder, and frighten the remaining black population into submission. There were, as it turned out, some important differences in the two situations. Governor Robertson, unlike Arkansas's Brough, did not turn the case over to local authorities and wash his hands of it, but instead remained engaged in developments throughout. And Tulsa's white population does not seem to have been as bent on further retribution as those in Phillips County; possibly, as a much larger majority for whom cheap black labor was more of a convenience than an economic dependency, Tulsa's whites felt less threatened than the Arkansas delta plantation owners. Or maybe the city leadership was just more sensitive to bad publicity.

Nevertheless, when the grand jury began hearing witnesses on the afternoon of June 9, Freeling and his team—Van Leuven, Short, Goldsberry, and an assistant attorney general named Tom Wallace—ignored the black informants lining the courthouse corridor, begging to be heard, to take testimony from white law officers and a few selected African Americans such as Barney Cleaver and the courthouse custodian.[89] The newspapers reported that almost two hundred witnesses were subpoenaed, and on June 16, as it wrapped up its work, the grand jury invited anyone who wished to testify to do so.[90] Sixty-four indictments were issued that day, all for black men; twenty-four more indictments followed, of which a dozen were reportedly for whites. The whites' names were not published, but none seems to have been of particular note.[91]

At least two of the African Americans indicted, Curley Walker and Ed Howard, were dead. Three others—John Smitherman, "Peg Leg" Taylor, and Andy Brown—were in jail.[92] The remaining African Americans included, unsurprisingly, J. B. Stradford and Andrew Smitherman, as well as Will Robinson, the man singled out by Barney Cleaver, and O. B. Mann, who had been identified by O. W. Gurley. The alleged drug dealer and Gustafson associate Smithee also made the roster. Several were identified by nicknames or partial names, such as "Fatty," "Russel," "Sullivan," "Big Fred," "Chummy," and "three others unknown." All were charged with "unlawfully, knowingly, willfully, riotously and feloniously" assembling, and armed "with rifles, shotguns, pistols, razors and other deadly weapons," disturbing the peace by "brandishing and discharging firearms and threatening and challenging to fight." Their actions, the document continued, resulted in a riot that caused the death of "one Walter Daggs, and other peaceable citizens of this city."[93]

Daggs apparently was a genuinely innocent bystander, an oil company employee who lived near the courthouse and was supposedly killed by a stray bullet.[94] Who actually fired the bullet was not known, but under the law—or at least the law as Freeling saw it—that did not really matter. Those responsible for the riot also bore the legal responsibility for everything that happened during it.[95]

After a four-day recess, the grand jury resumed its investigation on June 22. Three days later it indicted Chief John Gustafson on five counts, only one of which was related to the riot. It also indicted Officers Roy Meacham and Bay Ward on two counts each—for dereliction of duty during the riot and involvement in the alleged auto theft ring—and charged Sand Springs police chief B. F. Waddell and one of his officers, F. E. Williams, with car theft, as well.[96]

The *World* published the grand jury's final report in full on Sunday, June 26, under the headline "Grand Jury Blames Negroes for Inciting Race Rioting; Whites Clearly Exonerated."

We find that the recent race riot was the direct result of an effort on the part of a certain group of colored men who appeared at the courthouse on the night of May 31, 1921 for the purpose of protecting one Dick Rowland. . . . We have not been able to find any evidence either from white or colored citizens that any organized attempt was made or planned to take from the sheriff's custody any prisoner; the crowd assembled about the courthouse being purely spectators and curiosity seekers resulting from rumors circulating about the city. There was no mob spirit among the whites, no talk of lynching and no arms. The assembly was quiet until the arrival of armed negroes, which precipitated and was the direct cause of the entire affair.

While we find the presence of the armed negroes was the direct cause of the riot, we further find that there existed indirect causes more vital to the public interest than the direct cause. Among these was agitation among the negroes of social equality, and the laxity of law enforcement on the part of officers of the city and county.[97]

Freeling and his local allies had gotten almost everything they wanted. The city's administration, and to a lesser extent the county, had been discredited, and the social status quo reaffirmed: "We find that certain propaganda and more or less agitation had been going on among the colored population for some time. This agitation resulted in the accumulation of firearms among the [black] people and the storage of quantities of ammunition, all of which was accumulative in the minds of the negro[,] which led them as a people to believe in equal rights, social equality and their ability to demand the same."[98] The grand jury said it was "glad to exonerate" the majority of Tulsa's African Americans, but recommended discontinuing the use of black police officers. It also recommended that "indiscriminate mingling of white and colored people in dance halls and other places of amusement be positively prohibited and every law be rigidly enforced to the end that a proper relationship may be maintained between the two races." It went on to cite loose enforcement of vice codes in general, recommend construction of a new city jail and, curiously, tartly suggest that traffic police should either wear jackets to conceal their firearms or stop carrying guns altogether as this "tends to give impression to the outside world of a spirit of lawlessness that does not exist."[99]

The report is a remarkable statement of white Tulsa's frame of mind in June 1921: self-assured and completely oblivious to the way things looked from the other side of the literal and figurative railroad tracks. On June 18, with the grand jury's work almost finished, Freeling told a Tulsa civic group that as blacks had become better educated and "race papers" spread dangerous ideas of equality, the white man had come to be regarded as an oppressor instead of a friend. With a blithe lack of self-awareness typical of that time and place, Freeling summarized the problem briefly: "The negro is not the same man he was 30 years ago when he was content to plod along his own road accepting the white man as his benefactor."[100]

Hopefully, he almost certainly added silently, Tulsa's Negroes had been taught a lesson.

12

THE NEW NEGRO

Prince Freeling was right about one thing. The black American of 1921 was not the black American of the 1880s or 1890s. The term "New Negro" had been around for twenty-five years at the time of the Tulsa riot, but was beginning to come into vogue only with the dawn of the Harlem Renaissance.[1] The decades after Reconstruction had been a disaster for African Americans, especially in the South. Civil rights and economic opportunity disappeared into the darkness like white-robed vigilantes. Officially, the Ku Klux Klan had been put out of business, but really it had only taken off its mask and moved into state capitols, county courthouses, and city halls. With *Plessy v. Ferguson* in 1896, state-sponsored segregation and discrimination became a federally protected institution. Jim Crow proliferated. And the release of D. W. Griffith's incendiary *Birth of a Nation* and William J. Simmons's creation of the new Ku Klux Klan, both in 1915, glamorized the violence that made subjugation of an entire race possible.

From this new oppression emerged the New Negro, successive generations of African Americans increasingly disinclined to accept less than their share. The New Negro manifested himself not only in the formation of the National Association for the Advancement of Colored People but also in the Arkansas Delta farmers who demanded fair dealings from their white landlords. It could be seen in W. E. B. DuBois's Talented Tenth, but also in the dreams and determination of Greenwood's shopkeepers and schoolteachers, in the chronicles of Mary Parrish, and in the bitter anger of the ex-serviceman O. B. Mann.

As a World War I veteran, Mann belonged to a class of blacks many whites found particularly unsettling. These were men who had been in a fight, who had tasted blood and known victory. Most importantly, they had seen a world beyond the one they knew.

To be sure, most of the 270,000 African Americans who entered the military during the United States' short but decisive participation in the war to end all wars were kept as far from the front lines as possible. The majority of those who made it to France were employed as stevedores, truck drivers, construction workers, and common laborers. They were treated badly, sometimes abominably so, but that did nothing to dampen their conviction that they were invested more than ever in their country, and that their country owed them something in return.[2]

About forty thousand men were in the army's two black combat divisions, the Ninety-Second and the Ninety-Third. The Ninety-Third, made up mostly of National Guardsmen from New York, Chicago, Washington, D.C., Cleveland, and Massachusetts, was commanded by the National Guard's senior infantry officer, Brigadier General Roy Hoffman of Oklahoma. Attached to the French army, the Ninety-Third earned considerable acclaim, especially the "Harlem Hellfighters" of the 369th Regiment. The Hellfighters were renowned not only for their courage in combat but also for a jazz band led by James Reese Europe. The Ninety-Second Division, made up of draftees, suffered from poor training and a rift between its commanding officer, Brigadier General Charles Ballou, and his superior, Lieutenant General Robert Bullard of the U.S. Second Army. Bullard disparaged the Ninety-Second at every turn, portraying the black troops as incompetent cowards, thugs, and rapists. By the end of the war, however, the Ninety-Second had received several commendations from the French.[3]

African Americans, at home and abroad, viewed the war as not just a way to make the world safe for democracy, but to bring real democracy to their own country and their own people. When the Hellfighters returned to Harlem in 1919, DuBois wrote in the *Crisis*: "*We return. We return from fighting. We return fighting.* Make way for Democracy! We saved it in France, and by the Great Jehovah, we will save it in the United States of America, or know the reason why."[4]

This was exactly what many whites feared.

"It is my opinion that the principal [cause of the riot] was the drafting of negroes into the army," Harold Cooke told the *St. Louis Post-Dispatch*, "and their recognition by the United States government as soldiers on the same plane as white soldiers." That, explained Cooke, encouraged dangerous ideas and attitudes. "The United States placed them on the same footing in the army as white soldiers, and many of them when they returned walked through the streets with an arrogance they would never have dreamed of assuming before the war," continued Cooke. "White people have been forced to step aside on the sidewalk or be brushed aside by negroes. Negroes have ignored the Jim Crow laws on the street cars. . . . They have overflowed into the white sections of the car and have remained seated there while white women were forced to stand in the aisle."[5] In his June 18 speech to the City Club, Freeling suggested that the war had taught African Americans "the value of organization." With that organization, he said, "had come a force of blacks liable to start trouble at any time."[6]

For all this hand-wringing about black war veterans, it was white war veterans who continued to be more of a menace to the citizenry. The American Legionnaires organized as special deputies had been carrying out liquor raids around the county, much to the delight of the law-and-order crowd, and patrolling the burned district.[7] These were supposed to be trusted men well-known to the community, but Walter White, the NAACP's light-skinned investigator, seems to have talked his way onto this squad despite being a total stranger to town. "That evening in the City Hall I had to answer only three questions—name, age and address," White wrote eight years later. "I might have been a thug, a murderer, an escaped convict, a member of the mob itself which had laid waste a large area of the city none of these mattered; my skin was apparently white, and that was enough."[8]

Maurice Willows thought the legionnaires more hindrance than help, and urged their disbandment.[9] The fun ended after less than a week when one of the Legion men shot a local farmer during a midnight raid on a wheat field. The farmer, E. L. Meadows, and three companions said they were digging for buried treasure. The legionnaires, commanded by a man McCullough did not remember deputizing, had seized a carload of liquor at a dance in the southern part of the county when they came across Meadows's party. One thing led to another, and one of the Legion men, apparently firing wildly, shot Meadows in the shoulder. Meadows filed a criminal complaint with Seaver two days later;[10] soon after, the Legion squad was cut to twenty-seven men restricted to limited duty. They, too, were soon dismissed.[11]

It must be said that the vast majority of war veterans, white and black, behaved honorably during and after the riot, but the faith placed in white males simply because they were ex-servicemen defied logic. Cowboy Long, one of the town's most notorious hoodlums, was said to be a war veteran.[12] So, too, were the men who fatally wounded the white motorist R. L. Osborne as he entered the city on the Sand Springs road four days after the riot.[13] Colonel Rooney said white men in uniforms who did not belong to the National Guard caused considerable confusion and mischief during the riot.[14] But in the psychology of the moment, white veterans were perceived as trustworthy heroes and black veterans as dangerous malcontents.

With the effective dissolution of the American Legion squad, the money allocated by the city for that purpose was redirected to relief efforts.[15] On June 10, with the relief fund balance at about $15,000, the Public Welfare Board appointed a ten-member committee to raise $75,000 to $100,000 for what was described as temporary assistance. E. Roger Kemp, an oil executive who had led a quarter-million-dollar Red Cross drive during the war, was put in charge.[16] "This action was taken as a means of assuring the Red Cross the active support of the business men of Tulsa, following the transfer of full responsibility for receiving and administering the relief funds to the Red Cross by the Public Welfare Board," the *Tribune* reported. "The question of permanent reconstruction or housing will not be considered by this committee, which is named solely to gather funds for temporary relief work of an urgent nature."[17]

The Public Welfare Board's H. C. Tyrrell, who was also a director of the local Red Cross, said that about fifty African Americans were still hospitalized, and some of those would require medical care for at least another six months. The Red Cross's primary expense for the foreseeable future, Tyrrell said, would be for "medical attention, sanitation and tentage supervision." Responding to Cooke's complaints about the treatment of whites wounded in the riot, Tyrrell reported that most of the fifty to sixty whites treated in local hospitals during and immediately after the riot left without giving names or addresses and that only one white man had asked for help since.[18]

Kemp's committee had little time to work. On June 14, the simmering animosity between the city commission and the chamber of commerce exploded into the open: Evans appointed his own "reconstruction committee" and ordered the chamber and the Public Welfare Board, which was largely the chamber's creation, out of their offices in city hall. Three other business organizations were told they had to go, too. When City Attorney Frank Duncan told the commission that it could not evict the chamber without cause, Evans ally O. A. Steiner replied, "What's the use putting camouflage on this motion? We want that room because of the damnable carping criticism of the chamber of commerce directors. Why not come out and say so?"[19]

Declaring that the chamber's office space should be turned over to the American Legion, Steiner said, "I'm tired of the horseplay carried on by these self-constituted, self-ordained so-called prominent businessmen. I'm going to run my own business from now on. I have gone more than half-way to the chamber of commerce once too often. From now on I will steer my own ship without 'em." Evans, who had remained quiet over the past two weeks, issued a sharply worded written statement absolving the police and the city government of blame and laying it squarely on the "armed negroes and their followers who started this trouble and who instigated it, and anyone who tries to put half the blame on white people are wrong and should be told so in no uncertain terms."[20]

Evans claimed that on at least two occasions before he became mayor, "armed mobs of negroes visited the white section of the city and made certain demands under threat of force."[21] A similar assertion was made by the incarcerated John Smitherman, who claimed that Dr. Bridgewater had led a delegation to the county jail in 1919 to stop the rumored lynching of Jewell Davis, a black man accused of murder.[22] Bridgewater strenuously denied even knowing about such a sortie,[23] and neither the World nor the Tribune's predecessor, the Democrat, reported such a thing at the time.

In telling the Public Welfare Board it was no longer needed and definitely not wanted, and replacing it with his own committee, Evans went all in with those eager to remove the African Americans from their old neighborhoods near the Frisco tracks to make way for warehouses and a union train depot. He appointed some of the most vocal advocates of removal to the committee: the voluble Tate Brady, dour and ruthless Stephen Riley "Buck" Lewis, and Frank Long, an acolyte of the philanthropic yet ever-acquisitive Charles Page.[24] Attorney A. J. Biddison, brother of Judge Valjean Biddison and the most distinguished member of the committee, might have been a moderating influence had he not left town for the summer one day after being appointed. Another member, bank president and former judge J. W. Woodford, quickly resigned when his bank was taken over by Grant McCullough's First National.[25]

Those displaced by what some considered the petulant actions of the mayor and city commission were furious. Fred Shaw, a businessman on the Public Welfare Board, came as close as anyone to calling Evans's Reconstruction Committee a sham. "We've got a certain amount of money to raise for relief work, and that other committee can't raise it," Shaw said. "There are some good men on that committee—and there are some that are not so good."[26]

Brady, for whom one of the streets running through the affected district was named, would at times over the subsequent years be singled out as the ringleader and mastermind of the removal effort, but he is not the only or even most logical suspect. Lewis was more cunning and cold-blooded, and probably had as much at stake financially; he, not Brady, was quickly chosen chairman of the Reconstruction Committee. The involvement of Frank Long, an officer in Page's Sand Springs Railroad, suggests that Page, too, had an interest in the project. A week earlier, on June 7, Page had offered free housing for up to 150 black women displaced by the riot.[27] Whether this was merely another display of Page's well-known charity or something more complicated and less altruistic is impossible to know.

The mayor and his three city commission allies—Herman Newblock voted against evicting the chamber and generally distanced himself from the situation— had a point. They were Tulsa's elected government; unless and until removed from office, they constituted legal authority in the city. The chamber of commerce sometimes forgot that. It was used to calling the shots on issues that mattered, and its expulsion from city hall was a development as tectonically significant to the workings of the community as the riot itself. "City Hall Breaks with C. of C." read the *Tribune*'s eight-column headline on June 14.

> The meeting in the commissioners' room at the city hall snapped with fire and oratory as one proposal after another came before the commission as an aftermath of the riot and the emergency it caused. Mayor Evans presented a long series of resolutions for the approval of the commissioners, who gave it by vote after expressing their approval of the sentiments therein and their disapproval of the Public Welfare Board's course of action. Commissioners Steiner and Adkison were especially severe in their criticism of what was termed the "carping criticism" and "usurped authority" of the citizens who took charge of the local situation after Adjutant General Barrett."[28]

With remarkable restraint, the Public Welfare Board resigned en masse at a meeting the next day. In doing so, it reiterated Tulsa's obligation to those injured and left homeless by the riot and urged continued support for the Red Cross.[29] The chamber's president, an equable Spanish-American and First World War veteran named Alva Niles, stayed calm, but others thought Evans's actions intemperate and even ridiculous. Several likened the city commission to ill-mannered brats. "The commissioners are like a bunch of peeved children trying to cover up their derelictions," said Frank Greer, a realtor and publisher of one of Oklahoma Territory's first newspapers. "The city fathers are running against rather stiff

opposition . . . when they start to oust the leading business interests of the city,"
said L. E. Abbott, co-owner of one of the city's largest department stores.[30]

Cyrus Avery and a banker named T. J. Hartman, working through Newblock,
arranged a peace conference in the city commission's meeting room a few days
later.[31] "City Commissioners and Chamber Bury the Hatchet," said *Tulsa World*
subheadlines, "Love Feast Results."[32] "Jealousies and hard feelings were forgotten
in the revival of old friendships that followed," the *Tribune* reported. "A general
handshaking took place, and Mayor Evans asked Major Niles to appoint three
of his directors to a committee to help select additional members for the reconstruction committee."[33] The eviction order was withdrawn, the Reconstruction
Committee expanded, and the relationship between the city and the chamber
of commerce, though still touchy, more or less went back to normal.[34]

Evans's action also had important and potentially crippling implications
for relief fundraising—which may have been the reason for it in the first place.
Contributions slowed, and relations between the city and the Red Cross steadily
deteriorated until early July, when the Tulsa County Commission stopped Evans's
attempt to put the local Humane Society—a social service rather than animal
protection organization at that time—in charge of relief.[35] Willows summarized
the situation in one of his reports:

> Plans were underway whereby the Welfare Board was to engineer a reha-
> bilitation and housing program. They expected to raise immediately a
> sum of $100,000 to start with.
>
> When everything was running smoothly, like a thunderclap out of
> a clear sky. . . . [Evans] declared the Welfare Board out of commission,
> and in its place appointed a new committee . . . which he called "The
> Reconstruction Committee."
>
> Thus, the backbone of financial support had been broken, most abruptly.
>
> The Red Cross therefore was placed in a position of having to deal with
> a new Reconstruction Committee. It was understood, at first, that the new
> committee was to function as the agent of the city in the same manner as
> the old committee. Time, however, has proven that the new committee
> is politically constituted and is chiefly interested in maneuvering for the
> transfer of negro properties and the establishment of a new negro district.[36]

Whatever willingness African American property owners may have had to
sell was quickly dissipating. They could not ever have had much confidence of
a square deal, and this latest development reduced their faith to almost zero.

"We don't like what we've seen in the papers," the Reverend H. T. F. Johnson told the Reconstruction Committee on June 18. "The negro race is naturally optimistic but this is the first time I have ever seen my people when they were unable to smile. Their faith in God has been shaken. They ask me where God was when their homes were burning and I have been pushed to answer them." Rev. E. N. Bryant, at the same meeting, said, "What we want to know is where is our stopping place? We are out of doors and want to know where to go."[37]

Almost 4,300 people lost their homes in the riot, according to Willows,[38] and almost all of those whose houses remained intact had suffered some degree of looting and vandalism.[39] Some number of African Americans—reports ranged from a few hundred to five thousand[40]—had left the city. Most of the rest were crammed into all sorts of habitations, including outbuildings and tents.[41] The fairgrounds may have actually been more comfortable for some, but those who remained there were subjected to great scorn by whites. They were accused of laziness and malingering, and the police tried to dump prisoners charged with loitering and other minor infractions on the camp.[42] When some of the unemployed men at the camp were put to work unloading crushed rock for roadwork, the World published a sarcastic story accusing them of being loafers "strenuously dodging work, knowing they had a haven of refuge and rest and 'three squares' a day at the fair grounds." Presented with the "opportunity" to "repay the city for its kindness," the World said, the men agreed to work for no more than three meals a day and a "reasonably good bed" at night.[43]

Newt Graham, who was in charge of the fairgrounds camp, sharply objected to this characterization, and insisted that everyone at the fairgrounds worked willingly at whatever was asked.[44] The fact was, as the chamber of commerce quietly admitted on June 22, that Tulsa had far more unemployed men, white and black, than it had work for them to do.[45] The bricklayers and hod carriers, who had been on strike for a month, went back to work on June 19 for a dollar a day less than they had been making before.[46] One man passing through town offered to trade his two-year-old son for a job.[47] A young woman, writing in the World, pleaded for help. "Yes, give the negroes work, clothes, money, assistance of any kind, but oh! fairminded Tulsa, look at the white men and women who are struggling, begging for a chance to even get by. . . . I am about to lose my home, the result of a lifetime effort, because I cannot raise $500."[48]

Quickly resolving the burned district's future would have alleviated some of this joblessness, but the impasse only deepened after the change in regime. Perhaps as a show of strength, the Reconstruction Committee toured the area on June 15, one day after being constituted, and proclaimed unequivocally that it would become an industrial district.[49] On June 16, the Real Estate Exchange dropped the proposed loan association to finance construction of African American homes and businesses and endorsed the concept of a union depot. Some of the realtors, though, were uneasy. A resolution to build the new depot in the burned district was shouted down, and many of those present were dismayed by press reports that they had been behind the destruction of Greenwood.[50]

"While no official motion was considered," reported the *Tribune*, "the sense of the Real Estate Exchange today was that members should not speculate in negro property at this time. This attitude was taken because of stories printed in outside papers to the effect that the real estate men were accused of having [a] hand in the riot to make it possible to gain possession of the negro property for industrial purposes."[51] This accusation had appeared in the *World* a day earlier, in a letter by Ira E. Moore of Drumright, an oilfield town thirty miles west of Tulsa. "In regard to the recent race rioting in your city," wrote Moore, "please allow me to say that viewed from the outside and judged by newspaper reports and current editorials that since the density of the smoke screen thus thrown out has somewhat lessened one can begin to see the major operations behind the scenes."[52]

Moore noted the involvement of the Real Estate Exchange and asked, "Some plot is it not? And could it be possible that such a scheme could be premeditated and pre-arranged by the said Tulsa of Oklahoma, or her residents who are so highly lauded as the best of the earth. . . . We have read of such means and worse being used to acquire the Indian lands in the early days of this great country of ours. Could it be possible? Very likely it could."[53]

The *World* followed with an editorial against "all forms of duress or intrigue" in negotiating for the burned district. "However desirable this property may be for city-building or city-beautifying purposes," the editorial said, "the fact remains that it belongs to those who own it, and [it] can be secured, if at all, only after satisfying their views."[54]

On June 17, the city commission annexed Gurley Hill and two other African American additions into the city, presumably to give the city more control of them.[55] That same day, somewhere between twenty-five and one hundred black property owners were invited—or perhaps summoned—to a meeting with the Reconstruction Committee the next afternoon.[56]

Steiner, although not a member of the committee, told the blacks that their only chance of recovering their losses was by selling their property. Citing public health concerns that were probably valid but do not seem to have bothered

authorities when people were actually living in the district, Steiner declared
that Greenwood's outdoor toilets would be demolished and replaced with a few
public facilities. Aside from Steiner's blunt assessment, though, the whites in
attendance seem to have listened more than talked. Johnson and Bryant had
their say, as did several others. Barney Cleaver and George Washington Hutchins
were willing to sell. Gurley and Frank Williams said that they would do what was
best for the city. Bridgewater, angered and perhaps wounded by public criticism,
nevertheless pressed for details. What about the restrictions on their property?
Where were they to secure the financing to rebuild? Until those questions were
answered, he would not sell. The schoolteacher J. W. Hughes was more emphatic.
He would not turn loose of his property until fully compensated for his losses.[57]

In what was no doubt intended as a demonstration of magnanimous good
faith, the black property owners were allowed to choose five representatives to
attend the Reconstruction Committee meetings. That this was something of an
insult of its own does not seem to have occurred to the committee, or, if it did,
to have troubled anyone much.[58] On June 20, the Reconstruction Committee
asked Evans and the city commission to pressure both the railroads and the state
corporation commission on behalf of the union depot, and to even ask the latter
to require the depot be built in the burned district.[59]

That same afternoon, Tulsa's black community met in a Baptist church that
had survived the riot.[60] Neither the *World* nor the *Tribune* reported on the meeting, and no record of what transpired exists, but three days later, on June 22,
the men representing black property owners at the Reconstruction Committee
meetings told the members that sentiment had turned against removal, at least
in part because the proposal did not allow for the replacement of churches and
other "public improvements" not destroyed in the riot. Both newspapers buried
this information on their inside pages, in stories about the need for donated
furniture and cookstoves.[61]

Meanwhile, a former state corporation commissioner named W. D. Humphrey
urged the city to initiate condemnation proceedings, and questioned the process
by which the burned area had been brought under the fire code. "If the act of the
city council was predicated solely upon [acquiring the land] . . . without reference
to the necessity of fire limits within the area mentioned and without reference
to the necessity of such control for the protection of property within the area
involved, I have some doubts about the validity of the ordinance."[62]

Amid this flurry of noisy inactivity, Willows's stern voice was barely heard.
"We must look into the future, and realize that the job we have undertaken is

one that will last for several months," he told the Reconstruction Committee even as it resolved to go forward on the removal scheme. "Although it seems far away now, winter is coming, and with it changed conditions that will require more drastic action."[63]

On June 10, the black man "H. Johnson" died in Morningside Hospital. According to brief reports in the *World* and *Tribune*, Johnson's spinal cord was severed by a stray bullet in the early stages of the riot. The *Tribune* said that doctors believed Johnson would be the last fatality among hospitalized riot casualties and put the known death toll at thirty-five—twenty-five African American and ten whites.[64] In fact, at least one more black riot victim, Commodore Knox, would die in a Tulsa hospital, and death certificates have been found for twelve white males, excluding the unfortunate motorist R. L. Osborne.[65]

Early on, local officials and the National Guard rather candidly said they did not know with certainty how many people died.[66] The NAACP's Walter White, writing in the *Nation*, put the death toll at 250, and quoted the Salvation Army's O. T. Johnson as saying that 47 men had been hired to dig one hundred graves;[67] fifty years later, a black woman named Eunice Cloman Jackson said that her stepfather had helped dig about fifty graves at Oaklawn Cemetery.[68]

The *World*, in a June 19 editorial entitled "A Period of Hysteria," sought to discredit the most jarring claims, comparing them to "Hans Andersen's fairy tales and old Mother Goose's jingles."

> Popular psychology at this precise time affords a most interesting study. The vast majority of people appear to be not only prone to expect the worse [sic] that can possibly happen in everything but to acquire a keen enjoyment from that frame of mind.
>
> Take, for instance, the stories following in the wake of the inter-racial conflict. Stories persist that hundreds of negroes were killed and their names deliberately suppressed. Who has not heard the stories? There will always be people who believe that truck loads of negro bodies were dumped into the Arkansas river or buried in a mythical trench or piled into a building which was later set on fire.
>
> There is not a shred of truth in any of them. Each one carries the sure ear-marks of sheer fabrication and grow as they pass from tongue to tongue.[69]

Whether they were truth, fabrication, or combinations of the two, written and visual depictions of the Tulsa riot were in great demand, and for a variety of purposes. Everyone had an angle, a cause, a motive. Grisly images of burned and bullet-riddled corpses soon appeared on postcards.[70] On June 12, Oklahoma City's Folly Theater announced that it would be the first to show "Fox News of Tulsa Race Riot," a newsreel, still in existence, taken by an unknown photographer.[71] Some newspapers seemed to compete for the most lurid—and outlandish—accounts, and political interests of all stripes sought to exploit it, from Cyril Briggs to the Ku Klux Klan. On June 14, Police Commissioner Adkison ordered the arrest of anybody photographing the riot area, something that in later generations would almost certainly have provoked a First Amendment lawsuit. "This action was taken especially as a precaution against the influx here of negroes from other cities seeking propaganda for their organizations," the *Tribune* explained. "Adkison states today that his men were on the lookout for such characters and would deal with them summarily if they are apprehended here."[72]

Late on June 13, under pressure from the moralist element, Adkison ordered the arrest of all black porters in about fifty "questionable" hotels, pool halls, and boarding houses, regardless of whether the men possessed a required "green card" or not. "Arrests of the negro porters in the questionable pool halls probably will be made this afternoon," the *Tribune* said the next day.[73] The Red Cross, however, put the kibosh to this dragnet by refusing to take the prisoners at the fairgrounds.[74]

A good many people were in and out of jail over a period of several months because of the riot, but the only one known to have served time because of a conviction was a black man named Garfield Thompson. On June 10, municipal judge S. C. Maxey sentenced him to thirty days for possession of a firearm during the riot. Police said that Thompson was arrested in the downtown area on the night of May 31 with pistol in his belt. Thompson, pleading his innocence, claimed that he was at home when arrested.[75]

On June 23, as the grand jury neared the end of its labors, the *World* announced the formation of the "Inter-Racial committee of Tulsa county" to "improve the condition of the negro, as a race" and "by all appropriate and wholesome means, to foster activities along all lines tending to improve the understanding and co-operative efforts of the races." It was this group that hired Mary Jones Parrish to collect the stories of black riot survivors, and that to some extent helped African Americans fend off pressure to move without fair compensation.[76]

The Inter-Racial Committee may have considered itself progressive, but it was still far from advocating true racial discourse. It swore to uphold "evenhanded and impartial justice" in the protection of property as well as life and limb, but ultimately sought to preserve the social and political status quo. All twenty-four charter members seem to have been white, and their idea of "appropriate and wholesome" interaction consisted mostly of them telling black people what to do.[77]

A statement of the committee's principles said that it intended to "recognize and, by its conduct, exemplify, a superior and dominant white citizenship in government, and in all the social relations of life, and while observing with gratification the remarkable progress of the American negro since slavery, to recognize also his immaturity as a race." The group opposed lynching "for any cause whatsoever" and "lawlessness and unlawful violence, the lawless and vicious associations of whites and blacks at the varied and increasingly numerous points of contact between the races, as well as to always condemn and decry the unthinking and misguided activities of radical agitators and breeders of racial strife."[78]

Chairman Mather Eakes lamented the inconsistent messages that black Tulsans had received. "The Tulsa negro has been unfortunately dealt with in the past," he said. "Some have sought to hold him as a political pawn; others have dangled before him visions of social prestige and unwholesome association; while yet others have contemptuously passed him up as incapable of learning good citizenship. This is wrong, and the error must be corrected." Instead, he said, "the negro must be shown the attractiveness of his own unique position in the social and industrial system and he must be taught to occupy the position with skillful effort and pride to worthy accomplishment."[79]

In Tulsa, and elsewhere, that "unique position" mainly involved menial jobs at low pay. When, on June 26, a truckload of household goods was distributed near the temporary Red Cross headquarters at Booker T. Washington High School, it was the white population that rejoiced. As the World put it, the delivery signaled "that once again the washing can be taken away from the house, kept a few days and returned in a state of virginal whiteness that was its weekly habit in the days before the riot." The demand for washer women exceeded the supply, the World explained, "because the women living in tents had lost their washday equipment as well as their homes."[80]

But the men and women who built Greenwood did not come to Tulsa to wash clothes and bus tables. They had come for opportunity, to own businesses and property and to direct their own fates. They would not surrender that freedom without a fight.

13

TRIALS AND TRIBULATIONS

June was unusually wet that year. Almost fourteen inches of rain fell in the four weeks following the riot, including nine inches between June 22 and June 26.[1] A final deluge submerged low areas, mostly in what was then the southern part of the city and west of downtown extending along the interurban line to Sand Springs, to depths of as much as eight feet. Train trestles were washed away, basements flooded, roads inundated.[2] For those living in tents and makeshift shelters on Greenwood's blasted heath, the rain must have seemed like the latest plague to befall them. This can only be surmised, for the riot refugees were hardly mentioned in reports of that week's storms. The exception was a June 27 story in the *World* about the delivery of the washtubs and other household goods. It noted that three hundred black people had been forced to take shelter at Red Cross headquarters—Booker T. Washington High School—during the most recent storm.[3]

The *World* said that "virtually" two thousand dollars' worth of lumber and six kegs of nails had been "donated since the flood" for the construction of sturdier tents. "There is about a yard of screen around each tent," said the story, "floored with wood and walled with canvas, and all of the work has been done by the negroes." About fifty of the tents had been erected and equipped, said Maurice Willows, at a cost of seventy-five to ninety dollars each, with many more needed. Slow as it might seem, Willows said, progress was being made—perhaps enough to lift black Tulsans' spirits. For the first time since "the trouble," the *World* reported, "the black people in the devastated belt were smiling and singing. They had something to do that was getting them somewhere; they were having a hand in reconstruction work and they were helping each other."[4]

Just how happy they really were can only be guessed; what remains clear in these few paragraphs is the continued effort by Willows and other sympathetic whites to portray the majority of African Americans as willing, industrious souls deserving of assistance. This, in turn, suggests that some whites, and perhaps quite a few, thought otherwise. Buck Lewis, for one, believed that blacks were being pampered and spoiled;[5] others grumbled about aid to African Americans while white laborers contended with high rents and reduced wages during the postwar recession.[6]

Willows generally spoke favorably, at the time and afterward, about the people with whom he worked in Tulsa. Lewis Lefko of the Better Business Bureau and O. V. Borden of the Purchasing Agents Association in particular helped secure donated and at-cost materials and supplies. Willows also lauded the medical professions and charitable organizations. It was the self-serving politics that drove him to distraction. Willows was used to dealing with the aftermath of hurricanes, earthquakes, and floods; rarely, if ever, had he been dropped into a situation so racially and politically charged. Nor had he ever stayed on site so long. Usually, he stayed one week, or two tops, just long enough to get an organization in place, and he was off. This assignment had stretched to nearly four weeks with no end in sight.[7] "The job has only just begun," Willows said on June 26, "and the size of it is not, I believe, generally realized by the majority of the Tulsa people."[8] He prodded the Ministerial Alliance to action the next day by again warning that Tulsa's homeless African Americans faced a bleak winter unless rebuilding began soon. The clergymen, several of whom belonged to the newly formed Inter-Racial Committee of Tulsa County, resolved to press the Reconstruction Committee on the matter, and to demand at least one pastor be included in the group.[9]

On June 28, a local realtor named Gordon Grady, who said he represented "a number of wealthy Tulsa merchants and businessmen," made a presentation to the Reconstruction Committee that was yet another variation on an increasingly familiar theme. Grady said his group would buy most of the burned district at prices based on values prior to the riot. The city, meanwhile, would buy land northeast of Tulsa, subdivide it, and sell it to the African Americans for less than they had received for their old lots, but at "a small profit" to the city. This "small profit," finally, would be divided among the black property owners according to their losses. "There is no use stating that we do not expect to realize a profit," Grady said frankly. "These lots are much more valuable for industrial purposes than for residences, and would be purchased at a price to allow the property owners there a handsome profit over prices they paid."[10] This seems somewhat disingenuous. Surely a fair price would have been based on appreciated value, not the amount originally paid.

Grady refused to say who his clients and/or partners were in this venture, but one of them could have been Charles Page. A little over a week later, Page tipped his interest in relocation by promising to extend electric service into the proposed new black business district on North Lansing Avenue, where Tate Brady said "15 or 20 houses" were already under construction.[11] The Reconstruction Committee agreed to evaluate Grady's proposal and one day later asked him to submit it in writing.[12] Whether he did is unclear.

The committee was also apprised of another reconstruction scheme, this one headed by O. W. Gurley's friend Reverend Bryant. Capitalized at $25,000, The Protective Investment Building and Loan Association's stated purpose was solicitation of funds to rebuild Greenwood through loans at 10 percent interest. The Reconstruction Committee was not happy about this.[13] Bryant's group was probably incapable of raising the money to fully rebuild Greenwood, but it was a complication outside the committee's control. Freelance operations of this nature concerned local authorities from the very start, and not only for selfish reasons. They worried not only about outright fraud but also well-meaning amateurs more likely to cause confusion than actually accomplish anything.

And, of course, there was the public relations angle to be considered. Tulsa was getting a lot of press and it was all bad. A man making the rounds of churches and charities in New Jersey claimed to represent fifteen thousand destitute black Tulsans whose needs were being completely ignored by state and local authorities.[14] One story in circulation had Stradford being lynched on the "courthouse lawn."[15] The truth was embarrassing enough without such embellishment, so Bryant's group did not help itself locally by distributing fundraising materials stating that five hundreds blacks had been killed in the riot; Lefko, as head of the Better Business Bureau, was detailed to investigate the Protective Investment Building and Loan Association—and, no doubt, shut it down if possible.[16]

The end of June and early July were important and perhaps decisive days in the legal and political battle for Greenwood. At a June 29 city commission meeting, Evans revealed that the supposedly cash-strapped city had $23,500 left over from the money allocated by the county to pay the American Legion men, and that the money had to be spent by midnight the next day or it would revert to the sinking fund used for bond payments and judgments against the city. The mayor further surprised at least some of those present by recommending that the money be spent on rifles, machine guns, ammunition, and a "whippet tank"—a light tank developed by the British at the end of the First World War. O. A. Steiner, who had suggested the tank, said that an armored vehicle with mounted guns and the ability to carry up to fifteen men should also be considered. Commissioner Adkison, slightly less enthusiastic, said fifty "high-powered rifles," twenty "one-man machine guns," and a "patrol wagon" would come in handy.[17]

City commissioners Younkman and Newblock were opposed.[18] "The news will spread throughout the country that the city is establishing a fortress in the city hall and the result will be that Tulsa will be given a black eye," said Younkman. Later, when the subject came up again, Younkman exclaimed, "If we had police-men who were not yellow we would not need to buy guns and ammunition."[19]

This naturally did not set well with Adkison, who demanded to know where Younkman had been during the riot. Apparently this question had not been asked before, for to everyone's astonishment, the mild-mannered druggist unloaded a broadside at Chief Gustafson and Fire Chief R. C. Alder. Younkman replied that he had been in the middle of the confusion at the police station and had heard three black officers tell Gustafson that "there were 200 armed negroes at the Frisco station marching on the business district. The chief told them to go back and hold those negroes at all costs but not to fire a shot." Younkman said that he had ordered Alder to turn a fire hose on the mob surrounding the police station but that Alder, much to Younkman's chagrin, had ignored him.[20]

Newblock, a former lawman, ridiculed Evans's proposed arms buildup. "What are you going to do with the machine guns?" he asked. "Are you going to hunt squirrels?"[21] Evans finally suggested turning the money over to the Red Cross but found no support even though that must have seemed the obvious use for it.[22] Certainly other people thought so. City Attorney Frank Duncan, by this time nearly as unpopular with the commission as auditor Mary Seaman, said that the city had no choice but to spend the money on relief.[23] The Red Cross, which Clark Fields described as "at the end of our rope," quickly submitted its claim.[24] "If we don't get some money at once, we are going to have to quit," Fields told the commission on June 30.[25]

A day earlier, just hours after Evans recommended spending the surplus funds on guns and armored vehicles, Fields read to the Reconstruction Committee a report prepared by Willows. In it, he summarized the Red Cross's work and the

expenses to date, and again urged authorities to stop dithering. "The responsibility for financing Red Cross operations must be fixed definitely and speedily,"
Willows wrote, "and a rehabilitation policy must be outlined before we can hope
to see daylight. The extent of relief work necessary will not diminish until some
authority, municipal or otherwise, sets in motion plans whereby these thousands
of homeless and destitute people can be restored to homes and earning power."[26]

Over the preceding month, Willows's report said, eight public health nurses
employed by the Red Cross had made 4,300 in-home contacts, administered first
aid to 531 individuals, and served a total of almost 6,500 people. Willows said
that about 3,500 people, most of them women and children, were "still without
adequate housing, tentage, bedding and clothing," and that 300 families were
without even temporary housing. The committee said that it would ask the
county excise board for some of the $60,000 set aside for emergencies arising
from the riot.[27]

Willows, Fields, and Borden took their case—and a bill for more than
$20,000—to the city commission the next day. Evans and Steiner had dropped
their proposal for a city arsenal but were still cranky about being pressured to
make good on a promise that, in their view, had been made by the chamber of
commerce–backed Public Welfare Board. When Willows criticized the decision
to refuse outside assistance, Evans countered that that had been the Public
Welfare Board's doing, not the city's. Willows was not having it. He claimed
that Evans had dismissed the Public Welfare Board just as it was organizing a
major fund-raising campaign and had done nothing to take it up. Evans then
said he was not sure whether the city could legally take responsibility for all of
the refugees, since many of them lived outside the city limits.[28] "It isn't a question
of what we would like to do," said Evans. "If we are within the law, I am in favor
of being liberal in this relief work."[29] Fed up, Borden replied, "We don't want any
quibbling between the county and city about this. We have a debt of $20,000
and we want to know now if you are going to let us have any of the $23,000."[30]

The three commission members present—Evans, Steiner, and Adkison—
grumped about what they said was a lack of documentation but finally agreed
to pay about $21,000 in outstanding bills. The only rejected claim was for $1,250
in damage to the Cinnabar building used as a temporary hospital. That claim, by
the building's owner, was declined on the advice of a physician, Dr. Ralph Smith.[31]

Buck Lewis, the Reconstruction Committee's chairman, unloaded two days
later, telling the *Tribune* that the Red Cross "had spent too lavishly" on Tulsa's
blacks and should shut down all of its relief work except for the hospital. He also

disapproved of "the best white nurses that can be found" caring for blacks when "colored nurses are . . . fully capable of taking care of them." Only truly destitute African Americans—principally the old—should be supported, Lewis opined. "Negroes are a servant class of people and there is no reason why the women should not work as well as men," he said. "Mr. Willows of the Red Cross told us that there were 300 applications for grocery orders [this week]. In my opinion that is entirely too many and I am frank to say that the Red Cross estimates of the Negroes who need help are entirely too high."[32]

Like Tate Brady, Lewis was among that generation of men who had managed to parlay sketchy claims on tribal membership into positions of wealth and power during the final days of the Indian Territory and the early days of the state of Oklahoma. His father, Alexander S. Lewis, had been born in the old Cherokee country of northern Alabama and claimed a vague Cherokee ancestry that came in handy when the family moved from Texas to the Cherokee Nation north of Tulsa in the 1880s. The younger Lewis was born in 1873 in Hill County, Texas, between Waco and Fort Worth, and was educated at a Quaker mission school near Skiatook, twenty miles north of Tulsa. Admitted to the territorial bar in 1902, Buck Lewis solidified his position by marrying into a prominent Cherokee family, the Schrimshers, who were kinsmen of humorist Will Rogers. Lewis specialized in untangling land titles, a tricky and often shady business in early-day Oklahoma. Lewis's family founded the community of Dawson, now part of the city of Tulsa, and became heavily involved in ranching, farming, and coal mining.[33]

Lewis was influential in the Democratic Party and, at one time, an ally of Brady. The two fell out around 1911, however, and hostilities escalated to the point that Lewis once "demolished" a chair over Brady's head. The pair reached some sort of cease-fire prior to the 1920 municipal elections, when they agreed to support Evans, a Republican, over incumbent Democrat Charles Hubbard. Hubbard, apparently, was viewed as a long-term threat to Brady's and Lewis's standing within the Democratic Party, which at that time dominated state politics. Evans indicated that he would serve only one term and that his only real interest was putting through the bond issue needed to connect Tulsa with a planned reservoir on Spavinaw Creek, ninety miles away on the western fringe of the Ozarks.[34]

Charles Page wanted the city of Tulsa to get its water from his Shell Creek reservoir northwest of Tulsa. Acting on Page's behalf, Brady brought the Spavinaw project to a screeching halt in 1919 with a successful lawsuit that voided a bond issue and forced a city charter amendment. Then, less than a year later, Brady endorsed a mayoral candidate whose sole platform plank was completion of the

Spavinaw water source. In the summer of 1921, as the dispute over Greenwood dragged on, Page again promoted Shell Creek as an alternative to the more expensive Spavinaw project.[35] His half-hearted campaign does not seem to have been taken very seriously, even by Page, but perhaps the single-minded Evans interpreted it as a warning. Perhaps the mayor's commitment to Spavinaw water, and his desire to keep Brady, and by extension Page, mollified, affected his decisions concerning Greenwood.

Oklahoma county government operated under a system in which all county officers were elected in November of even-numbered years, but county commissioners and the county treasurer did not assume their duties until the following July. So it was that two new Tulsa County commissioners, Ira Short and Charles Gilmore, took office on July 5, joining holdover Frank Wooden.[36] The next morning, the newly constituted commission and Treasurer Wayne Dickey met with Mayor Evans, Clark Fields, Maurice Willows, A. M. Welch from the Humane Society, and J. H. McBirney and Barney Meyers from the Reconstruction Committee. A day earlier, Lewis and the Reconstruction Committee had practically ordered the Red Cross to stop feeding able-bodied blacks and to turn all operations except medical care over to the Humane Society.[37] Evans now raised this issue with the county and the others present.[38]

Was the Humane Society up to the task? someone asked. Evans said they were. Welch, the head of the Humane Society, shook his head no. Willows definitively said the society was not. Evans pleaded poverty on behalf of the city, but the county was not sympathetic. It agreed to make $60,000 available above and beyond what had already been spent, as long as the city put in $40,000 and Willows and the Red Cross remained in charge. Evans agreed.[39]

It is not clear whether the change in the county commission had much to do with it, but this meeting of July 6 and the resolution that came from it doomed the removal plans. Although Lewis, Brady, and others would hold out for several more months, their inability to cut off relief funding and push aside Maurice Willows was their Gettysburg. Blacks had regained a foothold in Greenwood, albeit mostly in the form of tents and temporary housing. But the tents now had wooden floors and walls, and a few buildings that met the fire code were beginning to go up. A legal team, led in white Tulsa by Mather Eakes and in Greenwood by B. C. Franklin, P. A. Chappelle, Isaac Spears, and others, was developing its strategy and tactics.

But most of all, by early July it was increasingly apparent that the syndicate behind removal did not have the money to pull it off. On July 13, the *World* published a lengthy editorial in which it urged the Reconstruction Committee to pay up or shut up. The problem, the *World* said, was "an unwillingness to face courageously substantial facts" and "too much of a proneness to follow inclination and desire instead." Yes, the editorialist continued, an industrial district and union station might be desirable and a popular idea with the public, but somebody had to pay for it.[40]

More fundamentally, the *World* said, the Reconstruction Committee

must take on itself the responsibility of deciding to make full reparation for the losses sustained by the property owners. Unless such reparation is undertaken by the community as a whole and unless there is a willingness on the part of the property owners to part with their [land], the alternative confronting the committee is to not only permit the property owners to rebuild their properties, but to engage itself in affording aid and advice to them in the work of reconstruction.[41]

The editorial predicted legal challenges to attempts at securing the property without the full and free agreement of the owners, and asked "Where is the money? . . . It is reported that a great number of the colored people want to rebuild their property; that many of them have the instant means to do that. In the light of what has been said, what is the community's best interest if not its duty? Is it not to give them permission to proceed and aid them in every way to accomplish their purpose? That is our thought."[42]

With black Tulsa's future in limbo, white Tulsa's attention was diverted by a preliminary to Chief John Gustafson's ouster trial. On June 30, accused car thief Calvin Brady was hauled before Judge Redmond Cole for trial. Specifically, Brady was accused of knowingly receiving an automobile stolen at his own direction by a man named Ray Dickens. Dickens and county investigator F. J. Bays were the primary witnesses for the state. Gustafson, Roy Meacham, Bay Ward, J. W. Patton, and a detective named Squires all testified that Brady had agreed to take the car from Dickens as part of what today would be called a sting operation. Brady claimed that the plan was to get Dickens and the car's owner on insurance fraud, but that Bays had arrested Brady before the trap could be sprung. The jury did not believe it. After hearing a day and night of testimony, it took less than a half hour to find Brady guilty. Cole sentenced him to the maximum five years in prison.[43]

This was just one more ill omen for Gustafson, and for Meacham and Ward. A few days earlier, the *World* had published the names of eighteen people the newspaper said gave grand jury testimony detrimental to the police chief.[44] The list included Brady and Bays as well as the feisty city auditor, Mary Seaman. Also identified was former police matron Mattie Clark, who in May had told an attorney general's investigator—possibly Kathryn Van Leuven—that some police officers were in the habit of having sex at the police station with female inmates and on occasion even taking them out of the jail for rendezvous.[45] The other witnesses included Nick Remackel, a former traffic cop who had been accused of selling liquor while on the job; H. H. Townsend, the private detective who had wanted Gustafson's job; Tulsa police officer E. S. Fields; and W. E. Pinion, chief of police in the nearby town of Bixby. Seventeen of the eighteen named by the *World* appear to have testified mostly or entirely about things other than the riot. The exception was J. W. Magee (whose name was also spelled "Megee" and "McGee"), whose store was looted by white rioters.

And there were other developments.

Will Robinson, identified by Barney Cleaver as the "all-around bad negro" at the front of the armed courthouse contingent, surrendered on June 29.[46] Remarkably, Robinson's lawyer was Moman Pruiett, the state's and one of the nation's best-known criminal attorneys. Brilliant, alcoholic, and violent, Pruiett had served jail terms in two states before landing in the Oklahoma Territory and somehow getting a license to practice law. Irrepressible as a May tornado, Pruiett won a place in the state constitutional convention, and present-day Creek County, Oklahoma, would have been Moman County had he not succeeded in outraging both the floor leader, Charles Haskell, and the presiding officer, William H. Murray.[47]

Pruiett claimed to have won acquittals in 303 of 343 murder cases, and to never have had a client executed. How Pruiett came to represent Robinson is unknown but not out of character. A man whose sense of outrage simmered perpetually at the boil, Pruiett took on clients without regard to race, creed, color, or ability to pay.[48]

Interestingly, an enduring tale of uncertain provenance has it that Dick Rowland's lawyer was Washington Hudson, a leading figure in Tulsa's soon-to-be-revealed Ku Klux Klan. There is no contemporary mention of Hudson representing Rowland, but he certainly could have, and in any event it makes a good story. Besides his Klan connection, Hudson was a prominent figure in the city and state and remained so for some time. He would become Democratic leader of the Oklahoma Senate, and Lake Hudson, a large reservoir east of Tulsa, is named for him. His son Robert was a well-known jurist.[49] But it was Pruiett's largely overlooked defense of Will Robinson that changed the course of the legal proceedings stemming from the riot.

From Freeling on down, the prosecution team wielded the threat of murder charges like a club over the heads of everyone indicted for rioting and succeeded in having the few who were caught or surrendered jailed without bail. This was essentially the same tactic used to squeeze confessions from defendants in the Phillips County, Arkansas, cases. But at a June 29 bond hearing for Robinson and another riot defendant named Will Davis, Pruiett convinced Judge Cole to release Robinson and Davis, each on $7,500 bond. His argument, apparently, was that so many people had participated in the Tulsa riot that murder convictions would be almost impossible. Assistant county attorney John Goldsberry, representing the prosecution, finally conceded that this was true, thus effectively eliminating that weapon from the state's legal arsenal.[50]

One of Gustafson's last acts before his suspension as police chief had been to ban fireworks except on the Fourth of July,[51] causing midsummer to pass more quietly than usual. But there was some loud grumbling. The Reconstruction Committee threatened charges against anyone spreading rumors of renewed race trouble as well as "political cranks" seeking to "undermine the confidence" of African Americans in the ongoing relief efforts.[52] This was meaningless huffing and puffing, but also another indication of the committee's annoyance with the opposition to its plans for the burned district.

Louder still was the outrage emanating from veterans over the unsolved shooting of one of their comrades, the volunteer machine gun operator Ed Wheeler. Wheeler, who said he moved to Oklahoma for his health, was trying to stop some white men from firing into the black district early on the morning of June 1 when "This young fellow walked up and told me that I would have to beat it, as I was for the negroes. I told him he was mistaken and I wouldn't leave. He pushed his gun against my chest and pulled the trigger and then ran."[53] Wheeler survived, but just barely, and minus any leads in finding his assailant, the National Guard on July 1 promised to track down the villain.[54] On July 4, the Fitzhugh Lee Camp of the United Spanish War Veterans convened an "informal court of inquiry" at the National Guard Armory, where several witnesses were examined. "Virtually all of them saw the man who fired the shot into [Wheeler's] body," the *World* reported, "but because of the excitement that prevailed and the semi-darkness that enveloped them and made them little plainer than shadows, none retained a mental picture of [the shooter]."[55] And so, like almost all the evildoers from that night and the next morning, Wheeler's assailant was never identified or brought to justice.

One of the busiest men in town was Judge Redmond Cole, who was presiding over the remarkable series of criminal cases following one after another in Tulsa County court. A few months shy of his fortieth birthday, Cole heard most of the criminal cases in Tulsa County, and in adjoining Pawnee County, where he had been mayor and chief prosecutor before elected district judge in 1919.[56] By the time John Gustafson's trial began on July 11, Cole had in rapid succession handled the Sperry bank robbery cases, the Calvin Brady case, and, perhaps most titillating of all, the trial of two women accused of killing an elderly lawyer named John Devereux. The "aged jurist," as the newspapers called him, had been found May 10 in a seedy hotel room on North Main, dazed by a bloody bump on the head and apparently drugged. He died the next day. The two young women, sisters who went by the names Goldie Gordon and Mrs. Jesse James, claimed to be caretakers of sorts; James identified herself as a nurse, while the newspapers winkingly described her as an "artist's model." Devereux, it developed, had given the pair at least $1,000 shortly before his death, and his family and friends contended that a promissory note and Liberty bonds worth a total of $27,000 were missing from his safety deposit box. When the two were bound over on manslaughter charges May 28 following a preliminary hearing, the courtroom exploded in applause.[57]

Public opinion had shifted by the time the pair went on trial in early July. James's precocious four-year-old daughter, who accompanied her mother to court, charmed the spectators crammed into the benches and perched on stools inside the rail. Aloof and childless, Gordon made a less sympathetic defendant than her excitable sister, but she nevertheless won over the audience. The state lined up a good deal of circumstantial evidence against the two women, but it could not prove that they had done anything illegal. Closing arguments lasted through a hot Saturday afternoon and into the evening; after an hour-long dinner break, the jury quickly found the defendants not guilty.[58]

Women made up a disproportionate share of the spectators, according to the *World*, and many of them apparently felt an affinity for the defendants. In any event, the applause now was for James and Gordon's acquittal. James let out a sharp cry when the verdict was read, prompting her attorney to hit her with a rolled up sheaf of papers and tell her to be quiet—which caused her to break down in tears with only her daughter to comfort her. Gordon quietly thanked the jurors and disappeared into the night.[59]

Having brought down the curtain on this melodrama, Cole took off only one day, a Sunday, before plowing ahead with the Gustafson trial.

Gustafson was originally to have been tried with TPD officers Roy Meacham and Bay Ward, but Cole agreed to the prosecution's request for separate proceedings. The trials of Sand Springs police chief B. F. Waddell and assistant chief F. E. Williams, indicted by the grand jury on charges unrelated to the riot, were also delayed.

Gustafson's defense team was led by A. Flint Moss, a forty-one-year-old Kentucky native of striking appearance and powerful oratorical skills. Assisting were T. J. Leahy of Pawhuska and City Attorney Frank Duncan. Goldsberry, the assistant county attorney, handled most of the jury selection for the state, with Freeling and Van Leuven making occasional appearances. Voir dire took nearly two days as Moss, over Goldsberry's objections, aggressively interrogated prospective jurors. What did they think of Chief Gustafson? Did they vote in the last election? Did they have an interest in its outcome such that they could not be objective? Goldsberry complained at the scope of Moss's questions, but Cole, for the most part allowed them.[60] "Never in the criminal annals of Tulsa County, say attorneys present, has so much time been spent on selecting a jury," reported the *Tribune*, "and never before has such wide latitude been exercised in the form of questions put to the prospective jurors." The newspaper predicted a lengthy trial, judging from "the bitterness with which opposing counsel contested each minor legal point relative to their selections."[61]

The two sides settled on a final twelve at 4:00 P.M. on Tuesday, July 12. It was a fairly nondescript group, all male, all white. Most listed "oil business" or something related to oil and gas as an occupation, but there were also two farmers, a schoolteacher, and an electrician.[62] Remarkably, two jurors, including foreman J. D. Richards, were among those who had convicted Calvin Brady less than two weeks earlier; neither Gustafson nor his attorneys objected, saying afterward that they considered the two jurors "friends."[63]

The jury was not even sworn before Leahy asked Cole to dismiss the case because the accusation against Gustafson was vague and improperly worded. When Freeling, naturally, objected, Moss called his arguments "absurd" and the attorney general himself "ridiculous." On something of a technicality, Cole finally agreed to dismiss one of the five charges—that Gustafson had used his position as police chief to solicit business for his private detective agency.[64]

The wrangling continued the next day. Cole's courtroom was again packed despite the mid-July heat. Spectators, almost all men, filled the benches and stood against the walls, the attorneys among them scoring the proceedings like a boxing match. Freeling was up first, his opening statement methodically laying out the state's case. Moss followed with an hour-and-a-half response the *Tribune* rated "one of the most powerful arguments for acquittal of a defendant ever heard in a Tulsa county court room." Then, only a few minutes into Freeling's direct examination of Luther James, the state's first witness, Moss and Leahy leaped from their seats to object in unison.[65]

The state had decided to focus first on the grand jury indictment's last count, which accused Gustafson of dereliction of duty during the riot. James, a former county prosecutor, was asked to describe the scene at the courthouse shortly before the shooting began. James said he saw about one thousand "orderly and good-natured" whites, and twenty to twenty-five blacks in a truck "on the edge of the crowd" and another three or four "on the ground." Some of the African Americans had guns; as far as he could see, James said, none of the whites did.[66] "I remarked to Breckinridge that the white people were not going to stand for that long and the negroes ought to be disarmed before there was serious trouble," James testified.[67]

Freeling asked if Gustafson made any attempt to follow through on that suggestion, and it was at that point Leahy and Moss "leaped to their feet and objected."[68] The defense attorneys argued that Gustafson's actions were irrelevant unless they were undertaken with "evil or corrupt purposes." The jury was dismissed, and two hours of lawyerly bickering ensued, at the end of which Cole ruled in the defense's favor.[69] "That the case will resolve itself into one of the greatest legal battles ever heard in the southwest has already become apparent," the *Tribune* said. "Attorneys for the defense took every opportunity to raise technical points throughout the morning session and argued each one at great length."[70]

More significantly, Gustafson's trial was the first public airing of many of the most shocking details of the riot. This was especially true of those involving the police. Most of the testimony, no doubt, had been told the grand jury, and whispered around town, but in Judge Cole's hot, stuffy courtroom it emerged into the open and was inscribed into the public record.

James's testimony set the tone for the state's case against Gustafson on the riot charge. Cole's ruling that the state must prove willful intent to remove the police chief from office does not seem to have altered Freeling's strategy or tactics. After James, Feeling summoned two more witnesses intended to reinforce his theme that Gustafson could have defused the riot by confronting the African American men at the courthouse.[71] The next witness, though, expanded the scope of Freeling's inquiry. John Oliphant, the former police commissioner, recounted not only Dr. Jackson's cold-blooded murder but the impunity with which whites burned and looted the more affluent black residences on the morning of June 1.[72]

Then came the bombshell.

"Judge Oliphant startled the courtroom into amazement," the *World* said, "when he testified that four men, one of whom he knew to be a policeman, named Brown, and the other three of whom were wearing stars, were the leaders of the firing squad which burned the best negro residential district. 'Cowboy Long,' notorious bootlegger, was also a member of the band, he said." Again and again, Oliphant testified, he requested assistance from the police and the National Guard, but no help ever came.[73]

Barney Cleaver gave the day's final testimony, a summary of his attempts to convince the black men at the courthouse that Dick Rowland was in no danger.[74]

Bill McCullough picked up the thread the next morning. Still in Freeling's sights himself, the sheriff described in detail the steps he had taken to protect Dick Rowland. He had received several telephone calls from black leaders during the evening, McCullough said, and each time he had assured them there was no chance of a lynching. "It would have been impossible for the mob to have taken the prisoner from the county jail," McCullough told the court. "We had a barricade in the jail and we could have shot members of any mob as fast as they came in sight.[75] "The only entrance to the jail was by means of a narrow stairway up which only one man at a time could go," McCullough said. "And at the top was a steel door leading into the jail. One man could have stood at the top and kept down an army, and I had several men up there."[76]

But McCullough had not been sufficiently convincing. African Americans kept coming to the courthouse, and each time they did the crowd of whites had grown larger. McCullough, a lawyer named C. B. Rogers, and former police detective Pete Joyce were on Boulder Avenue, on the west side of the courthouse, talking to a carload of black men when the shooting began. After first taking cover in the entry of the nearby Cadillac Hotel, McCullough crossed back into the courthouse and ascended to the jail.[77]

It was then that McCullough uttered the statement that would haunt him the rest of his long life. He had spent the night in the jail, he said, unaware of all that was going on around him. Even after talking to Gustafson and Adkison at 1:30 A.M., McCullough said, he did not understand the severity of the situation. "Sheriff Slept through Tulsa Riot" announced a banner headline in the next morning's *World*. "Admits Offering No Assistance to Chief of Police," read the subhead. The story, though, does not actually say that McCullough slept through the riot, only that he had been of "practically no assistance." Still defending Gustafson and the

Evans administration, the newspaper pointed out that the sheriff had made no more of an effort to disarm the black men at the courthouse than Gustafson.[78]

A number of other witnesses, including the wounded volunteer Ed Wheeler (sometimes identified as D. L. Wheeler), testified to the riot's general mayhem. A white man named Horrigan (or Harrigan, in some accounts) said shots were fired into his business near the east edge of the black district and that he and another man did their best to save the homes in their vicinity. Horrigan said he saw Commissioner Steiner and two officers, who promised assistance, but none arrived. A white man named W. C. Kelly said he was sitting in the lobby of the Hotel Tulsa when two groups of black men went by between 9:30 and 10:00 P.M. on the evening of May 31. Former chief deputy U.S. marshal Harry Blake said that Gustafson lost control of the police and that for a while on the night of May 31 a vaudeville performer named Murphy was giving orders outside the police station.[79]

The black deputy sheriff V. B. Bostick related his story of a man in a traffic officer's uniform leading an arson squad that set fire to Bostick's house. O. W. Gurley's account included the claim that the police department's black officers fled to the countryside during the riot, a charge that may partially explain Freeling's demand for their badges a few weeks earlier.[80]

Also testifying were J. W. Magee, the owner of the ransacked sporting goods store, who said his establishment was stripped not only of guns and ammunition but also of fishing tackle and just about everything else; J. W. Hickok, who lived across the street from the courthouse; and the private detective H. H. Townsend, who on cross-examination denied having had an interest in the police chief's job, then or ever.[81]

A white man named Fred Cook testified that he saw Wheeler shot and chased the gunman. Another white man, named Gibson, claimed that several whites set fire to a black barbershop while police watched.[82] Ira Gibbons, a respected early Tulsan, shocked the spectators with his testimony that a special deputy arrested him as a "negro sympathizer" when he badgered law officers on the scene to stop the looting and arson on the morning of June 1.[83]

The most titillating—and ultimately immaterial—testimony came from C. O. McInturff, a former police officer working for the Frisco Railroad. McInturff claimed to have observed a man wearing a star enter a black residence, change into a suit of clothes he found in the residence, and leave with twelve silk shirts and a second suit. He said the house was then set on fire by putting a mattress in a closet and lighting it. How McInturff managed to see all of this without going into the house himself was not addressed, but cross-examination revealed that

McInturff had been fired from the force after Bay Ward and officer Doc Bissett caught him "in a rooming house with a girl." McInturff implied that the young woman either worked for or was involved with one or both of the two officers. "Riotous laughter followed," said the *World*'s report, "and even after minutes of pounding his gavel Judge Cole was unable to suppress many giggles."[84]

A few days later, Meacham, Bissett, and an officer named Zimmerman were riding in an automobile when they spotted McInturff walking along the street. A confrontation ensued, with McInturff pulling a knife and he and Meacham both winding up in jail for disturbing the peace.[85]

Friday, July 15, began with the brickmason Laurel Buck testifying to the police's ineffectiveness and in some cases complicity in the riot. Under Van Leuven's direct examination, Buck related the now-infamous "get a gun and get a nigger" instructions from someone at the police station, and the apparent police involvement in the burning of buildings along North Cincinnati Avenue. Laurel Buck's father, I. J. Buck, followed. The elder Buck said he watched a building he owned burn and related his encounter with the officer who told him, "You ain't got no business building buildings for negroes to live in."[86]

The state then called Louis Hoffman, a white man who owned a grocery store in the black district, and Henry Sowders, the white projectionist at the Dreamland Theater. Hoffman told a story similar to I. J. Buck's, while Sowders (identified as "Souther" in some accounts) described the scene inside Greenwood minutes before the shooting started. They were followed in quick succession by a white former policeman named W. M. Wilson, Charles Daley, a white man named Charles Hahn and the black health inspector C. F. Gabe, who was the state's final witness on the riot-related charge against Gustafson.[87]

The chief's attorneys then moved to dismiss the count, arguing that none of the testimony indicated criminal or malicious intent on Gustafson's part.[88] And they correctly pointed out that none of the witnesses could or would identify the law officers they said engaged in looting and burning Greenwood. Laurel Buck, especially, was pressed on this matter, but when challenged by the defense, said he doubted he could pick out the officers he encountered at the police station or saw setting fire to buildings.[89] This, ultimately, was an important aspect of the trial. Without witnesses willing or able to name names, the prosecution began and ended with Gustafson; Freeling, for all of his bluster, might not have wanted it to go further.

Judge Cole denied the defense motion. The dereliction of duty charge related to the riot stayed in, and the trial proceeded to the car theft ring that allegedly included Gustafson. This portion of the trial began late on July 15, a Friday, with the state presenting witnesses through Saturday morning and the following Monday with complaints about the TPD auto theft detail. Bixby police chief W. E. Pinion said that Bay Ward had instructed him to cut the serial number of a stolen vehicle into the engine block of another automobile and turn it over to the owner of the first car. Others established suspicious links among Ward, his suspect son, Meacham, and others on both sides of the law[90]—although, as an aside, the most striking feature of this testimony for the modern reader is the frequency with which automobiles seem to have been stolen and resold in this era.

Witnesses continued to portray Gustafson and his department unfavorably, but their testimony did not directly bear on the riot. Then, late on July 18, Goldsberry unexpectedly concluded the state's case by dropping the two remaining charges, which alleged failure to control bootlegging and bawdy houses.[91]

> The dismissal came like a bolt out of a clear sky. The big crowd was astounded, the listening attorneys were puzzled and even the counsel for the defense was surprised. Many had looked on the vice counts, backed by the mass of testimony gathered by Assistant Attorney General VanLeuven [sic] prior to the grand jury investigation to afford the prosecution its strongest fighting points.
>
> Assistant Attorney General John Goldsberry, who served notice of the action on the court, offered no explanation. It was said later that proof on these counts would have caused the trial to drag on for several weeks and the state considered it had already made its case against the chief sufficiently strong.[92]

So that was it. After fulminating for months, if not years, about cleaning up Tulsa, Freeling walked away from the two counts that could have exposed the workings of bootlegging, prostitution, and police corruption in the Oil Capital. And one cannot help but wonder why. No doubt, talking about stamping out liquor and prostitution was one thing, but turning over the necessary rocks proved to be something else entirely. It is possible that some important people did not really want what was underneath exposed. Money may have been a factor, too. The courts, county attorney, and the attorney general all struggled to make ends meet on limited budgets. The Sperry bank robbery trials, the attorney general's investigation, and proceedings stemming from the riot had already soaked up an inordinate share of the available resources.[93] Perhaps, as the *Tribune* suggested, Freeling believed he had enough to force out Gustafson, which seemed to be his first priority, and decided to move on.

Adkison was the first defense witness. In great detail, he described the organization of the police department and his activities on the afternoon and evening of May 31. He recounted the anonymous call threatening Rowland's life; unasked, apparently, was why anyone who intended to carry out such a threat would alert the police to it. McCullough had been advised to take Rowland out of town, Adkison said, and declined the services of the entire police department. Adkison disputed the assertion that the police did little to deter armed blacks, claiming that he and Officer Pack turned back seventy such men who reached Third Street and Boulder Avenue just before the shooting began; the whites at the courthouse, Adkison said, were mere "spectators" who appeared to be unarmed and posed no real danger. Adkison said that he tried to get the names and addresses of the special officers he commissioned, but eventually gave up. Altogether, he said, about four hundred men were deputized.[94] "It was originally intended to throw a guard line around the colored district, but this plan had to be abandoned as impossible," Adkison said.[95]

Leahy began direct examination of Gustafson the next morning, June 19. The chief maintained that he and his men tried to intercept as many armed black men as possible, but the police response was hampered by it being the last day of the month, when officers switched day and night shifts. Gustafson explained that he and Captain George Blaine disarmed one isolated man at the courthouse without much difficulty, but the two lawmen deemed such a confrontation with the larger group too risky to attempt.[96]

Mr. Blaine and I discussed it for a moment and decided it would be practically suicide to start a fight in this crowd on account of the people, especially the women and children[.] It would have been an impossibility to have prevented a fight without shooting and for that reason we decided the only thing to do, if possible, was to get the negroes out peaceably, if we could, and away from the business section of the city.

For the next few minutes I pleaded with negroes and whites alike to leave here and prevent trouble. . . . Mr. Blaine . . . was doing the same thing in that respect.

My judgment would be that there were at least fifteen hundred or two thousand people. The streets were crowded, the streets were lined with automobiles, with men, women and children. The sidewalks were crowded, the streets were crowded.[97]

Blaine, described as a reluctant witness, followed Gustafson to the stand and largely corroborated the chief's testimony. C. M. Anderson, a former cop who headed the Cosden refinery security force; Major Kirkpatrick of the National Guard; and Chief of Detectives J. W. Patton presented testimony so unremarkable that empty seats appeared in the spectator section for the first time since the trial began. A silent groan must have gone around the room when the flamboyant Moss announced that he had no alternative but to call all eighty-four members of the police department to refute state testimony that unidentified officers had participated in the burning and looting of Greenwood—and perhaps in the murder of Doctor Jackson—on Gustafson's orders.[98]

Such a parade of witnesses might have produced a great many answers about the race riot. Or it might not. The only questions Moss and Leahy intended to ask each officer were whether he killed Jackson and whether he participated in the depredations on black homes and businesses. Moss called a few officers who answered in the negative, after which the state stipulated that all other officers would be asked the same questions and give the same answers.[99]

Almost everyone was ready for the trial to be over. "Throughout yesterday [July 21] afternoon the proceedings ground listlessly on," the Tribune reported. "The trial had lasted too long for the excessively hot weather. The jury seemed tired, the attorneys peevish at times and the court almost worn out by the labors in both the Devereux and Gustafson cases. Even the spectators looked fagged and there was a sigh of relief when the case came to an abrupt close."[100]

Some additional relevant testimony was given before the trial went to the jury. Detective Ike Wilkerson and Sergeant Claude Brice related their encounter with Deputy John Smitherman, and Officer J. L. Wilson said that he stepped off a streetcar into about 250 armed blacks late on the night of May 31, only to be rescued by a black preacher. Other defense witnesses with testimony bearing on the riot included Lieutenant Colonel Rooney; Officer D. B. Mondler, who accompanied Gustafson and Blaine to the courthouse; oilman R. H. Whitney; automobile dealer R. E. Sipes (or Siepe), who witnessed E. S. MacQueen's disastrous attempt to disarm a black man at the courthouse; and the suspended officer Ward.[101]

Defense testimony related to the riot ended late in the afternoon of Wednesday, July 20.[102] Testimony on the other remaining charge, that Gustafson was part of a conspiracy to defraud automobile owners and insurers, continued through Thursday.[103]

On Friday, July 22, Kathryn Van Leuven became the first woman to address a jury in a Tulsa courtroom. With Freeling absent, Van Leuven and Goldsberry summarized the state's case, emphasizing Gustafson's alleged involvement in the auto theft conspiracy. Then, turning to the riot count, Van Leuven said that the state "never contended that any law was violated after that trouble at the courthouse. After those armed negroes started shooting and killed a white man—then those who armed themselves for the obvious purpose of protecting their lives and property violated no law. The chief neglected to do his duty and the citizens after seeing their police fail took matters into their own hands. No, we don't contend they violated the law."[104]

Moss and Leahy argued that the state had produced no evidence that Gustafson was willfully derelict in his duty or had engaged in criminal activity. The jury deliberated six hours before returning verdicts of guilty on both counts. The vote was unanimous on the riot charge, 10–2 on the conspiracy count.[105]

Gustafson's was not the only trial of interest that July. In Chicago, eight members of the 1919 Chicago White Sox defended themselves against charges that they had fixed that year's World Series; they would be acquitted on August 2 but banned from baseball for life.[106] In Cleveland, the spectacularly unstable Eva Kaber was found guilty of arranging the murder of her wealthy husband in a bizarre plot involving spiritualists, potions, and a shadowy knife-wielding assassin.[107]

In Washington, a congressional committee investigating the escape of celebrated draft evader Grover Cleveland Bergdoll was disrupted when Representative Johnson of Kentucky tried to crawl across a table to get at Bergdoll's brother after each had called the other a liar.[108]

In Tulsa, there was a growing concern about typhoid. City health superintendent L. C. Presson told the *Tribune* on July 6 that he feared an outbreak because of conditions at the city dump located less than a mile northwest of downtown. Specifically, he was concerned about the large number of dead animals, especially horses, piling up, which he blamed on the lack of an incinerator or other resources to dispose of the carcasses.[109]

The next day, July 7, Barney Meyers of the Reconstruction Committee told the city commission that 150 to 200 black families were living in tents without access to sanitary facilities and drawing water from a single nearby well in danger of contamination. An epidemic, he said, was "likely to break out at any time." Then, wittingly or unwittingly, Meyers really got the committee's attention.[110]

"These negro women go into the homes of white people here," he said, "and if an epidemic did break out it probably would spread to the whites."[111]

The outbreak did reach "important proportions" in white neighborhoods over the next few weeks, but officials blamed careless handling of household garbage, not African American domestics, many of whom had been vaccinated by the Red Cross.[112]

On July 14, African American attorney and property owner G. W. Hutchins filed suit against the city and the National Fire Insurance Company of Hartford, Connecticut, seeking $3,500 for the loss of his home at 413 North Elgin and his office at 212 East Archer.[113] Appeals by local insurance agents and, apparently, the Reconstruction Committee to pay claims regardless of riot clauses do not seem to have had much effect, judging from the number of lawsuits like Hutchins's filed over the next two years.[114]

Meanwhile, the Reconstruction Committee's dogged commitment to removing the black district continued to encounter passive resistance, or maybe just disinterest. Several civic clubs adopted resolutions favoring a union railroad depot, but did not always specify a location.[115] On July 14, the committee acknowledged that a number of residences meeting the new code requirements had been built in the target area, and others were planned.[116] A few days later, with the Gustafson trial dominating the front pages, representatives of the chamber of commerce, Retail Merchants Association, and Ad Club asked the city commission to rescind the new building restrictions altogether. The economic recession, they said, made financing unlikely for the proposed union depot and industrial district; furthermore, they contended, the situation was unfair to black Tulsans and bad publicity for the city.[117] "We not only have not helped the negroes much, we have prevented them from helping themselves," said the chamber's Frank White.[118]

White and E. S. Hutchison claimed that African Americans were refusing to work and were saying that "the white people burned up our homes and now they can take care of us." Allowing black property owners to rebuild, White and Hutchison argued, would ease resentment and save white Tulsa continuing embarrassment.[119] "Everyone knows that a negro who has lost all his property in a fire cannot secure funds to build a brick building now," said White. "It is being said all over the country that the white people have with premeditation started the fire so they could put the negroes out of possession of their own section. If we allow them to build such homes as they can afford, we will cut the props out from under that malicious and false story."[120]

The city commission, however, would not budge. Instead, it asked Evans to meet with the Reconstruction Committee on the matter. Buck Lewis, the committee chairman, promptly called a public hearing in an effort to rally support for the removal plan.[121] The chamber of commerce proposal, Lewis said in announcing the hearing, would be "an invitation to take a backward step for Tulsa." Insisting that he had no personal interest in "any one plan," Lewis said that "it would be a great failure to let this low ground near the railroads be built up again with shacks and shanties. It only invites conflagration, one of which might prove disastrous to the business section." Cheaper, wood-frame homes, he said, were already being built in additions north and east of the fire zone, with plans for city waterlines and paved streets.[122]

On July 21, as Gustafson's trial rumbled noisily toward a conclusion, the Reconstruction Committee marched out a parade of prominent white citizens urging it to hold firm to the removal policy. Speakers included Mayor Evans, Colonel Rooney, W. O. Buck, Tate Brady, Buck Lewis, and Lilah Lindsey, a pioneer Tulsan and perhaps the most respected woman in town. Committee secretary Fred Kitchen, hinting at a new tactic to minimize objections to removal, announced that his analysis of the burned district found only 82 of 338 affected property owners were black and that whites probably owned a majority of the square footage.[123] How Kitchen came up with this figure is unclear, but it is possible that he counted mortgage holders, not those taking out the loans, as the property owners. In any event, there was enough opposition to Kitchen's claim that several weeks later it nearly led to fisticuffs between Boston Avenue Methodist Church's assistant pastor, C. J. Allen, and committee member E. E. Short, who was also the city treasurer.[124]

Brady and Lewis were particularly adamant, both in defending their plan for the burned district and in denying direct financial interest in the scheme. Both said that they had divested themselves of ownership in the district long before the riot. Lewis banged his fist on a table and offered one thousand dollars to anyone who could show otherwise.[125] "I understand a rumor has been circulated that I own much property there, and I want to say that anyone that says I do is a malicious coward," the agitated Lewis proclaimed.[126]

Apparently, no one accepted Lewis's challenge, but that does not resolve the issue of whether he expected to benefit, either directly or indirectly, from removal. Almost certainly Brady did, if for no other reason than it would have been good for his fading hotel at Main and Archer. During the meeting, Brady went on at some length about the necessity of modernizing Tulsa's railroad facilities and appealed to the spirit that had changed Tulsa's trajectory in its early days.

> When similar fire limits have been extended into white districts in the past, they have conformed to them without quibbling. There are some who appear to believe the committee should have erected a $3,000,000 union station and half a dozen large wholesale warehouses in the burned area by this time. We hope to have them, but these things are not obtainable at will. If everyone will stand up now like the Tulsans did who lifted Tulsa from the cowpath village it once was, we may have the city here we expect.
>
> I am most emphatically not with those who would turn back at this stage. If you want to see what is going on in the negro section, go out and look for yourself. This thing is solving itself. Probably a hundred houses have already been erected out there. To turn back now would hold Tulsa back for 25 years. We must get factories here and develop Tulsa's trade territory, and that is the logical place for them to locate. If the chamber of commerce won't move out and help Tulsa get its share of this trade that is rightfully hers, I want to say I will lend my humble efforts toward organizing a bunch that will.[127]

At this same meeting, Oklahoma City businessman George Gardner recommended the creation of a holding company that would acquire the entire burned district either through purchase or condemnation. The western half of the district, he said, should be converted to warehouses while the eastern half would be occupied by an "incubator"—a large building owned by its tenants through a stock issue.[128] The committee—and the *Tribune*—remained quite enthusiastic,[129] but the *World* was not. On July 22, it editorialized in support of the chamber of commerce proposal.

> In asking the city commission to repeal the ordinance extending the fire limits over the burned negro district and recommending to the reconstruction committee that it abandon all plans for converting that district into an industrial section, the chamber of commerce directors evince a grasp of the situation that is refreshing. Also they correctly interpret public opinion.
>
> Every practical consideration calls for such action. Neither the industrial section idea or the union depot project is practical at this time.[130]

The reasons for this impracticality, the editorial says somewhat mysteriously, "are recognized and therefore need not be enlarged upon." The efforts in question, while made in "good faith," had been "misunderstood" and "misrepresented abroad."[131]

"The reconstruction committee will find," the editorial went on, "that by turning its attention to aiding, morally at least, those who not only desire to rebuild but who needs must rebuild before the winter comes on, and allowing times and natural, orderly tendencies to take their course, that which appears to be a great problem will gradually disappear."[132] Of particular note here is the editorial's assertion that "public opinion"—and by this it meant white public opinion, and even more narrowly the opinion of whites with money and influence—did not support the removal scheme. This, again, is different than actually opposing it, but under the circumstances ultimately produced the same effect.

The mention of "well-known" but unstated reasons the enterprise was deemed impractical is intriguing. Perhaps it is another reference to general financial conditions. A month earlier, local banks had to move aggressively to tamp down rumors that at least some were overextended in the shrinking postwar economy, and in danger of failure.[133] Such rumors, when the Federal Reserve was in its infancy and federal deposit insurance and other safeguards did not yet exist, could trigger bank runs and panic. In this case, perhaps there was more to the rumors than anyone cared to let on.

The Real Estate Exchange, which had initially carried the ball on the removal effort, formally retired to the sideline on July 28. E. S. Hutchison, speaking for the chamber of commerce, said that the city would be responsible for feeding, clothing, and housing the city's black population unless it was allowed to begin rebuilding immediately. The exchange's president, Merritt Glass, argued otherwise, but the motion to end support for removal passed on a voice vote. Newspaper reports of the meeting were suspiciously sparse. That, coupled with the *Tribune*'s statement that "many members of the exchange . . . expressed their views," suggests the possibility of a heated exchange.[134]

Still, the Reconstruction Committee refused to budge. Meeting a short time after the Real Estate Exchange, it reaffirmed its commitment to enforcing the new building code, which at least some members seemed to think would root out undesirable elements of the old Greenwood. A white woman named Eunice Davis told the committee, "I would like to remind the negroes that members of their own race started this dreadful thing. . . . Reports are rife that a lawsuit against the city of Tulsa is the only means of securing justice. This is dangerous ground—but I do not believe we are in a humor to be bluffed."[135]

Davis shared the widespread notion among whites that the old Greenwood harbored crime and disease because African Americans wanted it that way, or were too lazy or ignorant to do anything about it; in fact, black leaders had complained frequently about conditions in the more squalid streets of the district, and been ignored.[136] "My plan," Davis said, "would be to settle with the negro for his property honestly, and if he wants the assistance of a committee to select a lot and erect a neat home with sanitary surroundings he should be encouraged to co-operate with decent people in making his addition to Tulsa a place of respectability, a place to be proud of instead of a hiding place for corruption and a protection to the lowest of the low."[137]

John Gustafson's motion for a new trial was rejected the day after it was filed.[138] His lawyers promised an appeal to the state Supreme Court, but local attention had already shifted to the Creek County Courthouse a dozen miles away in the town of Sapulpa. There, the peripatetic Prince Freeling was prosecuting a bribery charge against district judge Lucien Wright, whose ruling in a complicated oil lease case involving Charles Page, $2 million, and a dead and perhaps fictitious infant Creek allottee with at least three mothers, had raised some very important hackles.[139]

Freeling continued for a while to make desultory noises about seeking McCullough's removal[140] but never pursued the matter. The corruption charges against Sand Springs police chief B. F. Waddell were dismissed on a technicality and he resigned.[141] Bay Ward and Roy Meacham resigned from the Tulsa force, thus avoiding trial. Ward, it was said, had gone to Mexico, where he was prospecting for gold.[142] Meacham stayed and, with Freeling's help, eventually returned to the police force.[143] Charles Daley left the police department at the end of July. The *Tribune* said he departed out of frustration; Daley himself said it was for a job with an automotive supply company.[144] In any event, without him, Evans and Adkison were more firmly in control of the department than ever before; the new chief, George Blaine, though much respected for his courage, made few personnel or operational changes.[145] *Tribune* publisher Richard Lloyd Jones, who rather enjoyed the image of crusading newspaperman, said he had received threatening anonymous calls that he attributed to friends of Gustafson and Adkison.[146] The *World* called the charges "grotesque" and said "our contemporary"—the *Tribune*—could not have been more damaging to the city if it had been "in the pay of certain lawless interests that have exerted a terrifying influence on municipal conditions since the first hour of statehood."[147] The implication here, despite their protests to the contrary, was that Jones and the *Tribune* were part of a Democratic machine whose control of state politics had been far more corrupt than anything the local Republican administration could be accused of.

Governor Robertson pressed the nearly forgotten Public Welfare Board, through Cyrus Avery, for the $12,700 that General Barrett said it cost to bring in the National Guard during and after the riot.[148] A total of 423 men were deployed, Barrett reported, from a few days to more than two weeks.[149] Robertson ultimately relented and arranged for the state to pick up the tab.[150]

In early May, the parents of a teenage boy claimed that he had been married to his pregnant girlfriend literally at gunpoint by the Reverend Harold Cooke, after being kidnapped by the Ku Klux Klan and driven to secluded woods southwest of the city. Cooke, too, said had been kidnapped by masked men—he did not identify them as Klansmen—but the newspaper accounts seem to imply that Cooke was suspected of instigating the bizarre incident.[151]

Two months later, men in masks took a white waiter from the Muskogee restaurant where he worked and beat him until he confessed to involvement in the kidnapping of a teenage boy, who, it later turned out, had simply left town on a lark.[152] "The Ku Klux Klan apparently has reached Muskogee in its spread northward," the *Tribune*'s Stivers observed. Oklahoma City's crusading mayor, the Socialist sympathizer J. C. Walton, ordered an investigation of local "night riders."[153] A Ku Klux Klan organizer was reported in Bartlesville, fifty miles north of Tulsa.[154] One hundred miles to the west, at Enid, masked vigilantes flogged a white man accused of beating his wife.[155] With some wonder, the *World* reported on July 29 that "Muskogee Klan No. 3" had laid aside its tar and feathers to contribute fifty dollars to a day nursery's milk fund.[156]

Two weeks later, about 2,500 people—mostly men—turned out on a steamy Thursday night to hear the Reverend Caleb Ridley, a leader in the national Ku Klux Klan organization. The Klan's noble cause, he said, had in many cases been besmirched by the "deviltry" of "cowardly sneaks" in the guise of Knights of the Invisible Empire. The Klan, he allowed, could be tough, but only when necessary to preserve a white, Protestant, native-born America.[157] "The Catholics say [the Klan] is anti-Catholic—and it is. But we put it the other way. The Catholics are anti-Ku Klux Klan. . . . We are not against the negroes, though we don't admit them to membership. We draw no color line in protecting innocent and persecuted people against their aggressors. But we stand ready to stop trouble if some elements of the black folks start it." In particular, Ridley mentioned W. E. B. DuBois as the sort of "black folk" the Klan did not approve of. "The Klansmen," Ridley said, "will never surrender this white civilization . . . until every one of them is dead."[158]

Sixty-five "frame houses or shacks," in addition to several brick buildings, had been erected or were under construction by the end of the first week of

August. J. H. Goodwin, Vernon AME Church, the white businessman William Redfearn, and apparently others had obtained building permits, but most had not. Black property owners said they were being encouraged to build by white friends and employers, some of whom were lending them the money to do it.[159] Building inspector H. E. Kopp told the city commission that most of the work was being done at night and early in the morning, outside his department's normal working hours. Kopp suggested that police enforce the building ban, but that does not seem to have happened.[160]

For some time, blacks and whites had grumbled about selective enforcement of the ban. On July 26, a black minister and "medical research scientist" named Dearman complained to the Reconstruction Committee that C. F. Gabe and other favored African Americans were being given preferential treatment. "The negroes are all dissatisfied with the way things are going," Dearman said. "C. F. Gabe and other negroes specially favored by the city have been allowed to put up buildings in the burned district. It looks like partiality to us and what we want is for everybody to be treated alike."[161]

Dearman said that lawyers from as far away as Chicago were ready to sue the city on behalf of 1,500 black property owners. Dearman maintained that he had "been advised by the presidents of two banks that our claims are just and that we can recover from the city." He recommended the formation of a corporation by businessmen to settle the blacks' $4 million in claims stemming from the riot. The corporation, Dearman said, could then file a "friendly lawsuit" against the city to recover its original outlay. "We are not going to sell our property for an industrial section or any other purpose until settlement for our losses is made," said Dearman.[162]

Questioned by the *Tribune* on August 6, Gabe readily confirmed that Adkison had told him to resume work on what was described as a "long frame building with 16 rooms"—apparently an apartment building—after inspectors ordered him to stop. O. W. Gurley said that Mayor Evans had given similar verbal permission to a man named P. W. Ross, whose house at 511 North Elgin Avenue was already completed. Redfearn's new five-story Red Wing Hotel on Greenwood was nearly so. And the *Tribune* reported that it had no trouble finding other dwelling places—some permanent, some temporary—going up in plain sight of the police. Gabe and Gurley told the *Tribune* that more and more black property owners had decided to force the issue because of the Reconstruction Committee's inaction.[163]

"They better get the jail ready for us 'cause we're sure enough goin' to keep buildin'," Gabe told the *Tribune* good-naturedly.

What Gabe said was repeated by several other leading negroes who are rebuilding houses on their property. His plea was something along this line: We own this land, which we bought and paid for and built our homes on. We don't expect to get our losses paid for, but we want a chance to live. We feel the white people of the city will be fair with us if they only understand the situation. It isn't much of a place to build a home now, with the ruins all around here and no water or sewers fixed, but it's all we have and we don't want to part with it.[164]

Gurley was even more emphatic: "There is not much behind this talk about giving us better prices for our land as factory sites—not one offer has been made through the Reconstruction Committee to really buy. So we are building frame shacks on the rear of many lots to live through the winter in. The sentiment is to go ahead and build, regardless of the restrictions, and take a case through to the supreme court if we are prevented."[165]

White property owners were also becoming impatient. Twenty-five of them, including Redfearn and City Commissioner C. S. Younkman, met on August 1.[166] They met again a week later and agreed the city should be held responsible for their losses, and if not the city, the county or the state. According to the *Tribune*, white owners estimated their losses at $500,000;[167] this amounted to only one-tenth of the $5 million in claims black property owners had filed against the city,[168] and seems at odds with the Reconstruction Committee's assertion that more than half the affected property belonged to whites. It was also far more than the Real Estate Exchange's estimate of $1.5 million to $2 million,[169] which if nothing else illustrates the huge disparity between what the black property owners were being offered and what they were willing to accept.

The Reconstruction Committee, in exploring the possibility of leveraging anticipated damages against the city to finance the removal scheme, once again asked three attorneys to assess the city's potential liability. The three—City Attorney Frank Duncan, Buck Lewis's law partner W. D. Humphrey, and H. L. Browning of East St. Louis, Illinois—were perhaps not the most objective of arbiters, but even if statute and legal precedent had not been clear on the issue, opinions at variance from the earlier ones would have been surprising. As Browning put it, "specific negligence" would have to be shown for claimants to have a case. They would have to prove that city officials directed Greenwood's destruction. Apparently, the police chief's conviction—which, by definition, included willful misconduct—did not constitute that proof.[170]

The Reconstruction Committee demonstrated its continued resolve by asking the local school board to rebuild the burned Dunbar elementary school in the "new black district."[171] It was unmoved when a thunderstorm on the night of August 7 knocked down tents and displaced at least fifty women and children. Renewed warnings that up to four thousand black men, women, and children still had no permanent homes with winter drawing ever closer were similarly ignored.[172]

"We must never again allow the disgraceful shacktown that was burned to be rebuilt," Tate Brady said on August 13.[173] Brady was responding to a suit filed the previous day by Joe Lockard, a thirty-nine-year-old black man who, with his wife, had operated a diner at 316 E. Archer Street. Filed by local African American attorneys B. C. Franklin, P. A. Chappelle, and Ike Spears, the petition sought to overturn the city commission's extension of the fire code.[174] A separate but similar suit was filed on behalf of the Reverend R. A. Whitaker, pastor of Mount Zion Baptist Church. Both suits' primary argument was that the proposed ordinance was not properly published prior to the city commission's vote, but they also advanced other points in an effort to undermine the assertion that the code had been extended for health and safety reasons.[175]

The *World*, without mentioning the Lockard suit, called for repeal of the fire ordinance in an August 14 editorial. The ordinance had been "a mistake in the first instance," and its continued existence presented "the making of a very disagreeable situation." The article continued: "It is significant that practically all organizations more or less in sympathy with the plans for rehabilitation of the burned area have found it necessary, or at last compatible with their judgment, to reverse themselves. The union depot proposition is so utterly impracticable under existing conditions that it amounts to bunc; the industrial addition is even more absurd because of the impossibility of its realization."[176]

Brady held that the ordinance was not discriminatory because it applied equally throughout the city. Public health and well-being, he maintained, were the primary objectives, and he would fight to the "last ditch" to see the ordinance upheld. "There has never been an hour since the uprising that a negro could not get a permit to build in that district if he complied with the law. The extension of the fire limits in this district was simply made to comply with that of the white district across the tracks. . . . What we want is to insist on the negro district being built up in a respectable manner."[177]

Again, as Brady knew quite well, the problem was that few black families had the resources to rebuild according to the fire code. And, interestingly enough, the concerns cited by Brady and others for imposing the fire code on Greenwood apparently did not extend to the proposed resettlement addition.

Mayor Evans, in an attempt to prove popular support for the redevelopment project, solicited comment by mailing out one thousand letters with return postcards. A few days later he reported sentiment running five-to-one in favor of the proposal, but acknowledged that only about 20 percent of the cards had been returned. It was not clear whether any black Tulsans had been asked for their opinion.[178]

The three district judges, sitting en banc on August 25, ruled that the fire code ordinance had been passed improperly and granted the injunction sought by Reverend Whitaker. Their decision, though, effectively included only the blocks brought into the fire zone by the city commission's June vote. It did not help Lockard or any of the property owners along Archer or in the Greenwood business district. Those areas, the judges observed, had been covered by the fire code for several years and therefore were not affected by the new ordinance.[179]

The victory may have seemed a small and fleeting one. Maurice Willows estimated that only about half the homes burned in the riot could be replaced as a result of the injunction—and that was only if the injunction became permanent.[180] The court did not take up the case's broader issues, and the city commission had only to pass the ordinance again, this time with proper notification, to bring it into compliance. This the commission did as soon as possible, rejecting City Attorney Frank Duncan's recommendation to allow the construction of temporary housing. Evans said such housing "once erected, will be removed with difficulty."[181]

Duncan may have understood the situation more clearly than the commission or the Reconstruction Committee. The August 25 hearing had been a trial run for the fire code's opponents, a chance for them to make their case before all three district judges at once, to gauge the court's reaction, and to win another public relations battle. Another lawsuit, this one on behalf of twelve property owners, was filed as soon as the new ordinance passed, and this one would decide the matter once and for all.

White Tulsans had more on their minds than Greenwood. Workers' wages continued shrinking in the postwar recession.[182] Teens loitering about the streets were becoming such a nuisance that a nine-thirty curfew was imposed.[183] On consecutive nights near Red Fork, women shot and killed their abusive husbands.[184] Presson, the prickly health superintendent, ordered twenty water wells closed as health hazards and another thirty cleaned.[185] Sheriff's deputies raided Cowboy Long's roadhouse east of town on Federal Drive and confiscated one hundred pints of choc beer.[186] Dismayed Kiwanians were read a United Communist Party pamphlet urging white workers to rally to the aid of their black brothers fighting the oppression of capitalism in Tulsa.[187]

More troubling, the main roads between Tulsa and the surrounding towns had become infested with roving bands of holdup men who ambushed automobiles and made off with the occupants' belongings and occasionally the vehicles themselves. In one case, near Red Fork, the thieves apologized but said they were hungry and had not been able to find legitimate work. They relieved the occupants of eight dollars in cash and their car but promised to leave the latter where it could be easily found.[188] In Tulsa, two streetcars were held up within ten minutes of each other.[189]

The foul mood even permeated the sports world. On August 8, Western League umpires Will Guthrie and Ducky Holmes pleaded guilty to beating up a disabled veteran named Haines after a quarrelsome doubleheader at the local ballpark. Guthrie and Holmes, it seems, believed that Haines had been one of the spectators throwing pop bottles at them during the course of the afternoon.[190]

Perhaps most alarming to the general public, and certainly to homeowners outside the original Tulsa townsite, were the lawsuits filed in the wake of the Crosbie Heights decision of the previous April. That case clouded the titles of all ninety-eight additions to the city of Tulsa, comprising more than 4,600 acres, and prompted legal challenges to the ownership of three of them in addition to Crosbie Heights. One of the suits was brought by Rachel Perryman, widow of the esteemed George Perryman and a matriarch of early Tulsa.[191] The suits all claimed that the land had not been properly transferred from the original Creek or freedman allottees to the white developers.[192] True or not, such charges would not have been too surprising, given the complex restrictions on the sale of the allotments and the regularity with which they were circumvented. Equally unsurprising would have been a scam cooked up by unscrupulous attorneys.

"Citizens in Arms against Shysters" read the headline bannered across the August 24 *World*; the accompanying story described a meeting of five hundred howling property owners at Convention Hall, demanding disbarment of the attorneys bringing the lawsuits and congressional intervention.[193] If any of these white property owners recognized any irony or parallels in their situation and that of their African American neighbors, they kept it to themselves.

For Evans and the city commission, Greenwood instantly became a side issue. As they saw it, the entire city was at stake, so much so that Adkison suggested using the remaining reconstruction money to hire attorneys for the affected homeowners.[194] And in the midst of all this, Steiner and Adkison, Evans's two closest allies on the commission, continued to cross swords with Mary Seaman, the implacable city auditor.

Seaman refused to reimburse Steiner's auto supply company for $1,128 worth of tires and parts bought by the city in what she declared a violation of state law. Seaman also questioned the $1,700 in fees paid to Adkison for writing city employees' surety bonds. The commission, in turn, had ordered the firing of Seaman's head bookkeeper. Evans at first said that it was because Keefe was a Democrat, then because he was a Catholic—which he was not. Seaman refused. The commission again ordered Keefe to be fired, this time because, in Evans's words, he was "a meddler and mischief maker." The *Tribune*, always critical of Evans, suggested that the real reason may have been that the mayor suspected Keefe of feeding information to the attorney general. Frustrated, Evans said that Seaman was nothing more than a "clerk" and suggested that the commission could "fire" her, too, even though she was an elected official. Ultimately, Seaman agreed to terminate Keefe on September 1,[195] and the commission went back to fussing with Maurice Willows and A. L. Farmer of the Red Cross.

The Red Cross had spent about $52,000 on its relief activities by mid-August, and Willows complained that the city and the Reconstruction Committee were unresponsive to his requests for payment. Farmer said the Red Cross would pull out altogether if the situation was not resolved. But Kitchen, who had been put on the city payroll at $250 a month while acting as the Reconstruction Committee secretary, replied that all vendors had been paid. Farmer agreed that they had, but by the Red Cross. Petulantly, Evans and Kitchen countered that Willows had not made it clear he was asking for reimbursement. This back and forth went on for several days before the city commission relented and agreed to reimburse the relief agency $11,000.[196]

The stories laid out in single columns on the *Tribune*'s September 1 front page included one reporting the initiation of three hundred Ku Klux Klan members in the Osage Hills northwest of Tulsa, and another about what was described as a final, definitive lawsuit on the fire code extension.

The first story claimed that a *Tribune* reporter was one of 1,500 to witness the first initiation of Tulsa Klansmen;[197] the *World*, perhaps put out at being scooped, grumpily asserted the next morning that the ceremony involved only thirty initiates and three hundred spectators, and that previous initiations had taken place in Convention Hall.[198] Either way, the news was ominous.

The other *Tribune* story's tortured lead informed readers, "The question of whether or not the city has the legal right to pass a fire ordinance for the express purpose of preventing negroes rebuilding frame shacks in the burned area" was being "settled for all time" by the three district judges, once again sitting en banc, in a case brought by a dozen black property owners.[199]

Neither newspaper had mentioned the lawsuit until the hearing before the three judges was already underway on September 1. The suit specifically challenged the second fire code extension, passed only a few days before, so maybe the newspapers were caught off guard or were preoccupied with the title challenges to the white residential additions. It may be deduced that Duncan, at least, knew what was coming, because of his recommendation to the city commission to allow temporary housing in Greenwood. In any event, the general public did not know about the suit until arguments were well underway.

Tradition credits Franklin, Spears, and Chappelle with the case, and no doubt they did the bulk of the work. Certainly they did in the two earlier lawsuits.[200] Mather Eakes, though, was the attorney of record in this suit,[201] and this may have been a key point. The judges' decision to hear the case together, to present a unified front, suggests that they were under considerable pressure to rule in favor of the city and against the black plaintiffs. A white attorney arguing the case, instead of one of the three African American lawyers, surely made it easier for them to decide for the plaintiffs. Perhaps in the end it did not matter, but it certainly did not hurt.

Eakes maintained the fire code extension was unconstitutional because the intent was to prevent the rebuilding of the burned area and, ultimately, force owners to sell.[202] "We are raising the question in this case," Eakes explained, "that this ordinance is a direct attempt to take property without due process of law, and therefore violates the constitution of the United States and also the constitution of Oklahoma, which provides that property cannot be taken for private purposes, either with or without compensation, without the consent of the owner."[203]

Eakes accused the city of acting in bad faith in passing the fire code ordinance, and produced Mary Seaman as his star witness. Over what the *World* described as Duncan's vigorous objections, Seaman testified regarding a June 7 city commission meeting at which the Real Estate Exchange's proposal and the potential impact of extending the fire code were discussed. Several black people also testified about conditions in the burned zone. The hearing dragged well into the night, with the city's defense resting chiefly on the testimony of the state and local fire marshals. Finally, at 10:00 P.M., Judge W. B. Williams read the unanimous opinion. The ordinance was illegal.[204]

The fight for Greenwood was over.

THE YEARS SINCE

The next morning, Commissioner Adkison ordered city inspector H. E. Kopp to ignore the court's decision and reject building permit applications for the burned district. "Let them mandamus us," Adkison said. "If the district court is going to run this city, I'm in favor of making them do it legally."[1] Kopp seems to have ignored the outburst, either by his own judgment or on the advice of cooler heads. And, indeed, further resistance seemed futile. The *Tribune* reported on September 2 that seventy-five houses had been completed in the burned district. So, after initially filing a notice of appeal, the city dropped the case, and the rebuilding of Greenwood began in earnest.[2] Evans kept the Reconstruction Committee together for a while but admitted that it had little to do except push through a township road bond issue that would pave Lansing Avenue north from the city limits.[3]

Cool weather in late September and early October, the *Tribune* reported, found "Darkeytown . . . diggin' in." With the Red Cross and Tulsa businessmen supplying lumber and tents and the assistance of "white friends," the paper said, the old district had been "practically rebuilt." The reporter's definition of "rebuilt" may not have fit with the residents', however, for many of the "shacks" were in fact tents with wood floors and sidewalls. The description of these as "comfortable and . . . good shelters from rain and cold even in winter weather" seems more than a little presumptuous.[4] By implying that the district had been rebuilt entirely through the largesse of white benefactors, the *Tribune*'s account also ignored the resourcefulness of African Americans who applied their own money, materials, and labor to the task. The Mann family told Tim Madigan, several generations later, that the family was able to rebuild because its savings were deposited in a downtown bank.[5] Many people in those days did not trust banks and kept their cash and other valuables close at hand, hidden under mattresses, locked in safes, and buried in backyards. In the riot, many of those nest eggs were stolen or destroyed.

Although the fire code applied to new buildings in the section of Greenwood nearest the railroad tracks, that does not seem to have been a problem. By the end of September, numerous building permits had been issued to various individuals for projects, including C. G. Coggeshall, chairman of the white property owners group, 300 block of East Archer; R. J. Hill, 100 block of North Greenwood, two-story brick valued at $6,000; M. M. Dicks and J. C. Murphy, apartment building, 505 North Greenwood; American Supply office building, 511 East Brady; African Methodist Episcopal Church, 207 North Frankfort; Dr. R. T. Bridgewater, store and office, 330 North Greenwood; A. T. Wolf, residence, 503 North Elgin; William Walker, residence, 326 North Frankfort; and O. Morrow, residence, 528 North Elgin.[6] Joe Piro obtained a loan from his insurance company and rebuilt the rooming house at 511 East Archer that Dave and Alice Rowland had operated, though they did not return to that address.[7]

Also in September, it was reported that J. B. Stradford had sued his insurer from exile in Illinois, claiming the "danger of a Ku Klux Klan jury is too great" for the case to be tried in Oklahoma.[8] The Klan was indeed successful at rigging jury selection in many places; whether that included Tulsa at this time is unknown, but at the very least Stradford had plenty of reason for wariness. He was a fugitive as far as Oklahoma was concerned, charged as one of the chief instigators of a riot in which dozens of people died and millions in property damage had occurred.

Stradford's $65,000 suit ultimately failed.

One day after the big Klan gathering in the Osage Hills, a white man named J. E. Frazier was snatched off a Tulsa street shortly after being questioned and released by police in connection with the car thefts and hijackings afflicting the countryside. Wishing maximum coverage, the kidnappers notified both newspapers and even offered transportation to reporters. The *World* reporter was picked up by "a large car with the side curtains drawn," blindfolded, and driven to a place near the small town of Owasso, northeast of Tulsa. The *World* reporter recounted that "100 masked vigilantes, armed to the teeth," stripped Frazier to the waist, tied him to a tree, and "whipped him until he begged for mercy."[9] The *Tribune* told a similar story, except it put the number of masked men at twenty.[10] Neither newspaper explicitly identified the masked men as Klansmen, but the implication was clear.

The Tulsa Klan quickly grew larger and bolder. *Birth of a Nation*, re-released and frequently shown with direct or indirect Klan sponsorship, began a five-day, sold-out run at Convention Hall in late September.[11] In December, mourners at the graveside service of Harry Aurandt, Adkison's secretary, were startled by the appearance of a dozen Klansmen in full regalia, each of whom laid a rose on Aurandt's casket and filed silently away.[12]

Aurandt had died a hero from wounds suffered in a roadside shootout with four hoodlums. Bleeding and in pain, Aurandt managed to drive his seriously wounded companion, Chief Detective Ike Wilkerson, to a nearby house. Aurandt saved Wilkerson's life but took a turn for the worse and quickly died. Three of the lawmen's assailants were captured and taken to the Tulsa County jail; when rumors of a lynching reached Sheriff McCullough, he hastily smuggled the accused out of town rather than risk another second-guessing.[13]

Aurandt left behind a widow and three-year-old son,[14] who at fourteen went to work at Tulsa's first radio station; eventually, under the name Paul Harvey, the younger Aurandt became one of America's best-known radio personalities.[15]

By the following spring, the Tulsa Klan had grown in size and influence to such an extent that it was poised to seize control of local government. On April 1, just ahead of the city elections, some 1,700 robed and hooded members marched through downtown Tulsa while an airplane with a lighted cross fixed to the underside of its wings and fuselage flew overhead. Evans and McCullough tried to stop the demonstration but failed; McCullough insisted on walking at the head of the procession to discourage provocation.[16] Klan-backed candidates swept the city offices; all incumbents except Herman Newblock, who had remained quiet during the riot crisis, were turned out, including the plainspoken Mary Seaman.[17] Newblock, a confirmed Klansman,[18] won the first of his four two-year terms as mayor. How active Newblock was in the Klan is not clear; as mayor, he kept his distance from it but never denounced it, either. In 1924, the rabid Klansman G. S. Long—older brother of future Louisiana strongman Huey Long—challenged Newblock in the Democratic primary and lost badly.[19] An able administrator, Newblock presided over many improvements to the city—and what is probably the second-most notorious period in Tulsa's history.

In early August 1923, a suspected bootlegger named Nathan Hantaman was grabbed after being questioned by the police, in much the same manner as J. E. Frazier two years earlier and the union men in 1917. Also, as in those two cases,

Hantaman was driven into the country and severely beaten. Whereas those men had gone quietly away, however, Hantaman took his case to Governor J. C. Walton.[20]

J. C. "Jack" Walton, the crusading former Oklahoma City mayor, had been elected governor the previous November on an anti-Klan platform and when he heard about Hantaman's beating had him brought to the capital. A physical examination confirmed that Hantaman had been subjected to an unusually brutal attack, which he said lasted more than two hours. Furthermore, it had been administered only a few days after a Tulsa municipal judge complained about police mistreatment of prisoners appearing in his court. Already at war with the Klan, Walton declared martial law in Tulsa and eventually all of Tulsa County. Over the next six weeks, a series of military tribunals were held to investigate beatings carried out by the Klan with the aid and encouragement of local officials. By this time, McCullough and other county officers not friendly to the Klan had been replaced, leaving the group in complete control of city and county government. Little of the vigilantism uncovered was directed at African Americans; most singled out individuals judged guilty of drug or alcohol trafficking, immorality, or disloyalty. Hantaman, for instance, was nabbed not because he was Jewish, but because he sold illegal liquor and lived with a woman to whom he was not married.[21]

Walton was impeached and removed from office in November, after just ten months on the job. His effort to break the Klan's hold on Tulsa failed, but the group's influence nevertheless began to wane, and within a few years it disappeared as a political force.

The view of the world that created it, however, did not.

On the same day in September 1921 that *Birth of a Nation* opened at Convention Hall, charges against Dick Rowland were dropped. By this time, Tulsans seem to have been more concerned about film star Roscoe "Fatty" Arbuckle's pending murder trial in California than what happened to Dick Rowland. The dismissal rated only a brief mention in the *World*, which said the "white girl" involved had asked the county attorney by letter not to prosecute the case.[22]

Cases against six other African Americans charged with inciting and participating in the riot were continued during the same proceeding.[23] None seems to have ever come to trial. In late November, a white woman named Mrs. J. C. Eads—also known as Marie Riggins—went on trial for stealing a suit of clothes and four books from black businessman O. W. Williams.[24] The outcome is unknown.

White Tulsans and probably many blacks as well were content to let all or most of the riot-related criminal cases disappear into the judicial fog. Politics of the matter aside, district courts were clogged, and defendants and witnesses who wanted to disappear could do so easily. Forty-four murder cases were on the Tulsa County District Court docket that September.[25] Of the 485 cases assigned to Judge Cole, nearly half had to be dismissed or postponed because of missing witnesses and defendants. The court clerk put the value of forfeited bonds at no less than $225,000.[26]

One person neither in jail nor on the lam was Cowboy Long. On September 10, he and some ex-servicemen identified as his bodyguards barricaded themselves in Long's drug store on East Second Street. Long said he had received a threatening note signed "Vills," and while he did not take it too seriously, he was not taking any chances. Police, apparently suspecting a ruse to keep them away, raided the store two days later and arrested Long and an employee for possessing a quart of Jamaica ginger—a patent medicine with a high alcohol content—and twenty empty bottles they said smelled strongly of the stuff.[27] Given the city's thriving illegal drug and liquor trade, this raid on Long seems more like a rousting, especially since seven officers were deemed necessary to carry it out. Officials may not have been willing or able to bring Cowboy Long to justice for arson and possibly murder during the riot, but perhaps they were agreeable to running him out of town for being an all-around bad actor. In an October 3 letter to Freeling, county attorney Seaver refers to Long by saying, "I am starting up some business in that line 'ere long,"[28] In any event, the white man most likely to have been criminally prosecuted for his role in the Tulsa riot soon disappeared from the scene.

E. S. MacQueen, the would-be sheriff whose foolish attempt to forcibly disarm a black man at the courthouse resulted in the first shot of the riot, lost his job as a constable that September. Initially fired for drunkenness and malfeasance, MacQueen was later arrested for carrying a concealed weapon, on a complaint lodged by County Commissioner Ira Short.[29]

Whites and probably some blacks as well continued to blame lax enforcement of segregation for society's ills, including the riot. On the night of October 1, officers under the direction of the county attorney raided a choc joint—a dive that sold a homemade brew called Choctaw beer, or "choc"—at Pine and Greenwood and arrested nine whites and thirteen blacks "drinking and carousing together."[30] This illicit mingling of the races in northside clubs and dance halls would continue for decades, until changing mores and the end of segregation rendered it a moot issue.

The pettiness of the city commission's feud with the chamber of commerce reached its limit in September when the commission, at Evans's urging, refused to pay a seventeen-dollar printing bill incurred by the original Public Welfare Board.[31] The chamber accepted responsibility, and the two parties managed to put aside their differences long enough to sell voters on a $6.8 million bond issue for the Spavinaw water project. The reservoir and pipeline were essential to the city's long-term growth, but the bond issue's passage by a nearly four-to-one margin again demonstrated Tulsa's capacity to raise money—when it wanted to.[32]

In 1922, a corporate front for the Tulsa Klan called the Benevolent Association built a meeting hall at 501 North Main Street, a site formerly occupied by the Tigert Memorial Methodist Episcopal Church, South, forerunner of Rev. Harold Cooke's Centenary Methodist. Tigert Memorial had closed in 1920 when its congregation moved to the new Centenary Methodist a few blocks away on North Denver Avenue, across the street from Tate Brady's replica of Robert E. Lee's Arlington House.[33]

Cooke, whose rhetoric fed the fires of racism before and after the riot, left Centenary in November 1921 for a position with the planned Southern Methodist college several prominent Tulsans were trying to start.[34] The school never materialized, though, and Cooke continued to agitate the public against local law officers, particularly Sheriff McCullough, and complained about a change of venue motion for Aurandt's accused killers, saying, "Justice can be meted out in this county as well as in any other county."[35] Cooke was assigned to an Oklahoma City church in late 1922,[36] and ultimately returned to his home state of Texas, where he served sixteen years as president of McMurry College until his death in 1958.[37]

Brady's personal and financial fortunes continued to deteriorate, and the unexpected death of his favorite son finally unhinged him. Brady began walking the four miles to the gravesite at Rose Hill Cemetery and back every day, sobbing and crying out as he trudged along. Finally, on the morning of August 29, 1925, he sat down in the kitchen of the big house, picked up a pistol, and shot himself in the head. Brady's funeral was one of the largest ever seen in Tulsa.[38]

Mayor T. D. Evans never sought public office again. In 1923, he, Steiner, and Younkman were among the founders of the anti-Klan Daylight Republicans.[39] Evans lived quietly, practiced law as a title attorney, and when he died in 1948, his obituary did not mention the 1921 riot. Instead, Evans was praised, albeit mutedly, for his role in completing the Spavinaw water project. His friend O. A. Steiner took possession of Evans's papers and presumably destroyed them.[40]

Police Commissioner J. M. Adkison was defeated for reelection and ran unsuccessfully for Congress in 1924, but remained active in the Republican Party. He served six years as postmaster when the job was a political appointment, was a delegate to two national GOP conventions, and made an unsuccessful run for mayor in 1938. Adkison's name, like Newblock's, appears on a local Klan roster from the late 1920s. He died in 1953.[41]

John Gustafson returned to his private detective agency, and soon exacted a certain amount of revenge against his adversary Richard Lloyd Jones. Employed by some of Jones's enemies to discredit the *Tribune* publisher, Gustafson rented room 502 of the Hotel Tulsa in March 1922. The adjacent room 500 was kept by Jones as a second office and, more to the point, for almost daily assignations with his assistant Amy Comstock. A Dictaphone receiver was hidden in room 500, and one of Gustafson's detectives and a succession of other men spied on the couple through the keyhole of a door to the connecting bathroom. The men then testified to a grand jury. Peeping through the bathroom as they did, the witnesses conveyed a good deal more than one might have thought necessary about the toilet habits of the two people in question but still related enough salacious details to get Comstock and Jones indicted on morals charges. Embarrassed and a little concerned that they might be arrested in the heat of the ongoing political campaigns, Comstock and Jones left town until the matter blew over.[42]

Richard Lloyd Jones died in 1963.[43]

The coming of radio and then television proved the undoing of afternoon newspapers. In 1941, Jones and his family entered into a joint operating agreement with the rival *World*; the two papers remained editorially independent but combined other operations including advertising, circulation, and production. In 1992, the *World* ended the agreement, bought the *Tribune* from the Jones family, and closed it. The Lorton family, which had been involved in the operation of the *World* since 1911, and owned it since 1917, sold the paper to BH Media, a subsidiary of Berkshire Hathaway, in 2013.[44]

The intrepid Charles Daley entered the insurance business and moved to Oklahoma City. In 1935, he became the first head of the state Bureau of Criminal Identification and Investigation, forerunner of the Oklahoma State Bureau of Investigation. Daley died unexpectedly in 1941.[45]

George Blaine, the imposing twenty-four-year-old police captain who became chief upon Gustafson's ouster, lost his job in the 1922 Klan sweep of city and county offices. Blaine descended into alcoholism in the early 1930s but recovered and over a forty-year career was chief of detectives, police chief, and Tulsa County sheriff three times each. As sheriff in the 1940s, Blaine achieved considerable notoriety for his crusade against a gambling syndicate, and for his refusal to include the TPD in his operations. Blaine died in 1958, at the age of sixty-one.[46]

Andrew Smitherman fled to Boston and then to Buffalo, where he became prominent in the African American community.[47] His younger brother John, the sheriff's deputy who spent a month in jail, not only remained in Tulsa but spent most of the rest of his life in law enforcement, either with the sheriff's office or the Tulsa Police Department. He also remained active in politics. In March 1922, Smitherman was kidnapped from his room at the Red Wing Hotel and taken to a remote spot northeast of the city, near the town of Claremore, where he was severely beaten and one of his ears cut off. Smitherman said his assailants, who were never caught, warned him to stop encouraging African Americans to vote in Democratic primaries. Almost a quarter century later, in 1946, Smitherman was suspended from the TPD because of a controversy involving accusations he supposedly made against Blaine, then the newly elected county sheriff. Smitherman was reinstated in 1948 and died in 1956.[48]

O. W. Gurley, perhaps the single person most responsible for Greenwood's early reputation, never recovered financially from the riot. Like many black Tulsans—and many black Americans of the era—Gurley soon moved to California, but returned periodically to testify in legal proceedings arising from the riot.[49]

C. F. Gabe, the city health inspector whose testimony is a valuable piece of the riot's written record, started a construction company after the riot but died in 1925.[50]

B. C. Franklin and P. A. Chappelle, two of the young attorneys who successfully fought African American relocation, became patriarchs of families that remain prominent in Tulsa to this day.

P. A. Chappelle's son, the Reverend T. Oscar Chappelle Sr., led Morning Star Baptist Church for nearly a half century, and was succeeded by his son T. Oscar Chappelle Jr. Another of P. A. Chappelle's grandsons, Carlos Chappelle, became Tulsa County District Court's first African American presiding judge; a great-grandson, Danny Williams, became U.S. attorney for the Northern District of Oklahoma.[51]

B. C. Franklin's son John Hope Franklin became Tulsa's most decorated scholar, a student of African American history whose writing and teaching continues to influence generations of Americans of all races. John Hope's son, John

W. Franklin, was a key figure in the development of the Smithsonian Institution's National Museum of African American History and Culture. B. C. Franklin's daughter Mozella taught in the Tulsa Public Schools for nearly four decades, and her husband and son were prominent attorneys. Few Tulsa attorneys, black or white, were more respected in their time than B. C. Franklin, and Tulsa's Franklin Park honors the father, not the internationally acclaimed son.[52]

Only a few copies of Mary Jones Parrish's manuscript were published originally, and for decades its existence was largely unknown except to a few scholars and her family. Parrish's nephew Clarence Love, a Tulsa bandleader and nightclub owner, succeeded in bringing out two editions in the 1990s, but the book is once again out of print.[53]

Damie Rowland said in 1971 that Dick Rowland wound up in the Pacific Northwest, and died there in the 1950s.[54] The Tulsa Race Riot Commission spent considerable time and effort trying to track down Rowland and Sarah Page and came away with nothing concrete. Thus the two people whose encounter on an elevator set in motion the events leading to the Tulsa disaster have been lost to history.

Dozens of lawsuits were filed as the tolling of the two-year statute of limitations for civil suits approached in May 1923. Most of the plaintiffs were black, but whites also sued, among them Tate Brady, I. J. Buck, and William Redfearn,[55] with Redfearn's suit ultimately serving as the test case for all the others. A sampling of the African American lawsuits indicates that most if not all were brought by either Elisha Scott of Topeka, Kansas, or Franklin, Spears, and Chappelle. The two firms each developed their own boilerplates into which they inserted clients' names, addresses, descriptions of losses, and dollar amounts. Generally, the suits named all of the city and county commissioners at the time of the riot as well as George Blaine, John Gustafson, and the companies that had provided the surety bonds for the elected officials.[56]

Many of Scott's petitions echoed a 1921 *Chicago Defender* story in claiming that Blaine "did ride in an airplane, drop and caused to be dropped turpentine balls and bombs down and upon the houses of the plaintiff and diverse other people." They also asserted that city commissioners conspired to "kill citizens and to destroy the property of certain colored citizens of Tulsa." Regardless of the merits of these charges, Scott did not help his clients by repeating basic errors in virtually every filing. He identified George H. Blaine as "J. A." and sometimes "J. R." Blaine and maintained that the airplanes used by authorities during the riot were furnished by "St. Clair" Oil, an apparent reference to Sinclair Oil.[57] There is no sign that any of Scott's cases progressed past the filing stage, and many remained open until 1937, when Scott moved to dismiss them.[58]

Franklin and his partners also alleged a conspiracy involving the city's white leadership, but hewed closer to testimony given in open court. Their petitions churned with outrage at the injustices inflicted not only on their clients but on themselves and even, to a certain extent, the lawbreakers. In more than one petition, Franklin and his associates wrote: "The streets of Tulsa became all agog with a seething, surging sea of humanity, a veritable army of mad men—with passions long pent up, fanned into white heat by racial hate and racial prejudice, as an immediate, proximate and direct result . . . of said officials . . . [whose] illegal and unlawful command was, as aforesaid, in substance, "Go out and kill you a d_m nigger."[59]

The lawsuits never really had much of a chance. The grand jury findings and Gustafson's trial had failed to establish the legal foundation for the conspiracy claims; whether this in itself was contrived can only be guessed but is not an unreasonable suspicion. Indisputably, the odds were against the plaintiffs. If white property owners could not get favorable judgments, blacks almost certainly could not.

Years later, in the autobiography he wrote with his son John Hope Franklin, B. C. Franklin said, referring to the murders of Dr. Jackson and real estate man Ed Howard, "There was never the slightest evidence that any responsible white resident of the city had anything to do with these murders. . . . [but] I don't think . . . the city and county officials handled the situation with the degree of intelligence, firmness and care that they should have."[60]

The material and psychological damage of the riot and its aftermath was deeply felt and enduring, B. C. Franklin wrote. Income that might have otherwise been invested in homes or businesses or saved for retirement was spent on rebuilding. Stigma attached to the riot's violence dampened Tulsa's once indomitable spirit.

> Mob violence and lawlessness have never done a community any good and never will. Tulsa had been given a black eye in 1921, and the entire city felt the aftermath of the riot. This was especially true of the colored section. Negroes from Tulsa traveling elsewhere or abroad were taunted and ridiculed about what had taken place. As is too often true, people everywhere of all races thought Tulsa was an unsafe place in which to locate and do business, and most of them thought there was not a good white person in the entire city.[61]

To counter this stain on its reputation, Tulsa campaigned for and was awarded the 1925 National Negro Business League Convention. Whites joined in the effort, and Governor Martin Trapp and Mayor Newblock attended. Franklin noted that the convention coincided with the decline of Klan influence in the state and thought the two were related.[62] "I'm inclined," he wrote, "to the view that this meeting of Negro businessmen from all over the nation, and the favorable publicity that resulted from it, served to show the uninformed that the Negroes, as a whole, were good, decent and dependable citizens; and gave the good white citizens added strength to support their already good intentions."[63]

Commerce returned to Greenwood Avenue and spread northeast onto Lansing, the street the white promoters of relocation had envisioned as Greenwood's replacement. Black subdivisions, initially hemmed in by restrictive covenants barring them from white neighborhoods, stretched northward along the spine of what is now Peoria Avenue.[64] The little frame clinic built by the Red Cross on the site of the burned Dunbar School and named for Maurice Willows was taken over by the city, which in 1932 replaced it with a two-story brick hospital at Greenwood and Pine; the third generation of Willows's hospital, by now called Morton Comprehensive Health Services and built as part of a countywide capital improvement program, opened a few blocks away in 2006.[65] Booker T. Washington High School, a cornerstone of the community and refuge for so many after the riot, moved north after World War II. At the time, federal courts, the Truman Justice Department, and the NAACP were chipping away at *Plessy v. Ferguson*, the foundation of segregation, and white school officials were eager to prove that their classrooms could be both separate and equal. So a new high school complex was built about a mile to the northeast, in the heart of new African American neighborhoods. Two decades later, with Tulsa Pubic Schools still largely segregated and court-ordered busing a distinct possibility, Washington was designated a magnet school with high-level academic programs intended to attract white students. The decision's ramifications have been complicated and not entirely positive, but it did produce two desired results: the creation of one of the most successful high schools in the country, and integration without the levels of violence or white flight seen in many other American cities.

Slowly, legal constraints on African Americans loosened. Housing covenants were ruled unconstitutional. Schools and public transportation were desegregated. Public accommodation ordinances were passed. Court-ordered reapportionment assured African American representation in the legislature for the first time in nearly sixty years.

But it would be a mistake to think that white Tulsa—or, to some extent, black Tulsa—embraced integration. For decades, Tulsa was known as a highly segregated city where blacks and whites kept their distance, separated by engrained fears and suppressed memories. Black Tulsans retained a fierce independence and pride in their community, and white Tulsans had no interest in disturbing the status quo. Former state senator Judy Eason McIntyre, recalling the insular world of her north Tulsa childhood during the 1950s and 1960s, says she rarely interacted with white people and did not really understand racism until she attended the University of Oklahoma.[66] In 1965, when the Oklahoma legislature formally repealed two unconstitutional Jim Crow laws related to public transportation, Representative Perry Butler of Tulsa cast the House's only dissenting vote. There had been "too much agitation and talk," Butler said, and "a lot of colored people don't want integration. . . . I was in Tulsa when they had a race riot," he said. "I don't want to see it again."[67]

A white newspaper editor who moved to Tulsa as a youth in the 1960s once privately likened the riot to a Southern Gothic "crazy old aunt in the attic." "Everybody knew about it," he said, "but nobody wanted to talk about it."

The phrase "conspiracy of silence" has been applied to the muted decades that followed Tulsa's great conflagration.[68] It began almost immediately after the local district judges set aside the fire code extension, so that a few years later the Tulsa papers hardly mentioned district judge Edwin McNeill's order for a directed verdict in the William Redfearn case—the last hope for those trying to recover riot losses—and the *World* mistakenly identified Redfearn as black.[69] As decade piled upon decade, many children grew to adulthood without the faintest notion of what had happened.

But it is not true that all mention of the riot was suppressed. Several books, including Charles Barrett's multivolume history of Oklahoma, included fairly lengthy (if usually one-sided) accounts. A history of Tulsa written by chamber of commerce secretary Clarence Douglas and published in 1921, includes a section on the riot. W. E. B. DuBois revisited the riot in the pages of the *Crisis* in April 1926, following a speaking engagement in the city.[70] Readers seem to have had no difficulty understanding that Frances W. Prentice's short story "Oklahoma Race Riot" was about Tulsa when *Scribner's* magazine published it ten years after the event, in 1931.[71]

Infrequently, and in oddly offhand ways, references appeared in the *World* and *Tribune*, perhaps most notably in a 1941 *Tribune* profile of George Blaine that devotes several paragraphs to his role in the "negro race riot." Remarkably, the story got both the date (June 2) and the year (1922) of the riot wrong.[72]

The riot was a traumatic event in the lives of Tulsans, and in the life of Tulsa. Some dealt with this trauma the same way trauma is often dealt with—by trying to block it out, by refusing to acknowledge or discuss it. And that fear is understandable. The passions unleashed that night and morning were so powerful, so destructive, and so deadly they seem to have affected all but the most hardened personalities. But such silence also covered shame and guilt, denied virtue, and preserved the status quo. The "race riot" became the "Negro riot," in which only faceless agitators and a few long-gone bad actors—J. B. Stradford, Andrew Smitherman, Dick Rowland—bore any significant blame.

Not everyone kept the past bottled up. Stories were told and retold, through generations of black and white families, and from these tangled threads was spun a narrative subject to many interpretations but only one honest conclusion. The memory of the race riot of 1921 seems to have been kept alive predominantly by African Americans and white middle- and working-class households. Thus Bill LaFortune, Tulsa's mayor in the early 2000s and a third-generation Tulsan whose grandfather made his fortune in the oil and gas business, could say that he had never heard of the riot,[73] while the son of a white laborer raised in the flood-prone slums west of downtown could give a fairly detailed account. Summarizing the riot to a reporter in 2000, the man said, "I wasn't born yet so I don't remember it. My father told me all about it, though. He said it happened 'cause the blacks—he didn't call 'em blacks—wouldn't get off the sidewalks for white women."[74]

Family stories told by whites tend to be about African Americans hidden or taken in, or consist of passive observations about the actions of others. Some whites behaved badly, but not our family. Black family stories tend toward the heroic, with larger-than-life characters such as Peg Leg Taylor, who was said to have fought off white rioters with his prosthetic limb.[75] In some African American tellings, white casualties outnumbered black, and whites won only because they did not fight fair—disarming potential defenders of black Tulsa while bringing machine guns, airplanes, and explosives to bear. Of course, the fundamental moral of this version is indisputable, even if some details are, for there was no honor in the destruction of Greenwood.

With the approach of the riot's fiftieth anniversary, the curtain began to lift. *Tulsa*, a magazine published by the chamber of commerce, commissioned a piece from local historian Ed Wheeler (not to be confused with the wounded ex-serviceman of the same name), but his inquiries made some white Tulsans uneasy. Wheeler began receiving threats, and the chamber refused to publish his story. The *World* and *Tribune* passed on it, too. But Don Ross, editor of a new publication called *Oklahoma Impact*, did not.[76] As a schoolboy, Ross had learned about the riot from W. D. "Bill" Williams, a longtime history teacher in the city's segregated black schools. Williams's parents had owned the Dreamland Theater and several other Greenwood businesses destroyed in the riot. They survived and rebuilt, but the wounds never quite healed. And Williams made sure that his students knew the story, even if the white kids south of the railroad tracks did not.[77]

Oklahoma Impact may not have had a large circulation, but it put the riot narrative into play. At about this time, Ruth Avery began collecting oral histories, including Damie Rowland's. In 1975, Oklahoma historian R. Halliburton Jr. published the first scholarly paper on the riot since Loren Gill's 1946 master's thesis. A few years after that, one of John Hope Franklin's Duke University graduate students, Tulsa native Scott Ellsworth, began gathering material for what would become *Death in a Promised Land*, the first book-length account of the riot. Ellsworth used newspapers and other documentary evidence but also relied heavily on oral history, especially as related by African American survivors such as W. D. Williams and others. Importantly, Ellsworth seems to have been the first to systematically record these stories, which are now archived in the University of Tulsa's McFarlin Library.

By this time the old Greenwood was all but gone, reduced to a single block by urban renewal, migration, big box retailers, an interstate highway, and the simple passage of time. *Oklahoma Eagle* publisher E. L. Goodwin Sr. and a few others strove mightily to preserve what little remained, and in the end succeeded, at least after a fashion.[78] Ross, elected in 1982 to the first of ten terms in the Oklahoma House of Representatives, was at least as intent on preserving the memory of Greenwood, and of the devastation it survived. In 1997, with term limits about to catch up to him, Ross cajoled the Oklahoma legislature into authorizing a commission to investigate the riot.[79]

Ross was aided by a confluence of circumstances, including establishment of the Washita Battlefield National Historic Site in western Oklahoma and the Oklahoma City National Memorial, both of which commemorated large-scale acts of violence. Ross also had the support of the Democrat-controlled legislature and Republican governor Frank Keating, a Tulsan.[80] But there was also wariness and deep disagreements about the commission and its mission. The reparations movement was gaining some traction nationally in the late 1990s,[81] and its proponents were searching for arguments to overcome legal obstacles such as long-tolled statutes of limitation. A Florida commission similar to Oklahoma's had resulted in payments of up to $150,000 each to a handful of survivors of a 1923 race war that destroyed the Gulf Coast community of Rosewood.[82] A few years earlier, the U.S. government had paid reparations to Japanese Americans interned during World War II.[83] The goal of some people, inside the race riot commission and out, was to establish local, state, and possibly even federal responsibility for the riot in order to obtain compensation for the victims, either through the courts or by legislative action.[84]

Ross originally intended to ask for $5 million in payments to riot survivors, who at the time were thought to number about twenty, and $1 million for children's programs, but concluded that would be a nonstarter. Instead, he and his legislative partner, Senator Maxine Horner, whose district also included Greenwood, settled for the commission in the hope that it would develop such compelling evidence that even conservative white Oklahoma would agree to some form of restitution.[85]

The commission was given two and a half years to investigate the riot and issue a report. It was a difficult order. Some politicians were slow to appoint their members to the commission.[86] Once appointed, the twelve commissioners were often at odds.[87] They came from varied occupations and backgrounds, with equally varied ideas about what the commission should be doing. Few really qualified as historians or knew much about research techniques.[88] Bob Blackburn, then the deputy director of the Oklahoma Historical Society and chairman of the commission, wanted a methodical approach that would lay the groundwork for a National Park Service site similar to the one he had helped create at the Washita Battlefield.[89] Others sought a quick, headline-grabbing discovery that would marshal public support for restitution. In particular, they hoped to find one of the long-rumored mass graves.[90]

Some members and many observers feared that the commission would be used to minimize the riot's impact on the black community or to shift blame to avoid responsibility. They believed it their duty to make sure that the oral histories, especially those of African American survivors, were validated by the commission as the official story of the riot. This is understandable, given the extent to which African American history in general, and the 1921 race riot specifically, had been ignored or disparaged. Ross, for one, did not want a blanket apology. He wanted whites to accept a sort of personal guilt for the misdeeds of their ancestors. "An apology without recompense, in my view, is subterfuge if not altogether hot air," Ross said shortly after the commission was authorized in 1997. "It does finally say that, 'We as a people are responsible for the sins of our fathers,' which most whites don't want to admit."[91]

The two legislators on the panel, Representative Abe Deutschendorf of Lawton and Senator Robert Milacek of Waukomis, while not entirely unsympathetic, made clear their opposition to reparations—or at least reparations paid by the state. "If this is presented to the Legislature, it is unlikely to get much support," Milacek said when a subcommittee recommended reparations similar to those paid the Rosewood survivors. "People are going to say, 'If we do this for Tulsa, where does it stop?' What about the Mennonites whose homes were burned during World War I? And the American Indians. We could go on forever."[92]

Deutschendorf, a longtime educator (and uncle of singer John Denver), said that he did not see that the state bore any responsibility for the riot. "Who's at fault?" Deutschendorf said. "What I'm hearing is the state. Sorry . . . you did not make that argument convincing to me, and I would not be able to make that argument to my colleagues."[93]

The commission had turned up quite a bit of information—and found more than one hundred black riot survivors, instead of the one or two dozen expected—but not the definitive proof of official conspiracy some had hoped for. Ground-penetrating radar failed to locate a mass burial site. A reward—amount negotiable—for the long-sought "To Lynch Negro Tonight" editorial[94] went unclaimed. There were no letters or documents indisputably linking Mayor Evans, Tate Brady, or anyone else of note to a planned attack on Greenwood. Even with such evidence, reparations would have been a tough sell. Without it, they were impossible.[95]

The white population of Oklahoma and even of Tulsa felt no connection to the riot or responsibility for it. It was a terrible thing, but it had nothing to do with them. A memorial and acknowledgment of the riot's general injustice was fine with many—though by no means with all—and they were willing to consider indirect restitution such as a scholarship program for the descendants of riot survivors. But direct payments, as Senator Milacek had said, were a potential Pandora's box that lawmakers could not easily explain to the mostly white, mostly conservative voters back home.

At best, reparations were viewed as a perhaps well-intentioned but ultimately misguided notion whose acceptance in the Tulsa case would create a dangerous precedent. At worst—and this may have been the dominant view—reparations were suspected of being little if any short of a scam, especially when persons other than actual survivors entered the picture as potential recipients. "What happened was wrong but I had nothing to do with it and neither did my family," was a frequent rejoinder of white Oklahomans. Some were outright racists, but most simply could not or would not connect the past to the present, and frankly had little incentive to do so.

Survivors themselves tended to be somewhat ambivalent on the subject. "I don't see any need that I'd be asking for any money," said Ernestine Gibbs, who was eighteen at the time of the riot "Where would the money come from, anyway? You've got to think about that."[96]

The time for restitution had been in 1921, when their families were destitute.

"What can you do about it now but let bygones be bygones?" asked survivor Annie Beaird in 1999.[97]

In a three-hour meeting on February 4, 2000, the commission voted to recommend payments to survivors and their heirs, but did not suggest an amount. It also recommended a memorial, business incentives for Tulsa's black neighborhoods, and a scholarship program. The resolution adopted by the committee concluded that restitution was "good public policy" that would "do much to repair the emotional as well as physical scars of this most terrible incident."[98]

Deutschendorf thought the commission was making a mistake. "What has the best chance in the House and the Senate is educational scholarships," he said. "A memorial has a chance. Restitution for survivors is iffy."[99]

Eldoris McCondichie, who fled Tulsa in a hail of bullets as a young girl, said she had "mixed emotions" about restitution payments. "I'm not saying they wouldn't be a welcomed gesture. But after all these years, it's not about the money. "A memorial," McCondichie said, "would make people remember long after we're all gone."[100]

Indeed, riot survivors tended to be less adamant about restitution than some of the younger African Americans. Eddie Faye Gates, an educator and local historian who collected the stories of older black Tulsans, was particularly firm on this point. "We have to press this issue," Gates said. "It's a matter of justice—a matter of doing the right thing."[101]

The commission filed a preliminary report a few days later and asked to be authorized one more year in order to complete a more detailed account.[102] The request was reluctantly granted.[103] Blackburn, not entirely satisfied with progress to date, warned the commissioners that the hard work lay ahead. "For the final report, I think we should take each issue, one at a time, and go through it," said Blackburn. "It's going to take some time, but it is what we should do."[104]

Two months later, Blackburn resigned as chairman.[105] He had moved up to executive director of the Oklahoma Historical Society and was responsible for raising money for and overseeing construction of a new state history museum in anticipation of the state's centennial in 2007. Blackburn said that as chairman of the commission he had been intent on letting everyone have their say and reluctant to express his own views; now, he continued, he could better serve the commission as an independent historian and analyst.[106]

Blackburn was replaced by T. D. "Pete" Churchwell, president of the electric utility Public Service Oklahoma.[107] Affable, fair-minded, and patient, Churchwell needed all of his executive skills to keep the commission on track and moving toward a final report that would, in effect, be the state of Oklahoma's official findings concerning the race riot. The commission had made use of several consultants, most of them unpaid, to research specific subjects, such as airplanes, the Oklahoma National Guard, and death records, and each submitted individual reports. Scott Ellsworth wrote two pieces, one with John Hope Franklin, but found his overall role somewhat reduced after a falling out with Blackburn.[108] Danney Goble, a University of Oklahoma professor considered, with Blackburn, one of the preeminent authorities on Oklahoma history, was brought on to write a summary of the commission's findings and conclusions. Folksy, colorful, and perceptive, Goble would soon tell a reporter that it was the most difficult and frustrating job of his career.[109]

Every sentence, every syllable had to meet with each commissioner's approval, Goble explained, and that proved well-nigh impossible. "I sat at the computer for 12 hours one day and wrote two paragraphs. I threw them away the next day," Goble said near the end of his ordeal. When the commission met for what was supposed to be the last time on January 26, 2001, Goble's "thirtieth draft" still was not good enough, and more changes were ordered. He had too often mentioned the confirmed number of deaths—thirty-nine, including the stillborn infant and the man shot on June 5—and had not given enough weight to less substantiated but firmly believed estimates as high as three hundred or more.[110]

"People who don't want what we want will look at that and say, 'See, it wasn't as bad as everybody says,'" said Commissioner Vivian Clark-Adams, a strong proponent of reparations and one of those most concerned that African American voices would not be sufficiently represented in the final report.[111]

A lot of voices feared that they were not being sufficiently heard. A cadre of six to twelve people attended virtually every commission meeting; most were not bashful about letting their thoughts be known. Among these were a few elderly riot survivors and, usually more vocally, their children and grandchildren.[112] Particularly critical of the commission's direction were Beryl Ford and Bill O'Brien, two elderly white men with substantial knowledge of local history and understanding of the city. Ford had accumulated an extensive collection of newspapers, images, documents, and artifacts related to Tulsa history;[113] O'Brien's father had been the municipal judge whose complaints about the treatment of prisoners appearing in his courtroom helped trigger the 1923 probe of Ku Klux Klan influence in Tulsa County.[114] Neither disputed that the riot was a despicable affair, but both complained that the commission was not rigorously investigating some of the assertions being made. O'Brien wrote his own unpublished account of the riot and commission, "Who Speaks for Us?" in which he raises some worthwhile points but also advances a few far-fetched scenarios of his own, including the possibility of direct Soviet involvement in fomenting the riot.[115]

If there was a consensus among the commissioners, it was that there was no consensus, at least not beyond agreement that a great wrong had been done to Tulsa's African American population. The details—who had done what and why, and the state's and the community's responsibility after eighty years—remained in dispute.

"I didn't think there would be as much discussion as there was, especially over the same things," Pete Churchwell said at the January 26, 2001, meeting. "I'm not sure the changes are going to improve Danney's report, but my gut tells me that if I were black I would [want them]."[116]

"One of the things I've learned is how difficult it is to reach consensus," said Eddie Faye Gates. "Everybody sees things through their own eyes."[117]

These discussions roiled the community and prompted many a complaining letter to the editor, but they also fulfilled a purpose.

"Dr. Franklin brought in this idea of a conspiracy of silence," Blackburn said in 2016. "Everybody agreed not to talk about what happened, because it could happen again. And it was an embarrassment. So there was a conspiracy of silence. We had to break that down."

"We knew we had to have this dialogue," Blackburn said.[118]

The final report was presented to Governor Keating, legislative leadership, and Tulsa Mayor Susan Savage on February 28, 2001. Churchwell cast the commission's findings in a contemporary context. "Today in Oklahoma we would not tolerate the actions that took place during the riot," he said. "Now is the time to send a message to the world that we reject racism, violence and horror."[119]

"We accept this report with an open heart," said Keating. "I do not know what the Legislature will do, but I assure you something will be done."[120]

In fact, not much was. The state did not bury the report, as such documents often are, but it did not enthusiastically embrace the recommendations, either. In May, House Republicans briefly delayed the Oklahoma Historical Society's annual appropriation because it included $750,000 for a race riot memorial.[121] A Race Riot Reconciliation Act narrowly passed despite the opposition of state senator Charles Ford, Beryl Ford's brother, who said the bill "tries to accuse every white person of being a bunch of thugs who did something wrong. That's not right." He and other Republicans demanded that some of the language be removed or altered, but Senator Maxine Horner declined.[122]

In August, Governor Keating said he could support up to $5 million in state funding for business incentives and a memorial but did not think the commission findings justified payments to survivors. Mayor Savage, speaking at the same event as Keating, said she supported restitution but did not believe it was something the state could do without a court judgment. She noted a movement underway to raise money privately.[123] This was led by the Tulsa Chamber of Commerce and its chairman, John Gaberino, who said the hope was to pay each of the 138 documented survivors five thousand dollars through a foundation established for that purpose.[124] Those hopes never materialized. Whatever chance they had vanished when rumors of a high-profile lawsuit soured potential donors. Separately, Tulsa Metropolitan Ministries distributed $28,000 in checks of roughly two hundred dollars each in April 2002. Most of the money—$20,000—came from the Unitarian Universalist Association.[125]

The lawsuit *Alexander, et al. v. Oklahoma* was filed in February 2003, in U.S. District Court in Tulsa, with a Who's Who of civil rights and tort lawyers on board. Best-known to the general public was Johnnie Cochran, one of the defense attorneys in O. J. Simpson's murder trial, but Charles Ogletree of Harvard Law was actually in charge. The suit named the City of Tulsa, the Tulsa Police Department, and the State of Oklahoma as defendants, with more than two hundred survivors and descendants of riot victims as plaintiffs.[126]

Ogletree, who was cochairman of a slavery reparations movement and had published several newspaper and journal articles on the subject, thought that he saw a way to overcome the huge obstacle presented by the statute of limitations. He and his legal team, most notably litigator Michael Hausfeld, argued that the clock did not begin ticking in 1921, but when the race riot commission issued its report in 2001. Before that, Ogletree and his team asserted, potential plaintiffs did not fully understand the legal recourse available to them, or, if they did, they could not have been assured a fair trial. The old rules, they said, should not prevail if they stood in the way of justice.[127]

The trial judge, James O. Ellison, did not agree, and neither did the appellate courts. Ellison dismissed the suit a little over a year after it was filed, on March 19, 2004,[128] and was upheld by the Tenth Circuit.[129] The U.S. Supreme Court declined to hear an appeal.[130]

A memorial design committee authorized by state law in 2000 had gotten off to a slow start. Savage, with her ten years as mayor drawing to a close, proposed using surplus capital improvement funds and federal grants to help convert the Vernon AME Church at 311 North Greenwood Avenue into a museum,[131] but the city council, including the councilor representing Greenwood, thought that the money would be better spent elsewhere.[132] Blackburn and the committee's chairman, Julius Pegues, were often at odds over money and the project's direction. A parcel of land was finally identified near Mt. Zion Baptist Church and purchased two days before the initial *Alexander* filing in 2003.[133]

The state's contribution to the memorial was to have been $5 million, paid out over several years, but changing political realities and an economic downturn soon had the legislature not only refusing to meet its commitment, but demanding the money already appropriated be returned. Pegues deemed it prudent not to spend or obligate money until it was all in hand; legislators struggling to make the state's ends meet saw only a ready source of cash.[134] In October 2003, a state representative demanded to know why the Oklahoma Historical Society was furloughing employees and canceling contracts while the race riot memorial account held $1.4 million "with no concrete plans on how to spend the money."[135]

Private funds were drying up, too, largely as a reaction to the *Alexander* lawsuit.

"People are mad," Ross said in April 2003. "The people with money are mad."[136]

"That's why I was so disappointed when they brought in Cochran and the others," Blackburn said in 2016. "That set us back so far."[137]

Reconciliation had always been a stated objective of the memorial committee, but this rising resistance caused it to shift the discussion from violence and fixing blame to something less threatening, and to choose as its talisman the slender, genial figure of John Hope Franklin.[138]

"This isn't going to be a statue of people dead on the ground with a white man standing over them with a gun," Ross said. "That's never what this was about and we need to make that clear."[139]

Franklin could not exactly be described as a favorite son; nearing ninety, by the early 2000s his accomplishments were probably more appreciated nationally and internationally than by the average Tulsan. But Franklin had been a hero to a generation of black Tulsans growing up in the civil rights movement that his research and writing helped set in motion. Now, his involvement with the race riot commission and then the memorial committee reintroduced Franklin to his hometown. He was no softy, even at his age, but Franklin possessed the rare ability to impart hard truths while minimizing animosity, and his willingness to lend his name and reputation to the memorial project soothed frayed feelings.

But not even Franklin's involvement was enough to raise the kind of money Pegues had in mind. A retired aeronautical engineer and Booker T. Washington graduate who had been the first black varsity basketball player at the University of Pittsburgh, Pegues brought personal gravitas and family history to the committee leadership. His uncle, J. C. Latimer, had been an architect and builder and was one of Mary Parrish's informants; after the riot, Latimer had encouraged Pegues's father, a carpenter, to move to Tulsa from South Carolina.

Pegues initially envisioned an $18 million facility that would include archives and exhibits that drew visitors and researchers from around the world. Pegues's cautious decision to wait until all $18 million had been raised before spending a dime was quickly overruled by politics and pragmatic consideration.[140] Money was proving difficult to raise, and people more knowledgeable about state government advised Pegues that the cash on hand should be spent or at least encumbered quickly before lawmakers changed their minds and took it back. So in 2003 the committee bought almost three acres from the Tulsa Development Authority—the city's urban renewal trust—for $405,000.[141] At the urging of Mayor Bill LaFortune, the City of Tulsa eventually agreed to offset the purchase price by donating infrastructure improvements and utility relocations of equal value.[142] At the suggestion of the mayor's wife, Kathy LaFortune, a member of the design committee, the decision was made in September 2003 to go forward with a "reconciliation park" to serve as a sort of placeholder until the larger dreams of Pegues and the committee could be realized.[143]

That wait continues. Early on, Pegues and Blackburn disagreed on key points. Pegues feared that the state money held by the OHS would be diverted to other purposes. Blackburn thought Pegues's independent streak alienated too many major players. Blackburn believed sticking to a proven blueprint that included the National Park Service (NPS) designation was the best way to proceed. Pegues, too, hoped for NPS affiliation, but resisted surrendering control of the memorial's message. "We did not want someone to come in and dictate what we were doing," Julius Pegues said in 2016. "We would like to have [the National Park Service] involved, but we did not want them or anyone dictating and controlling."[144]

As it was, the NPS piece presented nettlesome challenges. Few physical assets from the riot era remain, and none are in the immediate Greenwood neighborhood. And, First District congressman John Sullivan aside, there was not much enthusiasm for the project among Oklahoma's delegation to Washington. Tom

Coburn, elected Oklahoma's junior senator in 2004, sat on the committee overseeing the NPS but opposed additions to the park system, even in his home state;
his predecessor, Don Nickles, had been crucial to the formation of the Battle of
the Washita National Historic Site.

Ground was not broken on John Hope Franklin Reconciliation Park until
November 2008. At ninety-three, Franklin himself made the arduous journey
from North Carolina for one of his final public appearances before his death four
months later.[145] The park opened in 2010 and is operated by the John Hope Franklin
Center for Reconciliation, a nonprofit foundation set up in 2007. The foundation and
its work, ultimately, are the race riot commission's most visible legacy. Its annual
conference, on the anniversary of the riot, examines aspects of conflict, communica-
tions, and resolution, mostly but not entirely in the context of race. The center also
sponsors programs that bring together people of varied backgrounds in an effort
to foster understanding. The center's work is respected and its annual dinner is
almost always sold out. Privately, though, some lament that these efforts, like many
attempts to foster honest racial dialog in America, are mostly preaching to the choir.

Pegues, the foundation's chairman, disagrees. "We've impacted the conversation in the city of Tulsa," he said. "We still have a ways to go, but there has
been significant progress. We have people involved in the dialogue who were
not particularly engaged before. It is not an easy job overcoming the fears and
misgivings of three or four hundred years," Pegues continued. "There are things
to be talked out. We are slowly making improvements."[146]

On April 6, 2012—Good Friday—two men, one American Indian and the
other white, went on a shooting spree in north Tulsa, killing three African
Americans and wounding two others. The incident attracted national attention
and immediate comparisons to the 1921 riot. In fact, there were few similarities
between the two events. The Good Friday shooters turned out to be a couple of
sad sacks named Jacob England and Alvin Watts, who had worked themselves
into a rage over the death of England's father in a fight with a black man two years
earlier. England and Watts were soon caught and quickly confessed, and each
was ultimately sentenced to five life terms without parole. The reaction of local
leaders, though, was interesting. Aware of the particular scrutiny the city would
come under because of its history, they assembled a task force of local, state, and
federal law enforcement agencies. The mayor, Dewey Bartlett, vowed that the
killers would be quickly apprehended and brought to justice, and they were.[147]

Three years later, a white Tulsa County reserve sheriff's deputy named Robert
Bates accidentally shot and killed an unarmed black man named Eric Harris after

an undercover sting operation went bad. Bates, a seventy-three-year-old insurance executive and friend of Sheriff Stanley Glanz, was allowed to accompany
full-time deputies on potentially dangerous operations, including the one that
led to Harris's death. Harris was an unlikely martyr, a thief and occasional drug
dealer who had agreed to illegally sell a gun to an undercover officer. When he
realized he had walked into a trap, Harris ran. Five deputies tackled him and
seem to have had Harris under control when Bates walked up, announced that
he was going to fire a Taser, and instead pulled his .38 caliber revolver and shot
Harris in the side. Harris died a short time later in a Tulsa hospital.[148]

This incident, like the Good Friday shootings, attracted national attention,
but this time in the context of a rash of deaths across the country involving law
officers and unarmed African Americans. The Bates case, though, was more
analogous to the riot than the Good Friday shootings had been. During the
riot, civilian volunteers operating under the color of Tulsa Police Department
authority ran amok, and in fact seem to have been chiefly responsible for the
worst of it. Bates, too, was a civilian volunteer, a law enforcement wannabe who
overstepped his bounds with tragic results. Bates insisted that he drew and fired
his gun by mistake, and evidence seemed to indicate his actions were probably
more reckless than malicious. But they were no less deadly, and Harris's family—and others—clamored for retribution. Speculation immediately arose as to
whether Bates's money and connections would protect him from prosecution.[149]

The sheriff's office did, in fact, try to shield itself and Bates by declaring no
crime or policy violation had occurred. District Attorney Steve Kunzweiler,
however, charged Bates with felony second-degree manslaughter and prosecuted
the case diligently. Under the scrutiny of the press and a citizens group that
gathered enough petition signatures to force a grand jury investigation, Stanley
Glanz's twenty-six years as sheriff were reduced to rubble. Under the same statutes
used to remove John Gustafson ninety-five years earlier, the grand jury indicted
Glanz on two misdemeanors and recommended his ouster. Glanz, still defiant,
resigned.[150]

In April 2016, a little more than a year after Eric Harris's death, an all-white
jury convicted Robert Bates of second degree manslaughter and recommended
the maximum penalty—four years in prison.[151]

In 1921, Tulsa did not hold law enforcement accountable; in 2016, in this one
case, it did. But one should be careful about drawing too many conclusions from
that. The riot was mayhem and lawlessness on a much larger scale in a much
different time. Bates, who often came across as arrogant and tone deaf to the

commotion around him, made an unsympathetic figure; but he was no Cowboy Long or one of the law officers seen setting fire to Greenwood. There is no evidence that Bates went out the morning of the shooting intent on killing someone.

But it is fair to say that the legal system did what it was supposed to do in the case of Eric Harris in a way that it did not for those whose lives were ended or forever altered by the Tulsa riot. Some thought Bates's punishment unduly harsh, but others viewed it as not only warranted in this particular case but as a statement about the relationship between law officers and the people they are sworn to protect. At trial, Bates's defense was that Harris did not die from Bates's gunshot, but from a heart attack brought on by drug abuse; in closing, Bates's attorney read off Harris's criminal record and suggested that he got what he deserved. To some, this echoed faintly of the labeling as drug dealers and arrogant agitators the African Americans who in 1921 went to the Tulsa County Courthouse, and blaming them for everything that followed.

This argument worked in 1921. It did not work this time. The jury decided that, although Eric Harris may not have been a model citizen, he did not deserve to die, and especially did not deserve to die at the hands of a reserve deputy who mistook a .38 caliber pistol for a Taser and then fired off a shot that not only struck Harris but came within inches of at least one deputy's head.

So some things have changed—but some things have not.

Five months after Robert Bates's conviction, a white Tulsa Police Department officer named Betty Shelby encountered a disoriented black man named Terence Crutcher wandering in the vicinity of his empty vehicle on a north Tulsa street. When Crutcher ignored Shelby's commands and walked away from her and toward his car, Shelby fired a single fatal shot that struck Crutcher in the chest; at the same instant, a second officer, Tyler Turnbough, deployed a Taser. The episode was captured on video taken from a TPD helicopter flying overhead—and in which Shelby's husband, David Shelby, was coincidentally a passenger—and to a lesser extent by a police cruiser's dashcam.[152]

Shelby told investigators that she believed Crutcher was reaching inside his vehicle, possibly for a gun. But there was no gun, or any other weapon. As Shelby suspected, Crutcher was under the influence of the drug PCP, which can make users behave erratically and almost impervious to pain, including the electrical charge from a Taser. Otherwise, Terence Crutcher posed no immediate threat.[153]

With the entire nation on edge about police shootings, authorities immediately recognized the gravity of the situation. Two days after Crutcher's death, police showed the videos from the TPD helicopter and Turnbough's dashcam to the

Crutcher family and African American leaders. The videos were made public the next day, an unusually quick turnaround in such cases.[154]

Black leaders were furious about what the images revealed. "It was not apparent at any angle from any point that [Crutcher] lunged, came toward, aggressively attacked or made any sudden movements that would have been considered a threat or life-threatening toward the officer," said Pastor Rodney Goss after viewing the video with Crutcher's family.[155]

An added irritant, though it apparently played no part in Shelby's decision to shoot Crutcher, were the words of the helicopter pilot, Michael Richert, to David Shelby: "Looks like a bad dude, too. Could be on something." Police insisted that Betty Shelby could not hear the comment, but many observers believed it revealing.[156]

"Because of this presumption of 'big, bad dude,'" said civil rights attorney Benjamin Crump, Terence Crutcher had been killed; the same presumption, he said, was at the root of many violent encounters between law enforcement and young black men.[157]

Tulsa police chief Chuck Jordan did not attempt to minimize the situation. At a press conference a few days after the shooting, he called the video of the shooting "very disturbing" and "very difficult to watch," and promised justice.[158] Later, Jordan would say, "I think it's important that we show our public what we saw. To find ways to delay release of the video, legal reasons or other reasons, especially video as absolutely important as this, I think you're making a mistake and losing the trust of the public."[159]

The relationships that had gotten city officials and the African American community through the Good Friday shootings and the Bates affair were now tested. Not long before Terence Crutcher's death, Jordan had gotten a standing ovation after telling a predominantly African American audience, "Black lives matter to us."[160] Now people white and black wondered if that was true. The police union rallied to Shelby's defense, and Blue Lives Matter demonstrations popped up in opposition to marches and rallies demanding criminal charges against the officer.[161]

But the lid stayed on, even when riots enveloped Charlotte, North Carolina, just a few days following the Crutcher incident, after police shot and killed a black man named Keith Scott. Tulsa's African American pastors praised local authorities,[162] and President Barack Obama called Mayor Bartlett to compliment him on the city's handling of the situation.[163]

Former state senator Judy McIntyre, an African American, reflected on black Tulsans' aversion to violent demonstrations. "Somewhere in our DNA is something telling us we don't want to go down that road," she said.[164]

The district attorney, Steve Kunzweiler, filed first-degree manslaughter charges against Officer Shelby the day after Obama's call, triggering surprise, elation, and anger.[165] That the city did not erupt was all the more remarkable considering this was not the only ongoing case involving a TPD officer's shooting of an unarmed young black man.

More than two years earlier, on August 5, 2014, an off-duty officer named Shannon Kepler had gunned down nineteen-year-old Jeremey Lake as Lake walked with Kepler's troubled daughter along a street just west of downtown. Using department computers, Kepler had decided that Lake was not a suitable companion for eighteen-year-old Lisa Kepler. Shannon Kepler and his wife, Gina Kepler, also a TPD officer, had adopted Lisa and her two younger sisters when the girls were small, but found it increasingly difficult to cope with the reactive attachment disorder developed by all three girls in early childhood. Particularly exasperated with Lisa, the adult Keplers had dropped her at a homeless shelter after kicking her out of their house a few days before the shooting.[166]

Shannon and Gina Kepler continued monitoring their daughter through her Facebook posts, though, and in this manner learned about Jeremey Lake. Using police department resources, Shannon Kepler ran a background check on Lake and then went looking for him. After twenty-four years with the TPD, Kepler had nary a mark on his record. For much of his career he had worked with children and youth. But this situation sent him flying off the tracks.[167]

Lake was of mixed ancestry but generally identified as African American; whether race had anything to do with what happened next was never clear. Shannon Kepler simply drove up to the house where Lake and Lisa Kepler were living with Lake's aunt, and when he found them outside, opened fire. Lake was killed, and a bystander, Lake's younger brother, was injured by a ricochet. Lisa Kepler claimed that her father also shot at her before driving away, although that was not proved. Later Kepler would plead self-defense claiming that Lake had a gun, but no gun was found, and witnesses—including Lisa Kepler—said Lake was unarmed.[168]

Now, after numerous delays, Kepler was about to go on trial, charged with murder.[169]

The Kepler case did not attract the national attention that the Crutcher shooting did or stir local passions to the same extent, but it did further stoke conversations about not only race and police violence but also race and justice. Defense teams for both defendants suggested that their clients were being unfairly prosecuted because they were white and the men they killed were black. Shelby's attorney, Shannon McMurray, said Kunzweiler charged the officer "out of fear," and against the recommendation of TPD's chief homicide detective, to mollify those clamoring for a conviction in the case. The prosecution and the trial judge in Kepler's case would accuse his lawyers of doing everything they could to exclude African American jurors, and lead defense attorney Richard O'Carroll ultimately claimed that Kepler was singled out because he was a white police officer. Throughout, O'Carroll did his best to portray Lake in ways many found stereotypically racist.[170]

This may not have been the way it looked to African American leaders—or to many whites, for that matter—but they continued to counsel patience and restraint while exhorting law enforcement officials to rethink their tactics.

"We are hopeful that justice will prevail, particularly in light of the way the city leaders have acted expeditiously and in an attempt for transparency," Rev. M. C. Potter of Antioch Baptist Church, speaking on behalf of a group of black clergyman, said after Officer Shelby was charged.[171] "We believe their actions have helped us to minimize the negative impact that an already tragic event has caused," Potter said, before adding, "We are deeply concerned about the culture of policing the community of color. We are convinced that the current culture of policing fosters violence against black people, and black males in particular."[172]

A few days later, during a service at Morning Star Baptist Church, Reverend Goss said, "We have to learn how to find our strength right here in Tulsa . . . to stand on our own feet and demand justice. . . . We pray that this night will be a night of unity, prayer and love, because that's what's going to get us through this time."[173]

"Tulsa is really great at 'we came together tonight,'" said city councilor Jack Henderson, a black man. "But what if we did this all the time. I'm sick and tired of people thinking we have a tale of two cities. We should have everyone standing together for the same cause."[174]

There were protests and marches in support of both Crutcher and Shelby but no confrontations with law enforcement.

"We are not anti-law enforcement. We are anti-injustice," said Rev. T. Sheri Dickerson of Black Lives Matter in Oklahoma. "We understand that this can be somewhat of an uncomfortable conversation to start, but we have to have these conversations and begin that dialogue so that we can actually evoke and initiate real change."[175]

Social media and the comments sections of local news outlets became the battleground. TPD disabled its Twitter account for a while and began deleting profanity and threats from its Facebook page. Officers were told to be extra alert. Terence Crutcher, his family, and supporters, and groups such as Black Lives Matter came in for harsh criticism.[176] Yet somehow it never boiled over into outright violence.

Shelby could have claimed that she shot Crutcher accidentally; some thought her firing only one shot suggested that she had not intended to pull the trigger. But, like Kepler, she insisted that she acted in self-defense, that she believed Crutcher was going for a gun, or might have been going for a gun, and followed protocol.[177]

"I saw a threat and I used the force I felt necessary to stop a threat," Shelby told CBS's 60 Minutes.[178]

"I have sorrow that this happened that this man lost his life but he caused the situation to occur. So in the end, he caused his own [death]," she said.[179]

Richert, the helicopter pilot, later testified that Shelby told him, "I can't believe he made me do it."[180]

Shelby told 60 Minutes reporter Bill Whitaker that race was no factor in her encounter with Crutcher, but others disagreed.

"Race had everything to do with her pulling the trigger that day," said the Reverend Roy Owens, pastor of Metropolitan Baptist Church. "Betty Shelby very likely viewed Terence Crutcher as a 'bad dude,'" Owens told Whitaker. "Is she a racist? Does she, you know, have some ill will toward black people? I doubt it. But if she is like so many people in our nation, she assumes too quickly that a black male, especially out on the streets at night, is a threat and not a citizen. Is a suspect and not—a decent human being."[181]

Would a white Tulsan have been treated the same? Whitaker asked.

"I don't think that a young white male would be dead today," Owens replied.[182]

Shelby's trial began on May 8, 2017, with much national and even international attention. Press access to the courtroom was tightly controlled, and photography even in the hallway outside was limited. The week of testimony that followed revealed just how much of a rift the case had opened between the district attorney's office and the TPD, but most of all it underscored just how far apart law enforcement and Tulsa's African Americans were in their understanding of each other.[183]

The jury, which included two African American women, deliberated nine hours before finding Shelby not guilty. But it did not exactly exonerate her, either, or law enforcement in general. A letter the jury foreman asked be included in the case file explained that the jurors concluded that they could not convict Shelby, but neither were some of them satisfied with the way she handled the situation—or the way law officers seemed to be trained.[184]

The jury concluded that any officer put in that situation at that exact moment and regardless of the skin color, gender or size of the suspect, would have performed the same way, which is in accordance with law enforcement training. . . . That moment, according to the evidence presented, was unfortunate and tragic, but justifiable due to the actions of the suspect.

While Officer Shelby made a justifiable decision at the very moment she pulled the trigger according to her training, when reviewing the moments before she discharged the weapon, the jury wonders and some believe that she had other options available to subdue Mr. Crutcher before he reached his car.

Many on the Jury could never get comfortable with the concept of Betty Shelby being blameless for Mr. Crutcher's death, but due to the lack of direct or even circumstantial evidence that she was acting outside of her training in the 30 feet prior to Mr. Crutcher reaching the window of that SUV, the Jury was forced by the rule of law to render a not guilty verdict.[185]

The jury goes on to explain that it could not discern from the testimony whether Shelby's training included some of these "other options," and for that reason it did not believe she could be held criminally responsible. But at least some of the jurors believed that Shelby demonstrated a lack of judgment that seemed to pervade law enforcement. And, the foreman's note articulated succinctly the concerns of many outside of law enforcement: "The jury under the confines of the law found Betty Shelby Not Guilty, yet we question her judgment as a law enforcement officer. It is possible she acted exactly as her training would dictate and no option was available otherwise, but to people not trained in law enforcement, it seems an option might have been there."[186]

As Shelby, her husband, and some supporters celebrated the verdict in a hotel near the Tulsa County Courthouse, angry crowds spilled into surrounding streets, disrupting traffic and venting their outrage. The officer's colleagues and friends said the decision proved Shelby should never have been charged; Crutcher's family and allies believed it confirmed that racism continued to rig the justice system against people of color.[187]

"We're concerned about the message this sends to young black males, and males, period, about the value of your life, and that you can be shot with your hands up, and they will find a way to say that you were still in violation, and get off [after] shooting you," said Pastor Warren Blakney of the North Peoria

Church of Christ. "When you get shot with your hands up, and no weapons on you, and you're walking away from the person doing the shooting, that doesn't send a very good message to a young black man who deals with police . . . that your life is devalued because of your color."[188]

"It's becoming a new norm," said Goss, the Morning Star Baptist Church pastor. "It's almost an expectation that there really is no justice. It seems that it's just us. I try very hard to believe that the system is fair, and that the system works. But how much evidence do you need to prove that something is horribly wrong?"[189]

With the anniversary of the 1921 riot approaching, Mayor G. T. Bynum, who had succeeded Bartlett in December, acknowledged both the Crutcher family's pain and the difficulties of law enforcement, and the lack of real communication between black and white Tulsa.

> We have to acknowledge that a divide exists in our city. We can't work to address it until we acknowledge it exists. . . . We have a long way to go as a city when one part of our city is synonymous with an entire race. We have a long way to go as a city when people keep expecting lawlessness from African-Americans in response to an incident or a verdict. I would remind Tulsans that our history shows us African-Americans in Tulsa have not been the instigators of lawlessness and riots; they have been the victims of them. So I would ask that we not keep assuming the worst from a part of our community that has been exposed to the worst in this city's history. We acknowledge the divide, and we acknowledge the long, difficult road that we have as a city to equity.[190]

Shelby was assigned desk duty after her acquittal and soon resigned. She accepted a deputy position in neighboring Rogers County, whose sheriff, Scott Walton, was a former Tulsa police officer and had been loudly critical of Jordan and Kunzweiler. In October, the courts granted Shelby's request to expunge her record of all mention of the charge against her.[191]

The Kepler case, meanwhile, was finally drawing to a conclusion.

Shannon Kepler had been tried for murder three times by the fall of 2017. All three trials ended in hung juries, including the third time, when jurors were given the option of finding Kepler guilty of manslaughter. Kunzweiler refused to drop the case, insisting it had to be settled one way or the other. In early October 2017, the fourth Kepler trial began.[192]

Jeremey Lake's shooting never elicited the same emotional response that Terence Crutcher's did, even though in most ways it was more straightforward.

Lake exhibited no signs of intoxication or impairment and a postmortem drug screening came back clean. There was no question of him ignoring a police order or reaching through a car window. Shannon Kepler said that Lake had a gun but could find no one to corroborate it. Kepler used police resources to track Lake down and fled after shooting him.[193]

Lake's family was not as well known as Crutcher's, which may have had something to do with the lesser interest in his death. Kepler was off-duty and out of uniform and did not kill Lake while acting as a law officer. Clearly, he had been pushed to the brink and beyond by his relationship with his daughter Lisa, and perhaps this created some sympathy for him. But Kepler never claimed emotional distress in his defense, and the law does not allow distraught parents to shoot their daughter's boyfriends, no matter how objectionable they might be.

Kepler insisted that he killed Lake in self-defense, not because he was angry or believed Jeremey Lake was a bad influence on Kepler's daughter. In the end, few people seem to have believed it, even on the hung juries. The fourth jury found Shannon Kepler guilty of first-degree manslaughter; perhaps ironically, it declined to convict him of murder, the forewoman said, because they believed the shooting was indeed a "crime of passion." Kepler was sentenced to fifteen years in prison.[194]

At Kepler's sentencing, O'Carroll unloaded a diatribe that seemed to encapsulate the anger of both Shelby's and Kepler's defenders. The two law officers were not killers; they were victims. They were only doing what anybody would have under the circumstances. Kepler was a "scapegoat for the state," O'Carroll said, a white man handed "token injustice" to appease those who complained about the disproportionate share of prison inmates who are people of color. "He's the great white whale," O'Carroll continued. "I'm saying that this was political, and it was a gesture, and it was a token gesture, and he was a pawn. And if it wasn't for the fact that he was a police officer and he was white and they [the state] put so many people of color in jail, they would never have tried this case four times. That's what I'm saying."[195]

Shannon Kepler and Betty Shelby were not known as trigger-happy cops. Neither had ever fired their weapon in the field before the mere seconds that so dramatically changed their lives and ended two others. Yet their reactions (or what they said were their reactions) to the situations in which they found themselves—resorting to preemptive deadly force in the anticipation of a threats that turned out not to exist—and O'Carroll's summation go to the heart of black America's complaint and white America's reluctance to listen.

On the night of October 12, 2017, something happened in Tulsa that had not happened in a long time, or maybe ever. A sitting member of Oklahoma's congressional delegation went onto black Tulsans' turf to hear what black Tulsans had to say.

Republican U.S. senator James Lankford held one of what he calls "community conversations" in the Big 10 Ballroom, a former north Tulsa nightclub where the likes of Ella Fitzgerald, Ray Charles, and James Brown had once performed, and is being restored by a small foundation called Pocketful of Hope. Elected to the Senate in 2014, Lankford had made a concerted effort to concern himself with what might be considered the greater Greenwood area, and in particular with its economic and community development. He had also agreed to an appointment to the commission overseeing the 1921 race riot centennial and made a point of visiting the Tulsa exhibit at the newly opened National Museum of African American History and Culture, where John W. Franklin, son of John Hope Franklin, was a senior administrator.[196]

Lankford, a conservative Republican by any measure, had gone to one of the most reliably Democratic enclaves in Oklahoma, at a time when conservative Republicans were finding public meetings not nearly as friendly as they used to be, even in Oklahoma. And yet this one came off with very little rancor.[197]

"People have been saying to me, 'What you doing with Sen. Lankford? He's a Republican. You're a Democrat. What are you doing going down there,'" said state representative Regina Goodwin, a Democrat whose family has been in Greenwood since before the 1921 riot. "This is what I'm doing going down here. There's something about being civil. . . . Sen. Lankford is one of the folks I can call on any given day and he picks up the phone and he has conversations [with me]."[198]

Having someone listen is important to the people of Greenwood. It is important because to them it seems that they have always been told what they are getting instead of being asked what they want. It was true in 1921, and many black Tulsans remain on vigilant lookout for the same a century later. In 2015, a huge furor erupted when Tulsa County made preliminary inquiries about building a new $40 million juvenile justice center on a hill three miles north of downtown, in an area for which black residents had other plans. The proposal, in truth, was not a bad one, but it was not what people wanted.[199]

State senator Kevin Matthews and other African American Tulsans envisioned a greater Greenwood revival based in part on cultural tourism—monetization of north Tulsa's historical legacy, musical traditions, and hospitality. "We don't have a hundred millionaires," Matthews said in explaining the strategy, "but we're rich in history, culture, entertainment and have some of the greatest food in the world. How can we harness that?"[200]

An obvious answer was the approaching centennial. Restoration of the Big 10 Ballroom fit into those plans. So did a reawakening of Greenwood's entrepreneurial spirit. Matthews, a retired Tulsa firefighter who had developed several sideline businesses while still in the department, had for years encouraged young black Tulsans to start their own small businesses. This was a message others before had preached for decades, insisting that birth and rebirth be as much a part of Greenwood's story as its destruction.[201]

Matthews promised that the centennial observation would do that. The resolution authorizing the centennial commission, he noted, had passed the state house and senate unanimously. The city and state's elected white leadership, including Lankford and Bynum, were outspoken in their support. But the real test was yet to come, as the actual dates of the centennial drew nearer and competing interests and truths and versions of the truth vied for supremacy. Would the relationships evolved so slowly over the decades and strained by countless missteps, misunderstandings, and betrayals hold under the strain of international attention? Could this newfound sense of brotherhood survive the constant reminders of all that had passed, not only the riot but the years of segregation and discrimination and ingrained prejudices and unresolved grievances never fully exorcised? In the fall of 2018, Bynum confirmed that the city would reopen the search for group burial sites, a potentially explosive undertaking but one many thought necessary.[202]

Lankford described the scrutiny Tulsa would come under, and the standard it would be expected to meet, in a speech on the Senate floor in 2016, as the ninety-fifth anniversary of the riot approached.

"Ninety-five years ago this week the worst race riot in American history broke out in Tulsa, Oklahoma," Lankford said. "And in five years the entire country will pause and will look at Oklahoma and will ask a very good question: What's changed in 100 years? What have we learned in 100 years?"[203]

A lot, it is fair to say. And yet sometimes it seems not so much.

KEY FIGURES

J. M. Adkison • Tulsa police commissioner.

R. C. Alder • Tulsa fire chief.

Cyrus S. Avery • Civic leader instrumental in rebuilding efforts, later known as the "Father of Route 66."

Gen. Charles Barrett • Oklahoma's adjutant general, commander of the Oklahoma National Guard.

F. J. Bays • Chief investigator for the Tulsa County attorney; uncovered car theft ring involving Tulsa Police Department (TPD).

Maj. James A. Bell • Tulsa National Guard battalion commander.

Roy Belton • a.k.a. Tom Owens, a white man lynched in Tulsa in 1920.

A. J. Biddison • Tulsa civic leader, brother of Judge Valjean Biddison.

Judge Valjean Biddison • Signed telegram requesting National Guard assistance; member of three-judge panel to rule on fire code case.

Capt. George Blaine • High-ranking TPD officer; named acting chief after John Gustafson's suspension.

Dep. V. B. Bostick • Black sheriff's deputy; testified that white police officer burned his house.

Calvin O. Brady • Central figure in car theft ring associated with TPD (not related to W. Tate Brady).

W. Tate Brady • Prominent early Tulsan and businessman; among the leaders of group seeking to move African American neighborhood following the riot.

Dr. R. T. Bridgewater • Prominent black physician and property owner.

Cyril Briggs • Founder of the African Blood Brotherhood.

Maj. Paul Brown • White Tulsa physician and commanding officer of National Guard medical company; arranged for care of African Americans injured in the riot.

Rev. E. N. Bryant • Prominent black Tulsan and unsuccessful county commission candidate.

Laurel Buck • Testified he was told to "get a gun and get a nigger" by Tulsa Police officer; son of I. J. Buck.

I. J. Buck • Tulsa builder and Greenwood property owner; father of Laurel Buck.

P. A. Chappelle • Prominent black Tulsa attorney; instrumental in fire code cases.

Jim Cherry • Prominent black businessman and property owner.

Barney Cleaver • Respected African American lawman and major Greenwood property owner. Testified that a white police officer led a group of men that burned his house after allowing him to remove his possessions. Key figure in trying to calm courthouse crowd.

Judge Redmond Cole • District court judge who presided over Gustafson trial.

Rev. Harold Cooke • Pastor of Centenary United Methodist Church, South; ardent segregationist and critic of city administration.

Maj. Charles Daley • National Guard inspector general and TPD assistant chief. Said to have single-handedly held off invasion of Greenwood.

Frank Duncan • Tulsa city attorney.

Mather Eakes • White attorney on legal team that fought the fire code extension.

T. D. Evans • Tulsa mayor.

B. C. Franklin • Member of legal team challenging fire code extension. Later represented clients in unsuccessful liability lawsuits stemming from the riot. Father of historian John Hope Franklin.

S. Prentiss "Prince" Freeling • Oklahoma's attorney general.

C. F. Gabe • African American health inspector and key witness in Gustafson and Redfearn trials.

Merritt J. Glass • President of the Real Estate Exchange.

John Goldsberry • Assistant county attorney; member of the state's prosecution team.

Newt Graham • Civic leader in charge of fairgrounds detention camp.

O. W. Gurley • Early Greenwood resident and businessman; owner of the Gurley Hotel.

John Gustafson • Tulsa police chief; convicted of dereliction and removed from office following the riot.

Ed Howard • Greenwood insurance man killed in riot.

Patrick Hurley • World War I hero and later U.S. secretary of war; made "special assistant" to Sheriff Bill McCullough after the riot.

Henry Jacobs • African American whose statement to investigators identified J. B. Stradford and the Smitherman brothers as encouraging the march on the Tulsa County Courthouse.

Dr. A. C. Jackson • African American surgeon murdered in front of his house by white assassins.

Luther James • Former Tulsa County prosecutor; key witness in Gustafson trial.

Rev. H. T. F. Johnson • Prominent Greenwood clergyman; member of the Inter-Racial Commission and the person who hired Mary Jones Parrish to interview black riot survivors.

Richard Lloyd Jones • Publisher of the *Tulsa Tribune*.

Maj. Byron Kirkpatrick • Aide to General Barrett. Maintained that accurate accounting of the dead was difficult because the bodies were not handled in a "systematic manner."

Fred Kitchen • Secretary of the Reconstruction Committee.

Tom Latta • *Tulsa Daily World* editorial page editor.

T. J. Leahy • One of John Gustafson's attorneys.

S. R. "Buck" Lewis • White businessman; chairman of the Reconstruction Committee; and among the most vocal advocates of relocating the black district after the riot.

Joe Lockard • Black business owner who brought an unsuccessful suit to repeal fire code extension.

E. L. "Cowboy" Long • White businessman, bootlegger, roadhouse operator, and hoodlum identified as a leader of the Greenwood arson squads.

E. S. MacQueen • Former investigator for the Tulsa County attorney's office and unsuccessful candidate for sheriff whose attempt to disarm a black man at the county courthouse resulted in the shot that touched off the riot.

O. B. Mann • Greenwood merchant and World War I veteran identified by O. W. Gurley as a leader of the black men at the county courthouse.

Col. B. H. Markham • National Guard officer.

L. J. Martin • Former Tulsa mayor chosen by business leaders to chair Public Welfare Board. Refused all outside offers of assistance, insisting that Tulsans must pay for destruction of Greenwood themselves.

Sheriff W. M. "Bill" McCullough • Tulsa County sheriff charged with protecting Dick Rowland. Sharply criticized after the riot for not dealing more forcefully with African Americans at the courthouse.

Capt. John McCuen • National Guard officer whose rifle company became involved in intense fire fights.

Roy Meacham • Controversial Tulsa police officer indicted by grand jury for activities unrelated to the riot.

A. Flint Moss • Chief John Gustafson's lead defense attorney.

Herman Newblock • Tulsa finance commissioner, former law officer, and future mayor.

Alva J. Niles • Tulsa banker and chamber of commerce president.

John Oliphant • Former Tulsa police commissioner and white neighbor of Dr. A. C. Jackson. Important witness in Gustafson and Redfearn trials.

Henry Pack • Black Tulsa police officer.

Sarah Page • Young white elevator operator whose encounter with Dick Rowland set in motion events leading to the riot.

Mary Jones Parrish • Young black woman hired by Inter-Racial Commission to interview riot survivors. Report published as *Race Riot 1921: Events of the Tulsa Disaster*.

J. W. Patton • TPD chief of detectives who maintained that Dick Rowland grabbed Sarah Page's arm but did not assault her as reported in the *Tribune*.

Moman Pruiett • Nationally known defense attorney who played a small but important part in unraveling state's attempt to prosecute African Americans for murder following the riot.

William Redfearn • White Greenwood merchant and theater operator whose lawsuit to recover fire losses became test case for hundreds of similar actions.

Caleb Ridley • National Ku Klux Klan leader; spoke to large crowd at Convention Hall two months after the riot.

Gov. J. B. A. Robertson • Governor of Oklahoma; outraged by riot.

Will Robinson • Identified by Barney Cleaver as a leader of the black men at the courthouse; released on bond after intervention of Moman Pruiett.

Lt. Col. L. J. F. Rooney • Senior National Guard officer in Tulsa.

Damie Rowland • Relative of Dick Rowland interviewed in 1972.

Dick Rowland • Young black man arrested for allegedly assaulting Sarah Page, setting in motion events leading to riot.

Elisha Scott • African American attorney from Kansas involved in many post-riot lawsuits, none of which came to trial.

Mary Seaman • Tulsa city auditor. Often clashed with all-male city commission. Key witness for plaintiffs in fire code cases.

W. F. Seaver • Tulsa County attorney (sometimes spelled "Seavers").

George S. Short • Assistant attorney general and member of state's prosecution team.

A. J. Smitherman • Editor and publisher of the *Tulsa Star*; sought on a fugitive warrant after the riot. Later a newspaper publisher in Buffalo, N.Y. Brother of sheriff's deputy John Smitherman.

Dep. John Smitherman • African American lawman charged with inciting riot; jailed for thirty days but never brought to trial. Ear severed during kidnapping, allegedly by Klansmen, two years later. Brother of A. J. Smitherman.

Isaac Spears • African American attorney who worked with B. C. Franklin and P. A. Chappelle on fire code and liability lawsuits.

O. A. Steiner • Tulsa street and sewer commissioner.

J. B. Stradford • Greenwood hotel owner accused of being a leading instigator of the riot; fled Tulsa to avoid arrest.

Kathryn Van Leuven • Assistant attorney general; member of the state's prosecution team. Investigating crime and corruption in Tulsa County at the time of the riot.

Bay Ward • Head of TPD's auto theft division; accused of masterminding car theft ring.

James T. A. West • African American teacher who gave extensive testimony to Mary Jones Parrish.

Rev. R. A. Whitaker • Pastor of Mt. Zion Baptist Church whose successful lawsuit helped stop extension of fire code in burned area.

Walter White • NAACP investigator.

Det. Ike Wilkerson • TPD officer whose testimony led to the jailing of Dep. John Smitherman.

Maurice Willows • Director of Red Cross relief operations.

C. S. Younkman • Tulsa water and sewer commissioner critical of police and fire departments during riot.

CHRONOLOGY

May 30

Morning White elevator operator Sarah Page tells police that a young African American man identified as Dick Rowland grabbed her arm, causing her to scream.

MAY 31

Morning Rowland arrested by Tulsa police and placed in city jail.

10 A.M.–2 P.M. *Tulsa Tribune* publishes front-page account of elevator incident and Rowland's arrest under headline "Nab Negro for Attacking Girl in an Elevator."

3 P.M.–4 P.M. Police Commissioner J. M. Adkison receives a telephone call at police station threatening Rowland's life. Adkison and Police Chief John Gustafson decide to move Rowland to the county jail on top floor of the Tulsa County Courthouse.

4 P.M. Adkison and Gustafson advise Sheriff Bill McCullough to sneak Rowland out of town; McCullough declines, convinced Rowland is safer in jail.

Rumors of an attempted lynching circulate through white and black communities. Telephone volume increases.

Evening Crowd begins forming at courthouse, mostly white but also African Americans concerned for Rowland's safety.

McCullough orders six deputies to take the courthouse's only elevator to the jail on the top floor and disable it, then barricade themselves inside the jail and shoot anyone who tries to come up the stairs.

Three white men enter the courthouse, where they are met by McCullough and county commissioner–elect Ira Short. McCullough threatens to shoot the men. They leave.

Men meet at the offices of A. J. Smitherman's *Tulsa Star* to plan Rowland's defense. One threatens to kill O. W. Gurley, who has been to the courthouse, when Gurley says the situation seems to be under control.

McCullough, Deputy Barney Cleaver, and others try to persuade everyone at the courthouse to go home. They have some success with African Americans, but when the whites refuse to disperse, the African Americans become more suspicious; because many of the African Americans are armed, whites become increasingly belligerent.

Two Oklahoma National Guardsmen go to the home of Major James A. Bell to apprise him of the situation; Bell begins assembling men.

Shorthanded, Gustafson sends a small number of police officers to intercept black men headed to courthouse.

Whites appear at National Guard Armory demanding weapons. Bell refuses and threatens to fire on them if they do not disperse, which they do.

Increasingly alarmed, Gustafson asks Bell for men to "clear the streets of Negroes." Bell tells Gustafson he must have orders from the governor.

10 P.M.　E. S. MacQueen, a former county prosecutor and unsuccessful candidate for sheriff, attempts to disarm a black man, possibly Johnny Cole. The gun fires, setting off the riot.

Whites begin looting pawnshops and sporting goods stores, at first taking guns and ammo and then most everything else of value.

Guns are distributed at the Dreamland Theater on Greenwood.

Hundreds of "special deputies" are turned loose on Tulsa streets by the Tulsa Police Department.

Street fighting in downtown Tulsa continues for about two hours, until African Americans retreat into Greenwood.

10:40 P.M.　Although not officially activated, local National Guard units ordered to make themselves available to authorities. Lieutenant Colonel L. J. F. Rooney in command.

June 1

Midnight–5 A.M.　Gunfire from both sides of the Frisco tracks separating Greenwood from white Tulsa continues through the night.

Rooney deploys about thirty National Guardsmen and a truck with a disabled machine gun on the back to patrol Detroit Avenue on the west side of the Greenwood District.

National Guard officially activated

Several African American–occupied buildings on the north side of the Frisco tracks set on fire; white rioters begin preventing firefighters from extinguishing blazes.

Daley momentarily holds back white mob at Frisco depot.

5 A.M. Organized assault on Greenwood begins, signaled, according to some, by a loud whistle. Many Greenwood residents flee northward out of the city, Mary Parrish and daughter among them. Those who remain are taken into custody and are interned, or stay behind and fight.

Six airplanes circle overhead. Authorities say the planes were used strictly for reconnaissance, but others say the craft attacked with guns and bombs.

African Americans interned first at Convention Hall, than at McNulty Park, the local minor league baseball stadium.

Captain John McCuen's rifle company engages in series of gun battles with bands of African Americans.

As Greenwood is emptied of residents, homes and businesses are looted and set ablaze, with police and special deputies participating.

7:30 A.M. Dr. A. C. Jackson is shot to death outside of his home by a white man in "a white shirt and a cap."

Mount Zion Baptist Church is set on fire to drive out snipers in its tower.

9:30 A.M. Adjutant General Charles Barrett and one hundred National Guardsmen arrive by train from Oklahoma City.

10 A.M. Greenwood "beyond the power of all human agency to save" as fire engulfs business district and spreads to residential neighborhoods.

11:15 A.M. Governor J. B. A. Robertson declares martial law. Fighting, arson, and looting have mostly stopped by this time.

Noon An estimated six thousand African Americans are held at Convention Hall and McNulty Park. Many others are sheltered at Tulsa churches. Those held at the ballpark and Convention Hall are released as whites vouch for them. A few residents filter back into Greenwood by early afternoon

1–5 P.M. Second train carrying another one hundred National Guardsmen arrives.

African American detainees transferred to fairgrounds on the eastern edge of the city.

The first funeral for a riot victim, an elderly black man named John Wheeler, is held.

About thirty whites are charged with "pillaging."

Armed National Guardsmen patrol downtown Tulsa.

10 P.M. Mary Jones Parrish and daughter and a large band of African Americans settle in for the night in a field thirteen miles northeast of Tulsa.

June 2

Barrett blisters local leaders during meeting at city auditorium. Former mayor L. J. Martin is chosen to lead what becomes known as the Public Welfare Board, which assumes control of all activities related to riot recovery.

Major Byron Kirkpatrick says an accurate death count is difficult because "bodies were not handled in a systematic manner." Reports spread of bodies dumped in the Arkansas River, thrown in coal pits, or disposed of in other ways.

Thirteen black men, five of them unidentified, are reported buried at Oaklawn Cemetery.

Real Estate Exchange proposes extending fire code to larger share of Greenwood and converting part of the district into an industrial area.

Barrett orders J. B. Stradford's arrest.

June 3

Public Welfare Board rejects all outside aid.

Mary Jones Parrish and daughter return to Tulsa aboard a truck loaded with displaced African Americans.

Maurice Willows arrives to supervise Red Cross activities.

Thirty tents erected in Greenwood.

Martial law ends.

June 4

John Stradford arrested in Coffeyville, Kansas, but bonds out and disappears.

Deputy John Smitherman is jailed.

National Guard verifies thirty-five dead—twenty-six black, nine white—and says more may have been secretly disposed of.

June 5

R. L. Osborne, a white man from Colorado, killed by "guards" on the road between Tulsa and the nearby town of Sand Springs. Sometimes counted with riot dead.

June 6

Small stores open in Greenwood District.

County attorney W. F. Seaver files rioting charges against Stradford and three other black men.

June 7

City commission extends fire code in burned area at urging of Real Estate Exchange.

Thirty-two whites are charged with grand larceny stemming from riot.

About four hundred people, mostly women and children, remain at fairgrounds camp.

African Americans are required to display identification cards.

June 9

Grand jury convenes.

June 14

Mayor T. D. Evans appoints his own Reconstruction Committee; chamber of commerce–backed Public Welfare Board resigns en masse the next day.

June 18

Grand jury recesses after returning eighty-eight indictments, mostly against African Americans.

About one hundred black property owners meet with mayor's Reconstruction Committee to hear buyout proposal.

June 20

"Community meeting" in Greenwood church spared from fire; afterward, opposition to buyout proposal intensifies.

McCullough says most of those indicted cannot be found.

Cowboy Long is charged with setting fires during riot; apparently never is prosecuted.

June 22

Grand jury resumes.

June 25

Grand jury indicts Gustafson on five counts, only one of which—dereliction of duty—is related to the riot. Grand jury report blames armed black men and "agitation" for "social equality" for the riot.

July 11

Jury selection begins for Gustafson ouster trial.

July 13

Tulsa World editorial calls for lifting of restrictions on construction in burned district. Reconstruction Committee continues pressing for relocation of African Americans.

Testimony begins in Gustafson ouster trial.

July 22

Gustafson convicted of dereliction of duty during riot and conspiracy in auto theft ring and removed from office. No criminal charges are filed.

July 31

Several Greenwood property owners are issued building permits.

August 5

Building inspector H. E. Kopp says he is unable to stop unauthorized construction in the burned area because most work is being done at night.

August 8

White Greenwood property owners announce plans for $500,000 lawsuit against city.

August 10

Thousands pack Convention Hall to hear national Ku Klux Klan leader Caleb Ridley speak.

August 14

World editorial calls for repeal of fire code in burned district, calls Reconstruction Committee's proposal "bunc."

August 25

Three-judge District Court panel rules insufficient notice was given before vote on fire code extension. City commission passes the extension again the next day, this time in compliance with the law.

August 31

KKK "naturalization" ceremony held near Tulsa.

September 1

Three-judge District Court panel rules fire code extension unconstitutional. City decides not to appeal.

January 12, 1926

Oklahoma Supreme Court upholds lower court decision in *Redfearn v. American Central Insurance*, ending Greenwood property owners' last hope of recovering damages.

NOTES

Chapter 1. May 30, 1921

1. "All Tulsa Pays Homage to Dead," *Tulsa Daily World*, May 31, 1921, p. 1.

2. Lampe, *Tulsa County*, 1–54, 164–183.

3. "'No Hyphenates, Only Americans,'" *Tulsa Daily World*, April 29, 1921, p. 1.

4. "The Purest American State," *Tulsa Daily World*, April 30, 1921, p. 4.

5. "I.W.W. Members Flogged, Tarred and Feathered," *Tulsa Daily World*, Nov. 10, 1917, p. 1.

6. Lampe, *Tulsa County*, 69–70.

7. "All Tulsa Pays Homage to Dead"; "Tulsa Bows in Honor of Dead Heroes," *Tulsa Tribune*, May 30, 1921, p. 1.

8. "Citizens of Tulsa Tell of Conditions Preceding the Race Riot," *St. Louis Post-Dispatch*, June 5, 1921, Editorial Section, p. 1.

9. "All Tulsa Pays Homage to Dead"; "Tulsa Bows in Honor of Dead Heroes."

10. Ibid.

11. "Nab Negro for Attacking Girl in an Elevator," *Tulsa Tribune*, May 31, 1921, p. 1.

12. Goble, *Tulsa!* 45; U.S. Census Bureau, *Fourteenth Census of the United States: Statistics for Oklahoma*, Population—Oklahoma, table 10.

13. Goble, *Tulsa!* 96–98.

14. "City, Country Overrun with Drug Peddlers," *Tulsa Tribune*, May 8, 1921, p. 8.

15. Gosnell, "Federal Report on Vice Conditions in Tulsa," April 21–26, 1921, Oklahoma State Archives, box 25, case 1062.

16. "Should Group Social Agencies," *Tulsa Daily World*, Feb. 20, 1921, p. 12.

17. Ibid.

18. Johnson, "Ghosts of Greenwood."

19. *Polk-Hoffhine Directories of Tulsa, Okla.*, 1921, 658–60.

20. Parrish, *Race Riot 1921*, 17.

21. Testimony of John A. Gustafson, in *State of Oklahoma v. John A. Gustafson*, Oklahoma State Archives, box 25, case 1062, pp. 5–6.

22. Whitaker, *On the Laps of the Gods*; "Charge Peonage 'All over South," *Tulsa Daily World*, March 29, 1921, p. 1.

23. Comstock, "Over There."

24. Parrish, *Race Riot 1921*, 17.

25. DuBois, "Let Us Reason Together," 231.

26. Franklin, "African Americans."

27. "Tulsa County Tally of Primary Election," *Tulsa Daily World*, Aug. 4, 1920, p. 5.

28. "The Facts Remain the Same," *Tulsa Star*, Sept. 18, 1920, p. 8.

29. "White Man Shot in Race Trouble," *Tulsa Daily World*, April 17, 1921, p. 1.

30. "Thought He Owned the Car," *Tulsa Tribune*, May 12, 1921, p. 8.

31. "Probe Bares Police Failures," *Tulsa Tribune*, May 21, 1921, p. 1–2; "Thirty Witnesses Fail to Link Police with Vice," *Tulsa Daily World*, May 21, 1921, p. 1; H. H. Townsend, "Special Report on Vice Conditions In and Around Tulsa," Oklahoma State Archives, box 25, case 1062.

32. "Probe Bares."

33. "Freeling Probes Far into Night," *Tulsa Daily World*, June 23, 1917, pp. 1, 4; "Eddie Shouquette Convicted," *Tulsa Daily World*, April 2, 1921, pp. 1, 11.

34. "Impeachment of Police Falls Flat," *Tulsa Daily World*, May 20, 1921, pp. 1–2; "Thirty Witnesses"; "Probe Bares."

35. Statement of Barney Cleaver, Oklahoma State Archives, box 25, case 1062; "Negro Officers in North Side Battle," *Tulsa Daily World*, March 22, 1919; "'Dope' Worth $2,000 Seized, Negress Held," *Tulsa Tribune*, May 18, 1921.

36. "City Turns on Police Critics, Plans Inquiry," *Tulsa Tribune*, May 17, 1921; "City Calls Bluff of Police Critics," *Tulsa Daily World*, May 18, 1921, p. 1, 13; "City Shining Spotlight in Own Inquiry," *Tulsa Tribune*, May 18, 1921, p. 4.

37. "Impeachment of Police Falls Flat."

38. Halliburton, *Tulsa Race War of 1921*, 3, 7; "Nab Negro"; "Nine Whites, Sixty-five Negroes Killed in Tulsa," *St. Louis Post-Dispatch*, June 1, 1921, p. 1; Gates, *They Came Searching*, 71.

Chapter 2. Tulsa

1. Goble, *Tulsa!* 13–17; Hall, *Beginning of Tulsa*; Meserve, "Perrymans," 166–84; Saunt, *Black, White, and Indian*, 170; Woodhouse, *Naturalist in Indian Territory*, 136.

2. Goble, *Tulsa!* 13–17.

3. Irving, *Tour on the Prairies*, 10–11.

4. Ibid., 11–19.

5. Goble, *Tulsa!* 13–17; Meserve, "Perrymans."

6. Meserve, "Perrymans."

7. Woodhouse, *Naturalist in Indian Territory*, 136.

8. Meserve , "Perrymans."

9. Saunt, *Black, White, and Indian*, 170; Robert Littlejohn, interview with author, February 29, 2000.

10. Fischer, *Civil War Era*; Rampp and Rampp, *Civil War in the Indian Territory*; Goble, *Tulsa!* 28–30.

11. Meserve, "Perrymans."

12. Ibid.

13. Debo, *From Creek Town to Oil Capital*, 70.

14. Hall, *Beginning of Tulsa*, 9–10, 71; Meserve, "Perrymans."

15. Meserve, "Perrymans"; Debo, *From Creek Town to Oil Capital*, 67.

16. Hall, *Beginning of Tulsa*, 10; Goble, *Tulsa!* 33.

17. Hall, *Beginning of Tulsa*, 10; Goble, *Tulsa!* 33–34.

18. Debo, *From Creek Town to Oil Capital*, 54–60; Hall, *Beginning of Tulsa*, 2, 6, 9–10.

19. Goble, *Tulsa!*; 44–45; Hall, *Beginning of Tulsa*, 4, 42; Oklahoma Conservation Commission, "Abandoned Coal Mines in Tulsa County"; Tulsa Preservation Commission, "Industry"; "Smith Brothers Coal Pit."

20. Hall, *Beginning of Tulsa*, 91; "Leading Men Pay Tribute to Brady," "A City Builder is Dead," "Brady Funeral Plans Awaiting His Children," all in *Tulsa Tribune*, Aug. 30, 1925, p. 1; "W. Tate Brady, City Builder, Kills Himself," *Tulsa Daily World*, Aug. 30, 1925, p. 1.

21. Everett, "Charles E. Page"; "We Knew He Wouldn't Do It," *Tulsa Daily World*, June 24, 1919, p. 1; "Brady Hopes to Stop the Spavinaw Bonds," *Tulsa Daily World*, June 23, 1919, p. 16; Krehbiel, *Tulsa's "Daily World,"* 11–15.

22. Clinton, "First Oil and Gas Well," 312–32; Forbes, "History of the Osage Blanket Lease," 70–81; Weaver, "Glenn Pool Field."

23. Hall, *Beginning of Tulsa*, 46.

24. Paul Monies, "Several Oklahoma Bills Target Local Drilling Bans," *Oklahoman*, Jan. 26, 2015.

25. Hall, *Beginning of Tulsa*, 63–64.

26. Doulgas, *History of Tulsa*, 195–198, 536; Goble, *Tulsa!* 58–59.

27. U.S. Census Bureau, *Thirteenth Census of the United States*, table 1, 588.

28. Goble, *Tulsa!* 89–99.

29. U.S. Census Bureau, *Abstract of the Fourteenth Census of the United States*, 8.

30. "Negro Suburbs for Annexation," *Tulsa Daily World*, March 12, 1921, p. 6; "A Negro Writes Ably," Barometer of Public Opinion, *Tulsa Daily World*, Aug. 1, 1919, p. 4.

31. O'Dell, "Wallace N. Robinson."

32. Lampe, *Tulsa County in the World War*, 1–28, 59–69, 73–76, 104–105, 139–41, 151–54, 164–83, 221–22, 224.

33. "I.W.W. Plot Breaks Prematurely in Blowing Up of Pew Residence," *Tulsa Daily World*, Oct. 30, 1917, p. 1.

34. "I.W.W. in Tulsa Raided by Police," *Tulsa Daily World*, Nov. 6, 1917, p. 1; "I.W.W. Members Flogged, Tarred and Feathered," *Tulsa Daily World*, Nov. 10, 1917, p. 1; "I.W.W. Danger in Tulsa Not Ended," *Tulsa Daily World*, Nov. 11, 1917, p. 1.

35. "I.W.W. Members Flogged, Tarred and Feathered"; "I.W.W. Danger in Tulsa Not Ended"; Lampe, *Tulsa County in the World War*, 221–22.

36. L. A. Brown, Report to Rodger Baldwin, National Civil Liberties Bureau, March 20, 1918, Princeton University, NCLB Oklahoma Documents.

37. Lampe, *Tulsa County in the World War*, 221–22.

38. Tucker, *History of Governor Walton's War*, 11–14.

39. Lampe, *Tulsa County in the World War*, 51–70, 91–95, 221–22, 224–26; Hilton, "Oklahoma Council of Defense and the First World War," 18–42; Wilson, "Oklahoma Council of Defense."

40. Lampe, *Tulsa County in the World War*, 51–70, 73–76, 91–95.

41. Ibid.

42. Phillips, *Wealth and Democracy*, 59–63.

43. Menard, "Omaha Race Riot."

44. Krugler, *1919*, 50–58.

45. "Blacks Who Fear Mob Are Quieted," *Tulsa Daily World*, March 21, 1919, p. 1.

46. "Negro Writes Ably."

47. Ibid.

Chapter 3. Greenwood

1. DaNeen L. Brown, "All Black Towns across America: Life Was Hard but Full of Promise," *Washington Post*, March 27, 2015.

2. Tulsa County land records, Tulsa County Clerk's Office.

3. Franklin, "African Americans"; Abel, *American Indian as Slaveholder*.

4. Littlejohn interview.

5. Campbell, *Campbell's Abstract*, 7; Debo, *Road to Disappearance*.

6. Smith, "Resource Protection Planning Project," 1–3.

7. U.S. Census Bureau, *Twelfth Census of the United States*, 427, 686–97, 702–705.

8. Hall, *Beginning of Tulsa*, 16, 47.

9. "Population of Oklahoma and Indian Territory 1907," 89.

10. Original Townsite ledger, Blocks 23, 46–48, Tulsa County Clerk's Office.

11. Hall, *Beginning of Tulsa*, 62–63; O'Dell, "Daniel Webster Patton."

12. Original Townsite plat, Tulsa County Clerk's Office; Hall, *Beginning of Tulsa*, 63.

13. Debo, *From Creek Town to Oil Capital*, 81–82.

14. O'Dell, "Daniel Webster Patton."

15. Original Townsite ledger.

16. Ibid.

17. Ibid.

18. Ellsworth, *Death in a Promised Land*, 1–3.

19. Turley Addition plat, Tulsa County Clerk's Office.

20. Turley Addition and Original Townsite ledgers, Tulsa County Clerk's Office.

21. Cleaver statement; Cleaver individual census entries, 1870, 1880, 1900, 1910; *Hoffhine Directories of Tulsa, Okla.*, 1910 and 1911; *R. L. Polk's Directory of Tulsa, Okla.*, 1912; *Polk-Hoffhine Directories of Tulsa, Okla.*, 1913–1920; Turley Addition ledger; "Break Up Negro

'Choc' Party," *Tulsa Daily World*, Nov. 21, 1920, p. 12; "Negro Officer Is Heavy Loser in Race Riots," *Tulsa Tribune*, June 2, 1921.

22. Cleaver statement; Cleaver individual census entries, 1910 and 1920; *Hoffhine Directories of Tulsa, Okla.*, 1910–1911; *R. L. Polk's Directory of Tulsa, Okla.*, 1912; *Polk-Hoffhine Directories of Tulsa, Okla.*, 1913–1922; *Polk's Tulsa City Directories*, 1923–1956.

23. Cleaver individual census entries, 1910 and 1920; Turley Addition ledger; *Hoffhine Directories of Tulsa, Okla.*, 1909–1911; *R. L. Polk's Directory of Tulsa, Okla.*, 1912; *Polk-Hoffhine Directories of Tulsa, Okla.*, 1913–1920; Cleaver statement.

24. Cleaver individual census entries, 1880 and 1910; Ancestry.com database of Missouri marriage licenses.; City Directories, 1909–1920; Parrish, *Race Riot 1921*, 45.

25. Draft registration cards, U.S. Selective Service System, *World War I Selective Service System Draft Registration Cards, 1917–1918*, M1509, National Archives and Records Administration, Washington, D.C. (accessed through ancestry.com). Cleaver individual census entry, 1930; *Polk-Hoffhine Directories of Tulsa, Okla.*, 1914–1917.

26. U.S. Census Bureau, *Twelfth, Thirteenth, and Fourteenth U.S. Censuses of the United States*.

27. *Moore's Directories of the City of Muskogee, Okla.*; *Polk-Hoffhine Directories of Tulsa, Okla.*, 1913; Nevergold, "A. J. Smitherman"; White, "William Henry Twine"; "Facts Remain the Same," *Tulsa Star*, Sept. 18, 1920, p. 8.

28. *Polk-Hoffhine Directories of Tulsa, Okla.*, 1917.

29. Draft registration cards.

30. *Polk-Hoffhine Directories of Tulsa, Okla.*, 1917.

31. U.S. Census Bureau, *Fourteenth Census of the United States*, enumerator records.

32. "Stradford, John the Baptist 'J. B.'"

33. *Stratford [sic] v. Midland Valley R. Co.* 128 P. 98 (Okla. 1912).

34. U.S. Census Bureau, *Ninth Census of the United States*, enumerator records.

35. *Gould's City Director of St. Louis*.

36. "Stradford, John the Baptist 'J. B.'"

37. *Coffeyville, Kan., City Directory*; ancestry.com (date of Bertie's death).

38. *Coffeyville, Kan., City Directory*.

39. Turley Addition ledger.

40. *Hoffhine Directories of Tulsa, Okla.*, 1911; *R. L. Polk's Directory of Tulsa, Okla.*, 1912; *Polk-Hoffhine Directories of Tulsa, Okla.*, 1913–1920.

41. *Polk-Hoffhine Directories of Tulsa, Okla.*, 1920.

42. *Hoffhine Directories of Tulsa, Okla.*, 1911.

43. *Polk-Hoffhine Directories of Tulsa, Okla.*, 1921.

44. "No Dodging the Y.M. Campaign," *Tulsa Daily World*, April 17, 1921, p. 2.

45. Tulsa Preservation Commission, "Education."

46. *Polk-Hoffhine Directories of Tulsa, Okla.*, 1921.

47. U.S. Census Bureau, *Fourteenth Census of the United States*; *Polk-Hoffhine Directories of Tulsa, Okla.*, 1921; "Ceremony to Dedicate Standpipe Hill Historical Marker."

48. *Polk-Hoffhine Directories of Tulsa, Okla.*, 1921; Report of Capt. John McCuen to Lt. Col. L. J. F. Rooney, May 31, 1921, Oklahoma State Archives, box 25, case 1062.

49. "Negro Writes Ably."

50. "Negro Suburbs for Annexation."

51. U.S. Census Bureau, *Thirteenth Census of the United States*, table 1, 588; *Fourteenth Census of the United States*, Population—Oklahoma, table 10.

52. Parrish, *Race Riot 1921*, 11.

53. See, for example, Hart, "Peonage and the Public," 43; and "Peonage Farming," 1.

54. "Recover Eleven Bodies of Negroes Murdered in Georgia Slave Case," *Tulsa Daily World*, March 28, 1921, p. 1; "Georgia Planter Gets Life Term," *Tulsa Daily World*, April 10, 1921, p. 13.

55. "Officers Catch Ex-Governor," *Tulsa Daily World*, May 22, 1921, p. 6.

56. Although more African Americans were moving into manufacturing, they remained disproportionately concentrated in lower-paying agriculture and domestic and personal services jobs. It is reasonable to assume that the small number achieving professional status earned less than their white counterparts because their patients and clients had less to pay them. U.S. Census Bureau, *Fourteenth Census of the United States*, vol. 4, p. 340, table 3, and vol. 2, p. 1050.

57. Lichtman, *Embattled Vote in America*, 70–98, 147–79.

58. Franklin, *Mirror to America*, 24–25; "No Money for Muskogee Schools," *Tulsa Star*, Dec. 11, 1920, p. 1; "Black Teachers Watch Tax Bill," *Tulsa Daily World*, March 1, 1921, p. 6.

59. *Polk-Hoffhine Directories of Tulsa, Okla.*, 1921.

60. Brophy, "Tulsa Race Riot of 1921."

61. Parrish, *Race Riot 1921*, 81.

62. Original Townsite plat.

63. "Sub Post Office Is Robbed—Baker Is Arrested for the Crime," *Tulsa Star*, June 12, 1920, p. 2.

64. "Negro Library Asks Equipment," *Tulsa Daily World*, March 21, 1921, p. 6.

65. "Two Republicans Get Pluralities," *Tulsa Daily World*, April 3, 1912, p. 1; "Shall Tulsa Be Muskogeeized," *Tulsa Democrat*, April 4, 1912, p. 4.

66. "Followers of Jefferson Strangle Many Votes by Most Unfair Methods," *Tulsa Daily World*, April 17, 1912, p. 1.

67. Brophy, "*Guinn v. United States*"; "NAACP Victory in *Guinn v. United States*."

68. Smallwood, "Segregation."

69. Bruce, "A. C. Hamlin"; Scales and Goble, *Oklahoma Politics*, 44–47.

70. Smallwood, "Segregation."

71. Smallwood, "Segregation"; Bruce, "A. C. Hamlin."

72. U.S. Census Bureau, U.S. Census, 1907 ("Population of Oklahoma and Indian Territory 1907"), 1910, and 1920 data for Oklahoma.

73. "New Paper for Tulsa," *Tulsa Star*, March 27, 1920, p. 1; "Colored Democrats Hold Rally," *Tulsa Star*, April 3, 1920, p. 1; "The Truth Shall Set You Free," *Tulsa Daily World*, Oct. 26, 1920, p. 1.

74. *Tulsa Star*, Oct. 30, 1920, pp. 1–2, 4–7, 11.

75. "Negroes Cheer the Democrats," *Tulsa Daily World*, March 30, 1912.

76. "Negro Writes Ably."

77. "Kicks on Negro for Berth as Registrar," *Tulsa Daily World*, April 18, 1921, p. 1.

78. "Penrose the Impossible," *Tulsa Daily World*, April 10, 1921, p. 1.

79. "'Penrose the Impossible,'" letter to the editor, *Tulsa Daily World*, April 18, 1921, p. 4.

80. "Answering Noonan," *Tulsa Daily World*, April 20, 1921, p. 4.

81. Gates, "New Negro and the Black Image."

82. Rudolph, *Encyclopedia of Modern Ethnic Conflicts*, 746–57.

83. "Our Best Citizens Favor Mayor Hubbard," *Tulsa Star*, March 15, 1920, p. 1; "Just a Straight Democrat, Please," *Tulsa Star*, March 27, 1920, p. 1; Nevergold, "A. J. Smitherman."

84. "Truth Shall Set You Free."

85. "Nailing the Lie," *Tulsa Star*, Dec. 11, 1920, p. 8.

86. "Race Harmony Foreshadowed?" *Tulsa Star*, Nov. 27, 1920, p. 1; "As to Race Legislation," *Tulsa Star*, Nov. 27, 1920, p. 8.

87. "As to Race Legislation."

88. "City Briefs," *Tulsa Daily World*, March 8, 1921, p. 13.

89. Van Prooyen, "Henry Lowery (Lynching of)."

90. Ibid.; "Negro Begs to Die," *Tulsa Daily World*, Jan. 23, 1921, p. 3; "Negro Taken from Train by Mob," *Tulsa Tribune*, Jan. 26, 1921; "Mob Burns Negro at the Stake," *Tulsa Daily World*, Jan. 27, 1921, p. 1; "Mob Burns Negro after 100-Mile Trip," *New York Times*, Jan. 27, 1921, p. 1.

91. Whitaker, *On the Laps of the Gods*.

92. Rudolph, *Encyclopedia of Modern Ethnic Conflicts*, 746–57.

Chapter 4. "The Story That Set Tulsa Ablaze"

1. Damie Rowland, interview by Ruth Sigler Avery, 1972, Ruth Sigler Avery Collection, Special Collections and Archives, Oklahoma State University–Tulsa (hereafter "Avery Collection"); Oklahoma Commission to Study the Tulsa Race Riot of 1921, *Tulsa Race Riot*, 66 (hereafter "Race Riot Commission report").

2. U.S. Census Bureau, *Fourteenth Census of the United States*; Polk-Hoffhine Directories of Tulsa, Okla., 1921; *Polk's Tulsa City Directories*, 1932 and 1946.

3. "Nab Negro"; "Arrest of Young Negro on Statutory Charge Caused Battle between the Races," *Tulsa Daily World*, June 1, 1921, final edition, p. 1.

4. Halliburton, *Tulsa Race War of 1921*, p. 3.

5. *Polk-Hoffhine Directories of Tulsa, Okla.*, 1921.

6. U.S. Census Bureau, *Fourteenth Census of the United States*.

7. Rowland interview.

8. Gates, *They Came Searching*, 41–42.

9. Ibid., 71.

10. See, for example, ibid., 41–42, 71; "Arrest of Young Negro"; and "Nab Negro." See also Littlejohn interview.

11. Randy Krehbiel, "Opposing Theories Offered on Race Riot," *Tulsa Daily World*, March 5, 2000.

12. "Nab Negro."

13. Ibid.

14. "All Tulsa Pays Homage to Dead."

15. Advertisement, *Tulsa Daily World*, May 29, 1921, p. B-1.

16. Littlejohn interview; Krehbiel, "Opposing Theories Offered on Race Riot," p. 1; "Union Station Is Endorsed by Realty Dealers," *Tulsa Tribune*, June 16, 1921.

17. "Nab Negro."

18. "Arrest of Young Negro."

19. *Polk-Hoffhine Directories of Tulsa, Okla.*, 1921.

20. Gates, *They Came Searching*, 69–71, 246.

21. "Nab Negro."

22. Gustafson testimony, 7.

23. "Arrest of Young Negro."

24. "Nab Negro."

25. White, "Eruption of Tulsa," 909–10.

26. "The Trial and Lynching of Leo Frank"; "Duluth Lynchings."

27. "The Attorney General's Investigation," *Tulsa Daily World*, April 15, 1921, p. 4; "City Calls Bluff of Police Critics, *Tulsa Daily World*, May 18, 1921, p. 1; Statement of H. H. Townsend dated May 18, 1921, Oklahoma State Archives, case 1062.

28. "Brady Hopes to Stop Spavinaw Bonds," *Tulsa Daily World*, July 23, 1919, p. 16; "R. L. Jones Purchases *Tulsa Democrat*," *Editor & Publisher*, Nov. 6, 1919, p. 36; "Negroes on Lansing," *Tulsa Daily World*, July 8, 1921, p. 9.

29. "Negro Lynched by Holdenville Mob/Mobs Threaten Two Other Jails," *Tulsa Daily World*, Dec. 6, 1920, p. 1; "Oklahoma Disgraced Again by Mob Violence," *Tulsa Star*, Dec. 11, 1920, p. 2; "Negro Lynched, Shot," *Tulsa Daily World*, March 16, 1921, p. 1; "Mob Denies Negroes Pleas," *Tulsa Daily World*, March 23, 1921, p. 1; "Mob Lynches Negro," *Tulsa Daily World*, April 30, 1921, p. 1.

30. "Fleeing Negro Outraces Cops," *Tulsa Daily World*, Jan. 3, 1921, p. 6.

31. Parrish, *Race Riot 1921*, 43–44; Race Riot Commission report, 59.

32. *Tulsa Tribune*, May 31, 1921, Tulsa Public Library and World Media., microfilm.

33. "The False Story Which Set Tulsa on Fire," *Black Dispatch*, July 1, 1921, p. 1.

34. Krehbiel, "1921 Race Riot: Tribune Mystery Unsolved," *Tulsa Daily World*, p. 1.

35. Gill, "Tulsa Race Riot," 21–22.

36. *Tulsa Tribune*, June 1, 1921, "mail" edition; Krehbiel, "1921 Race Riot."

37. "False Story."

38. White, "Eruption of Tulsa," 909–10.

39. "Story of Attack on Woman Denied," *Tulsa Daily World*, June 2, 1921, p. 14.

40. "Officials Under Fire at Meeting," *Tulsa Daily World*, June 3, 1921, p. 1; Barrett, *Oklahoma after Fifty Years*, 206.

41. "Arrest of Young Negro." Emphasis added.

42. "Nab Negro"; "Arrest of Young Negro."

43. "Inefficiency of Police Is Denied," *Tulsa Daily World*, July 19, 1921, p. 1; "Chief Tells Own Story about Riot," *Tulsa Tribune*, July 19, 1921, p. 1.

44. Parrish, *Race Riot 1921*, 43–44.

45. "Inefficiency of Police"; "Chief Tells Own Story."

46. "Twelve Escape County Jail," *Tulsa Tribune*, May 26, 1921, p. 1.

47. "Sheriff Tells of Plans to Guard Negro," *Tulsa Tribune*, July 14, 1921, pp. 1, 11; "Sheriff Slept through Tulsa Riot," *Tulsa Daily World*, July 15, 1921, pp. 1, 8; "Inefficiency of Police"; "Chief Tells Own Story."

48. This and the following paragraph draw from "Mob Lynches Tom Owens," *Tulsa Daily World*, Aug. 29, 1920, pp. 1, 9; "High Court Refuses to Oust Woolley," *Tulsa Tribune*, Sept. 10, 1920, pp. 1, 13; "Tom Owen's Victim Dies," *Tulsa Daily World*, Aug. 28, 1920, p. 1; "Another Jailed in Holdup Case," *Tulsa Daily World*, Aug. 25, 1920, pp. 1, 12; "Girl Confesses Plot in Tragedy," *Tulsa Daily World*, Aug. 24, 1920, p. 1; and "Bandits Club and Shoot Taxi Driver," *Tulsa Daily World*, Aug. 22, 1920, p. 1.

49. "Probe Belton Lynching," *Tulsa Daily World*, Aug. 30, 1920, pp. 1, 3.

50. "Complete Vote of Tulsa County for County Officials," *Tulsa Daily World*, Nov. 4, 1920.

51. "Uncle Bill McCullough, 87, Early Day Sheriff, Dies," *Tulsa Tribune*, July 23, 1954, pp. 1, 3; "Another Pioneer Story Ends with McCullough Rites Today," *Tulsa Daily World*, July 24, 1954; "Freeling Probes Far into Night," *Tulsa Daily World*, June 23, 1917, pp. 1, 4; "Sheriff Removal Appears Certain," *Tulsa Daily World*, June 24, 1917, p. 1; McCullough Case Dismissed by Court," *Tulsa Democrat*, Oct. 9, 1917, p. 1; "Crowd Curious to See Gallows," *Tulsa Daily World*, March 31, 1911, p. 5; "Henson Has Paid Penalty by Death," *Tulsa Daily World*, April 1, 1911, p. 5.

52. Statement of Bill McCullough, Oklahoma State Archives, box 25, case 1062.

53. "Local findings on record of Jno. A. Gustafson," Oklahoma State Archives box 25, case 1062; Van Leuven to Hill, May 13, 1921, Oklahoma State Archives box 25, case 1062.

54. *Redfearn v. American Central Insurance*, Brief of Plaintiff Error in Brief, Supreme Court of the State of Oklahoma, 19–20.

55. Ibid.

56. "We Can't Forget," *Tulsa Star*, Oct. 23, 1920, p. 8.

57. *Redfearn*, 19–21.

58. Statement of Henry Jacobs, Oklahoma State Archives, box 25, case 1062; *Redfearn*, 19–21.

59. *Redfearn*, 19–21.

60. Ibid., 17–21; "Sheriff Slept"; "Chief Tells Own Story"; "Chief and Officers Take Witness Stand," *Tulsa Daily World*, July 20, 1921; "Armed White Parties to Be Disbanded," *Tulsa Daily World*, June 1, 1921, third extra, pp. 1, 3; "Martial Law Halts Race War," *Tulsa Tribune*, June 1, 1921, p. 1.

61. Parrish, *Race Riot 1921*, 18; police notebook, p. 43, Oklahoma State Archives, box 25, case 1062.

62. Parrish, *Race Riot 1921*, 18, 115.

63. Gustafson testimony, 16; *Redfearn*, 17–18; Statement of Luther James, Oklahoma State Archives, box 25, case 1062; "Lawyers Halt Chief's Trial," *Tulsa Tribune*, July 13, 1921, pp. 1–2; "State Elects to Try Gustafson First on Riot Action Charge," *Tulsa Daily World*, July 14, 1921, pp. 1, 2.

64. "First Detailed Story of How the Tulsa Race Riot Began," *St. Louis Post-Dispatch*, June 3, 1921, pt. 2, p. 1; "Armed White Parties"; "Martial Law"; police notebook, 44–45.

65. "Two Whites Dead in Race Riot," *Tulsa Daily World*, June 1, 1921, final edition, pp. 1, 8.

66. "First Detailed Story"; police notebook, 32, 46.

67. "First Detailed Story."

68. Ibid.; "Two Whites Dead"; *Redfearn*, 17–19.

69. *Redfearn*, 13–14, 18–19; "Sheriff Says Telephone Call Started Riot," *Tulsa Tribune*, June 3, 1921, p. 1; "Citizens of Tulsa"; "Police Accused from Stand," *Tulsa Tribune*, July 15, 1921, pp. 1, 9; "Instruction Is Denied by Court," *Tulsa Daily World*, July 16, 1921, pp. 1–2; "Impact Raps with W. D. Williams."

70. *Redfearn*, 18–19; "Police Accused from Stand"; "Instruction Is Denied"; "Citizens of Tulsa."

71. "Tulsa in Remorse to Rebuild Homes; Dead Now Put at 30," *New York Times*, June 3, 1921, pp. 1–2.

72. "First Detailed Story"; "Sheriff Slept"; "Chief Tells Own Story"; Report of Major James A. Bell to Lt. L. J. F. Rooney, July 2, 1921, Oklahoma State Archives, box 25, case 1062; police notebook, 16–19.

73. "Martial Law."

74. "Two Whites Dead."

75. "Arsenal for City Hall," *Tulsa Tribune*, June 29, 1921, pp. 1–2.

76. "Two Whites Dead"; "Martial Law"; Chief Tells Own Story"; "Chief and Officers Take Witness Stand"; Gustafson testimony, 12–18.

77. "Arsenal for City Hall."

78. "Two Whites Dead"; "Martial Law"; Chief Tells Own Story"; "Lawyers Halt Trial"; "Chief and Officers Take Witness Stand"; Gustafson testimony, 12–18.

79. Bell to Rooney.

80. Ibid.

81. Ibid.

82. Ibid.

83. Ibid.; Capt. Frank Van Voorhis, 1st Lt. Ernest V. Wood, and 1st Lt. Emmett L. Barnes to Lt. Col. L. J .F. Rooney, July 30, 1921; Major Paul Brown to the Adjutant General of Oklahoma, July 1, 1921, both in Oklahoma State Archives.

84. Bell to Rooney; "Two Whites Dead."

85. Bell to Rooney.

86. "Citizens Uphold Officers' Story," *Tulsa Daily World*, July 21, 1921, pp. 1, 3; "Meacham at Bar for Chief, Denies Plot," *Tulsa Tribune*, July 21, 1921, pp. 1, 5; police notebook, 26.

87. "Citizens Uphold Officers' Story."

88. "Martial Law"; Judge Redmond Cole to James G. Finley, June 6, 1921, Oklahoma State Archives, box 25, case 1062; E. S. MacQueen for Sheriff advertisement, *Tulsa Tribune*, July 18, 1920; "Vote in County Falls Far Short," *Tulsa Daily World*, Aug. 5, 1920, pp. 1, 8; Statement of E. S. MacQueen, Oklahoma State Archives, box 25, case 1062.

89. "Martial Law."

Chapter 5. Chaos

1. Major C. W. Daley to Lt. Col. L. J. F. Rooney, July 6, 1921, Oklahoma State Archives.

2. Douglas, *History of Tulsa*, 3:710–13.

3. "Oklahomans Off for Mexico City," *Tulsa Tribune*, Nov. 26, 1920, p. 1; "Daley Enthused over Mex Jaunt," *Tulsa Daily World*, Dec. 10, 1920, p. 15.

4. Whitlock, *Rock of Anzio*, 18.

5. Douglas, *History of Tulsa*, 3:710–13; "Major Daley Quits Police, Displeased," *Tulsa Tribune*, July 21, 1921, p. 1.

6. "Many More Whites Are Shot," *Tulsa Daily World*, June 1, 1921, second extra, p. 1.

7. Parrish, *Race Riot 1921*, 18; "Warning against Further Trouble," *Tulsa Daily World*, June 4, 1921, p. 1; Daley to Rooney.

8. Major Frank Van Voorhis, interview by Effie S. Jackson, Oct. 25, 1937, Indian-Pioneer Papers, Western History Collection, University of Oklahoma.

9. Daley to Rooney.

10. Franklin, *My Life and an Era*, 196–97.

11. Douglas, *History of Tulsa*, 1:620–24.

12. Daley to Rooney.

13. "Two Whites Dead"; "Martial Law Halts Race War."

14. James Leighton Avery, interview by Ruth Sigler Avery, Dec. 2, 1980, Avery Collection.

15. "Two Whites Dead"; "Many More Whites Are Shot"; "State Troops in Charge," *Tulsa Daily World*, June 1, 1921, third extra, 1; "Martial Law Halts Race War"; "The Dead," *Tulsa Tribune*, June 1, 1921, p. 1; "The Known Dead," *Tulsa Daily World*, June 2, 1921, p. 1; Race Riot Commission report, 109–22.

16. "The Dead"; "Young Wife Finds Mate in Morgue," *Tulsa Tribune*, June 1, 1921; "Known Dead"; Race Riot Commission report, 109–22.

17. "State Troops in Charge."

18. "Panic in Lobby of Hotel Tulsa When Negroes Cut Loose," *Tulsa Tribune*, June 1, 1921.

19. "Two Whites Dead"; "Many More Are Whites Shot"; "State Troops in Charge"; "Martial Law Halts Race War"; W. R. Holway, interview by Ruth Sigler Avery, Avery Collection; Major Byron Kirkpatrick to Lt. Col. L. J. F. Rooney, July 1, 1921, Oklahoma State Archives; "Inefficiency of Police"; police notebook, 17–18.

20. "People of Coffeyville Say 'Enough!'"

21. "'Shoot to Kill' Is Police Advice," *Tulsa Daily World*, Dec. 28, 1921, p. 1.

22. "Police May Use Special Officers," *Tulsa Daily World*, Jan. 1, 1921, p. 7.

23. Cleaver statement.

24. Tulsa City Commission minutes, 1921.

25. "Citizens Uphold Officers' Story"; Van Voorhis, Wood, and Barnes to Rooney.

26. "Inefficiency of Police."

27. Littlejohn interview; Hower, *1921 Tulsa Race Riot*; "Negro District May Be Restored," *Tulsa Daily World*, July 20, 1921, p. 18; "City Balks at Rebuilding of Burned Area," *Tulsa Tribune*, July 20, 1921, p. 1.

28. "Two Whites Dead."

29. "Heavy Losses Sustained by Gun Store Men," *Tulsa Tribune*, June 3, 1921, p. 4.

30. Laurel Buck testimony, Oklahoma State Archives, box 25, case 1062, pp. 2–4; "Police Accused from Stand," *Tulsa Tribune*, July 15, 1921, pp. 1, 9; "Instruction Is Denied by Court."

31. Kirkpatrick to Rooney.

32. Thoburn and Wright, *Oklahoma: A History*, 3:109.

33. Kirkpatrick to Rooney.

34. Memo to author from Robert D. Norris, Jr. (Tulsa Race Riot Commission researcher); Norris, "Oklahoma National Guard," 69–71.

35. Thoburn, Standard *History of Oklahoma*, 2:1230.

36. Bell to Rooney.

37. Norris memo; Van Voorhis, Wood, and Barnes to Rooney.

38. Bell to Rooney; Van Voorhis, Wood, and Barnes to Rooney.

39. Bell to Rooney; McCuen to Rooney.

40. Chen, "Browning Automatic Rifle"; Gander, *Machine Guns*, 92–96.

41. Van Voorhis, Wood, and Barnes to Rooney; Bell to Rooney.

42. "More Police on Stand at Chief's Trial," *Tulsa Tribune*, July 20, 1921, pp. 1, 5; "Citizens Uphold Officers' Story."

43. Kirkpatrick to Rooney.

44. "More Police on Stand."

45. Parrish, *Race Riot 1921*, 37.

46. *Redfearn*, 13–14.

47. Ibid., 18–19.

48. Ibid.; "Police Accused from Stand" (Sowders was incorrectly identified in article as "Souther"); "Instruction Is Denied by Court."

49. "State Troops in Charge"; "Martial Law Halts Race War."

50. "Two Whites Dead"; "Meacham, at Bar for Chief, Denies Plot."

51. "State Troops in Charge"; "Martial Law Halts Race War"; *Redfearn*, 31, 35; "85 Whites and Negroes Die in Tulsa Riot as 3,000 Armed Men Battle in Streets; 30 Blocks Burned, Military Rule in City," *New York Times*, June 2, 1921, pp. 1–2; "Whites Advancing into 'Little Africa;' Negro Death List is About 15," *Tulsa Daily World*, June 1, 1921, first extra edition, p. 1.

52. "Whites Advancing."

53. Parrish, *Race Riot 1921*, 18–19.

Chapter 6. "Mob Spirit and Fever Heat"

1. Lt. Col. L. J. F. Rooney and Major Charles W. Daley to Adj. Gen. Charles Barrett, June 3, 1921, Oklahoma State Archives.

2. Ibid.

3. Kirkpatrick to Rooney.

4. Daley to Rooney.

5. "Citizens Uphold Officers' Story."

6. Ibid.

7. Ibid.; Kirkpatrick to Rooney; Van Voorhis interview.

8. Gustafson testimony, 3–5.

9. Police notebook, 12; Norman Bickers, Grand Jury Witness Note, Oklahoma State Archives, box 25, file 1062.

10. Gustafson testimony, 3–9; "Sheriff Slept"; "Chief Tells Own Story"; "Chief and Officers Take Witness Stand."

11. Daley to Rooney; "Chief Tells Own Story"; "Chief and Officers Take Witness Stand."

12. "Citizens Uphold Officers' Story."

13. Kirkpatrick to Rooney.

14. "Martin Blames Riots to Lax City Hall Rule," *Tulsa Tribune*, June 2, 1921; "Mayor Warned of Uprising Negro Avers," *Tulsa Tribune*, June 6, 1921.

15. Daley to Rooney; "Chief Tells Own Story"; "Chief and Officers Take Witness Stand." "Citizens Uphold Officers' Story."

16. Ibid.

17. Rooney and Daley to Barrett.

18. "More Police on Stand."

19. McCuen to Rooney.

20. Gander, *Machine Guns*, 21–29.

21. Testimony of John Oliphant, in *Oklahoma v. Gustafson*, 15, 29; "More Police on Stand"; "Citizens Uphold Officers' Story."

22. "More Police on Stand."

23. Rooney and Daley to Barrett; Van Voorhis, Wood, and Barnes to Rooney.

24. Rooney and Daley to Barrett.

25. Van Voorhis, Wood, and Barnes to Rooney.

26. Daley and Rooney to Barrett; Daley to Rooney; "Martial Law Halts Race War."

27. "Military Control Is Ended at Tulsa," *New York Times*, June 4, 1921, p. 1; Statement of Henry Jacobs, Oklahoma State Archives, box 25, case 1062.

28. Rooney and Daley to Barrett.

29. Daley to Rooney; "Martial Law Halts Race War"; "More Police on Stand."

30. Daley to Rooney.

31. Ibid.

32. *Polk-Hoffhine Directories of Tulsa, Okla.*, 1921.

33. "Two Whites Dead."

34. *Redfearn*, 35.

35. Ibid., 32.

36. "Martial Law Halts Race War."

37. Daley to Rooney.

38. "Two Whites Dead."

39. "Whites Advancing."

40. Daley to Rooney.

41. "Rioter Wantonly Injured Veteran," *Tulsa Daily World*, July 2, 1921, pp. 1, 8; "White Who Shot Legion Member Is Being Sought," *Tulsa Tribune*, July 2, 1921; "Sheriff Tells of Plan to Guard Negro."

42. Van Voorhis Wood, and Barnes to Rooney; "Sheriff Slept."

43. Race Riot Commission report, 109–22.

44. "Funeral of Second White Victim Will Be Held Tomorrow," *Tulsa Tribune*, June 3, 1921, p. 1.

45. *Redfearn*, 30.

46. "Frustrate Attempt of Pair to Escape from Jail," *Tulsa Daily World*, June 1, 1921, first extra, p. 1.

47. Parrish, *Race Riot 1921*, 37.

48. U.S. Census Bureau, *Fourteenth Census of the United States*.

49. "Martial Law Halts Race War"; "Dead Estimated at 100; City is Quiet," *Tulsa Daily World*, June 2, 1921, pp. 1–2; "Church Dedicated Sunday," *Tulsa Daily World*, April 8, 1921, p. 7; "Splendid New Colored Church Opened Today," *Tulsa Daily World*, April 10, 1921, p. 32 (photo); Rooney and Daley to Barrett; Van Voorhis, Wood, and Barnes to Rooney.

50. Parrish, *Race Riot 1921*, 60–61.

51. *Redfearn*, 17–18.

52. Ibid.

53. Ibid.

54. Parrish, *Race Riot 1921*, 19.

55. Smitherman, "Descriptive Poem of the Tulsa Race Riot and Massacre."

56. *Redfearn*, 22.

57. Ibid., 19; "Negro Deputy Sheriff Blames Black Dope-Head for Inciting His Race into Rioting Here," *Tulsa Daily World*, June 3, 1921, p. 1.

58. "Two Whites Dead"; Kirkpatrick to Rooney."

59. "Two Whites Dead"; "Sheriff Slept."

60. "Two Whites Dead."

61. *Redfearn*, 19; "Negro Deputy Sheriff Blames Black Dope-Head"; "Citizens of Tulsa."

62. *Redfearn*, 19.

63. Ibid., 20.

Chapter 7. Retribution

1. *Redfearn*, 18.

2. Ibid., 22.

3. Ibid., 19–20.

4. Parrish, *Race Riot 1921*, 37.

5. Ibid., 45.

6. "Innovation Here in New Whistle," *Tulsa Daily World*, Oct. 21, 1920, p. 6.

7. Parrish, *Race Riot 1921*, 45.

8. Daley to Rooney.

9. "Mob Held Back by Major Daley for Two Hours," *Tulsa Tribune*, June 5, 1921.

10. Ibid.

11. "More Police on Stand"; Van Voorhis, Wood, and Barnes to Rooney; Parrish, *Race Riot 1921*, 43.

12. "Whites Advancing," second and third extras.

13. Van Voorhis, Wood, and Barnes to Rooney; McCuen to Rooney.

14. Parrish, *Race Riot 1921*, 19–20.

15. McCuen to Rooney.

16. Van Voorhis, Wood, and Barnes to Rooney.

17. Ibid.

18. Ibid.

19. Ibid.

20. Carlson, "Tulsa Race Riot of 1921."

21. Van Voorhis, Wood, and Barnes to Rooney.

22. Ibid.

23. "Armed White Parties"; "Inefficiency of Police."

24. "Dead Estimated at 100"; "When Riot Stalked in Tulsa," *Tulsa Daily World*, June 2, 1921, p. 7.

25. "Armed White Parties."

26. David C. MacKenzie, "A Lovely Lady Turns 75," *Tulsa Daily World*, Aug. 20, 1989.

27. "Armed White Parties"; "Fire Razes Black District; All Negroes Interned as Guardmen Patrol City," *Tulsa Tribune*, June 1, 1921, p. 1; "Negroes Shuffle to Safe Retreat Hands Held High," *Tulsa Tribune*, June 1, 1921; Parrish, *Race Riot 1921*, 60–61.

28. Faith Hieronymus, "Negroes Gladly Accept Guards," *Tulsa Daily World*, June 2, 1921, p. 1, 7; "5,000 Negro Refugees Guarded in Camp at County Fairgrounds," *Tulsa Daily World*, June 2, 1921, p. 1–2; Parrish, *Race Riot 1921*, 41, 53, 61.

29. "5,000 Negro Refugees."

30. "White Woman Shot 6 times By a Sniper," *Tulsa Tribune*, June 1, 1921; Rooney and Daley to Barrett; McCuen to Rooney; "85 Whites and Negroes Die"; Tulsa City Commission minutes, July 1, 1921.

31. McCuen to Rooney.

32. Ibid.

33. Van Voorhis, Wood, and Barnes to Rooney.

34. McCuen to Rooney.

35. "Fire Razes Black District."

36. Rooney and Daley to Barrett; Bell to Rooney; "City Will Be Open Tonight, Barrett Says," *Tulsa Tribune*, June 2, 1921, p. 1.

37. Parrish, *Race Riot 1921*, 37.

38. McCuen to Rooney.

39. Ibid.

40. Ibid.

41. *Polk-Hoffhine Directories of Tulsa, Okla.*, 1921.

42. "Negro Tells How Others Mobilized," *Tulsa Tribune*, June 4, 1921, p. 1.

43. *State of Oklahoma v. Robinson, et al.*

44. Madigan, *Burning*.

45. Transcript of T. J. Essley, interview by unidentified relative, 1987, annotated, in Tulsa Race Riot Commission Collection, Oklahoma Historical Society, box 1, folder 1 (hereafter "Race Riot Commission Collection"). Annotated by Robert Norris. The following four paragraphs draw on the Essley interview.

46. McCuen to Rooney.

47. Van Voorhis interview.

48. "Citizens of Tulsa."

49. Ibid.

50. Van Voorhis interview, 1937.

51. Parrish, *Race Riot 1921*, 37–38.

52. *Redfearn*, 17–18; "Witness Says Cop Urged Him to Kill Black," *Tulsa Tribune*, July 15, 1921; "Instruction Is Denied by Court."

53. "Known Dead"; "When Riot Stalked in Tulsa."

54. "Witness Says Cop Urged Him."

55. "Whites Advancing"; "Air Observers Watched Blacks for the Police," *Tulsa Tribune*, June 2, 1921; Parrish, *Race Riot 1921*, 62, 65; Race Riot Commission report, 103–108; Franklin, *My Life*, 197; "Bombs Hurled From Aeroplanes in Order to Stop Attacks on the Whites," *Chicago Defender*, June 4, 1921, p. 1; "Armed White Ruffians Who Begged for Guns to Help Murder," *Chicago Defender*, June 11, 1921, p. 1; "Ex-Police Bares Plot of Tulsans," *Chicago Defender*, Oct. 14, 1921, p. 1.

56. Keyes, "Long-Lost Manuscript."

57. Franklin, *My Life*, xiii–xiv.

58. Prentice, "Oklahoma Race Riot."

59. Race Riot Commission report, 103–108.

60. Parrish, *Race Riot 1921*, 62.

61. Ibid., 65; Franklin, *My Life*, 197; "Bombs Hurled from Aeroplanes"; "Armed White Ruffians"; "Ex-Police Bares Plot."

62. National Air and Space Musuem, "Curtiss JN-4D Jenny."

63. Parrish, *Race Riot 1921*, 20.

64. McCuen to Rooney.

65. "Sheriff Slept"; "Witness Says Cop Urged Him"; Deputy Sheriff Bostick, Notes on Witnesses, Oklahoma State Archives, box 25, case 1062.

66. The following six paragraphs draw from *Redfearn*, 20–27.

67. Buck testimony, 3–5; "Witness Says Cop Urged Him"; "Instruction Is Denied by Court."

68. "Witness Says Cop Urged Him"; "Instruction Is Denied by Court."

69. *Redfearn*, 20–27; Buck testimony, 5; "Witness Says Cop Urged Him"; "Instruction Is Denied by Court."

70. "When Riot Stalked in Tulsa"; "Insurance Men Say Policies Won't Be Paid," *Tulsa Tribune*, June 2, 1921.

71. *Redfearn*; "Insurance Suit in Riot Wake on Today," *Tulsa Daily World*, April 16, 1924.

72. Riot Commission Excel file, in Tulsa Race Riot Commission Collection; Race Riot Commission report, 143–50; *Redfearn*.

73. Oliphant testimony, 3. The following ten paragraphs draw from Oliphant testimony, 1–28.

74. *Polk-Hoffhine Directories of Tulsa, Okla.*, 1921.

75. "Martial Law Halts Race War"; McCuen to Rooney.

76. "5,000 Negro Refugees."

77. Hower, *1921 Tulsa Race Riot*, 187.

78. "The Disgrace of Tulsa," *Tulsa Daily World*, June 2, 1921, p. 4.

79. Parrish, *Race Riot 1921*, 56.

Chapter 8. Aftermath

1. Adj. Gen. Charles F. Barrett to Lt. Col. L. J. F. Rooney, telegram, June 1, 1921, file 1062, Oklahoma State Archives; Barrett, *Oklahoma after Fifty Years*, 212; "Armed White Parties."

2. "Armed White Parties."

3. Oliphant testimony, 6, 9, 12–13, 19–20, 24–25, 27.

4. Prentice, "Oklahoma Race Riot."

5. Barrett, *Oklahoma after Fifty Years*, 212; *Redfearn*, 20; "Dick Rowland Is Spirited Out of City," *Tulsa Tribune*, June 1, 1921, p. 6.

6. Barrett, *Oklahoma after Fifty Years*, 212.

7. Ibid.; "Barrett Placed in Full Command, Governor Comes," *Tulsa Tribune*, June 1, 1921, p. 1.

8. Barrett, *Oklahoma after Fifty Years*, 213–15.

9. Ibid., 214.

10. Ibid., 215; "Armed White Parties"; "5,000 Negro Refugees"; Norris, "Oklahoma National Guard," 223.

11. "5,000 Negro Refugees."

12. "Tulsa in Remorse to Rebuild Homes; Dead Now Put at 30," *New York Times*, June 3, 1921, pp. 1–2.

13. U.S. Census Bureau, *Fourteenth Census of the United States*.

14. "5,000 Negro Refugees."

15. Barrett, *Oklahoma after Fifty Years*, 214.

16. "Police Seize 30 in Riot Wake," *Tulsa Tribune*, June 4, 1921, p. 1.

17. "Whites Named in New Batch of True Bills," *Tulsa Tribune*, June 18, 1921, p. 1; "88 Indicted in Race Riot Probe," *Tulsa World*, June 19, 1921, p. 2; "White Woman Is Arrested on Looting Charge," *Tulsa Tribune*, June 21, 1921, p. 1.

18. Charles Barrett vertical file, 45th Infantry Museum, Oklahoma City.

19. "5,000 Negro Refugees"; "Tulsa in Remorse."

20. "5,000 Negro Refugees"; "Barrett Placed in Full Command."

21. Parrish, *Race Riot 1921*, 20–21.

22. Ibid.

23. Ibid., 22–23.

24. "Negroes from Tulsa Flee to Other Towns," *Tulsa Tribune*, June 2, 1921.

25. "Capture 33 at Catoosa," *Tulsa Tribune*, June 1, 1921.

26. "Fire Razes Black District."

27. "Two Negro Doctors and Wives Found in Hills," *Tulsa World*, June 3, 1921, p. 13; "Many Refugees Hiding in Hills," *Tulsa World*, June 4, p. 15.

28. "60 Tulsa Negroes Find Refuge Here," *Daily Oklahoman*, June 19, 1921, p. 36.

29. "Aide to Police Answers Critics," *Tulsa World*, June 5, 1921, p. 13.

30. "Armed White Parties"; "Fire Razes Black District."

31. Parrish, *Race Riot 1921*, 39, 42, 50; "5,000 Negro Refugees."

32. *Redfearn*, 31.

33. Brown to Adjutant General.

34. Parrish, *Race Riot 1921*, 53, 59; Hieronymus, "Negroes Gladly Accept Guards"; "Fire Razes Black District."

35. Hieronymus, "Negroes Gladly Accept Guards." The following paragraphs detailing Hieronymus's account of the ballpark detainees draw from this article.

36. "Nine Whites and 68 Blacks Slain in Race War," *Tulsa Tribune*, June 1, 1921, p. 1; "Bulletins," *Tulsa Tribune*, June 1, 1921, p. 1.

37. "Dead Estimated at 100," 1.

38. "Search Cuts Known Death List to 27," *Tulsa Tribune*, June 2, 1921, p. 1.

39. Race Riot Commission report, 109–22; "Another Negro Victim of Riot Dies Friday," *Tulsa World*, June 12, 1921. The *Tribune* maintained its own list of dead, which was at odds with the official list submitted by Maj. Paul Brown of the Oklahoma National Guard. Brown reported thirty-six deaths prior to Johnson's. "4 More Blacks Dead, Total of Known Dead 31," *Tulsa Tribune*, June 5, 1921, p. 1.

40. "5,000 Negro Refugees."

41. James Leighton Avery interview.

42. Hower, *1921 Tulsa Race Riot*, 164.

43. A version of this story was related by Phillip Rhees, who said it had been told to him by an older brother, during an interview in 2000.

44. "5,000 Negro Refugees"; White, "Eruption of Tulsa."

45. Andrew Wilkes and Margaret Wilsey, interview by Ruth Sigler Avery, July 8, 1972, Avery Collection.

46. White, "Eruption of Tulsa."

47. Robert H. Patty, interview by author, and personal memo, June 13–14, 2000.

48. Littlejohn interview.

49. "Incinerator Needed," *Tulsa World*, May 12, 1920, p. 14; "Ask for Bids on New Incinerator," *Tulsa World*, July 20, 1921, p. 9.

50. "Citizens Object to Odors," *Tulsa World*, May 18, 1921, p. 3.

51. "5,000 Negro Refugees"; White, "Eruption of Tulsa."

52. "Story of Attack on Woman."

53. Ibid.

54. Statement of Mrs. W. H. Clark to attorney general's investigator, Oklahoma State Archives, box 25, case 1062.

55. "Officials Under Fire."

56. Barrett, *Oklahoma after Fifty Years*, 206.

57. "*World* Statement False," *Tulsa Tribune*, June 2, 1921, p. 1.

58. "Martin Blames Riots."

59. "85 Whites and Negroes Die."

60. "Warning against Further Trouble."

61. This is stated in a few pages of photocopied typescript purported to be from Stradford's unpublished memoir given the author in 2000. See also, "Account of J. B. Stradford," in Race Riot Commission Collection.

62. "Negro Deputy Sheriff Blames Black Dope-Head."

63. Redmond S. Cole to James Findlay, June 6, 1921, Redmond S. Cole Papers, Western History Collections, University of Oklahoma.

64. "Local Red Cross Is Reorganized," *Tulsa World*, June 3, 1921, pp. 1–2.

65. "Ready to Report Spavinaw Costs," *Tulsa World*, Oct. 25, 1921, p. 1.

66. "Evans and Bigger Tulsa Ticket Elected," *Tulsa World*, April 7, 1920, pp. 1, 5.

67. "Assign New City Officials Places," *Tulsa World*, April 18, 1920, pp. 1, 4.

68. "Mayor Warned of Uprising Negro Avers."

69. "Barrett Placed in Full Command."

70. "Agitators Were Cause of Riot," *Tulsa World*, June 3, 1921, p. 2.

71. "Henson Has Paid Penalty by Death," *Tulsa World*, April 1, 1911, p. 5; Toby LaForge, "'The Right's Always the Law,'" *Tulsa Tribune*, May 3, 1951; "Uncle Bill McCullough, 87, Early-Day Sheriff, Dies," *Tulsa Tribune*, June 23, 1954; "Another Pioneer Story Ends with McCullough, Rites Today," *Tulsa World*, June 24, 1954.

72. "Attorney General May Arrive This Week," *Tulsa World*, June 18, 1917; "Freeling Probes Far into Night," *Tulsa World*, June 23, 1917, pp. 1, 4; "Sheriff Removal Appears Certain," *Tulsa World*, June 24, 1917, p. 1; "M'Cullough Case Dismissed by Court," *Tulsa Democrat*, Oct. 9, 1917; "Sheriff Ouster Case Passed Up," *Tulsa World*, Oct. 10, 1917.

73. *State of Oklahoma ex rel S. P. Freeling, Attorney General, v. William W. McCullough*, Oklahoma State Archives, box 25, case 1062. Petition was originally prepared with McCullough's name as defendant but was altered with pencil to substitute the name of the police chief of Healdton, Oklahoma.

74. "Blaine High on City Hall Police Roster," *Tulsa Tribune*, July 24, 1921, pp. 1–2. Statement of John Burnett; *State of Oklahoma v. John A Gustafson*, accusation; Statement of J. W. Russell; Kathryn Van Leuven to A. A. Gordon, June 4, 1921; "Local Findings on record of Jno. A. Gustafson"; Kathryn Van Leuven to Mr. Hill, May 13, 1921; "Marie Weber—Extortion"; and Statement of Walter Duckett to R. E. Maxey, all in Oklahoma State Archives, box 25, case 1062.

75. "Burns to Contest Case against Him," *Tulsa World*, Nov. 14, 1915, p. 1; "Blaine High on City Hall Police Roster."

76. "Police Department to Be Reorganized by Chief Gustafson," *Tulsa World*, April 28, 1920, p. 1; "Police Chief Leaves," *Tulsa World*, July 26, 1921, p. 3; "City Orders Police Force Increased," *Tulsa World*, Dec. 22, 1920, p. 1; "City Asks More Police and Money," *Tulsa Tribune*, Dec. 22, 1920, p. 1; "Big Sisters Move Begins in Tulsa," *Tulsa World*, April 14, 1921, p. 1; "Go to New York for Convention," *Tulsa World*, April 30, 1921, p. 2; Blaine High on City Hall Police Roster."

77. "Getting Results," *Tulsa Star*, Jan. 15, 1921, p. 2.

78. Statement of Grace Dowty, witness notes, Oklahoma State Archives, box 25, case 1062.

79. Burnett statement; Statement of Loren Conway, Oklahoma State Archives, box 25, case 1062.

80. Statement of Lee Pullin and E. S. Fields, witness notes, Oklahoma State Archives, box 25, case 1062.

81. Clark statement.

82. "Policeman Whips Episcopal Rector," *Tulsa World*, March 3, 1921, p. 1; "Detective Who Struck Pastor Suspended," *Tulsa Tribune*, March 3, 1921, pp. 1–2; "Attack on Crum Arouses Storm," *Tulsa World*, March 4, 1921, pp. 1, 11.

83. Clark statement.

84. "Chief Gustafson Indicted," *Tulsa Tribune*, June 25, 1921, p. 1; "Freeling After More Oustings?," *Tulsa World*, June 26, 1921, pp. 1, 8.

85. Statement of Dan White; and Statement of E. W. Meyers to R. E. Maxey, both in Oklahoma State Archives, box 25, case 1062. "Instruction Is Denied by Court"; "Star Witness in Brady Case Goes on Stand," *Tulsa Tribune*, July 16, 1921, p. 1.

86. MacQueen statement; Statement of M. C. Rodolf, Oklahoma State Archives, box 25, file 1062.

87. "Commissioners Send Business to Own Firms," *Tulsa Tribune*, Aug. 12, 1921, p. 2. Mary Seaman to Kathryn Van Leuven, May 13, 1921; and city auditor to J. M. Adkison, Nov. 20, 1920, both in Oklahoma State Archives, box 25, case 1062.

88. "Newblock Named for Police Head," *Tulsa World*, April 10, 1920; "Assign New City Officials Places," *Tulsa World*, April 18, 1920, pp. 1, 4; "Blaine High on City Hall Roster."

89. "Big Sisters Move Begins in Tulsa"; "Go to New York for Convention."

90. "City Vote Passes Strict Taxi Law," *Tulsa World*, Jan. 22, 1921, p. 7.

91. "Sentimentality Helps Crook; Straw Bonds Encourage Them," *Tulsa World*, Nov. 28, 1920, pp. C-1, C-5.

92. Ibid.

93. "Enforce the Law, Police Are Told," *Tulsa World*, March 1, 1921, pp. 1, 13.

94. Ibid.; Statement of W. F. Seaver, Oklahoma State Archives, box 25, case 1062.

95. "Crime Outbreak Believed Ended," *Tulsa World*, Nov. 18, 1920, p. 8.

96. "City Orders Police Force Increased"; "City Asks More Police and Money."

97. "'Shoot to Kill' Is Police Advice," *Tulsa World*, Dec. 28, 1920, p. 1.

98. "Restore Order," *Tulsa Tribune*, June 1, 1921, p. 1.

99. Parrish, *Race Riot 1921*, 41, 53, 61.

100. Hieronymus, "Negroes Gladly Accept Guards"; "5,000 Negro Refugees."

101. Parrish, *Race Riot 1921*, 41, 53–54.

102. Hower, *1921 Tulsa Race Riot*, 4–5.

103. "5,000 Negro Refugees"; "Free Interned Negroes; Red Cross Is in Charge," *Tulsa Tribune*, June 2, 1921, pp. 1, 13; "Order Replaces Chaos in Camp," *Tulsa World*, June 3, 1921, p. 8; "Tulsa Churches in Mercy Work," *Tulsa World*, June 3, 1921, p. 9; Parrish *Race Riot 1921*, 50.

104. Parrish, *Race Riot 1921*, 22–25; "Two Negro Doctors"; "Negroes from Tulsa Flee"; "Capture 33 at Catoosa."

Chapter 9. "Wounds of Passion"

1. "Disgrace of Tulsa," *Tulsa Daily World*, June 2, 1921, p. 4.

2. "On Race Legislation," *Tulsa Daily World*, Nov. 26, 1920, p. 4; "On Race Legislation," *Tulsa Star*, Nov. 27, 1920, p. 8; "Penrose the Impossible," *Tulsa Daily World*, April 10, 1921, p. B-4; Thoburn and Wright, *Oklahoma: A History* 3:41–42.

3. "Disgrace of Tulsa."

4. Ibid.

5. Parrish, *Race Riot 1921*, 24–25.

6. Ibid.

7. Ibid.; "Free Interned Negroes"; "City Will Be Open Tonight Barrett Says," *Tulsa Tribune*, June 2, 1921, p. 1.

8. Parrish, *Race Riot 1921*, 24–25; "5,000 Negro Refugees."

9. Parrish, *Race Riot 1921*, 24–25.

10. Ibid.

11. "City Will Be Open Tonight."

12. "All Blacks Must Wear Green Tags," *Tulsa Daily World*, June 7, 1921, p. 9; "Blacks Must Be Self-Sustaining," *Tulsa Daily World*, June 8, 1921, p. 15.

13. All Blacks Must Wear Green Tags."

14. "Free Interned Negroes."

15. "Order Replaces Chaos." The next five paragraphs describing the fairground detainees draw from this article.

16. Adj. Gen. Charles Barrett, Field Order No. 4, in Barrett, *Oklahoma after Fifty Years*, 216.

17. "City to Meet Demands Out of Own Purse," *Tulsa Tribune*, June 3, 1921, p. 1.

18. Adj. Gen. Charles Barrett, Field Order No. 3, in Barrett, *Oklahoma after Fifty Years*, 216.

19. "Free Interned Negroes."

20. "Tulsa Churches in Mercy Work."

21. Ibid.

22. Parrish, *Race Riot 1921*, 26.

23. "Two Negro Doctors."

24. "Many Refugees Hiding in Hills."

25. "Tulsa Churches in Mercy Work."

26. "Took Whole Family of Negroes to Her Home," *Tulsa Daily World*, June 3, 1921, p. 13.

27. "Jury Inquiry Is Demanded by Governor," *Tulsa Tribune*, June 2, 1921, p. 1; "Grand Jury to Probe Rioting Called," *Tulsa Daily World*, June 3, 1921, pp. 1, 8.

28. Gov. J. B. A. Robertson to Atty. Gen. S. P. Freeling, June 3, 1921, Oklahoma State Archives, box 25, case 1062.

29. "Vivid Contrast in Two Nights," *Tulsa Daily World*, June 2, 1921, p. 1.

30. Barrett, *Oklahoma after Fifty Years*, 214–18; "City Will Be Open Tonight"; "Grand Jury to Probe Rioting Called."

31. "Martin Blames Riots to Lax City Hall Rule"; "Officials Under Fire."

32. "Blood Shed in Race War Will Cleanse Tulsa," *Tulsa Tribune*, June 4, 1921.

33. "Martin Blames Riots to Lax City Hall Rule"; "Officials Under Fire."

34. *Polk-Hoffhine Directories of Tulsa, Okla.*, 1920; "Optimistic Note Is Sounded Here," *Tulsa Daily World*, Jan. 19, 1921, p. 13.

35. Randy Krehbiel, "Early Day Banker's Persistence Prefaced Carnegie Library for Tulsa," *Tulsa World*, April 2, 2001.

36. Douglas, *History of Tulsa*, 3:430.

37. "$2,000 to Start Fund for Relief," *Tulsa Daily World*, June 2, 1921, p. 1.

38. Hall, *Beginning of Tulsa*, 66.

39. "Tulsa's Future Is on the Horizon," advertisement, *Tulsa Daily World*, March 14, 1920, p. 43; *Moody's Manual of Railroad and Corporation Securities*, 895; advertisement, *Oil and Gas News*, Feb. 5, 1920, p. 36; *Texas Trade Review and Industrial Record*, 16.

40. Kelly, *Father of Route 66*.

41. "Martin Blames Riots to Lax City Hall Rule."

42. Ibid.

43. Ibid.

44. Hower, *1921 Tulsa Race Riot*, 110–11.

45. Douglas, *History of Tulsa*, 2:183–84.

46. "Free Interned Negroes"; "Local Red Cross Is Reorganized"; "Order Replaces Chaos"; Hower, *1921 Tulsa Race Riot*, 111.

47. "Lost Bureau Is Operated by the Y.M.C.A.," *Tulsa Tribune*, June 3, 1921; "Reorganize for Relief Work," *Tulsa Daily World*, June 4, 1921, p. 1.

48. "When Riot Stalked in Tulsa."

49. Ibid.

50. Hower, *1921 Tulsa Race Riot*, 110.

51. Ibid.

52. American Red Cross, "Our History."

53. Hower, *1921 Tulsa Race Riot*, 110–11.

54. Ibid.

55. Ibid.

56. "Free Interned Negroes"; "Local Red Cross Is Reorganized"; "Reorganize for Relief Work."

57. "Vote $21,000 for Emergency Work," *Tulsa Daily World*, July 1, 1921, p. 8.

58. Hower, *1921 Tulsa Race Riot*, 111; "Free Interned Negroes"; "Local Red Cross Is Reorganized"; "Order Replaces Chaos"; "City to Meet Demands"; "Reorganize for Relief Work.

59. "Red Cross in Field until All Are Well," *Tulsa Tribune*, June 4, 1921, pp. 1, 6.

60. "City to Meet Demands."

61. "Warning against Further Trouble," *Tulsa Daily World*, June 4, 1921, pp. 1, 11.

62. "$2,000 to Start Relief Fund"; "*World*'s Fund," *Tulsa Daily World*, June 4, 1921, p. 1.

63. "City to Meet Demands."

64. "*World*'s Relief Fund at $4,447," *Tulsa Daily World*, June 3, 1921, p. 1.

65. "Red Cross Fast Helping Blacks," *Tulsa Daily World*, June 5, 1921, pp. 1, 3.

66. "Red Cross in Field."

67. "Total Loss in Fire Is Fixed at $1,500,000," *Tulsa Tribune*, June 5, 1921, p. 1; Hower, *1921 Tulsa Race Riot*, 148.

68. "May Finance Building of Homes for Negroes," *Tulsa Daily World*, p. 9.

69. "'Give at Once' Avery's Plea to Save City," *Tulsa Tribune*, June 5, 1921, p. 1.

70. "Hiring Negro Help," *Tulsa Tribune*, June 5, 1921.

71. "When Riot Stalked in Tulsa."

72. Race Riot Commission report, 115; "Bury First White Victim of Riots This Afternoon," *Tulsa Tribune*, June 2, 1921.

73. Race Riot Commission report, 118.

74. "No Graves Dug, Bodies of 18 Negroes Held," *Tulsa Tribune*, June 2, 1921.

75. "Riot Death Toll Reduced to 30 by Re-Checking," *Tulsa Daily World*, June 3, 1921, p. 1.

76. Race Riot Commission report, 118.

77. "Riot Death Toll Reduced."

78. Race Riot Commission report, 117.

79. Ruth Sigler Avery, "African-American S. M. Jackson (Mortician) and his wife, Eunice Cloman Jackson on June 26, 1971," Avery Collection.

80. "Dead Estimated at 100," p. 1.

81. "Search Cuts Known Death List."

82. "4 More Blacks Dead."

83. "When Riot Stalked in Tulsa."

84. "Known Dead Is 33," *Tulsa Daily World*, June 7, 1921, p. 3; "Two More Negroes Dead, Total Death Toll to 34," *Tulsa Tribune*, June 7, 1921.

85. Brown to Adjutant General.

86. "Known Dead"; "White Injured," *Tulsa Daily World*, June 2, 1921; "Negroes Wounded," *Tulsa Daily World*, June 2, 1921, pp. 1–2.

87. Brown to Adjutant General.

88. "The Injured," *Tulsa Tribune*, June 2, 1921.

89. "Reorganized for Relief Work"; "Relief Hospital Cares for Sick," *Tulsa Daily World*, June 5, 1921, p. 3.

90. "Many Dismissed from Hospitals," *Tulsa Daily World*, June 3, 1921, p. 13.

91. "Looking for His Family," *Tulsa Tribune*, June 4, 1921.

92. "Fine Vandal Who Admits Offense, *Tulsa Daily World*, June 4, 1921, p. 16.

93. "One Held on Charges of Inciting Riot," *Tulsa Tribune*, June 4, 1921, p. 1.

94. Ibid.

95. "Court Orders $225,000 in Bonds Seized," *Tulsa Tribune*, Sept. 12, 1921; "Court Forfeits Criminal Bonds," *Tulsa Daily World*, Sept. 13, 1921, p. 2.

96. "Charges Filed against 32 for Thefts in Riot," *Tulsa Tribune*, June 7, 1921, p. 1.

97. "Cars Are Stolen by Riot Vandals," *Tulsa Daily World*, June 3, 1921, p. 13.

98. "Special Officer Is Charged with Theft," *Tulsa Daily World*, June 16, 1921, p. 16.

99. "Police Capture Big Distillery," *Tulsa Daily World*, June 5, 1921, p. 1; "Cleaner Is Sought by Police after Still Is Seized," *Tulsa Tribune*, June 6, 1921.

100. "Negro Finds $600 in Melted Gold in Ruins of His Home," *Tulsa Tribune*, June 2, 1921.

101. "One Held in Charges of Inciting Riot."

102. "Governor to Lift Martial Law at Once," *Tulsa Tribune*, June 3, 1921, p. 1.

103. "Warning against Further Trouble."

104. "C. of C. Asks Martial Law Be Continued," *Tulsa Tribune*, June 3, 1921, p. 1; Barrett, *Oklahoma after Fifty Years*, 217–18.

105. "Militia's Reign Brought to End," *Tulsa Daily World*, June 4, 1921, pp. 1, 10; "Hurley's Men Can Stop Riot in 30 Minutes," *Tulsa Tribune*, June 5, 1921, p. 1.

106. "Deputies Picked for Daring and Nerve by Hurley," *Tulsa Daily World*, June 6, 1921, p. 1.

107. "Man Shot by Guards," *Tulsa Daily World*, June 6, 1921, p. 1; "Guard Kills Autoist Who Didn't Halt," *Tulsa Tribune*," June 6, 1921, p. 1; Bert Martin to J. A. B. [*sic*] Robertson, July 14, 1921, Oklahoma State Archives, RG 8-D-1–3, box 3, FF 16.

108. "City to Meet Demands"; "Red Cross in Field."

109. "Moving Negroes to Central Camp," *Tulsa Daily World*, June 6, 1921, p. 9.

Chapter 10. "It Must Not Be Again"

1. "To Appraise All Loss by Negroes," *Tulsa Daily World*, June 3, 1921, p. 1; "Plan to Move Negroes into New District," *Tulsa Tribune*, June 3, 1921, p. 1; Greater Tulsa Association of Realtors, "GTAR History."

2. "To Appraise All Loss by Negroes"; "Plan to Move Negroes into New District."

3. "To Appraise All Loss by Negroes"; "When Riot Stalked in Tulsa."

4. "Plan to Move Negroes into New District."

5. "To Appraise All Loss by Negroes."

6. "Plan to Move Negroes into New District."

7. Ibid.

8. "Reconstruction Plans Approved," *Tulsa Daily World*, June 19, 1921, p. 2; "Ask Tramway Terminal in Burned Area," *Tulsa Tribune*, June 19, 1921, p. 1.

9. "Welfare Board to Be Augmented," *Tulsa Daily World*, June 17, 1921, p. 7.

10. "Plan to Move Negroes into New District"; "Negro Suburbs for Annexation."

11. "Restore Order."

12. "The State in Action," *Tulsa Tribune*, June 2, 1921, p. 1.

13. H. M. Stivers, "The Disinterested Spectator," *Tulsa Tribune*, June 2, 1921.

14. "Tulsa's Job," *Tulsa Tribune*, June 2, 1921.

15. "Tulsa Must Restore," *Tulsa Tribune*, June 3, 1921, p. 1.

16. "Realtors Start Task of Listing All Losses," *Tulsa Tribune*, June 3, 1921.

17. "Tulsa Will," *Tulsa Tribune*, June 3, 1921.

18. "Funeral of Second White Victim"; Operative no. 36 reports on the Regal Hotel, May 18, 1921, Oklahoma State Archives, box 25, case 1062.

19. "Police Say They Knew of 'War' Plans," *Tulsa Tribune*, June 3, 1921, p. 1.

20. "Warning against Further Trouble."

21. "Bad Niggers!," *Tulsa Daily World*, June 4, 1921, p. 4.

22. "Ex-Yanks on Guard; O.N.G. Troops Gone," *Tulsa Tribune*, June 4, 1921, p. 1; Tulsa County Jail booking records, Tulsa County Sheriff's Office.

23. "Which Is It to Be?" *Tulsa Daily World*, June 4, 1921, p. 4.

24. Stivers, "The Disinterested Spectator," *Tulsa Tribune*, June 4, 1921.

25. "Red Cross in Field."

26. "It Must Not Be Again," *Tulsa Tribune*, June 4, 1921.

27. Ibid.

28. "For Tulsa," *Tulsa Tribune*, June 4, 1921.

29. "Push Grand Jury," *Tulsa Tribune*, June 3, 1921, p. 1.

30. "Riot Outbreak Is Deplored by President," *Tulsa Tribune*, June 6, 1921, p. 1.

31. "Orders Federal Quiz Into Riot," *Tulsa Daily World*, June 4, 1921, p. 1; "Sub-Station of Postoffice (cq) Is Razed by Fire," *Tulsa Tribune*, June 4, 1921, p. 6.

32. "Press Scolds Tulsa; Editors Blame Police," *Tulsa Tribune*, June 5, 1921; "Comment in London Paper on Race Riot at Tulsa," *St. Louis Post-Dispatch*, June 6, 1921; "Behind the Massacre," *St. Louis Post-Dispatch*, June 3, 1921; "Tulsa," *New York Times*, June 3, 1921, p. 14; "Tulsa Still Target for Editors' Ire," *Tulsa Tribune*, June 7, 1921.

33. "Jury Inquiry Is Demanded by Governor"; "Grand Jury to Probe Rioting Called"; "Governor to Lift Martial Law at Once."

34. Gov. J. B. A. Robertson to Atty. Gen. S. P. Freeling, June 3, 1921, Oklahoma State Archives, box 25, case 1062.

35. "Rule by Guards Is Made Easier."

36. "Ex-Yanks on Guard."

37. "Accused Negro Leader Dodges State Hearing," *Tulsa Tribune*, June 16, 1921, p. 1; "Extradite Stratford [*sic*]," *Tulsa Daily World*, June 17, 1921, p. 1.

38. "Negro Victim of Riot Sues for $65,000," *Tulsa Tribune*, Sept. 24, 1921.

39. "Ex-Yanks on Guard."

40. Nevergold, "A. J. Smitherman."

41. Tulsa County Jail booking records; "Ex-Yanks on Guard."

42. Jacobs statement; Statement of John Henry Potts, Oklahoma State Archives, box 25, case 1062.

43. "Smitherman, Held for Inciting Riot, Released on Bail," *Tulsa Tribune*, July 11, 1921, p. 2; Tulsa County Jail booking records.

44. "Negroes Gladly Accept Guards."

45. "Military Control Is Ended at Tulsa," *New York Times*, June 4, 1921, p. 1.

46. "Negro Deputy Sheriff Blames Black Dope-Head."

47. *Cleaver v. City of Tulsa et al.*, No. 23331, Tulsa Race Riot Commission Collection, Oklahoma Historical Society, Oklahoma City; *Alexander et al. v. City of Tulsa et al.*, 03-CV-133-E.

48. "White Woman Is Arrested on Looting Charge," *Tulsa Tribune*, June 21, 1921, p. 1; "Long Is First White Man Arrested under Rioting Indictment," Tulsa Daily World, June 21, p. 1.

49. "Gets Injunction to Prevent Raid; Hearing June 27," *Tulsa Tribune*, June 19, 1921.

50. "Roadhouse Killing May Start Crusade," *Tulsa Democrat*, May 6, 1917.

51. "Jury Summons Being Issued for Riot Quiz," *Tulsa Tribune*, June 4, 1921, p. 6.

52. "Prison for Riot Chiefs," *Tulsa Tribune*, June 5, 1921, pp. 1, 3.

53. "Freeling Forms Distinct Court for Evidence," *Tulsa Tribune*, June 7, 1921, p. 1.

54. Harrison, *Me and My Big Mouth*, 65–66.

55. Oklahoma Heritage Association, "S. Prince Freeling."

56. Jackson, "Deadly Affair."

57. "Seaver Explains, Denies Friction," *Tulsa Daily World*, March 27, 1921, p. 1; "'My Inning Next,' Seaver Declares," *Tulsa Daily World*, March 29, 1921, p. 1.

58. "Identify Two as Sperry Robbers," *Tulsa Daily World*, March 31, 1921, pp. 1, 7; "Arrest 2 More in Sperry Case," *Tulsa Daily World*, April 1, 1921, pp. 1, 8; "Applause Greets Stanley's Story," *Tulsa Daily World*, April 6, 1921, pp. 1, 7.

59. "Arrest 2 More in Sperry Case."

60. "'Guilty' Verdict Quickly Reached," *Tulsa Daily World*, April 2, 1921, pp. 1, 11; "Applause Greets Stanley's Story"; "Stanley Guilty, Draws 15 Years," April 7, 1921, pp. 1, 7.

61. "Peeved Witness in Sperry Bank Robbery Case Knocks Lawyer through Glass Door," *Tulsa Daily World*, May 7, 1921, p. 1.

62. "'Guilty' Verdict Quickly Reached"; "Freeling Orders County Cleanup," *Tulsa Daily World*, April 5, 1921, p. 1; "Freeling Tired Out by Trial, Leaves for Capital to Rest; To Return Friday for Probe," *Tulsa Daily World*, April 7, 1921, p. 1.

63. "'Guilty' Verdict Quickly Reached."

64. "Nab Police Aide as Auto 'Fence,'" *Tulsa Daily World*, April 6, 1921, pp. 1, 10; "Brady Turns on Bay Ward; Arouses Doubt," *Tulsa Tribune*, April 6, 1921, p. 1.

65. MacQueen statement.

66. "Nab Police Aide as Auto 'Fence.'"

67. "Freeling Tired Out by Trial."

68. "About Politics and Politicians," *Harlow's Weekly*, Oct. 14, 1921, p. 2.

69. "Freeling Boom Officially Born," *Tulsa Daily World*, May 4, 1921, p. 1.

70. "The Attorney General's Investigation," *Tulsa Daily World*, April 15, 1921, p. 4.

71. "The Police Investigation," *Tulsa Daily World*, May 21, 1921, p. 4.

72. Edith Johnson, "Pretty Little Portia Gets the Gate," *Oklahoman*, June 28, 1925; Thoburn and Wright, *Oklahoma: A History*, 3:357; Amelia F. Harris, interview of Kathryn Nedry Van Leuven, July 13, 1937, Indian-Pioneer Papers, Western History Collection, University of Oklahoma.

73. Van Leuven to Hill.

74. "Thirty Witnesses Fail to Link Police with Vice," *Tulsa Daily World*, May 21, 1921, pp. 1, 17.

75. Seaman to Van Leuven; "Commissioners Send Business to Own Firms."

76. "Another Official Is Hit by Probe," *Tulsa Daily World*, March 12, 1921, p. 1; "House Votes in Soldier Bills," *Tulsa Daily World*, March 20, 1921, p. 1.

77. Hill, *History of the State of Oklahoma*, 2:344–45; "Municipal and County Affairs," *Harlow's Weekly*, Nov. 10, 1921, p. 11; U.S. Attorney's Office for the Northern District of Oklahoma, "History."

78. "Causes of Riots Discussed in Pulpits of Tulsa Sunday," *Tulsa Daily World*, June 6, 1921, pp. 1, 5.

79. Ibid.

80. The next several paragraphs (through the third Mouzon extracted quote) draw from "Black Agitators Blamed for Riot," *Tulsa Daily World*, June 6, 1921, pp. 1, 5.

81. "Causes of Riots Discussed."

82. Ibid.

83. "Vice at Bottom of Riot Charge of the Clergy," *Tulsa Tribune*, June 6, 1921.

84. Ibid.

85. "Causes of Riots Discussed."

86. The next five paragraphs discussing Cooke's sermon draw from "Vice at Bottom of Riot."

87. Ibid.

88. "Causes of Riots Discussed."

89. "Need Relief Funds," *Tulsa Tribune*, June 6, 1921, p. 1.

90. "Raise $10,000 for School," *Tulsa Daily World*, June 6, 1921, p. 9.

91. "School Fund Half Million," *Tulsa Daily World*, June 6, 1921, p. 9.

92. "Sunday Services in Concentration Camp," *Tulsa Daily World*, June 6, 1921, p. 9.

Chapter 11. Directed Verdict

1. "New Protective League Formed," *Tulsa Daily World*, June 6, 1921, pp. 1, 7; "Minute Men on Job for Fresh Break," *Tulsa Tribune*, June 6, 1921, p. 1.

2. "Hurley Discredits Reports of Further Outbreaks in Tulsa," *Tulsa Daily World*, June 6, 1921, p. 1; "Minute Men on Job"; "Local Situation is Well in Hand," *Tulsa Daily World*, June 6, 1921, p. 2; "Trip by Airplane Disproves Rumor," *Tulsa Daily World*, June 7, 1921, p. 7; "Red Bird Sends Peace Message," *Tulsa Daily World*, June 9, 1921, p. 9.

3. "Man Shot by Guards"; "Guard Kills Autoist"; "Trip by Airplane Disproves Rumor."

4. "Guard Kills Autoist."

5. "Negro Baptist Church, Destroyed at Tulsa, Was Arsenal of Black Bolshevists, Charge," *Sunday Oklahoman*, June 5, 1921, p. 34.

6. "Conditions Pointed To in Tulsa as Bearing upon the Race Riot," *St. Louis Post-Dispatch*, June 5, 1921, Editorial Section, p. 1.

7. "Urges Negroes Here to Arm Themselves," *New York Times*, June 6, 1921.

8. "Military Control Is Ended at Tulsa," *New York Times*, June 4, 1921, p. 1.

9. "Dr. DuBois Misrepresents Negrodom," *Crusader*, May 1919.

10. "Tulsa and the African Blood Brotherhood," *Crusader*, July 1921.

11. Hill, "Racial and Radical," v–lxvi.

12. Ibid.

13. "Denies Negroes Started Tulsa Riot," *New York Times*, June 5, 1921.

14. Ibid.

15. "Colored Republican Leaders Taking in Chicago," *Tulsa Star*, June 12, 1920, p. 2.

16. Advertisement, *Tulsa Star*, March 15, 1920, pp. 4, 5; advertisement, *Tulsa Star*, June 12, 1920, p. 3.

17. "Black Agitators Blamed for Riot."

18. "Denies Negroes Started Tulsa Riot."

19. "Tulsa and the African Blood Brotherhood."

20. Hill, "Racial and Radical."

21. "Refugees Declare Peonage Prevalent," *New York Times*, June 3, 1921, p. 2; "Negroes Forced to Leave State They Declare," *Tulsa Tribune*, June 3, 1921; "Luxury Prospect Lured Okmulgee Negroes Away," *Tulsa Daily World*, June 4, 1921, p. 1.

22. "Hide Black Who Shot White Man to Death," *Tulsa Daily World*, March 4, 1921, p. 3.

23. "Okmulgee Contractor Warned," *Tulsa Tribune*, June 2, 1921.

24. "Luxury Prospect Lured Okmulgee Negroes Away."

25. "Two Mobs Are Outwitted by Beggs Deputy," *Tulsa Tribune*, June 14, 1921.

26. "Weapons Are Being Seized by Officials," *Tulsa Tribune*, June 21, 1921, p. 9.

27. "Files Charges to Bring Back Negro Suspect," *Tulsa Tribune*, June 6, 1921, p. 1; "Bring Stratford [*sic*] Back for Trial," *Tulsa Tribune*, June 7, 1921, p. 3.

28. "Bring Stratford Back for Trial"; "Seek Return of Alleged Rioter," *Tulsa Daily World*, June 16, 1921; "Accused Negro Leader Dodgers State Hearing," *Tulsa Tribune*, June 16, 1921, p. 1.

29. "Files Charges to Bring Back Negro Suspect."

30. "Not Guilty Says Wallace," *Tulsa Daily World*, June 7, 1921; "Held for Auto Trial," *Tulsa Tribune*, June 7, 1921.

31. "Charges Filed against 32," *Tulsa Tribune*, June 7, 1921, p. 1.

32. "Freeling Forms Distinct Court."

33. "The Meaning of Government," *Tulsa Daily World*, June 7, 1921, p. 4.

34. "Freeling Forms Distinct Court"; "Freeling Heads Grand Jury Quiz," *Tulsa Daily World*, June 8, 1921, p. 8; "Gustafson to Face Prison on 1 Count," *Tulsa Tribune*, June 26, 1921, pp. 1–2.

35. "Freeling Forms Distinct Court."

36. Ibid.

37. "Jury Probe of Riot Blocked; Inquiry Is On," *Tulsa Tribune*, June 8, 1921, p. 1.

38. "Freeling," *Tulsa Tribune*, June 8, 1921.

39. "Probe Cause of Race Riot," *Tulsa Daily World*, June 8, 1921, p. 18.

40. "The Grand Jury Investigation," *Tulsa Daily World*, June 9, 1921, p. 4.

41. J. H. Welch, "Unquestionably So," *Tulsa Daily World*, June 9, 1921, p. 4.

42. B. F. Ingraham, "In Defense of Officers," *Tulsa Daily World*, June 9, 1921, p. 4.

43. "'Go to Bottom' Courts Order to Grand Jury," *Tulsa Tribune*, June 9, 1921, p. 2; "The Grand Jury," *Tulsa Daily World*, June 10, 1921, p. 1.

44. "'Go to Bottom.'"

45. "Hundreds to Be Called in Probe," *Tulsa Daily World*, June 10, 1921, p. 1.

46. "Judge Biddison's Instructions to Grand Jury," *Tulsa Tribune*, June 9, 1921, pp. 1–2; "The Principal Points," *Tulsa Tribune*, June 10, 1921, p. 1.

47. "Negro Section Abolished by City's Order," *Tulsa Tribune*, June 7, 1921, p. 1; Tulsa City Commission minutes, June 7, 1921; "Burned District in Fire Limits," *Tulsa Daily World*, June 8, 1921, p. 2.

48. "Negro Section Abolished."

49. Ibid.

50. "Corporation to Re-Build Homes, Plan," *Tulsa Tribune*, June 8, 1921, p. 1; "May Finance Homes for Negroes," *Tulsa Daily World*, June 9, 1921, p. 9.

51. "Corporations to Re-Build Homes."

52. "500 Perish When Flood Hits Pueblo," June 5, 1921, p. 1; "Flood's Death Toll Put at 500," *Tulsa Tribune*, June 5, 1921, p. 1; "New Flood Rises in Stricken Pueblo," *Tulsa Daily World*, June 6, 1921, p. 1; "Pueblo Flood Waters Recede," *Tulsa Tribune*, June 6, 1921, p. 1; City of Pueblo, Colorado, "History of Pueblo."

53. "Board Floats $25,000 Loan for Expenses," *Tulsa Tribune*, June 6, 1921, p. 1.

54. "Ask $25,000 for Rehabilitation," *Tulsa Daily World*, June 7, 1921, p. 9; Tulsa City Commission minutes, June 7, 1921; "Vote to Pay Riot Bill," *Tulsa Tribune*, June 7, 1921; "Get Emergency Fund," *Tulsa Daily World*, June 8, 1921, p. 9.

55. "Sound Citizenship in Action," *Tulsa Daily World*, June 7, 1921, p. 4.

56. "Welfare Board Drops Control of Relief Fund," *Tulsa Daily World*, June 9, 1921, p. 1.

57. "Refugee Feeding Is Systematized," *Tulsa Daily World*, June 7, 1921, pp. 1, 11.

58. "Reorganize for Work of Relief"; "Red Cross in Field."

59. "Local Red Cross Is Reorganized."

60. "Blood Shed in Race War"; "Blacks Must Be Self-Sustaining," *Tulsa Daily World*, June 8, 1921, p. 15; Hower, *1921 Tulsa Race Riot*, 82; "Reorganize for Work of Relief."

61. "Refugee Feeding Is Systematized"; "Blacks Must Be Self-Sustaining."

62. Hower, *1921 Tulsa Race Riot*, 152; "Blood Shed in Race War."

63. "Blacks Must Be Self-Sustaining"; Hower, *1921 Tulsa Race Riot*, 152–53.

64. "All Blacks Must Wear Green Tags," *Tulsa Daily World*, June 7, 1921, p. 9; "Police Order Idle Blacks to Fair Camp," *Tulsa Tribune*, June 7, 1921, p. 4; "Notice," *Tulsa Tribune*, June 8, 1921, p. 1.

65. "All Idle Blacks to Be Arrested by Zero Hour, 7 Tonight," *Tulsa Tribune*, June 10, 1921, p. 1.

66. "Police Order Idle Blacks to Fair Camp"; "Blacks Must Be Self-Sustaining."

67. "All Trains Out of City Jammed with Refugees," *Tulsa Tribune*, June 5, 1921; "Aide to Police Answers Critics," *Tulsa Daily World*, June 5, 1921, p. A-13; "'Bye, Bye Tulsa' Is Song of Many Blacks without Jobs Here," *Tulsa Tribune*, June 11, 1921.

68. "City Is Not Liable, Says Legal Board," *Tulsa Tribune*, June 7, 1921, p. 1; "Not Liable for Damages," *Tulsa Daily World*, June 8, 1921, p. 14.

69. Tulsa City Commission minutes, June 7, 1921; "Claim for Damages Filed against City," *Tulsa Daily World*, June 8, 1921, p. 2.

70. Riot Commission Excel database, in Race Riot Commission Collection.

71. Ibid.; Tulsa City Commission minutes, Sept. 27, 1921.

72. Tulsa City Commission minutes, July 8, 1921.

73. Parrish, *Race Riot 1921*, 78; Hower, *1921 Tulsa Race Riot*, 112; "City 'Dads' and Red Cross Agree," *Tulsa Daily World*, Aug. 12, 1921, pp. 1–2.

74. Hower, *1921 Tulsa Race Riot*, 133–36, 140–41, 173–78; "White Dead Are Forgotten, Rev. Cooke Charges," *Tulsa Tribune*, June 9, 1921; "Charges Neglect of Riot Victims," *Tulsa Daily World*, June 10, 1921, p. 20.

75. Hower, *1921 Tulsa Race Riot*, 177.

76. "Blood Shed in Race War."

77. "Took Whole Family of Negroes"; "All Blacks Must Wear Green Tags"; "Police Order Idle Blacks to Fair Camp"; "Blacks Must Be Self-Sustaining."

78. "First Home in Old Negro Belt Built by Gypsy Oil Co.," *Tulsa Tribune*, June 10, 1921.

79. "Negroes Plan Legal Fight against City," *Tulsa Tribune*, July 26, 1921.

80. Parrish, *Race Riot 1921*, 71–75.

81. "New Paper for Tulsa," *Tulsa Star*, March 27, 1921, p. 1.

82. Parrish, *Race Riot 1921*, 27.

83. "New Paper for Tulsa."

84. "Negroes Publish New Daily Newspaper," *Tulsa Daily World*, June 9, 1921, p. 7.

85. "Negroes Again Reprieved," *Tulsa Daily World*, June 10, 1921, p. 12.

86. Stockley, "Elaine Massacre"; Whitaker, *On the Laps of the Gods*.

87. Ibid.

88. Ibid.

89. "Peace Officers Give Testimony," *Tulsa Daily World*, June 11, 1921, p. 3; "Hundreds to Be Called in Probe"; "Police Still before Grand Jury Proers [*sic*]," *Tulsa Tribune*, June 10, 1921, p. 1.

90. Ibid.; "The Jury's Invitation," *Tulsa Daily World*, June 17, 1921, p. 1.

91. "Grand Jury Gives Report to Court," *Tulsa Daily World*, June 16, 1921, p. 1; "52 Indicted on Charge of Inciting Riot," *Tulsa Tribune*, June 16, 1921, p. 1; "Roundup of 64 Indicted Blacks Is On," *Tulsa Tribune*, June 17, 1921, p. 1; "Find Few Traces of Indicted Men," *Tulsa Daily World*, June 18, 1921, p. 15; "Whites Named in New Batch of True Bills," *Tulsa Tribune*, June 18, 1921, p. 1; "88 Indicted in Race Riot Probe," *Tulsa Daily World*, June 19, 1921, p. 2.

92. "Roundup of 64 Indicted Blacks Is On."

93. *State of Oklahoma v. Robinson, et al.*

94. "Known Dead."

95. "Jury Probe of Riot Blocked."

96. "Gustafson Eager for Trial, Certain of His Vindication; Commissioners Back Him Up," *Tulsa Daily World*, June 26, 1921, pp. 1, 8.

97. "Grand Jury Blames Negroes for Inciting Race Riot; Whites Clearly Exonerated," *Tulsa Daily World*, June 26, 1921, pp. 1, 8.

98. Ibid.

99. Ibid.

100. "Propaganda of Negroes Is Blamed," *Tulsa Tribune*, June 18, 1921, p. 1; "Race Equality Does Not Exist," *Tulsa Daily World*, June 19, 1921, p. 3.

Chapter 12. The New Negro

1. Gates, "New Negro and the Black Image."

2. Bryan, "Fighting for Respect"; Williams, "African Americans and World War I."

3. Ibid.

4. DuBois, "Returning Soldiers," 13.

5. "Citizens of Tulsa."

6. "Propaganda of Negroes Is Blamed."

7. "Legion Makes Raids," *Tulsa World*, June 8, 1921, p. 1; "Legion to Form Reserve Guard to Protect City," *Tulsa Tribune*, June 8, 1921; "Raid Liquor Joints," *Tulsa World*, June 10, 1921, p. 2.

8. White, "I Investigate Lynchings."

9. "Legion Guard Cut to 27 and More Go Today," *Tulsa Tribune*, June 17, 1921, p. 2.

10. "Jenks Farmers Seek Warrants for Legion Men," *Tulsa Tribune*, June 14, 1921.

11. "Legion Guard Cut to 27."

12. "'Cowboy' Defies 'Get Out' Order," *Tulsa World*, Sept. 11, 1921, pp. 1, 13.

13. "Man Shot by Guards"; "Guard Kills Autoist"; Martin to Robertson; Rogers S. Sherman to S. P. Freeling, June 11, 1921, Oklahoma State Archives, box 25, case 1062.

14. "More Police on Stand"; "Citizens Uphold Officers' Story."

15. "Legion Guard Cut to 27."

16. "Board Named to Raise Big Relief Fund," *Tulsa Tribune*, June 10, 1921, p. 1; "Want $100,000 for Relief Work," *Tulsa World*, June 11, 1921, p. 8; Douglas, *History of Tulsa*, 434.

17. "Board Named to Raise Big Relief Fund."

18. Ibid.; "Want $100,000 for Relief Work."

19. "City Hall Breaks with C. of C.," *Tulsa Tribune*, June 14, 1921, pp. 1–2; "Riot Statement Made by Mayor," *Tulsa World*, June 15, 1921, pp. 1, 7; "To Vacate City Hall," *Tulsa World*, June 15, 1921, p. 2; Tulsa City Commission minutes, June 14, 1921.

20. "City Hall Breaks with C. of C."; "Riot Statement Made by Mayor."

21. Ibid.

22. "Grand Jurors' Probe Takes a New Angle," *Tulsa Tribune*, June 13, 1921, p. 1.

23. Parrish, *Race Riot 1921*, 47.

24. "City Hall Breaks with C. of C."; "Riot Statement Made by Mayor"; "Ask Tramway"; "Prepare to Develop Big Osage Purchase," *National Petroleum News*, Nov. 20, 1918, p. 27.

25. "New Board to Study Housing Problem Today," *Tulsa Tribune*, June 16, 1921, p. 2.

26. "Public Welfare Board Quits Job," *Tulsa World*, June 16, 1921, pp. 1, 3.

27. "Hostess House for Negroes Being Erected," June 4, 1921, p. 6.

28. "City Hall Breaks with C. of C."

29. "Public Welfare Board Quits Job."

30. "Business Men Praise Public Welfare Board," *Tulsa Tribune*, June 15, 1921, pp. 1, 11.

31. "C. of C. and Commission Meet Today," *Tulsa Tribune*, June 17, 1921, p. 1.

32. "Ouster Order to C. of C. Rescinded," *Tulsa World*, June 18, 1921, p. 1.

33. "City Hall–C. C. Breach Healed by Handshakes," *Tulsa Tribune*, June 18, 1921.

34. "Ouster Order to C. of C. Rescinded"; "City Hall–C.C. Breach."

35. "Will Prosecute Rumor Starters," *Tulsa World*, July 6, 1921, p. 10; "City-County Combine to Aid Negroes," *Tulsa Tribune*, July 6, 1921, p. 1.

36. Hower, *1921 Tulsa Race Riot*, 157.

37. "Ask Tramway."

38. "Action on Union Station Project," *Tulsa World*, June 21, 1921, p. 14.

39. "When Riot Stalked in Tulsa."

40. "All Trains Out of Tulsa Jammed with Refugees"; "Negro Exodus Is Denied by Roads," *Tulsa World*, June 15, 1921, p. 16; "60 Tulsa Negroes Find Refuge Here," *Daily Oklahoman*, June 19, 1921, p. 36.

41. "Red Cross in Field"; Parrish, *Race Riot 1921*, 57.

42. "Police Order Negro Porters Out of Hotels," *Tulsa Tribune*, June 14, 1921, p. 1; "No Prisoners at Detention Camp," *Tulsa World*, June 15, 1921 p. 12.

43. "Work Negroes on City Street Job," *Tulsa World*, June 14, 1921, p. 16.

44. "No Prisoners at Detention Camp."

45. "Warns Workers in Small Cities of Labor Surplus Here," *Tulsa Tribune*, June 22, 1921.

46. "Bricklayers Agree to $1 Cut in Scale," *Tulsa Tribune*, June 19, 1921, p. 1.

47. "Broke, Salesman Offers to Trade Boy, 2, for a Job," *Tulsa Tribune*, June 19, 1921.

48. "A Heart Cry," *Tulsa World*, June 17, 1921, p. 4.

49. "Want Wholesale Houses in Tulsa," *Tulsa World*, June 15, 1921, p. 9; "New Welfare Board Tours Burned Area," *Tulsa Tribune*, June 15, 1921, pp. 1, 11.

50. "Union Station Is Endorsed Realty Dealers."

51. Ibid.

52. Ira Moore, "Cutting Sarcasm," *Tulsa World*, June 15, 1921, p. 4.

53. Ibid.

54. "A Friendly Suggestion," *Tulsa World*, June 16, 1921, p. 4.

55. Tulsa City Commission minutes, June 17, 1921.

56. "Invite Negroes to Meet Board," *Tulsa World*, June 18, 1921, p. 14; "New Committee Invites Blacks to Conference," *Tulsa Tribune*, June 18, 1921, p. 1.

57. "Ask Tramway"; Hower, *1921 Tulsa Race Riot*, 6.

58. Ibid.

59. "Action on Union Station Project."

60. "Reconstruction Plans Approved," *Tulsa World*, June 18, 1921, p. 2.

61. "Give Furniture to Needy Blacks," *Tulsa World*, June 23, 1921, p. 16; "Dishes, Cook Stoves, Need of Red Cross," *Tulsa Tribune*, June 23, 1921.

62. "Humphrey Urges Union Station," *Tulsa World*, June 24, 1921, p. 2.

63. "Action on Union Station Project."

64. "Another Negro Victim of Riot Dies Friday," *Tulsa World*, June 12, 1921, p. 12; "Thirty-Fifth Victim of Riot Dies after Spinal Cord Hurt," *Tulsa Tribune*, June 12, 1921, p. 12.

65. Race Riot Commission report, 109–21.

66. "5,000 Negro Refugees"; "4 More Blacks Dead."

67. White, "Eruption of Tulsa."

68. Eunice Cloman Jackson, interview by Ruth Avery, June 27, 1971, Avery Collection.

69. "A Period of Hysteria," *Tulsa World*, June 19, 1921, p. 28.

70. Race Riot Commission report, 26.

71. Advertisement, *Sunday Oklahoman*, June 12, 1921, p. 18.

72. "Police Boss Puts Ban on Camera Men in Destroyed Area," *Tulsa Tribune*, June 14, 1921.

73. "Police Order Negro Porters."

74. "No Prisoners at Detention Camp."

75. "Negro Sentenced for Toting Gun on Day of Riot," *Tulsa Tribune*, June 10, 1921.

76. "Good May Come Out of Rioting," *Tulsa World*, June 23, 1921, p. 7; Parrish, *Race Riot 1921*, 27, 77–78.

77. "Good May Come Out of Rioting."

78. Ibid.

79. Ibid.

80. "Wash Tubs Given to Negro Women," *Tulsa World*, June 27, 1921, p. 10.

Chapter 13. Trials and Tribulations

1. U.S. Department of Agriculture Weather Bureau, Climatological Data, Oklahoma Section, June 1921.

2. "Arkansas River Falling Rapidly," *Tulsa Daily World*, June 26, 1921, p. 1–2; "$10,000 Loss Done in City by Big Rains," June 27, 1921, p. 1.

3. "Wash Tubs Given to Negro Women."

4. Ibid.

5. "Red Cross too Free with Coin, Lewis Charges," *Tulsa Tribune*, July 3, 1921, p. 5.

6. "Heart Cry."

7. Hower, *1921 Tulsa Race Riot*, 110–17, 161–85.

8. "Wash Tubs Given to Negro Women."

9. "Welfare Board Is Criticized by Preachers," *Tulsa Tribune*, June 27, 1921.

10. "Reconstruction Plan Presented," *Tulsa Daily World*, June 29, 1921, p. 16; "Realty Dealer Proposes Plan," *Tulsa Tribune*, June 29, 1921, p. 5.

11. "Negroes on Lansing."

12. "Reconstruction Plan Presented"; "Realty Dealer Proposes Plan to Aid Blacks."

13. "Question Motive of Loan Company," *Tulsa Daily World*, June 29, 1921, p. 12.

14. "Spreading More Riot Propaganda," *Tulsa Daily World*, Sept. 2, 1921, p. 12.

15. "To Help Tulsa Sufferers," *Washington Bee*, July 2, 1921, p. 2.

16. "Question Motive of Loan Company."

17. "Arsenal Urged for City Hall," *Tulsa Tribune*, June 29, 1921, pp. 1–2; "Discuss Riot Arms," *Tulsa Daily World*, June 30, 1921, p. 3.

18. Ibid.

19. "Arsenal Urged for City Hall."

20. Ibid.

21. Ibid.

22. Ibid.

23. "City Will Pay Relief Bills with $23,500," *Tulsa Tribune*, July 1, 1921.

24. "Receive Report on Negro Relief," *Tulsa Daily World*, June 30, 1921, p. 14.

25. "Arsenal Fund Is Demanded by Red Cross," *Tulsa Tribune*, June 30, 1921, p. 1; "Vote $21,000 for Emergency Work," *Tulsa Daily World*, July 1, 1921, p. 8.

26. "Receive Report on Negro Relief."

27. Ibid.

28. "Arsenal Fund Is Demanded by Red Cross"; "Vote $21,000 for Emergency Work."

29. "Vote $21,000 for Emergency Work."

30. "Arsenal Fund Is Demanded by Red Cross."

31. Ibid.; "Vote $21,000 for Emergency Work."

32. "Red Cross Too Free with Coin."

33. Douglas, *History of Tulsa*, 435–36.

34. William N. Randolph, "Political Enemies Reunited," *Tulsa Tribune*, July 3, 1921, Magazine Section, P1; "Who'll Be the Next Mayor of Tulsa? Political Hypnotists Can't Answer," *Tulsa Daily World*, July 3, 1921, p. 2.

35. "Page Offers Water Supply at Low Cost," *Tulsa Tribune*, July 26, 1921, p. 1; "Page's Proposal Turned Down," *Tulsa Daily World*, Aug. 11, 1921, p. 1.

36. "County Is Now under Rule of Republicans," *Tulsa Tribune*, July 5, 1921, p. 1.

37. "Will Prosecute Rumor Starters."

38. "City-County Combine to Aid Negroes"; "Funds Combined for Negro Relief," *Tulsa Daily World*, July 7, 1921, p. 14.

39. Ibid.

40. "The Reconstruction Committee," *Tulsa Daily World*, July 13, 1921, p. 4.

41. Ibid.

42. Ibid.

43. "Police Under Cover Sleuth Faces Jury," *Tulsa Tribune*, June 30, 1921, p. 1; "Begin Trial of Auto Theft Case," *Tulsa Daily World*, July 1, 1921, pp. 1, 10; "Brady Is Guilty of Auto Larceny," *Tulsa Daily World*, July 2, 1921, p. 1.

44. "Obtain Names of Chief's Enemies," *Tulsa Daily World*, June 28, 1921, p. 3.

45. Clark statement.

46. "Not Guilty Plea to Riot Charge," *Tulsa Daily World*, June 29, 1921, p. 1.

47. O'Dell, "Moorman H. Pruiett."

48. Ibid.

49. Statement of Damie Rowland, Oklahoma State Archives, box 25, case 1062; Douglas, *History of Tulsa*, 698–702.

50. "Not Guilty Plea to Riot Charge"; "Admit Men to Bail," *Tulsa Daily World*, June 30, 1921, p. 1.

51. "By Order of Chief," *Tulsa Tribune*, June 21, 1921.

52. "Will Prosecute Rumor Starters."

53. "Sheriff Slept."

54. "Rioter Wantonly Inured Veteran," *Tulsa Daily World*, July 2, 1921, p. 1; "White Who Shot Legion Member."

55. "Probe Shooting of Capt. Wheeler," *Tulsa Daily World*, July 5, 1921, p. 1.

56. Misch, "Redmond Selecman Cole," 242–44.

57. "Lawyer Mysteriously Wounded, May Die," *Tulsa Daily World*, May 11, 1921, pp. 1, 11; "Devereux Dies, Mystery Is Unsolved," *Tulsa Daily World*, May 12, 1921, pp. 1, 15; "2 Women Charged with Killing Judge," *Tulsa Daily World*, May 13, 1921, pp. 1–2; "Sister Did Not Receive Wealth," *Tulsa Daily World*, May 16, 1921, pp. 1, 9; "Judge's Fortune Has Disappeared," *Tulsa Daily World*, May 17, 1921, pp. 1, 15; "Will Try Nurses This Afternoon," *Tulsa Daily World*, May 23, 1921, p. 1; "Accuse Goldie of 'Framing' Story," *Tulsa Daily World*, May 26, 1921, pp. 1, 3; "Obtain Trace of Jurist's Fortune," *Tulsa Daily World*, May 27, 1921, pp. 1, 15; "Women Bound Over in Devereux Case," *Tulsa Daily World*, May 28, 1921, pp. 1, 12.

58. "Devereux Death Trial This Week," *Tulsa Daily World*, July 2, 1921, p. 3; "Try Devereux Case," July 5, 1921, p. 1; "Goldie's Lawyer Flays the Press," *Tulsa Daily World*, July 6, 1921, pp. 1, 8; "Drawing Web around Two Nurses Accused of Slaying Devereux," *Tulsa Daily World*, July 7, 1921, pp. 1–2; "'Kill Old Devil' Goldie's Threat," *Tulsa Daily World*, July 8, 1921, pp. 1, 10; "Words of Dying Judge Admitted," July 9, 1921, pp. 1, 6; "Artist's Model and Nurse Go Free," *Tulsa Daily World*, July 10, 1921, pp. 1, 19.

59. "Artist's Model and Nurse Go Free," *Tulsa Daily World*, July 10, 1921, pp. 1, 19.

60. "Legal Battles Mark Opening of Police Case," *Tulsa Tribune*, July 11, 1921, pp. 1–2; "Chief of Police Faces Accusers," *Tulsa Daily World*, July 12, 1921, pp. 1–2; "Jury Box Not Yet Filled for Chief's Trial," *Tulsa Tribune*, July 12, 1921, p. 1; "Admits Demurrer in Chief's Trial," *Tulsa Daily World*, July 13, 1921, pp. 1, 8.

61. "Jury Box Not Yet Filled."

62. "Admits Demurrer."

63. "Chief Found Guilty on Two Counts," *Tulsa Daily World*, July 23, 1921, pp. 1, 11; "Jury Convicts Gustafson on Both Counts," *Tulsa Tribune*, July 23, 1921, pp. 1, 6; "Ousted Chief Wanted Brady Jurors in Case," *Tulsa Tribune*, July 24, 1921, p. 2.

64. "Admits Demurrer."

65. "Legal Fight Waged over Riot Evidence," *Tulsa Tribune*, July 13, 1921, pp. 1–2; "State Elects to Try Gustafson."

66. Ibid.

67. "Legal Fight Waged."

68. Ibid.

69. "State Elects to Try Gustafson."

70. "Legal Fight Waged."

71. Ibid.; "State Elects to Try Gustafson."

72. "State Elects to Try Gustafson"; "Sheriff Tells of Plans to Guard Negro."

73. Ibid.

74. Ibid.

75. "Sheriff Tells of Plans to Guard Negro."

76. "Sheriff Slept."

77. Ibid.; "Sheriff Tells of Plans to Guard Negro."

78. "Sheriff Slept."

79. Ibid.; "Sheriff Tell of Plans to Guard Negro."

80. "Sheriff Slept"; "Police Accused from Stand"; V. B. Bostick, Witness Notes, Oklahoma State Archives, box 25, case 1062.

81. "Police Accused from Stand."

82. Ibid.; Mr. McGee, Attorney Notes of Witness Testimony, Oklahoma State Archives, box 25, case 1062.

83. "Police Accused From Stand"; Ira H. Gibbons, Attorney Notes of Witness Testimony, Oklahoma State Archives, box 25, case 1062.

84. "Sheriff Slept."

85. "Trial Testimony Results in Fight between Officers," *Tulsa Daily World*, July 19, 1921, p. 1; "Charges Cops Beat, Robbed Him of Purse," *Tulsa Tribune*, July 19, 1921, p. 1.

86. Laurel Buck testimony transcript, Oklahoma State Archives, box 25, case 1062; "Witness Says Cop Urged Him"; "Instruction Is Denied by Court."

87. "Witness Says Cop Urged Him"; "Instruction Is Denied by Court"; H. C. Souders, Attorney Notes of Witness Testimony, Oklahoma State Archives, box 25, case 1062; Lewis [sic] Hoffman, Attorney Notes of Witness Testimony, box 25, case 1062.

88. "Instruction Is Denied by Court"; "Star Witness in Brady Case."

89. Laurel Buck testimony; "Witness Says Cop Urged Him"; "Instruction Is Denied by Court."

90. "Star Witness in Brady Case"; "Gustafson Hits Back at State," *Tulsa Daily World*, July 17, 1921, pp. 1, 12; "State's Evidence Must Touch on Gustafson, Judge Cole Declares," *Tulsa Tribune*, July 17, 1921; "Brady, Secret Sleuth, Bares Police Neglect," *Tulsa Tribune*, July 18, 1921, p. 1; "Dickens Story Is Contradicted," *Tulsa Daily World*, July 19, 1921, pp. 1–2; "Chief Tells Own Story." W. E. Pinion, Attorney Notes of Witness Testimony; Dan White, Attorney Notes of Witness Testimony; L. N. Ewing, Attorney Notes of Witness Testimony; and John Eckley, Attorney Notes of Witness Testimony, all in Oklahoma State Archives, box 25, case 1062.

91. "Dickens Story Is Contradicted"; "Chief Tells Own Story."

92. "Chief Tells Own Story."

93. Kathryn Van Leuven to R. J. Churchill, July 27, 1921; and Statement of W. F. Seavers [sic], both in Oklahoma State Archives, box 25, case 1062.

94. "Inefficiency of Police"; "Chief Tells Own Story."

95. "Inefficiency of Police."

96. "Chief Tells Own Story"; "Chief and Officers Take Witness Stand."

97. Gustafson testimony.

98. "Chief and Officers Take Witness Stand"; "More Police on Stand."

99. Ibid.

100. "Case Will Be Given to Jury by 4 O'Clock," *Tulsa Tribune*, July 22, 1921, pp. 1, 4.

101. "More Police on Stand"; "Meacham, at Bar for Chief, Denies Plot"; "Citizens Uphold Officers' Story"; police notebook, 26.

102. "Citizens Uphold Officers' Story"; "Meacham, at Bar for Chief, Denies Plot."

103. "Gustafson Case to Jurors Today," *Tulsa Daily World*, July 22, 1921, pp. 1, 7; Case Will Be Given to Jury by 4."

104. "Chief Found Guilty on Two Counts."

105. Ibid.; "Jury Convicts Gustafson on Both Counts."

106. Andrews, "The Black Sox Baseball Scandal."

107. Nash, *World Encyclopedia of 20th Century Murder*, 321–22.

108. "Bergdoll Probe Breaks Up When Senator Brands Witness Liar; Fight Is Barely Averted," *Tulsa Daily World*, July 24, 1921, p. 1.

109. "Typhoid Fever Menaces City, Says Presson," *Tulsa Tribune*, July 7, 1921, p. 2.

110. "City Dump to Be Cleaned Up, Says Presson," *Tulsa Tribune*, July 8, 1921, p. 1; Tulsa City Commission minutes, July 8, 1921.

111. "City Dump to Be Cleaned Up, Says Presson."

112. "Typhoid Fever Is Increasing Here," *Tulsa Daily World*, July 14, 1921, p. 2; "Enforce Fire Laws," *Tulsa Daily World*, July 14, 1921, p. 3.

113. "Sues for Insurance," *Tulsa Daily World*, July 15, 1921, p. 5.

114. "May Pay Fire Losses Sustained by Negroes," *Tulsa Daily World*, June 22, 1921, p. 8; "Will Prosecute Rumor Starters"; Riot Commission lawsuit database, in Race Riot Commission Collection.

115. "North Siders Endorse Plan for One Depot," *Tulsa Tribune*, June 29, 1921; "Favor Proposed New Depot Site," *Tulsa Daily World*, June 30, 1921, p. 7; "Investigate Depot Idea," *Tulsa Daily World*, July 8, 1921, p. 9; "Find Opposition to Union Station," *Tulsa Daily World*, July 8, 1921, p. 9; "Auto Insurance Here $7; but Only 80¢ in California," *Tulsa Tribune*, July 11, 1921, p. 2.

116. "Enforce Fire Laws."

117. "Launch Move to Abandon Factory Site," *Tulsa Tribune*, July 19, 1921, p. 9; "Negro District May Be Restored"; "City Balks at Rebuilding of Burned Area," *Tulsa Tribune*, July 20, 1921, p. 1.

118. "Negro District May Be Restored"; "City Balks at Rebuilding Burned Area."

119. Ibid.

120. "City Balks at Rebuilding Burned Area."

121. Ibid.

122. Ibid.

123. "To Stand Pat on First Decision," *Tulsa Daily World*, July 22, 1921, p. 3; "Burned Area Factory Site Plan Winner," *Tulsa Tribune*, July 22, 1921, pp. 1, 4.

124. "City 'Dads' and Red Cross Agree."

125. "To Stand Pat on First Decision"; "Burned Area Factory Site Plan Winner."

126. "To Stand Pat on First Decision."

127. Ibid.

128. Ibid.; "Burned Area Factory Site Plan Winner."

129. "Burned Area Factory Site Plan Winner."

130. "A Return to Reason," *Tulsa Daily World*, July 22, 1921, p. 4.

131. Ibid.

132. Ibid.

133. "Period of Hysteria."

134. "Realtors Quit Struggle for Factory Zone," *Tulsa Tribune*, July 28, 1921, p. 1; "Rescind Action in Burned Area," *Tulsa Daily World*, July 29, 1921, p. 3.

135. "To Stand Pat Upon First Decision," *Tulsa Daily World*, July 29, 1921, p. 10.

136. Ibid.; "Board Stands Pat on Negro Fire Zone Area," *Tulsa Tribune*, July 29, 1921.

137. "Board Stands Pat on Negro Fire Zone Area."

138. "Court Rulings Attacked by Chief's Lawyer," *Tulsa Tribune*, July 26, 1921; "Motion for New Gustafson Trial," *Tulsa Daily World*, July 27, 1921, p. 1; "Court Denies New Trial to Ousted Chief," *Tulsa Tribune*, July 27, 1921, p. 1; "Deny Gustafson Retrial," *Tulsa Daily World*, July 28, 1921, p. 1.

139. "Sapulpa Bribery Trial on Today," *Tulsa Daily World*, July 27, 1921, p. 1; "Witness Army Summoned at Judge's Trial," *Tulsa Tribune*, July 27, 1921, p. 1; "Says Wright Had Stacks of Money," July 28, 1921, pp. 1, 6.

140. "Trial of Sand Springs Chief is Under Way," *Tulsa Tribune*, July 25, 1921; "Freeling Makes New Threat to Try McCullough," *Tulsa Tribune*, Aug. 4, 1921.

141. "Springs Chief Dismissed on Liquor Charge," *Tulsa Tribune*, July 26, 1921; "Free Waddell of Neglect Charge, *Tulsa Daily World*, July 27, 1921, p. 1.

142. "Jury Convicts Gustafson on Both Counts"; "Blaine Will Follow Path of Old Chief," *Tulsa Tribune*, June 27, 1921, p. 1.

143. Roy Meacham to Prince Freeling, Dec. 19, 1921, and Jan. 30, 1922, Oklahoma State Archives, box 25, case 1062.

144. "Major Daley Quits Police; Displeased"; "Daley to Quit Police Duties on August 1," *Tulsa Tribune*, July 28, 1921.

145. "Blaine High on City Hall Police Roster"; "Blaine Is Acting Chief," *Tulsa Daily World*, July 26, 1921, p. 3; "Mrs. Blaine Is Dead," *Tulsa Daily World*, Sept. 24, 1921, p. 11.

146. "Who's Your Friend, Adkison?" *Tulsa Tribune*, July 25, 1921.

147. "An Indefensible Offensive," *Tulsa Daily World*, July 27, 1921, p. 4.

148. J. B. A. Robertson to Cyrus Avery, July 11, 1921, Oklahoma State Archives, box 25, case 1062; "$12,750 Is Cost of Race Riot to State," *Daily Oklahoman*, July 7, 1921, p. 3.

149. "$12,750 Is Cost of Race Riot."

150. "State Finally Agrees to Pay Guard Riot Bill," *Tulsa Tribune*, Aug. 25, 1921.

151. "Youth Kidnapped, Forced to Marry Divorcee, Charge," *Tulsa World*, May 3, 1921, pp. 1–2; "Minister, Himself Kidnapped, Tells of Night Wedding on Sapulpa Road," *Tulsa World*, May 3, 1921, p. 1; "Confessed Only to Save Life," *Tulsa World*, May 4, 1921, p. 2; "Forced Wedding Bonds Severed by Judge Cole," *Tulsa World*, June 4, 1921, pp. 1–2.

152. "Muskogeean Flayed by Masked Mob," *Tulsa Daily World*, July 7, 1921, p. 1; "Whip Suspect in Kidnapping at Muskogee," *Tulsa Tribune*, July 7, 1921, p. 1; H. M. Stivers, "The Disinterested Spectator," *Tulsa Tribune*, July 7, 1921.

153. "Capital Mayor Orders Night Rider Inquiry," *Tulsa Tribune*, July 19, 1921, p. 1.

154. "Klan at Bartlesville," *Tulsa Tribune*, July 26, 1921, p. 1.

155. "Masked Mob Applies Whip to Enid Man," July 13, 1921, p. 1.

156. "Peaceful Klan Aids Babes, No Tar, Just Milk," July 29, 1921, p. 1.

157. "Ku-Klux Keeps Laws While Cowards Hide Crime under Name of Klan Says Ridley," *Tulsa Daily World*, Aug. 11, 1921, p. 1; "Baptist Pastor Klan Defender Tells Its Aims," *Tulsa Tribune*, Aug. 11, 1921, pp. 1–2.

158. "Baptist Pastor Klan Defenders Tells Its Aims."

159. "Negroes Fear Winter, Build in Fire Zone," *Tulsa Tribune*, Aug. 8, 1921.

160. "Commission Orders Clerk Fired Again," *Tulsa Tribune*, Aug. 5, 1921, p. 1; "Want Police to Stop Building of Shacks in Burned District," *Tulsa Daily World*, Aug. 6, 1921, p. 16.

161. "Negroes Plan Legal Fight against City," *Tulsa Tribune*, July 26, 1921.

162. Ibid.

163. "Negroes Fear Winter, Build in Fire Zone."

164. Ibid.

165. Ibid.

166. "White Property Owners Organize," *Tulsa Daily World*, Aug. 2, 1921, p. 12.

167. "White Victims of Riot to Sue for $500,000," *Tulsa Tribune*, Aug. 8, 1921, p. 9; "Whites Seek Redress," *Tulsa Daily World*, Aug. 9, 1921, p. 10.

168. "Negroes Plan Legal Fight against City"; "Claims of 5 Million Filed against City by Negroes of Tulsa," *Tulsa Daily World*, July 27, 1921, p. 2.

169. "Total Loss in Fire Is Fixed at $1,500,000."

170. "City Not Liable for Riot Damages," *Tulsa Daily World*, Aug. 7, 1921, pp. 1–2; "City Purse Safe from Riot Claim," *Tulsa Tribune*, Aug. 7, 1921, p. 1.

171. "Committee Considers Rebuilding of School," *Tulsa Daily World*, Aug. 5, 1921, p. 16.

172. "Negroes Fear Winter, Build in Fire Zone."

173. "Fire Zone Area in Black Belt May Be Reduced," *Tulsa Tribune*, Aug. 14, 1921.

174. "Negro Sues to Rebuild Waste Area," *Tulsa Tribune*, Aug. 13, 1921, p. 1; "Negro Would Rebuild," *Tulsa Daily World*, Aug. 15, 1921, p. 1; "Hearing Postponed," *Tulsa Daily World*, Aug. 18, 1921; *Lockard v. Evans et al.*, Tulsa County District Court, Box 5, Folder 6, Tulsa Race Riot Commission Collection, Oklahoma Historical Society.

175. "Three Judges Hear Evidence in Negro Suit," *Tulsa Tribune*, Aug. 25, 1921, p. 1; "Can Reconstruct Restricted Area," *Tulsa Daily World*, Aug. 26, 1921, p. 3.

176. "Repeal the Fire Ordinance," *Tulsa Daily World*, Aug. 14, 1921, p. 4.

177. "Fire Zone Area in Black Belt May Be Reduced."

178. "Factory Site Project Leads in Straw Vote," *Tulsa Tribune*, Aug. 19, 1921.

179. "Three Judges Hear Evidence"; "Can Reconstruct Restricted Area."

180. "Three Judges Hear Evidence."

181. "Can Reconstruct Restricted Area"; "City Plans New Ordinance to Ban Building," *Tulsa Tribune*, Aug. 26, 1921; "City Will Fight Rebuilding Plan," *Tulsa Daily World*, Aug. 27, 1921, p. 5.

182. "Bricklayers Agree to $1 Cut"; "Pay Slashes Put in Effect on 210 Roads," *Tulsa Tribune*, June 27, 1921, p. 1; "All Rail Labor Feels Wage Cut," *Tulsa Daily World*, June 28, 1921, p. 1; "Carpenters Lop $1 Off Wage Scale," *Tulsa Tribune*, July 7, 1921, p. 1; "Wages of 40,000 Men Are Cut Ten Per Cent by Coal Mining Firm," *Tulsa Tribune*, July 30, 1921, p. 1.

183. "Enforce Curfew Law against All Tulsa Children," *Tulsa Daily World*, Aug. 5, 1921, p. 1.

184. "Scuffle for Gun Fatal to Husband," *Tulsa Daily World*, Aug. 8, 1921, p. 1; "Red Fork Woman Shoots Husband," *Tulsa Daily World*, Aug. 9, 1921, p. 1.

185. "Condemn City Wells," *Tulsa Daily World*, August 2, 1921, p. 10.

186. Officers Raid Road House," *Tulsa Daily World*, Aug. 15, 1921, p. 1.

187. "Pamphlet Shows Radicals in U.S," *Tulsa Daily World*, Aug. 2, 1921, p. 14.

188. "Robbers Are Polite," *Tulsa Daily World*, Aug. 4, 1921, p. 1.

189. "Rob Two Street Cars within 10 Minutes Monday," *Tulsa Daily World*, July 12, 1921, p. 1.

190. B. A. Bridgewater, "Bottle Throwing Mars Doubleheader; O. C. Wins Both," *Tulsa Daily World*, Aug. 8, 1921, p. 5; "Umps Fined for Attack on War Vet," *Tulsa Tribune*, Aug. 8, 1921, p. 1.

191. "Creek Claims Title to South Side Property," *Tulsa Tribune*, Aug. 13, 1921, p. 1; "Indian Claims Rich Property," *Tulsa Daily World*, Aug. 13, 1921, pp. 1, 3.

192. "City Will Help Homeowners," *Tulsa Daily World*, Aug. 17, 1921, pp. 1, 13; "Meet Next Week on Indian Suits," *Tulsa Daily World*, Aug. 19, 1921, p. 1; "Mass Meeting to Get Big Support," *Tulsa Daily World*, Aug. 20, 1921, p. 1; "Will Make Plans for Mass Meet," *Tulsa Daily World*, Aug. 22, 1921, p. 1; "Citizens Meet to Protect Property," *Tulsa Daily World*, Aug. 23, 1921, p. 1.

193. "Citizens in Arms against Shysters," *Tulsa Daily World*, Aug. 24, 1921, pp. 1, 3.

194. "City Will Help Homeowners."

195. "City Hall War Turns on Religion," *Tulsa Tribune*, Aug. 1, 1921, p. 1; "Mrs. Seaman Defies Mayor, Hires Clerk," *Tulsa Tribune*, Aug. 2, 1921, p. 1; "Commission Orders Clerk Fired Again"; "Stop Salary But He Stays on Job," *Tulsa Daily World*, Aug. 6, 1921, p. 16; "Mrs. Seaman Defies Evans, Keefe Works," *Tulsa Tribune*, Aug. 6, 1921, p. 1; "Keefe Disloyal So Says Mayor," *Tulsa Daily World*, Aug. 7, 1921, p. 2; "Keefe Quits Sept. 1," *Tulsa Daily World*, Aug. 13, 1921, p. 2.

196. "Claims City Has Paid Riot Bills," *Tulsa Daily World*, Aug. 11, 1921, p. 3; "Red Cross to Quit City if Row Develops," *Tulsa Tribune*, Aug. 11, 1921, pp. 1, 10; "City 'Dads' and Red Cross Agree"; "Commission Votes $11,000 for Red Cross," *Tulsa Tribune*, Aug. 12, 1921, p. 1; "Relief for Red Cross," *Tulsa Daily World*, Aug. 13, 1921, p. 16.

197. "1,500 Klansmen Take Oath at Cross of Fire," *Tulsa Tribune*, Sept. 1, 1921, p. 1.

198. "Klux Klan Initiates," *Tulsa Daily World*, Sept. 2, 1921, p. 5.

199. "Blacks Attack New Ordinance Passed by City," *Tulsa Tribune*, Sept. 1, 1921, p. 1.

200. "Three Judges Hear Evidence."

201. "Blacks Attack New Ordinance Passed by City"; "Cannot Enforce Fire Ordinance," *Tulsa Daily World*, Sept. 2, 1921, p. 1.

202. Ibid.

203. "Blacks Attack New Ordinance Passed by City."

204. "Cannot Enforce Fire Ordinance."

Chapter 14. The Years Since

1. "City May Not Appeal Fire Zone Ruling," *Tulsa Tribune*, Sept. 2, 1921, p. 1.

2. Ibid.; "No Appeal from Court Decision," *Tulsa World*, Sept. 3. 1921, p. 2.

3. "Mayor to Keep Reconstruction Board on Job," *Tulsa Tribune*, Sept. 3, 1921, p. 1.

4. "First Wintry Blasts Speeds Up Darkeytown," *Tulsa Tribune*, Oct. 2, 1921.

5. Madigan, *Burning*, 86, 242.

6. "Building Work Is Increasing," *Tulsa World*, Sept. 25, 1921, p. A-11.

7. Tulsa County land records, Tulsa County Clerk's Office; *Polk's Tulsa City Directories*, 1923.

8. "Negro Victim of Riot Sues for $65,000," *Tulsa Tribune*, Sept. 25, 1921, p. 1.

9. "Tulsa Vigilantes Flay Captive," *Tulsa World*, Sept. 3, 1921, p. 1.

10. "Masked Men Whip Suspect, Warn Others," *Tulsa Tribune*, Sept. 3. 1921, p. 1.

11. Advertisement, *Tulsa World*, Sept. 27, 1921, p. 7.

12. "Robed Klansmen Honor Dead While Hundreds Stand Agape at Funeral of Harry Aurandt," *Tulsa World*, Dec. 22, 1921, pp. 1, 9.

13. "Hijackers Shoot Two City Officers," *Tulsa World*, Dec. 19, 1921, p. 1; "Sheriff Spirits Trio from County," *Tulsa World*, Dec. 20, 1921, pp. 1–2; "Will Try Trio Early Next Year," *Tulsa World*, Dec. 21, 1921, pp. 1, 8.

14. "Robed Klansmen Honor Dead."

15. Dennis McLellan, "Paul Harvey Dies at 90; Radio Personality Known for His Distinctive Delivery," *Los Angeles Times*, March 1, 2009.

16. "Airplane Leads Klan Procession in Quiet Parade," *Tulsa World*, April 2, 1922, pp. 1–2.

17. "Elect Entire Democratic Ticket," *Tulsa World*, April 5, 1922, pp. 1, 3.

18. Ku Klux Klan ledger, Ku Klux Klan Papers, McFarlin Library Special Collections, University of Tulsa.

19. "Hadley Wins 3 to 2, Newblock 5 to 1," *Tulsa World*, March 19, 1924, pp. 1–2.

20. Tucker, *History of Governor Walton's War*, 11–14; Bynum, *Personal Recollections*, 70–73.

21. Ibid.; Alexander, *Ku Klux Klan in the Southwest*, 129–58; "Police Accused in Whipping Case," *Tulsa World*, Aug. 12, 1923, pp. 1, 5; "Tulsa Ordered under Martial Law," *Tulsa World*, Aug. 14, 1923, pp. 1, 5; "8 Klan Floggers Plead Guilty, Sent to Pen; 6 Others Named in Confessions Are Seized," *Tulsa World*, Aug. 24, 1923, pp. 1–2; "Rigid Martial Law for Entire County," *Tulsa World*, Sept. 1, 1923, pp. 1, 8; "Tulsans Get Walton's Treaty Terms," *Tulsa World*, Sept. 7, 1923, pp. 1–2.

22. "Continue Riot Cases," *Tulsa World*, Sept. 29, 1921, p. 7; "'Fatty' Is Freed Pending Trial," *Tulsa World*, Sept. 29, 1921, p. 1.

23. "Continue Riot Cases."

24. "White Woman Goes to Trial as Riot Looter," *Tulsa Tribune*, Nov. 30, 1921.

25. "44 Murder Cases Load One Docket," *Tulsa Tribune*, Sept. 11, 1921, pp. 1, 7.

26. "Court Orders $225,000 in Bonds Seized," *Tulsa Tribune*, Sept. 12, 1921, p. 1; "Court Forfeits Criminal Bonds," *Tulsa Tribune*, Sept. 13, 1921, p. 3.

27. "'Cowboy' Defies 'Get Out' Order"; "'Cowboy' Long's Store Is Raided by Police," *Tulsa World*, Sept. 13, 1921, p. 1.

28. W. F. Seaver to Prince Freeling, Oct. 3, 1921, Oklahoma State Archives, box 25, case 1062.

29. "Order Audit of Book of All Justices," *Tulsa Tribune*, Sept. 7, 1921, p. 3; "Fired, Wouldn't Quit, Constable Arrested Again," *Tulsa Tribune*, Sept. 16, 1921, p. 9.

30. "'Choc' Joint Raided," *Tulsa World*, Oct. 2, 1921, p. 1; "Black and White Party Raided and 22 Caught," *Tulsa Tribune*, Oct. 2, 1921, p. 1.

31. "Chamber Pays Bill," *Tulsa World*, Sept. 10, 1921, p. 3.

32. "Water Bonds Win by 4,233 Majority," *Tulsa World*, Nov. 30, 1921, pp. 1–2.

33. "Records Confirm Klan Has Temple," *Tulsa World*, Aug. 28, 1923, p. 1.

34. "Cooke Will Bid His Flock Goodbye in Last Sermon Sunday," *Tulsa Tribune*, Nov. 17, 1921.

35. "Citizens Defied," *Tulsa World*, March 7, 1921, pp. 1, 3.

36. "You Tell the World," *Tulsa World*, Nov. 14, 1922, p. 11.

37. "Dr. Cooke, McMurry President, Dies in Sleep," *Abilene Reporter-News*, March 17, 1958, p. 1.

38. "W. Tate Brady, City Builder, Kills Himself," *Tulsa World*, Aug. 30, 1921, pp. 1, 9; "A City Builder Is Dead," *Tulsa Tribune*, Aug. 30, 1921, p. 1; "Brady Funeral Plans Awaiting His Children," *Tulsa Tribune*, Aug. 30, 1921, pp. 1, 4.

39. "'Bill of Rights' by Republicans Attack on Klan," *Tulsa World*, Nov. 8, 1923, pp. 1, 8.

40. "Former Tulsa Mayor Dies," *Tulsa Tribune*, July 18, 1948; Carl Lawrence, "High Tributes Paid T. D. Evans, Ex-Mayor, at Funeral Services," *Tulsa World*, July 20, 1948; David DeShane (grandson of O. A. Steiner), interview with author, May 3, 2000; Rose Coffman, interview with author, May 11, 2000.

41. "Death Claims J. M. Adkison," *Tulsa World*, June 30, 1953; "Adkison Rites Set Wednesday," *Tulsa Tribune*, June 30, 1953; Ku Klux Klan ledger.

42. Arlie J. Cripe, grand jury testimony; I. G. Long, grand jury testimony; E. M. Bottom, grand jury testimony; D. H. Tibbetts, grand jury testimony; and Sam McCanee, grand jury testimony, all in Oklahoma State Archives, box 25, case 1062; Woodard, *In Re Tulsa*.

43. Jenkin Lloyd Jones, "The Last Tribune," *Tulsa Tribune*, Sept. 30, 1921, p. 1; Wilson, "*Tulsa Tribune*."

44. Wayne Greene, "*Tulsa World* to Be Sold to Warren Buffett's BH Media Group," *Tulsa World*, Feb. 26, 2013, p. 1.

45. "Charles Daley Dies after Heart Attack," *Daily Oklahoman*, June 18, 1941, p. 2.

46. "Blaine Named Police Chief in Quick Move," *Tulsa Tribune*, Nov. 8, 1941; Bob Foresman, "George Blaine Recalls When His Life Changed," *Tulsa Tribune*, Nov. 19, 1941; Curtis Huff, "Blaine Tells of Conversion; Praises Work at Missions," *Tulsa World*, May 8, 1942; "Blaine Asks Leave for Sheriff Race," *Tulsa World*, May 27, 1944; Gilbert Asher, "Blaine Balks at Revealing Warren Data," *Tulsa World*, Feb. 18, 1949; Nolen Bulloch, "Counties Join to Wipe Out Gaming Spots," *Tulsa Tribune*, Feb. 18, 1949; Gilbert Asher, "Blaine Tries Buck Passing in Car Fraud," *Tulsa World*, Feb. 19, 1949; Gilbert Asher, "Rift Revealed between City, County Units," *Tulsa World*, Feb. 21, 1949; "Law Enforcement Is a Profession," *Tulsa Tribune*, Oct. 23, 1954; "Blaine Quits after 40 Years on Job," *Tulsa Tribune*, Jan. 21, 1958; "Blaine Ends Long Career," *Tulsa World*, Jan. 22, 1958; "40 Years a Law Officer, George Blaine Dies Here," *Tulsa World*, May 27, 1958; June Moore, interview by author, Jan. 27, 2000.

47. Nevergold, "A. J. Smitherman."

48. "Negro Whipped, One Ear Cut Off by Masked Band," *Tulsa World*, March 12, 1922, pp. 1, 11; "Retired Negro Detective Dies," *Tulsa Daily World*, Oct. 8, 1956.

49. *Redfearn*, 20.

50. *Polk-Hoffhine Directories of Tulsa, Okla.*, 1922; *Polk's Tulsa City Directories*, 1923–1926; Oaklawn Cemetery Report, Tulsa City-County Library.

51. "Longtime District Judge, Carlos Chappelle, Dies," *Tulsa World*, June 30, 2015, pp. A1, A3.

52. Julie DelCour, "The Legacy of B. C. Franklin," *Tulsa World*, Jan. 17, 2016, pp. G1, G5.

53. Parrish, *Race Riot 1921*, 9–10, 138–40.

54. Damie Rowland interview.

55. Riot Commission database.

56. *Birdie Lynch Farmer v. T. D. Evans et al.*; *M. L. Gilliam v. T. D. Evans et al.*; *W. S. Holloway v. City of Tulsa et al.*; *Mrs. J. H. Goodwin v. City of Tulsa et al.*; *J. W. Williams v. City of Tulsa et al.*; *J. S. Gish v. T. D. Evans et al.*; *Jennie M. Wilson v. City of Tulsa et*

al.; *Daisy Williams v. City of Tulsa et al.*; *P. S. Thompson v. T. D. Evans et al.*, all in Race Riot Commission Collection, boxes 1–9.

57. Ibid.

58. Race Riot Commission report, 145; *Daisy Williams v. City of Tulsa et al.*

59. *P. S. Thompson v. T. D. Evans et al.*

60. Franklin, *My Life and an Era*, 200.

61. Ibid., 200–202.

62. Ibid.

63. Ibid., 202–203.

64. Coleman, "A Socioeconomic Analysis of the Greenwood District of Tulsa, Oklahoma: 1940–1980."

65. Morton Comprehensive Health Services, "History."

66. Randy Krehbiel, "The March to History," *Tulsa World*, Aug. 25, 2013, pp. A1, A12–A13.

67. "Tulsan Votes against 'Jim Crow' Repeals," *Tulsa Tribune*, Feb. 4, 1965.

68. Race Riot Commission report, 25.

69. "Negro Loses Big Insurance Suit," *Tulsa World*, April 20, 1924.

70. DuBois, "Opinion," 269–70; Franklin, *My Life and an Era*, 202n5.

71. Prentice, "Oklahoma Race Riot."

72. Foresman, "George Blaine Recalls When His Life Changed."

73. Larsen, "Tulsa Burning," 46.

74. Personal conversation with anonymous white caller, 2000.

75. Race Riot Commission report, 77.

76. Staples, "Unearthing a Riot," 69; Race Riot Commission report, 29–30.

77. "*Impact* Raps with W. D. Williams," 32–36.

78. Johnson, *Black Wall Street*, 113–17.

79. Brian Ford, "House Oks Riot Study Resolution," *Tulsa World*, March 14, 1997; Chuck Ervin, "'21 Race Riot Study Proposal Advances," *Tulsa World*, April 8, 1997; "Keating Signs Bill for Study of Riot," *Tulsa World*, April 23, 1997.

80. Bob Blackburn, interview by author, Jan. 21, 2016.

81. Randy Krehbiel, "Making Amends Possible," *Tulsa World*, Jan. 10, 2000; Robinson, *Debt*.

82. D'Oroso, *Like Judgement Day*.

83. "Payments to WWII Internees to Begin," *Los Angeles Times*, Oct. 1, 1990.

84. Rik Espinosa, "Apology Alone Just 'Hot Air,'" *Tulsa World*, June 22, 1997; Ford, "House Oks Riot Study Resolution."

85. Ibid.; Ervin, "'21 Race Riot Study Proposal Advances."

86. Michael Overall, "Mending Fences," *Tulsa World*, Aug. 17, 1997.

87. Randy Krehbiel, "Race Riot Commission: Panel at Odds on Report Details but Agree Riot Was Inexcusable," *Tulsa World*, Jan. 27, 2001.

88. "Those Who Look Back to See Ahead: The Tulsa Race Riot Commission Members," *Tulsa World*, Jan. 31, 1999.

89. Michael Overall, "City's 'Favorite Son,'" *Tulsa World*, Dec. 6, 1997; Randy Krehbiel, "Panel to Get New Chairman," *Tulsa World*, April 11, 2000; Krehbiel, "Tulsa Race Riot: Presentation of Findings at Center of Debate," Dec. 16, 2000; Blackburn interview.

90. Julie Bryant, "Unmarked Graves May Hold Riot Victims," *Tulsa World*, Jan. 29, 1999; Bryant, "Setting the Record Straight," *Tulsa World*, Jan. 31, 1999; Robert S. Walters, "Digging for the Truth," *Tulsa World*, May 28, 1999; Walters, "Grave Probe May Spur New Questions," *Tulsa World*, May 29, 1999; Rik Espinosa, "Cemetery Probe Yields Some Results," *Tulsa World*, July 27, 1999; Espinosa, "Race Riot Panelists OK Dig for Remains," *Tulsa World*, Aug. 10, 1999; Espinosa, "Oaklawn Excavation Pondered," *Tulsa World*, Aug. 11, 1999; Randy Krehbiel, "Victims' Graves a Mystery," *Tulsa World*, Jan. 14, 2000; Krehbiel, "Accord Reached on Dig," *Tulsa World*, Jan. 20, 2000; Krehbiel, "Race Riot Digging Cancelled," *Tulsa World*, Feb. 1, 2000.

91. Espinosa, "Apology Alone Just 'Hot Air.'"

92. Randy Krehbiel, "Panel Recommends Race Riot Reparations," *Tulsa World*, Nov. 23, 1999.

93. Ibid.

94. Dana Stirling, "Reward Offered for Missing Newspaper Article," *Tulsa World*, June 11, 1998.

95. Michael Overall, "Payments Panel's Top Priority," *Tulsa World*, Feb. 5, 2000.

96. Jean Pagel, "Can Victims Be Repaid?," *Tulsa World*, April 12, 1998.

97. Julie Bryant, "Peaceful Life Shattered," *Tulsa World*, Jan. 30, 1999.

98. Randy Krehbiel, "Riot Panel Votes for Reparations," *Tulsa World*, Feb. 5, 2000.

99. Ibid.

100. Overall, "Payments Panel's Top Priority."

101. Ibid.

102. Ford, "Bill Would Extend Riot Panel," *Tulsa World*, Feb. 13, 2000.

103. "Keating Renews Tulsa Race Riot Commission," *Tulsa World*, April 8, 2000.

104. Krehbiel, "Riot Panel Votes for Reparations."

105. Krehbiel, "Panel to Get New Chairman."

106. Ibid.; Blackburn interview.

107. Randy Krehbiel, "Race Riot Commission Sets Goals," *Tulsa World*, June 30, 2000.

108. Blackburn interview.

109. Krehbiel, "Race Riot Commission: Panel at Odds on Report Details."

110. Ibid.

111. Ibid.

112. Ibid.

113. "Rites Slated for Tulsa Historian," *Tulsa World*, May 10, 2009.

114. O'Brien, "Who Speaks for Us?"

115. Ibid.

116. Krehbiel, "Race Riot Commission: Panel at Odds on Report Details."

117. Ibid.

118. Blackburn interview.

119. "Riot: Reparations Report Wraps Up," *Tulsa World*, March 1, 2001.

120. Ibid.

121. Ford, "GOP Delays Appropriations Bill Which Includes Race Riot Memorial," *Tulsa World*, May 22, 2001.

122. Ervin, "Divided Senate Oks Race Riot Bill," *Tulsa World*, May 24, 2001.

123. Randy Krehbiel, "Keating: Riot Pay from State Not Likely," *Tulsa World*, Aug. 10, 2001.

124. Randy Krehbiel, "Leader Promises Action on Riot Issue," *Tulsa World*, April 27, 2001; John Gaberino Sr. and Jay Clemons to Tulsa Metro Chamber of Commerce directors, Oct. 12, 2001; Krehbiel, "Race Riot Provisions Backed," *Tulsa World*, Oct. 16, 2001.

125. Randy Krehbiel, "Checks in the Mail after 80 years," *Tulsa World*, April 9, 2002.

126. *John Melvin Alexander et al. v. Oklahoma et al.*; Randy Krehbiel, "Suit Filed for Riot Survivors," *Tulsa World*, Feb. 25, 2003; Krehbiel, "Big-Name Attorneys Join Riot Lawsuit," *Tulsa World*, Feb. 26, 2003.

127. *Alexander et al.*; David Harper, "Statute of Limitations Is First Issue of Debate in Riot Suit," *Tulsa World*, April 15, 2003.

128. Ellison order, March 19, 2004, in *Alexander et al.*

129. Tenth Circuit Court of Appeals opinion, Dec. 13, 2004, in *Alexander et al.*

130. Cert. denied, 544 U.S. 1044 (2005).

131. P. J. Lassek, "Councilors Back Plan for Church," *Tulsa World*, Dec. 21, 2001.

132. Curtis Killman, "Councilor Gives Alternative for Riot Memorial Funding," *Tulsa World*, Jan. 4, 2002; Killman, "Third-Penny Tax Use Plan Appears Dead," *Tulsa World*, Jan. 9, 2002.

133. Agenda, first meeting of Tulsa Race Riot Memorial of Reconciliation Design Committee, Oct. 23, 2000 (author's files); Patrick O. Waddel to Julius Pegues and Bob Blackburn, Feb. 19, 2003 (author's files); Randy Krehbiel, "Land for Museum Targeted," *Tulsa World*, Feb. 20, 2003; Krehbiel, "Land OK'd for Race Riot Memorial Museum," *Tulsa World*, Feb. 22, 2003.

134. Randy Krehbiel, "Race Riot Memorial: Action Urged to Protect Funding," *Tulsa World*, Aug. 20, 2003; Krehbiel, "Tulsa Race Riot Memorial to Start Small," *Tulsa World*, Sept. 5, 2003; Krehbiel, "Support for Riot Project Questioned," April 4, 2004; Brian Barber, "Council Oks Funds for Race Riot Park," *Tulsa World*, Oct. 17, 2008.

135. Rep. Randall Erwin to Speaker Larry Adair, Oct. 27, 2003 (author's files).

136. Randy Krehbiel, "Lawsuit Could Affect Riot Memorial," *Tulsa World*, April 12, 2003.

137. Blackburn interview.

138. Randy Krehbiel, "Riot Memorial May be Named for Historian," *Tulsa World*, May 17, 2003.

139. Krehbiel, "Lawsuit Could Affect Riot Memorial."

140. Randy Krehbiel, "'Healing Circle' Is Central Element of Riot Memorial," *Tulsa World*, March 22, 2003; *Dr. John Hope Franklin Greenwood Reconciliation Museum: Program and Conceptual Design Manual*.

141. Waddel to Pegues and Blackburn; Krehbiel, "Land for Museum Targeted"; Krehbiel, "Land Ok'd for Race Riot Memorial Museum."

142. Brian Barber, "Council OKs $500 Million Budget," *Tulsa World*, June 18, 2004.

143. Krehbiel, "Tulsa Race Riot Memorial to Start Small."

144. Julius Pegues, interview by author, Nov. 18, 2016.

145. Randy Krehbiel, "City to Break Ground on Park, Finally," *Tulsa World*, Nov. 8, 2008; Denver Nicks, "Harmony's Park," *Tulsa World*, Nov. 18, 2008.

146. Pegues interview.

147. "Good Friday Shootings in Tulsa," *Tulsa World* Good Friday Shootings web page.

148. Corey Jones and Arianna Pickard, "Bates Guilty," April 28, 2016, pp. A1, A3; Jones and Pickard, "Bates Sentenced to 4 Years," *Tulsa World*, June 1, 2016; Jones, "Officials Complete Probe of TCSO," *Tulsa World*, Oct. 18, 2016, pp. A9, A11.

149. Ibid.

150. Ibid.

151. Jones and Pickard, "Bates Guilty"; Jones and Pickard, "Bates Sentenced to 4 Years."

152. Corey Jones and Samantha Vicent, "Tulsa Police Chief on Fatal Shooting of Terence Crutcher: 'There Was No Gun,'" *Tulsa World*, Sept. 20, 2016.

153. Corey Jones and Samantha Vicent, "Update. Finding of PCP in Terence Crutcher's System Called 'Immaterial' by Family's Attorney," *Tulsa World*, Oct. 12, 2016.

154. Paris Burris and Arianna Pickard, "Family, North Tulsa Leaders View Fatal Shooting," *Tulsa World*, Sept. 19, 2016; Jones and Vicent, "Tulsa Police Chief on Fatal Shooting of Terence Crutcher: 'There Was No Gun.'"

155. Burris and Pickard, "Family, North Tulsa Leaders View Fatal Shooting."

156. "Terence Crutcher Slaying: Police Address Concerns Raised by 'Bad Dude' Statement in Chopper Video," *Tulsa World*, Sept. 20, 2016; Samantha Vicent, "'Color of Somebody's Skin' Was a Concern after Betty Shelby Shot Terence Crutcher, Officer Testifies," *Tulsa World*, May 10, 2017.

157. "Family of Terence Crutcher Calls for Criminal Charges, Urges Peaceful Protests," *Tulsa World*, Sept. 20, 2016.

158. Jones and Vicent, "Tulsa Police Chief on Fatal Shooting."

159. Corey Jones, "Words and Actions: Tulsa Police Chief Chuck Jordan Shows Leadership in Tough Situation," *Tulsa World*, Dec. 17, 2016.

160. Ibid.

161. Corey Jones, "Two Rallies Held to Support Law Enforcement as Al Sharpton Marches in Tulsa for Terence Crutcher," *Tulsa World*, Sept. 26, 2016; Paris Burris and Arianna Pickard, "Rev. Al Sharpton Rallies with Hundreds for Terence Crutcher in Downtown Tulsa," *Tulsa World*, Sept. 26, 2017; Paighten Harkins, "We the People Calls for TPD to Arrest Betty Shelby, Implement Community Policing Practices," *Tulsa World*, Sept. 20, 2016; Jones, "Tulsa Police Union Files Ethics Complaint against DA Steve Kunzweiler Alleging 'Rushed' Decision in Betty Shelby Case," *Tulsa World*, May 3, 2017.

162. Bill Sherman, "North Tulsa Pastors Praise Handling of Terence Crutcher Case, Express Concern for Policing People of Color," *Tulsa World*, Sept. 24, 2016.

163. Jarrel Wade, "President Obama Calls Tulsa Mayor Dewey Bartlett to Discuss City's Response to Fatal Police Shooting," *Tulsa World*, Sept. 22, 2016.

164. Randy Krehbiel, "Fragile Peace in Tulsa Following Terence Crutcher's Death the Work of Many," *Tulsa World*, Sept. 25, 2016.

165. Corey Jones and Samantha Vicent, "Office Betty Shelby Charged with Manslaughter, Free on Bond after Turning Herself In," *Tulsa World*, Sept. 23, 2017.

166. Kendrick Marshall, Corey Jones, and Samantha Vicent, "Police Report: Tulsa Officer Fatally Shoots Daughter's Boyfriend," *Tulsa World*, Aug. 5, 2014; Dylan Goforth, "Officer Accused of Killing Daughter's Boyfriend Had Never Been Disciplined in 24-Year Career," *Tulsa World*, Aug. 8, 2014; Goforth, "Tulsa Officer Charged With First-Degree Murder in Jeremey Lake Shooting," *Tulsa World*, Aug. 19, 2014; *State of Oklahoma v. Shannon James Kepler*, CF-2014-3952, Tulsa County District Court; Vicent, "Jury Selection Begins in Murder Trial for Former Police Officer," *Tulsa World*, Nov. 1, 2016.

167. Marshall, Jones, and Vicent, "Police Report: Tulsa Officer Fatally Shoots Daughter's Boyfriend"; Goforth, "Tulsa Officer Charged"; Samantha Vicent, "Shannon Kepler's Daughter to Testify Again Friday after Becoming Too Emotional to Continue Thursday," *Tulsa World*, Nov. 4, 2016.

168. Marshall, Jones, and Vicent, "Police Report: Tulsa Officer Fatally Shoots Daughter's Boyfriend"; Goforth, "Tulsa Officer Charged."

169. Samantha Vicent, "Former Officer's Murder Case on Track for Oct. 31 Trial with Ruling on Juror Questionnaire," *Tulsa World*, Oct. 13, 2016.

170. Samantha Vicent, "Defense for Shannon Kepler Accused of Trying to 'Purposefully' Eliminate Black Jurors; Opening Statements Set for Thursday," *Tulsa World*, Oct. 11, 2017; Vicent, "Officer Betty Shelby's Defense Claims Homicide Detective Told DA the Case against Her Is 'Unwinnable,'" *Tulsa World*, Jan. 12, 2017; F. Jones, "The Oklahoma Eagle Editorial: Kepler Trial Is Inescapably about Race," *Oklahoma Eagle*, Oct. 20, 2017; Vicent, "'Color of Somebody's Skin' Was a Concern"; Vicent, "Shannon Kepler Gets 15-Year Sentence for Fatally Shooting His Daughter's Boyfriend," *Tulsa World*, Nov. 20, 2017.

171. Sherman, "North Tulsa Pastors Praise Handling of Terence Crutcher Case."

172. Ibid.

173. Bill Sherman, "Local Pastors Urge Peace, Prayers in Wake of Terence Crutcher Shooting," *Tulsa World*, Sept. 28, 2016; Paris Burris, "Promoting Justice, Equality Focus of Youth Rally in Remembrance of Terence Crutcher," *Tulsa World*, Dec. 4, 2016.

174. Sherman, "Local Pastors Urge Peace."

175. Mike Averill and Paris Burris, "Supporters of Justice for Terence Crutcher Rally, Urge Continued Activism," *Tulsa World*, Sept. 25, 2016.

176. Paighten Harkins, "Tulsa Police Make Changes to Keep Officers, Public Safe in Wake of Terence Crutcher Shooting," *Tulsa World*, Sept. 23, 2016.

177. "Shots Fired"; Vicent, "'Color of Somebody's Skin' Was a Concern."

178. "Shots Fired."

179. Ibid.

180. Vicent, "'Color of Somebody's Skin' Was a Concern."

181. "Shots Fired."

182. Ibid.

183. Samantha Vicent, "Betty Shelby Not Expected in Court as Jury Selection Begins Monday in Manslaughter Trial," *Tulsa World*, May 8, 2017; Kyle Hinchey, "Betty Shelby Trial Day 1: News and Notes," *Tulsa World*, May 8, 2017; Vicent, "Jury Chosen for Betty Shelby Trial; Opening Statements Now Underway," *Tulsa World*, May 9, 2017; Hinchey,

"Betty Shelby Trial Day 2: News and Notes," *Tulsa World*, May 9, 2017; Vicent, "'Color of Somebody's Skin' Was a Concern"; Hinchey, "Betty Shelby Trial Day 3: News and Notes," *Tulsa World*, May 10, 2017; Vicent, "DA's Handling of Betty Shelby Charges Was Disrespectful, Homicide Detective Testifies," *Tulsa World*, May 11, 2017; Hinchey, "Betty Shelby Trial Day 4: News and Notes," *Tulsa World*, May 11, 2017; Hinchey and Vicent, "Betty Shelby Trial Day 5: News and Notes," *Tulsa World*, May 12, 2017; Hinchey, "Homicide Detective's Testimony, Emotional Video Highlights of First Week of Betty Shelby Trial," *Tulsa World*, May 13, 2017; Vicent, "Betty Shelby's Defense Rests after Unsuccessful Motion for Mistrial, Expert Defense Testimony," *Tulsa World*, May 15, 2017; Hinchey and Vicent, "Betty Shelby Trial Day 6: News and Notes," *Tulsa World*, May 15, 2017; Hinchey and Vicent, "Betty Shelby Trial Day 7: News and Notes," *Tulsa World*, May 16, 2017; Vicent, "Jury Begins Deliberations in Officer Betty Shelby's Manslaughter Trial," May 17, 2017; Paighten Harkins, "Crutcher Supporters Gather outside Tulsa Courthouse during Closing Arguments in Betty Shelby Trial," *Tulsa World*, May 17, 2017.

184. Samantha Vicent, "NOT GUILTY: Betty Shelby Acquitted; Multiple Jurors in Tears; Crutcher's Sister Says Police Tried to Cover Up Her Brother's Murder," *Tulsa World*, May 17, 2017; Notice of Letter, May 19, 2017, *State of Oklahoma v. Betty Jo Shelby*, CF-16-5138; F. Jones, "Betty Shelby Not Guilty Verdict Adds Fuel to the Fires of Racism and Discomfort in Tulsa," *Oklahoma Eagle*, May 19, 2017.

185. Notice of Letter, May 19, 2017, in *State of Oklahoma v. Betty Jo Shelby*.

186. Ibid.

187. Bill Sherman, "Pastors in North Tulsa Disappointed by Shelby Verdict, Hope for Peaceful Response from Community," *Tulsa World*, May 17, 2017; "Protest after Shelby Verdict Spills from Courthouse Plaza to Mayo Hotel, Then Blocks Traffic on Denver Avenue," *Tulsa World*, May 17, 2017; Paighten Harkins, "Crutcher Family Stunned after Not Guilty Verdict in Betty Shelby Case," *Tulsa World*, May 17, 2017; F. Jones, "The Oklahoma Eagle Editorial: Officer Betty Shelby Was Acquitted but Not Exonerated by the Jury," *Oklahoma Eagle*, May 25, 2017; Mike Averill, "Rogers County Sheriff Scott Walton Calls Out Tulsa County DA, Tulsa Police Chief in Open Letter on Facebook," *Tulsa World*, July 24, 2017.

188. Sherman, "Pastors in north Tulsa Disappointed by Shelby Verdict."

189. Ibid.

190. "G. T. Bynum: Racial Disparity Is the Great Moral Issue of Our Time in Tulsa," *Tulsa World*, May 19, 2017.

191. Corey Jones, "Officer Betty Shelby to get nearly $36,000 in Back Pay as She Moves to Administrative Duty," *Tulsa World*, May 24, 2017; Harrison Grimwood, "Betty Shelby Resigns from Tulsa Police after Reassignment to Desk Job Following Acquittal in Crutcher Slaying," *Tulsa World*, July 14, 2017; Jones, "Police Department Accepts Officer Betty Shelby's Resignation; Her Last Day of Work Is Aug. 3," *Tulsa World*, July 19, 2017; Averill, "Rogers County Sheriff Scott Walton Calls Out Tulsa County DA"; Samantha Vicent, "Betty Shelby Joining Rogers County Sheriff's Office," *Tulsa World*, Aug. 9, 2017; Vicent, "Betty Shelby Sworn In at Rogers County Sheriff's Office as Reserve Officer," *Tulsa World*, Aug. 10, 2017; Jones, "Seeking Privacy, Betty Shelby Seeks to Expunge Terence Crutcher

Manslaughter Case Records," *Tulsa World*, Aug. 22, 2017; Vicent, "Judge Grants Betty Shelby's Request for Manslaughter Case Records to Be Expunged," *Tulsa World*, Oct. 25, 2017.

192. Samantha Vicent and Corey Jones, "Fourth Trial Coming for Former Tulsa Police Officer Charged with Killing His Daughter's Boyfriend," *Tulsa World*, July 17, 2017; Vicent, "Shannon Kepler's fourth Murder Trial Gets Underway with Opening Statements," *Tulsa World*, Oct. 12, 2017.

193. Ibid.; Samantha Vicent, "Shannon Kepler Defends Leaving Scene after Shooting Daughter's Boyfriend," *Tulsa World*, July 6, 2017; Vicent, "No Gun Found on or Near Victim after Fatal Shooting, Police Officers Testify in Kepler Murder Trial," *Tulsa World*, Oct. 13, 2017; Vicent, "New Key Witness Brought to Tears by Shannon Kepler's Defense Attorney during Ex-Officer's Fourth Murder Trial," *Tulsa World*, Oct. 16, 2017.

194. Samantha Vicent, "Former Tulsa Police Officer Shannon Kepler Convicted of Manslaughter with 15-Year Term Recommended," *Tulsa World*, Oct. 18, 2017; Vicent, "'Crime of Passion': Shannon Kepler Juror Speaks Out about Convicting the Former Officer," *Tulsa World*, Oct. 29, 2017; Vicent, "Shannon Kepler Gets 15-Year Sentence."

195. Vicent, "Shannon Kepler Gets 15-Year Sentence."

196. Mike Averill, "A Pocketful of Hope Shows Off Future Home to U.S. Senator," *Tulsa World*, Sept. 1, 2016; Chris Casteel, "New D.C. Museum Features Tulsa Race Riot Exhibit," *Oklahoman*, Dec. 11, 2016; "Senator Lankford Joins Tulsa Leaders to Unveil Tulsa Race Riot Centennial Commission," Lankford Press Office, Feb. 24, 2017; "Sen. Lankford Hosts Town Hall on Tulsa Race Relations"; Bill Sherman, "Sen. James Lankford's Town Hall at Historic Big 10 Ballroom Spotlights Issues and the Future of North Tulsa," *Tulsa World*, Oct. 12, 2017; Ginnie Graham, Renovation of Big 10 Ballroom a Decade in the Making," *Tulsa World*, Oct. 25, 2017.

197. Sherman, "Sen. James Lankford's Town Hall at Historic Big 10 Ballroom"; Oklahoma State Election Board, *Voter Registration by District*.

198. "Sen. Lankford Hosts Town Hall."

199. Randy Krehbiel, "N. Tulsans Raise Concerns on Justice Center," *Tulsa World*, Sept. 29, 2015; Paighten Harkins, "North Tulsa Residents Air Grievances with Proposed Juvenile Center," *Tulsa World*, Oct. 4, 2015.

200. "Sen. Lankford Hosts Town Hall"; Randy Krehbiel, "Legislators Organize Mentoring Program for Black Youths," *Tulsa World*, July 30, 2014.

201. Randy Krehbiel, "Tulsa Race Riot Commission Announced," *Tulsa World*, Feb. 25, 2017; Krehbiel, "'Commemorate' but Not 'Celebrate': Race Riot Centennial Commission Discusses Plans for 2021 Event," *Tulsa World*, Sept. 12, 2017.

202. Kevin Canfield, "Mass Graves from the 1921 Tulsa Race Massacre? Mayor Plans to Re-Examine the Issue," *Tulsa World*, Oct. 2, 2018; Randy Krehbiel, "Mayor G. T. Bynum Hopes to Have Burial Search Plan by First Of Year," *Tulsa World*, Oct. 15, 2018.

203. "Senator Lankford Recognizes 95th Anniversary."

BIBLIOGRAPHY

Archival Sources

Avery, Ruth Sigler, Collection. Special Collections and Archives. Oklahoma State University, Tulsa.

Cole, Redmond S., Papers. Western History Collections. University of Oklahoma, Norman.

Oklahoma Documents. National Civil Liberties Bureau. Princeton University.

Oklahoma State Archives. Oklahoma Department of Libraries, Oklahoma City

Oaklawn Cemetery Report. Cemeteries and Death Records. Tulsa City-County Library.

Special Collections and University Archives. McFarlin Library, University of Tulsa.

    Ku Klux Klan Papers

    Norris, Robert D., Jr, "The Oklahoma National Guard and the Tulsa Race Riot of 1921: A Historical, Tactical and Legal Analysis." Unpublished manuscript, ca. 2000.

Tulsa County Clerk's Office, Tulsa, Oklahoma.

Tulsa Race Riot Commission Collection. Oklahoma Historical Society, Oklahoma City.

    Essley, T. J. Interview recorded summer 1987. Transcript annotated by Robert Norris. Box 10, Folder 1.

    O'Brien, William. "Who Speaks for Us?" Unpublished manuscript. Box 16, Folders 14–16.

Tulsa Race Riot Court Cases. Tulsa Historical Society, Tulsa, Oklahoma.

    Daisy Williams v. City of Tulsa et al.

    J. W. Williams v. City of Tulsa et al.

    Jennie M. Wilson v. City of Tulsa et al.

Vertical files. 45th Infantry Museum, Oklahoma City.

Works Progress Administration. Indian-Pioneer Papers. Western History Collections. University of Oklahoma Libraries, Norman, Oklahoma.

Government Documents

Oklahoma Commission to Study the Tulsa Race Riot of 1921. *Tulsa Race Riot: A Report.* Oklahoma City, February 28, 2001.

Oklahoma State Election Board. *Voter Registration by District.* January 15, 2017.

Tulsa County Jail booking records. Tulsa County Sheriff's Office, Tulsa.

Tulsa City Clerk's Office, Tulsa, Oklahoma

Tulsa City Commission minutes, June 7, 14, 17, July 1, 8, September 27, 1921.

U.S. Census Bureau

Abstract of the Fourteenth Census of the United States. Washington: Government Printing Office, 1923.

Cleaver, Barney. Individual U.S. Census entries for 1870, 1880, 1900, 1910, and 1920.

Fifteenth Census of the United States. Enumerator records.

Fourteenth Census of the United States Taken in the Year 1920: Statistics for Oklahoma. Washington: Government Printing Office, 1922.

Fourteenth Census of the United States. Enumerator records.

Ninth Census of the United States. Enumerator records.

"Population of Oklahoma and Indian Territory, 1907." Department of Commerce and Labor. *Bureau of the Census Bulletin* 89 (1907).

Tenth Census of the United States. Enumerator records.

Thirteenth Census of the United States Taken in the Year 1910: Statistics for Oklahoma. Washington: Government Printing Office, 1913.

Thirteenth Census of the United States. Enumerator records.

Twelfth Census of the United States Taken in the Year 1900. Washington: U.S. Census Office, 1901.

U.S. Department of Agriculture. Weather Bureau. Oklahoma Section, Climatological Data. June 1921.

Court Cases

Alexander et al v. City of Tulsa et al. 03-CV-133-E.

John Melvin Alexander, et al v. Oklahoma, et al.

Cleaver v. City of Tulsa et al. No. 23331.

Birdie Lynch Farmer v. T. D. Evans et al.

W. S. Holloway v. City of Tulsa et al.

M. L. Gilliam v. T. D. Evans et al.

J. S. Gish v. T. D. Evans et al.

Mrs. J. H. Goodwin v. City of Tulsa et al.

Lockard v. Evans, et al. Case no. 15,780. Tulsa County District Court.

Redfearn v. American Central Insurance. Brief of Plaintiff Error. Supreme Court of the State of Oklahoma. Oklahoma State Courts Network. https://www.oscn.net/dockets/Search.aspx.

State of Oklahoma v. Robinson, et al.

State of Oklahoma v. Betty Jo Shelby. CF-16-5138. Oklahoma State Courts Network. https://www.oscn.net/dockets/Search.aspx.

State of Oklahoma v. Shannon James Kepler, CF-2014-3952. Tulsa County District Court.

Stratford [sic] v. Midland Valley R. Co. 128 P. 98 Okla. 1912.

P. S. Thompson v. T. D. Evans et al.

Newspapers

Abilene Reporter-News, March 17, 1958.

Black Dispatch, July 1, 1921.

Chicago Defender, June 4, 1921–April 2, 1922.

Daily Oklahoman, June 19, 1921–June 18, 1941.

Los Angeles Times, October 1, 1990–March 1, 2009.

New York Times, January 27–June 6, 1921.

Oil and Gas News, February 5, 1920.

Oklahoma Eagle, May 19–October 20, 2017.

St. Louis Post-Dispatch, June 1–6, 1921.

Sunday Oklahoman, June 5–12, 1921.

The Oklahoman, January 26, 2015–December 11, 2016.

Tulsa Daily World, March 31, 1911–May 27, 1958.

Tulsa Democrat, April 4, 1912–October 9, 1917.

Tulsa Star, March 15, 1920–March 27, 1921.

Tulsa Tribune, July 18, 1920–September 30, 1992.

Tulsa World, August 20, 1989–November 20, 2017.

Washington Bee, July 2, 1921.

Washington Post, March 27, 2015.

Author Interviews

Blackburn, Bob. January 21, 2016.

Coffman, Rose. May 11, 2000.

DeShane, David. May 3, 2000.

Littlejohn, Robert. February 29, 2000.

Moore, June. January 27, 2000.

Pegues, Julius. November 18, 2016.

Rees, Phillip. March 10, 2000.

Patty, Robert H. June 13–14, 2000.

Villareal, Maury. April 14, 2000.

Books and Theses

Abel, Annie H. *The American Indian as Slaveholder and Secessionist.* Cleveland, Ohio: Arthur H. Clark, 1915.

Alexander, Charles C. *The Ku Klux Klan in the Southwest.* Norman: University of Oklahoma Press, 1995.

Barrett, Charles. *Oklahoma after Fifty Years*. Oklahoma City: Historical Record Association, 1941.

Brophy, Alfred. *Reconstructing the Dreamland: The Tulsa Race Riot of 1921, Race Reparations, and Reconciliation*. New York: Oxford University Press, 2002.

Bynum, E. T. *Personal Recollections of Ex-Governor Walton*. Oklahoma City: Self-published, 1924.

Campbell, J. B. *Campbell's Abstract of Creek Freedman Census Cards and Index*. Muskogee, Okla.: Phoenix Job Printing, 1915.

Coffeyville, Kan., City Directory. Coffeyville, Kans.: Journal Printing, 1904.

Coleman, Amanda. "A Socioeconomic Analysis of the Greenwood District of Tulsa, Oklahoma: 1940–1980." Master's thesis, Oklahoma State University, 2001.

Debo, Angie. *From Creek Town to Oil Capital*. Norman: University of Oklahoma Press, 1943.

———. *The Road to Disappearance*. Norman: University of Oklahoma Press, 1967.

D'Oroso, Michael. *Like Judgement Day: The Ruin and Redemption of a Town Called Rosewood*. New York: Berkley, 1996.

Douglas, Clarence. *The History of Tulsa, Oklahoma*. 3 vols. Chicago: Clarke, 1921.

Ellsworth, Scott. *Death in a Promised Land*. Baton Rouge: Louisiana State University Press, 1982.

Ferguson, Bessie. "The Elaine Race Riot." Master's thesis, George Peabody College for Teachers, Vanderbilt University, 1927.

Fischer, LeRoy Henry. *The Civil War Era in Indian Territory*. Los Angeles: L. L. Morrison, 1974.

Franklin, B. C. *My Life and an Era: The Autobiography of Buck Colbert Franklin* (Baton Rouge: Louisiana State University Press, 1997).

Franklin, John Hope. *Mirror to America: The Autobiography of John Hope Franklin*. New York: Farrar, Straus and Giroux, 2005.

Gander, Terry. *Machine Guns*. Ramsbury, UK: Crowood Press, 2003.

Gates, Eddie Faye. *They Came Searching: How Blacks Sought the Promised Land in Tulsa*. Austin, Tex.: Eakin Press, 1997.

Gill, Lauren L. "The Tulsa Race Riot." Master's thesis, University of Tulsa, 1946.

Goble, Danney. *Tulsa! Biography of the American City*. Tulsa, Okla.: Council Oak Books, 1997.

Gould's City Directory of St. Louis, for 1882. St. Louis: David Edwards, 1882.

Hall, J. M. *The Beginning of Tulsa*. Tulsa: *Tulsa Tribune*, 1933.

Halliburton, R. *The Tulsa Race War of 1921*. Saratoga, Calif.: R and E Research, 1975.

Harrison, Walter M. *Me and My Big Mouth*. Oklahoma City: Britton Printing, 1954.

Hill, Luther B. *A History of the State of Oklahoma*. 2 vols. Chicago: Lewis, 1909.

Hirsch, James. *Riot and Remembrance: The Tulsa Race War and Its Legacy*. New York: Houghton Mifflin Harcourt, 2002.

Hoffhine Directories of Tulsa, Okla. Tulsa, Okla.: Hoffine Directory, 1909–1911.

Hower, Bob, ed. *1921 Tulsa Race Riot and the American Red Cross, "Angels of Mercy."* Tulsa: Homestead Press, 1993.

Irving, Washington. *Tour on the Prairies*. Paris: A. and W. Galignani, 1835.

Johnson, Hannibal. *Black Wall Street: From Riot to Renaissance in Tulsa's Historic Greenwood District*. Austin, Tex.: Eakin Press, 1998.

Kelly, Susan Croce. *The Father of Route 66: The Story of Cy Avery*. Norman: University of Oklahoma Press, 2014.

Krehbiel, Randy. *Tulsa's Daily World: The Story of a Newspaper and Its Town*. Tulsa, Okla.: World Publishing, 2007.

Krugler, David F. *1919, the Year of Racial Violence: How African Americans Fought Back* Cambridge: Cambridge University Press, 2014.

Lampe, William T. *Tulsa County in the World War*. Tulsa, Okla.: Tulsa County Historical Society, 1919.

Lichtman, Allan J. *The Embattled Vote in America: From the Founding to the Present* Cambridge, Mass.: Harvard University Press, 2018.

Madigan, Tim. *The Burning: Massacre, Destruction, and the Tulsa Race Riot of 1921*. New York: Thomas Dunne, 2003.

Moody's Manual of Railroad and Corporation Securities. New York: Moody Publishing, 1921.

Moore's Directories of the City of Muskogee, Okla. Muskogee, Okla.: Model Printing, 1911 and 1912.

Nash, Jay Robert. *World Encyclopedia of 20th Century Murder*. Lanham, Md.: M. Evans, 1992.

Parrish, Mary E. Jones. *Race Riot 1921: Events of the Tulsa Disaster*. Tulsa, Okla.: Out on a Limb Publishing, 1998.

Phillips, Kevin. *Wealth and Democracy: A History of the American Rich*. New York: Broadway Books, 2002.

R. L. Polk's Directory of Tulsa, Okla. Tulsa, Okla.: R. L. Polk, 1912.

Polk's Tulsa City Directories. Kansas City, Mo.: R. L. Polk, 1923–1956.

Polk-Hoffhine Directories of Tulsa, Okla. Tulsa, Okla.: Polk-Hoffine Directory, 1913–1922.

Rampp, Donald A., and Lary C. Rampp. *The Civil War in the Indian Territory*. Austin: Presidial Press, 1975.

Robinson, Randall. *The Debt: What America Owes to Blacks*. New York: Dutton, 2000.

Rudolph, Joseph R., Jr., ed. *Encyclopedia of Modern Ethnic Conflicts*. 2nd ed. Santa Barbara, Calif.: ABC-CLIO, 2016.

Saunt, Claudio. *Black, White, and Indian: Race and the Unmaking of an American Family*. New York: Oxford University Press, 2005.

Scales, James R., and Danney Goble. *Oklahoma Politics: A History*. Norman: University of Oklahoma Press, 1982.

Stockley, Grif. *Blood in Their Eyes: The Elaine Race Massacres of 1919*. Fayetteville: University of Arkansas Press, 2001.

Thoburn, Joseph. *A Standard History of Oklahoma*. 5 vols. Chicago: American Historical Society.

Thoburn, Joseph L., and Muriel H. Wright. *Oklahoma: A History of the State and Its People*. 4 vols. New York: Lewis Historical Publishing, 1929.

Trekell, Ronald L. *History of the Tulsa Police Department, 1882–1990.* Tulsa, Okla.: Tulsa Police Department, 1989.

Tucker, Howard A. *History of Governor Walton's War on the Ku Klux Klan.* Oklahoma City: Southwest Publishing, 1923.

Whitaker, Robert. *On the Laps of the Gods: The Red Summer of 1919 and the Struggle for Justice that Remade a Nation.* New York: Crown, 2008.

Whitlock, Flint. *The Rock of Anzio: From Sicily to Dachau, a History of the U.S. 45th Infantry Division.* New York: Basic Books, 2005.

Woodard. John R. *In Re Tulsa.* Kansas City: Kansas City Law Print, 1935.

Woodhouse. S. W. *A Naturalist in Indian Territory: The Journals of S. W. Woodhouse 1849–1850.* Edited by John S. Tomer and Michael J. Brodhead. Norman: University of Oklahoma Press, 1992.

Other Publications and Documents

"About Politics and Politicians." *Harlow's Weekly.* October 14, 1921.

Brophy, Alfred. "The Tulsa Race Riot of 1921 in the Oklahoma Supreme Court." *Oklahoma Law Review* 54 (2001): 67–96.

"Ceremony to Dedicate Standpipe Hill Historical Marker." *Tulsa Business and Legal News,* June 12, 2014.

Clinton, Dr. Fred S. "First Oil and Gas Well in Tulsa County." *Chronicles of Oklahoma* 3 (Fall 1952): 312–32.

Comstock, Amy. "Over There: Another View of the Tulsa Riots." *Survey* 46 (July 2, 1921): 460.

"Dr. DuBois Misrepresents Negrodom." *Crusader* 1 (May 1919).

Dr. John Hope Franklin Greenwood Reconciliation Museum: Program and Conceptual Design Manual. Tulsa: EWC, June 18, 2003.

DuBois, W. E. B. "Let Us Reason Together." *Crisis* 18 (September 1919): 231.

———. "Opinion." *Crisis* (April 1926): 269–70.

———. "Returning Soldiers." *Crisis* 18 (May 1919): 13–14.

Forbes, Gerald. "History of the Osage Blanket Lease." *Chronicles of Oklahoma* 19 (March 1941): 70–81.

Golus, Carrie. "Legal Precedent." *University of Chicago Magazine* 105, no. 6 (July–August 2013): 40–41.

Grimshaw, Allen D. "Actions of Police and the Military in American Race Riots." *Phylon: The Atlanta University Review of Race and Culture* 24, no. 3 (1963): 271–89.

Hart, Albert Bushnell. "Peonage and the Public." *Survey* 46 (April 9, 1921): 43–4.

Hill, Robert A. "Racial and Radical: Cyril V. Briggs, *The Crusader* Magazine, and the African Blood Brotherhood, 1918–1922." Introduction to *The Crusader: September 1918–August 1919.* Vol. 1, edited by Robert Hill. New York: Garland, 1987.

Hilton, O. A. "The Oklahoma Council of Defense and the First World War." *Chronicles of Oklahoma* 20 (March 1942): 18–42.

"*Impact* Raps with W. D. Williams." *Oklahoma Impact.* June–July 1971.

Larsen, Jonathan Z. "Tulsa Burning." *Civilization* 4 (February/March 1997): 46–55.

McCuen, Capt. John, to Lt. Col. L. J. F. Rooney, n.d. Oklahoma State Archives. Oklahoma Department of Libraries. Oklahoma City.

Meserve, John Bartlett. "The Perrymans." *Chronicles of Oklahoma* 15 (June 1937): 166–84.

Misch, Fannie Brownlee. "Redmond Selecman Cole." *Chronicles of Oklahoma* 38, no. 3 (Fall 1960): 242–44.

"Municipal and County Affairs." *Harlow's Weekly*, November 10, 1921.

Nevergold, Barbara A. Seals. "A. J. Smitherman: Pen Warrior." *Chronicles of Oklahoma* 89 (Fall 2011): 288–311.

Oklahoma Conservation Commission. "Abandoned Coal Mines in Tulsa County." Oklahoma Geological Survey and Oklahoma Department of Mines, April 23, 2008. http://mines.ok.gov/coal-and-coal-combustion#tulsa.

"Peonage Farming." In *Farm Forecast: Crop and Live Stock Report for North Carolina*. North Carolina Department of Agriculture, Bulletin 46, January 1927.

Prentice, Frances. "Oklahoma Race Riot." *Scribner's* 90 (August 1931): 151–56.

"Prepare to Develop Big Osage Purchase." *National Petroleum News*, November 20, 1918.

"R. L. Jones Purchases Tulsa Democrat." *Editor & Publisher* 52 (November 6, 1919): 36.

"Senator Lankford Recognizes 95th Anniversary of the Tulsa Race Riot with Senate Speech." Lankford Press Office. May 16, 2016.

"Senator Lankford Joins Tulsa Leaders to Unveil Tulsa Race Riot Centennial Commission." Lankford Press Office. February 24, 2017.

"Sen. Lankford Hosts Town Hall on Tulsa Race Relations, Showcases Local Talent." KOKI Fox 23 News video. October 12, 2017. http://www.fox23.com/news/sen-lankford-hosts -town-hall-on-tulsa-race-relations-showcases-local-talent/623152474.

"Shots Fired." CBS *60 Minutes*. Season 49, Episode 28. April 2, 2017.

Smith, Michael D. "Resource Protection Planning Project: Patterns of White Settlement in Oklahoma 1889–1907." Oklahoma Historic Preservation Survey, Department of History, Oklahoma State University, 1986.

Staples, Brent. "Unearthing a Riot." *New York Times Magazine*, December 19, 1999.

Texas Trade Review and Industrial Record. February 1, 1917.

"Tulsa and the African Blood Brotherhood." *Crusader*, July 1921.

Tulsa Race Riot Memorial of Reconciliation Design Commmittee agenda, October 23, 2000. Author's files.

White, Walter F. "I Investigate Lynchings." *American Mercury*, January 1929.

———. "The Eruption of Tulsa." *Nation*, June 29, 1921.

Online Sources

American Red Cross. "Our History." http://www.redcross.org/about-us/who-we-are /history.

Ancestry.com. Database of Missouri marriage licenses.

Anderson, Elizabeth, and Jeffrey Jones. "Race, Voting Rights and Segregation: The Rise and Fall of the Black Voter, 1868–1922." The Geography of Race in the U.S., University of Michigan (September 2002), http://www.umich.edu/~lawrace/disenfrancise1.htm.

Andrews, Evan. "The Black Sox Baseball Scandal." October 9, 2014. History.com. https://www.history.com/news/the-black-sox-baseball-scandal-95-years-ago.

Brophy, Alfred L. "*Guinn v. United States (1915)*." In *Encyclopedia of Oklahoma History and Culture*. http://www.okhistory.org/publications/enc/entry.php?entry=GU001.

Bruce, Michael. "A. C. Hamlin." In *Encyclopedia of Oklahoma History and Culture*. http://www.okhistory.org/publications/enc/entry.php?entry=HA015.

Bryan, Jami. "Fighting for Respect: African American Soldiers in WWI." *On Point: The Journal of Army History*. January 20, 2015. https://armyhistory.org/fighting-for-respect-african-american-soldiers-in-wwi/.

Carlson, I Marc. "The Tulsa Race Riot of 1921." https://tulsaraceriot.files.wordpress.com/2012/06/tulsa.gif.

Chen, C. Peter. "Browning Automatic Rifle M1918 'BAR' Machine Gun." World War 2 Database. http://ww2db.com/weapon.php?q=52.

City of Pueblo, Colorado. "History of Pueblo." http://www.pueblo.us/119/History-of-Pueblo.

"Duluth Lynchings." Minnesota Historical Society. http://www.mnhs.org/duluthlynchings/index.php.

Everett, Diana. "Charles E. Page." Oklahoma Historical Society. In *Encyclopedia of Oklahoma History and Culture*. http://www.okhistory.org/publications/enc/entry.php?entry=PA003.

Franklin, Jimmie Lewis. "African Americans." In *Encyclopedia of Oklahoma History and Culture*. http://www.okhistory.org/publications/enc/entry.php?entryname=AFRICAN AMERICANS.

Gates, Henry Louis, Jr. "The New Negro and the Black Image: From Booker T. Washington to Alain Locke." Freedom's Story. TeacherServe. National Humanities Center. http://nationalhumanitiescenter.org/tserve/freedom/1917beyond/essays/newnegro.htm.

"Good Friday Shootings in Tulsa." December 16, 2013. Good Friday Shootings web page. *Tulsa World*. https://www.tulsaworld.com/good-friday-shootings-in-tulsa/collection_ae83ec02-66a7-11e3-89b9-001a4bcf6878.html.

Greater Tulsa Association of Realtors. "GTAR History." http://www.tulsarealtors.com/Pages/History.aspx.

Jackson, Ron J., Jr. "A Deadly Affair." Newsok Special. December 2013. http://newsok.com/article/3910896.

Johnson, Hannibal B. "The Ghosts of Greenwood: A Walk Down Black Wall Street." Hannibal B. Johnson website. May 11, 2009. http://www.hannibalbjohnson.com/the-ghosts-of-greenwood-past-a-walk-down-black-wall-street/.

Keyes, Allison. "A Long-Lost Manuscript Contains a Searing Eye-Witness Account of the Tulsa Race Massacre of 1921." *Smithsonian*, May 27, 2016. https://www.smithsonianmag.com/smithsonian-institution/long-lost-manuscript-contains-searing-eyewitness-account-tulsa-race-massacre-1921-180959251/.

Menard, Orville D. "Omaha Race Riot." In *Encyclopedia of the Great Plains*. http://plainshumanities.unl.edu/encyclopedia/doc/egp.afam.032.

Morton Comprehensive Health Services. "History of Morton Comprehensive Health Center." https://www.mortonhealth.com/about-us/our-history/.

"NAACP Victory in *Guinn v. United States.*" NAACP: A Century in the Fight for Freedom. Library of Congress. http://www.loc.gov/exhibits/naacp/founding-and-early-years .html#obj23.

National Air and Space Musuem. "Curtiss JN-4D Jenny." https://airandspace.si.edu /collection-objects/curtiss-jn-4d-jenny.

National Archives. Selective Service Records. https://www.archives.gov/st-louis /archival-programs/other-records/selective-service.html.

O'Dell, Larry. "Daniel Webster Patton." In *Encyclopedia of Oklahoma History and Culture,* http://www.okhistory.org/publications/enc/entry.php?entry=PA018.

———. "Moorman H. Pruiett." In *Encyclopedia of Oklahoma History and Culture,* http:// www.okhistory.org/publications/enc/entry.php?entry=PR022.

———. "Wallace N. Robinson." In *Encyclopedia of Oklahoma History and Culture,* http:// www.okhistory.org/publications/enc/entry.php?entry=RO009.

Oklahoma Heritage Association. "Kathryn Van Leuven." https://oklahomahof.com /member-archives/v/van-leuven-kathryn-1939.

———. "S. Prince Freeling." https://oklahomahof.com/member-archives/f/freeling -s-prince-1936.

"People of Coffeyville Say 'Enough!'" National Park Service reprint of *Coffeyville Journal,* October 7, 1892. https://www.nps.gov/nr/twhp/wwwlps/lessons/99condon/99facts3 .htm.

Smallwood, James M. "Segregation." In *Encyclopedia of Oklahoma History and Culture.* http://www.okhistory.org/publications/enc/entry.php?entry=SE006.

"Smith Brothers Coal Pit." Image. Beryl Ford Collection. Tulsa Historical Society. https:// tccl.bibliocommons.com/item/show/2139698063.

Smitherman, A. J. "A Descriptive Poem of the Tulsa Race Riot and Massacre." Self-published, ca. 1922. http://www.personal.utulsa.edu/~marc-carlson/riot/smithermanpoem .html.

"Stradford, John the Baptist 'J. B.'" In *Notable Kentucky African Americans Database.* http://nkaa.uky.edu/record.php?note_id=865.

Stockley, Grif. "Elaine Massacre." In *Arkansas Encyclopedia of History and Culture.* http:// www.encyclopediaofarkansas.net/encyclopedia/entry-detail.aspx?entryID=1102.

"The Trial and Lynching of Leo Frank." Topics in Chronicling America—The Trial and Lynching of Leo Frank. Library of Congress. https://www.loc.gov/rr/news/topics /leofrank.html#links.

Tulsa Preservation Commission. "Education." http://tulsapreservationcommission.org /tulsa-history/education/.

———. "Industry." http://tulsapreservationcommission.org/tulsa-history/industry/.

U.S. Department of Justice. U.S. Attorney's Office, Northern District of Oklahoma. "History." https://www.justice.gov/usao-ndok/history.

Van Prooyen, Anitra. "Henry Lowery (Lynching of)." In *Encyclopedia of Arkansas History and Culture.* http://www.encyclopediaofarkansas.net/encyclopedia/entry-detail .aspx?entryID=7064.

Weaver, Bobby D. "Glenn Pool Field." In *Encyclopedia of Oklahoma History and Culture*. http://www.okhistory.org/publications/enc/entry.php?entry=GL007.

White, Jimmie L., Jr. "William Henry Twine." In *Encyclopedia of Oklahoma History and Culture*. http://www.okhistory.org/publications/enc/entry.php?entry=TW006.

Williams, Chad. "African Americans and World War I." *Africana Age: African and African Diasporan Transformations in the 20th Century*. Schomburg Center for Research in Black Culture. New York Public Library. http://exhibitions.nypl.org/africanaage /essay-world-war-i.html.

Wilson, Linda D. "Oklahoma Council of Defense." In *Encyclopedia of Oklahoma History and Culture*. http://www.okhistory.org/publications/enc/entry.php?entry=OK038.

———. *"Tulsa Tribune."* In *Encyclopedia of Oklahoma History and Culture*. http://www .okhistory.org/publications/enc/entry.php?entry=TU016.

INDEX

References to illustrations appear in italic type.

CPSIA information can be obtained
at www.ICGtesting.com
Printed in the USA
LVHW050429140720
660554LV00002B/38/J